P...
WELCOME!
1997

The Animal Lovers' Holiday Guide

with Special Supplements
Kennels & Catteries
Holidays with Horses
Pet Friendly Pubs

FHG Publications

**Abbey Mill Business Centre, Seedhill,
Paisley PA1 1TJ
Tel: 0141-887 0428; Fax: 0141-889 7204**

36th Edition 1997
ISBN 1 85055 221 5

Cover design: Sheila Begbie
Cover photographs: Image Bank

Cartography by GEO Projects, Reading

Maps are based on Ordnance Survey Maps with the permission
of the Controller of Her Majesty's Stationery Office,
Crown Copyright reserved.

Typeset by FHG Publications Ltd, Paisley.
Printed and bound in Great Britain by Guernsey Press, Guernsey.

Published by FHG Publications Ltd,
Abbey Mill Business Centre, Seedhill, Paisley PA1 1TJ
(0141-887 0428; Fax: 0141-889 7204).

Distribution. **Book Trade**: WLM, Downing Road, West Meadows Ind. Estate,
Derby DE21 6HA
(Tel: 01332 343332 Fax: 01332 340464).
News Trade: USM Distribution Ltd, 86 Newman Street,
London W1P 3LD
(Tel: 0171-396 8000. Fax: 0171-396 8002). E-mail:usm.co.uk

Please note: owing to recent boundary changes
the following counties no longer exist:

England

Avon — see under Gloucester and Somerset
Cleveland — see under Durham
Humberside — see under Yorkshire(East) and Lincolnshire

Scotland

Banffshire — see under Moray and Aberdeenshire
Kincardineshire — see under Aberdeenshire
Kinross-shire — see under Perth and Kinross

In **Wales** the changes have been more extensive
and we have arranged the section as follows:
North Wales — formerly Clwyd and Gwynedd
Dyfed
Powys
South Wales — formerly Glamorgan and Gwent

CONTENTS

ENGLAND

WALES

SCOTLAND

IRELAND

PETS WELCOME!
1997

BIGGER and better than ever! This new edition of *Pets Welcome!* provides an even wider selection of accommodation, both board and self catering, where pets and owners will be made welcome.

An increasing number of us like to take short holidays and breaks during the year, as well as our main holiday, and finding alternative accommodation for the family pet can be inconvenient (and expensive). All the establishments featured here welcome pets with well behaved owners, but please remember to be considerate of others — what you may regard as perfectly acceptable behaviour for your animal may upset or offend your fellow guests.

As usual we include a small selection of Kennels and Catteries as an extra option, and, in the Holidays with Horses supplement, a choice of accommodation with facilities for horses — stabling, grazing etc — which we hope will be useful for those travelling to and from events and competitions as well as for holidays. The Golden Bowl Supplement of Pet-Friendly Pubs is an established feature, and lists pubs and inns where *all* members of the family will be welcome when stopping for refreshment.

Some proprietors offer fuller facilities for pets than others, and in the classified entry which we give each advertiser we try to indicate by symbols whether or not there are any special facilities and if additional charges are involved. However, we suggest that you raise any queries or particular requirements when you make enquiries and bookings.

Most of our entries are of long standing and are tried and tested favourites with animal lovers. However as publishers we do not inspect the accommodation advertised in *Pets Welcome!* and an entry does not imply our recommendation. If you have any problems or complaints, please raise them on the spot with the owner or his representative in the first place. We will follow up complaints if necessary, but we regret that we cannot act as intermediaries nor can we accept responsibility for details of acccommodation and/or services described here. Happily, serious complaints are few.

Finally, if you have to cancel or postpone a holiday booking, please give as much notice as possible. This courtesy will be appreciated and it could save later difficulties.

Please let us know if you have any unusual or humorous experiences with your pet on holiday. This always makes interesting reading! And we hope that you will mention *Pets Welcome!* when you make your holiday enquiries and bookings.

READERS' OFFER 1997 — VALID during 1997

Sacrewell Farm and Country Centre

Thornhaugh, Peterborough, Cambridgeshire PE8 6HJ Tel: (01780) 782254

GROUP RATE ADMISSION for all members of party

NOT TO BE USED IN CONJUNCTION WITH ANY OTHER OFFER

READERS' OFFER 1997 — VALID during 1997

DAIRYLAND FARM WORLD

Summercourt, Near Newquay, Cornwall TR8 5AA Tel: 01872 510246

One child **FREE** when accompanied by adult paying full admission price

NOT TO BE USED IN CONJUNCTION WITH ANY OTHER OFFER

READERS' OFFER 1997 — VALID Easter to October 1997

Tamar Valley Donkey Park

St Anns Chapel, Gunnislake, Cornwall PL18 9HW Tel: 01822 834072

10% OFF admission price for up to 6 people, free donkey ride for children included

NOT TO BE USED IN CONJUNCTION WITH ANY OTHER OFFER

READERS' OFFER 1997 — VALID during 1997

COARSE FISHING AT CROSSFIELD

Crossfield, Staffield, Kirkoswald, Cumbria CA10 1EU Tel: 01768 898711

ADMIT two children for the price of one; three adults for the price of two

NOT TO BE USED IN CONJUNCTION WITH ANY OTHER OFFER

READERS' OFFER 1997 — VALID during 1997

THE CUMBERLAND TOY AND MODEL MUSEUM

Banks Court, Market Place, Cockermouth, Cumbria CA13 9NG Tel: 01900 827606

One person **FREE** per full paying adult

NOT TO BE USED IN CONJUNCTION WITH ANY OTHER OFFER

The fascinating story of farming and country life with working watermill, gardens, collections of bygones, farm and nature trails. Excellent for young children. Campers and Caravanners welcome.

DIRECTIONS: Junction A1/A47, 8 miles west of Peterborough.

OPEN: daily all year.

FHG PUBLICATIONS, ABBEY MILL BUSINESS CENTRE, PAISLEY PA1 1TJ

Britain's premier farm attraction - milking parlour, Heritage Centre, Farmpark and playground. Daily events include bottle feeding, "Pat-a-Pet" and rally karts.

DIRECTIONS: 4 miles from Newquay on the A3058 Newquay to St Austell road.

OPEN: from early April to end October 10.30am to 5pm. Also open from early December to Christmas Eve 12-5pm daily.

FHG PUBLICATIONS, ABBEY MILL BUSINESS CENTRE, PAISLEY PA1 1TJ

Donkey and donkey cart rides for children. Feed and cuddle tame lambs, goats, rabbits and donkeys. Playgrounds, cafe, gifts.

DIRECTIONS: just off A390 Tavistock to Callington road at village of St Anns Chapel

OPEN: Easter to end October 10am to 5pm

FHG PUBLICATIONS, ABBEY MILL BUSINESS CENTRE, PAISLEY PA1 1TJ

Relax, escape and enjoy a great day out - Carp, Rudd, Tench, Bream, Crucians, Ide, Roach and (for fly) Rainbow and Brown Trout

DIRECTIONS: from Kirkoswald follow signs for Staffield, turn right (signposted Dale/Blunderfield); Crossfield is 200m up narrow road via cattle grid.

OPEN: flexible — please telephone to book your fishing

FHG PUBLICATIONS, ABBEY MILL BUSINESS CENTRE, PAISLEY PA1 1TJ

Winner of the 1995 National Heritage Shoestring Award. 100 years of mainly British toys including working tinplate Hornby trains, Scalextric cars, Lego etc. Free quiz.

DIRECTIONS: just off the market place in Cockermouth

OPEN: daily 10am to 5pm from 1st February to 30th November

FHG PUBLICATIONS, ABBEY MILL BUSINESS CENTRE, PAISLEY PA1 1TJ

READERS' OFFER 1997 VALID 28/3/97 TO 30/9/97

Heron Corn Mill and Museum of Papermaking

Waterhouse Mill, Beetham, Milnthorpe, Cumbria LA7 7AR Tel: 015395 63363

One child **FREE** with paying adult (not valid Bank Holidays)

NOT TO BE USED IN CONJUNCTION WITH ANY OTHER OFFER

FHG **READERS' OFFER 1997** VALID March to September 1997

Lowther Leisure and Wildlife Park

Hackthorpe, Penrith, Cumbria CA10 2HG Tel: 01931 712523

£2 off standard admission price (per person) up to maximum of 5 persons

NOT TO BE USED IN CONJUNCTION WITH ANY OTHER OFFER

FHG **READERS' OFFER 1997** VALID to end October 1997

HEIGHTS OF ABRAHAM

Matlock Bath, Derbyshire DE4 3PD Telephone: 01629 582365

FREE child entry with one full paying adult

NOT TO BE USED IN CONJUNCTION WITH ANY OTHER OFFER

FHG **READERS' OFFER 1997** VALID during 1997

The Big Sheep

Bideford, Devon EX39 5AP Telephone: 01237 472366

Admit one **FREE** with each paid admission

NOT TO BE USED IN CONJUNCTION WITH ANY OTHER OFFER

FHG **READERS' OFFER 1997** VALID during 1997

Plymouth Dome (and Smeaton's Tower)

The Hoe. Plymouth, Devon PL1 2NZ Tel: 01752 600608

One child **FREE** with one full-paying adult

NOT TO BE USED IN CONJUNCTION WITH ANY OTHER OFFER

Water-driven working corn mill; displays of milling and papermaking
through the centuries. Occasional demonstrations of hand-making of paper.

DIRECTIONS: one mile south of Milnthorpe off A6, follow brown tourist signs. Exit 35
off M6, north on A6 to Beetham, follow tourist signs

OPEN: 1st April to end Sep: Tuesdays to Sundays plus Bank Holiday Mondays

FHG PUBLICATIONS, ABBEY MILL BUSINESS CENTRE, PAISLEY PA1 1TJ

Attractions, rides, adventure play areas, circus and wildlife, all set in undulating
parkland amidst beautiful scenery, make Lowther the Lake District's
premier all-day attraction.

DIRECTIONS: travelling North leave M6 at J39, follow brown signs; travelling South
leave at J40, follow brown signs. A6 Shap Road, 6 miles south Penrith.

OPEN: March/April to September 10am to 5/6pm.

FHG PUBLICATIONS, ABBEY MILL BUSINESS CENTRE, PAISLEY PA1 1TJ

Cable car return journey plus two famous show caverns. Tree Top Visitor Centre with
restaurant, coffee and gift shops; nature trails and children's play areas.

DIRECTIONS: signposted from all nearby major trunk roads. On A6 at Matlock Bath.

OPEN: daily Easter to end October 10am to 5pm (later in High Season).

FHG PUBLICATIONS, ABBEY MILL BUSINESS CENTRE, PAISLEY PA1 1TJ

"England for Excellence" award-winning rural attraction combining traditional rural
crafts with hilarious novelties such as sheep racing and duck trialling.

DIRECTIONS: on A39 North Devon link road, 2 miles west of Bideford Bridge

OPEN: daily all year, 10am to 6pm

FHG PUBLICATIONS, ABBEY MILL BUSINESS CENTRE, PAISLEY PA1 1TJ

Award-winning centre sited on Plymouth's famous Hoe telling the story of the city,
from the epic voyages of Drake, Cook and the Mayflower Pilgrims
to the devastation of the Blitz. A must for all the family

DIRECTIONS: follow signs from Plymouth City Centre to the Hoe and seafront

OPEN: daily all year (Smeaton's Tower closed October to Easter)

FHG PUBLICATIONS, ABBEY MILL BUSINESS CENTRE, PAISLEY PA1 1TJ

Heavy horse and pony centre, also Icelandic riding stables. Cafe, gift shop. Facilities for disabled visitors.

DIRECTIONS: signposted from the centre of Verwood, which is on the B3081

OPEN: Easter to end October 10am to 5pm

FHG PUBLICATIONS, ABBEY MILL BUSINESS CENTRE, PAISLEY PA1 1TJ

Britain's best preserved lead mining site — and a great day out for all the family, with lots to see and do. Underground Experience — Park Level Mine now open.

DIRECTIONS: alongside A689, midway between Stanhope and Alston in the heart of the North Pennines.

OPEN: April 1st to October 31st 10.30am to 5pm daily

FHG PUBLICATIONS, ABBEY MILL BUSINESS CENTRE, PAISLEY PA1 1TJ

The home of rare breeds conservation, with over 50 breeding flocks and herds of rare farm animals. Adventure playground, pets' corners, picnic area, farm nature trail, Touch barn, Woodland Walk and viewing tower

DIRECTIONS: M5 Junction 9, off B4077 Stow-on-the-Wold road. 5 miles from Bourton-on-the-Water.

OPEN: daily 10.30am to 5pm April to September (to 6pm Sundays, Bank Holidays and daily in July and August).

FHG PUBLICATIONS, ABBEY MILL BUSINESS CENTRE, PAISLEY PA1 1TJ

---

3 floors of a Listed 7-storey Victorian warehouse telling 200 years of inland waterway history by means of video film, working exhibits with 2 quaysides of floating exhibits. Special school holiday activities.

DIRECTIONS: Junction 11 or 12 off M5 — follow brown signs for Historic Docks. Railway and bus station 10 minute walk. Free coach parking.

OPEN: Summer 10am to 6pm; Winter 10am to 5pm. Closed Christmas Day.

FHG PUBLICATIONS, ABBEY MILL BUSINESS CENTRE, PAISLEY PA1 1TJ

Beaulieu offers a fascinating day out for all the family. In the National Motor Museum there are over 250 vehicles from the earliest days of motoring; within the Palace House many Montagu family treasures can be viewed. Plus a host of rides and drives to enjoy.

DIRECTIONS: off Junction 2 of M27, then follow brown tourist signs.

OPEN: daily 10am to 5pm (Easter to September to 6pm). Closed Christmas Day

FHG PUBLICATIONS, ABBEY MILL BUSINESS CENTRE, PAISLEY PA1 1TJ

One of the UK's largest collections of rare farm animals, plus deer, llamas, miniature
horses, waterfowl and poultry in 30 beautiful coastal acres.

DIRECTIONS: on main south coast road A3055 between Ventnor and Niton.

OPEN: Easter to end October open daily 10am to 5.30pm;
Winter open weekends only 10am to 4pm

FHG PUBLICATIONS, ABBEY MILL BUSINESS CENTRE, PAISLEY PA1 1TJ

Over 2000 years of Britain's history is vividly re-created
at this award-winning attraction

DIRECTIONS: signposted on entry into Dover from M20/A20 and M2/A2

OPEN: Easter to end October 10am to 5pm;
November to end December 10am to3pm. Closed Christmas and Boxing Day.

FHG PUBLICATIONS, ABBEY MILL BUSINESS CENTRE, PAISLEY PA1 1TJ

Award-winning science and industry museum. Fascinating colliery tours and
"hands-on" displays including holograms, tornado and virtual reality.

DIRECTIONS: 10 minutes from Junction 22 M1 and Junction 13 M42/A42.
Well signposted along the A50.

OPEN: April to Oct.10am to 6pm; Nov. to March 10am to 5pm. Closed 25/26 Dec.

FHG PUBLICATIONS, ABBEY MILL BUSINESS CENTRE, PAISLEY PA1 1TJ

A marvellous collection of toys dating from the 1780s. Nostalgia and fun for all ages,
with push-buttons, old pier-end machines, silly mirrors,
videos of moving toys, music and lights

DIRECTIONS: approach Lincoln via A46, A15, A57 or A158. Opposite large car park at
foot of castle walls

OPEN: Easter to end Sep: daily except Mon (unless Bank Hol); Oct to Christmas
weekends and school holidays only. Groups by arrangement.

FHG PUBLICATIONS, ABBEY MILL BUSINESS CENTRE, PAISLEY PA1 1TJ

Lions, snow leopards, chimpanzees, penguins, reptiles, aquarium and lots more,
set amidst landscaped gardens.

DIRECTIONS: on the coast 16 miles north of Liverpool; follow the brown tourist signs.

OPEN: daily except Christmas Day. Summer 10am to 6pm; Winter 10am to 4pm.

FHG PUBLICATIONS, ABBEY MILL BUSINESS CENTRE, PAISLEY PA1 1TJ

Beautiful walled garden with nearly 900 types of herbs, woodland walk, nursery, shop.
Guide dogs only.

DIRECTIONS: 6 miles north of Hexham, next to Chesters Roman Fort.

OPEN: daily March to October/November.

FHG PUBLICATIONS, ABBEY MILL BUSINESS CENTRE, PAISLEY PA1 1TJ

A modern working farm with over 3000 animals including ducklings, deer, bees, rheas,
piglets, snails, lambs (all year). New pet centre.

DIRECTIONS: off the A614 at Farnsfield, 12 miles north of Nottingham.
From M1 Junction 27 follow "Robin Hood" signs for 10 miles.

OPEN: daily all year round.

FHG PUBLICATIONS, ABBEY MILL BUSINESS CENTRE, PAISLEY PA1 1TJ

Leading naval aviation museum with over 40 aircraft on display
— Concorde 002 and "Carrier". Based on an operational naval air station.

DIRECTIONS: just off A303/A37 on B3151 at Ilchester.
Yeovil rail station 10 miles.

OPEN: April to October 10am to 5.30pm; November to March 10am to 4.30pm

FHG PUBLICATIONS, ABBEY MILL BUSINESS CENTRE, PAISLEY PA1 1TJ

---

* Britain's most spectacular caves * Traditional paper-making * Fairground Memories *
* Penny Arcade * Magical Mirror Maze *

DIRECTIONS: from M5 Junction 22 follow brown-and-white signs via A38 and A371.
Wookey Hole is just 2 miles from Wells.

OPEN: Summer 9.30am to 5.30pm; Winter 10.30am to 4.30pm. Closed 17-25 Dec.

FHG PUBLICATIONS, ABBEY MILL BUSINESS CENTRE, PAISLEY PA1 1TJ

Planet Earth and Dinosaur Museum, Botanic Garden, model village, playland park,
garden centre and coffee shop

DIRECTIONS: signposted "Garden Paradise" off A26 and A259

OPEN: all year, except Christmas Day and Boxing Day.

FHG PUBLICATIONS, ABBEY MILL BUSINESS CENTRE, PAISLEY PA1 1TJ

READERS' OFFER 1997

VALID during 1997

The Arctic Penguin Maritime Museum

The Pier, Inveraray, Argyll PA32 8UY Tel: 01499 302213

One child **FREE** with each full-paying adult

NOT TO BE USED IN CONJUNCTION WITH ANY OTHER OFFER

READERS' OFFER 1997

VALID April 1997 to April 1998

EDINBURGH CRYSTAL VISITOR CENTRE

Eastfield, Penicuik, Midlothian EH26 8HB Telephone: 01968 675128

OFFER: Two for the price of one (higher ticket price applies).

NOT TO BE USED IN CONJUNCTION WITH ANY OTHER OFFER

READERS' OFFER 1997

VALID during 1997

MYRETON MOTOR MUSEUM

Aberlady, East Lothian EH32 0PZ Telephone: 01875 870288

One child **FREE** with each paying adult

NOT TO BE USED IN CONJUNCTION WITH ANY OTHER OFFER

READERS' OFFER 1997

VALID during 1997

Highland Folk Museum
Am Fasgadh

Duke Street, Kingussie, Inverness-shire PH21 1JG Tel: 01540 661307

One **FREE** child with accompanying adult paying full admission price

NOT TO BE USED IN CONJUNCTION WITH ANY OTHER OFFER

READERS' OFFER 1997

VALID during 1997

SPEYSIDE HEATHER CENTRE

Skye of Curr, Dulnain Bridge, Inverness-shire PH26 3PA Tel: 01479 851359

FREE entry to "Heather Story" exhibitions for two persons

NOT TO BE USED IN CONJUNCTION WITH ANY OTHER OFFER

A fascinating collection of Clyde maritime displays, memorabilia, stunning archive film and entertaining hands-on activities on board a unique three-masted schooner

DIRECTIONS: at Inveraray on the A83

OPEN: daily 10am to 6pm April to October, 10am to 5pm November toMarch

---

Visitor Centre with Exhibition Room, factory tours (children over 8 years only), Crystal Shop, gift shop, coffee shop. Facilities for disabled visitors.

DIRECTIONS: 10 miles south of Edinburgh on the A701 Peebles road; signposted a few miles from the city centre.

OPEN: Visitor Centre open daily; Factory Tours weekdays (9am-3.30pm) all year, plus weekends (11am-2.30pm) April to October.

Motor cars from 1896, motorcycles from 1902, commercial vehicles from 1919, cycles from 1880, British WWII military vehicles, ephemera, period advertising etc

DIRECTIONS: off the A198 near Aberlady, 2 miles from A1

OPEN: daily October to Easter 10am to 5pm; Easter to October 10am to 6pm. Closed Christmas Day and New Year's Day.

One of the oldest open air museums in Britain! A treasure trove of Highland life and culture. Live events June to September.

DIRECTIONS: Easily reached via the A9, 68 miles north of Perth and 42 miles south of Inverness.

OPEN: Easter to October: open daily. November to March: open weekdays. Closed Christmas and New Year.

Multi-award winning centre, "Heather Story" exhibition, gift shop/boutique, over 300 varieties of heather, gardens, trail.
Famous Clootie Dumpling Restaurant - "21 ways to have your dumpling"!

DIRECTIONS: signposted on A95 between Aviemore and Grantown-on-Spey

OPEN: daily 9am to 6pm (10am to 6pm Sun). Please check opening times in winter

FHG READERS' OFFER 1997   **VALID** during 1997

Alice in Wonderland Centre
3/4 Trinity Square, Llandudno, North Wales LL30 2PY Tel: 01492 860082

One child **FREE** with two paying adults

NOT TO BE USED IN CONJUNCTION WITH ANY OTHER OFFER

FHG READERS' OFFER 1997   **VALID** during 1997

Llanberis Lake Railway
Llanberis, Gwynedd LL55 4TY Telephone: 01286 870549

One child travels **FREE** with two full fare-paying adults

NOT TO BE USED IN CONJUNCTION WITH ANY OTHER OFFER

FHG READERS' OFFER 1997   **VALID** March to October 1997

PILI PALAS – BUTTERFLY PALACE
Menai Bridge, Isle of Anglesey LL59 5RP Tel: 01248 712474

One child **FREE** with two adults paying full entry price

NOT TO BE USED IN CONJUNCTION WITH ANY OTHER OFFER

FHG READERS' OFFER 1997   **VALID** during 1997

CENTRE FOR ALTERNATIVE TECHNOLOGY
Machynlleth, Powys SY20 9AZ Telephone: 01654 702400

One child **FREE** when accompanied by paying adult (one per party only)

NOT TO BE USED IN CONJUNCTION WITH ANY OTHER OFFER

FHG READERS' OFFER 1997   **VALID** July to Dec 1997

Techniquest
Stuart Street, Cardiff Bay, South Wales CF1 6BW Tel: 01222 475475

One child **FREE** with full-paying adult

NOT TO BE USED IN CONJUNCTION WITH ANY OTHER OFFER

Walk through the Rabbit Hole to the colourful scenes of Lewis Carroll's classic story set in beautiful life-size displays. Recorded commentaries and transcripts available in several languages.

DIRECTIONS: situated just off the main street, 250 yards from coach and rail stations

OPEN: 10am to 5pm daily Easter to November; closed Sundays November to Easter

FHG PUBLICATIONS, ABBEY MILL BUSINESS CENTRE, PAISLEY PA1 1TJ

A 40-minute ride on a quaint historic steam train along the shore of Llyn Padarn. Spectacular views of the mountains of Snowdonia.

DIRECTIONS: just off the A4086 Caernarfon to Capel Curig road. Follow the "Padarn Country Park" signs.

OPEN: most days Easter to October. Free timetable available from Railway.

FHG PUBLICATIONS, ABBEY MILL BUSINESS CENTRE, PAISLEY PA1 1TJ

Visit Wales' top Butterfly House, with Bird House, Snake House, Ant Avenue, Creepy Crawly Cavern, shop, cafe, adventure playground, picnic area, nature trail etc.

DIRECTIONS: follow brown-and-white signs when crossing to Anglesey; one-and-a-half miles from the Bridge.

OPEN: March to end October 10am to 5pm daily; November/December 11am to 3pm.

FHG PUBLICATIONS, ABBEY MILL BUSINESS CENTRE, PAISLEY PA1 1TJ

Europe's leading Eco-Centre. Water-powered cliff railway, interactive renewable energy displays, beautiful organic gardens, animals; vegetarian restaurant.

DIRECTIONS: three miles north of Machynlleth on the A487 towards Dolgellau.

OPEN: from 10am every day all year (last entry 5pm); times may vary when cliff railway closed ie November to Easter.

FHG PUBLICATIONS, ABBEY MILL BUSINESS CENTRE, PAISLEY PA1 1TJ

Science Discovery Centre with 160 interactive exhibits, Planetarium, Science Theatre and Discovery Room. Fun for all!

DIRECTIONS: A4232 from Juntion 33 of M4. Follow brown tourist signs to Cardiff Bay and Techiquest (10 minutes)

OPEN: weekdays 9.30am to 4.30pm; weekends and Bank Holidays 10.30am to 5pm

FHG PUBLICATIONS, ABBEY MILL BUSINESS CENTRE, PAISLEY PA1 1TJ

BERKSHIRE

COMPTON SWAN HOTEL ✿✿✿
Near Newbury, Berkshire RG20 6NQ

Situated in the heart of the Berkshire Downlands, the Hotel has 5 bedrooms with en suite bathrooms, satellite TV, beverage facilities and telephones. There is an extensive menu with traditional, exotic, vegetarian and special diets catered for. Our home-cooked meals are a speciality. Downlands Healthy Eating Award winner. Large walled garden where we have *al fresco* eating; BBQs. We are near the famous ancient Ridgeway National Trail and are an ideal base for walking, horse-riding and golf. Stabling and horsebox available. Real Ales and Bar Meals available. Entry in CAMRA Good Beer Guide and Good Pub Guide.

Phone Liz or Garry Mitchell FHCIMA on 01635 578269

Compton

Village 5 miles/7Km west of Streatley where Georgian houses are one of the notable sights on the banks of the Thames.

COMPTON SWAN HOTEL, NEAR NEWBURY RG20 6NQ (01635 578269). Situated in the heart of the Berkshire Downlands; 5 rooms en suite with satellite TV, beverage facilities and telephones. Extensive menu with special diets catered for. Large walled garden. ETB 3 Crowns.

CAMBRIDGESHIRE

St Ives

Town on River Ouse 5 miles east of Huntingdon.

ST IVES MOTEL, LONDON ROAD, ST. IVES, HUNTINGDON PE17 4EX (Tel & Fax: 01480 463857). RAC & AA 2 Stars. 16 rooms, all en suite, overlooking orchards and garden. Close to Cambridge and A14. Licensed bar and restaurant. [Pets £2-£5 per night depending on type of animal.

Welney

Village 5 miles north west of Littleport. Wildfowl refuge is noted for Bewick swans.

MRS C. H. BENNETT, STOCKYARD FARM, WISBECH ROAD, WELNEY PE14 9RQ (01354 610433). Rurally situated between Ely and Wisbech, this cosy former farmhouse is ideal for birdwatchers, anglers or touring. Miles of riverside dog walks. Conservatory breakfast room, TV lounge. 1 twin, 1 double. Central heating, washbasins, hot drinks. B&B £13 - £20. No Smoking. [🐾 pw!]

Chester

Former Roman city on the River Dee, with well-preserved walls and beautiful 14th century Cathedral. Liverpool 25 miles.

THE EATON HOTEL, CITY ROAD, CHESTER CH1 3AE (01244 320840; Fax: 01244 320850). In a perfect central location. All rooms have bath or shower (most with WC), colour TV, radio, telephone, hairdryers and tea making facilities. [🐕]

Sandbach

5 miles north-east of Crewe. Two large Saxon crosses in the market place.

MRS HELEN WOOD, ARCLID GRANGE, ARCLID GREEN, SANDBACH CW11 0SZ (01270 764750; Fax: 01270 759255). Set in own mature gardens in lovely countryside, yet within one mile of M6 Junction 17. All rooms with en suite bathroom, colour TV, tea/coffee making, telephone. Residential licence. Delicious home-cooked meals. Ample private parking. B&B from £20pp, Dinner from £12.50.

All the advertisers in PETS WELCOME! have an entry in the appropriate classified section and each classified entry may carry one or more of the following symbols:

🐕   This symbol indicates that pets are welcome free of charge.

£   The £ indicates that a charge is made for pets. We quote the amount where possible, either per night or per week.

pw!   This symbol shows that the establishment has some special provision for pets; perhaps an exercise facility or some special feeding or accommodation arrangements.

⌂   Indicates separate pets accommodation.

PLEASE NOTE that all the advertisers in PETS WELCOME! extend a welcome to pets and their owners but they may attach conditions. The interests of other guests have to be considered and it is usually assumed that pets will be well trained, obedient and under the control of their owner.

CORNWALL

NOTE

All the information in this book is given in good faith in the belief that it is correct. However, the publishers cannot guarantee the facts given in these pages, neither are they responsible for changes in policy, ownership or terms that may take place after the date of going to press. Readers should always satisfy themselves that the facilities they require are available and that the terms, if quoted, still apply.

Coombe Mill

The very Finest Self Catering Cottages & Log Cabins

Cabins - ETB 4 Keys Commended
Cottages - Up to ETB 5 Keys Highly Commended
Dogs Very Welcome plus other pets by arrangement.

Superb cottages and beautiful log cabins set in idyllic 30 acre river valley farm park. All cottages have log burners.

Farm animals and wildlife in abundance. BBQ's, fishing lakes and 2 miles of river fishing, fresh spring water, woodland walks, landscaped gardens. Sandy beaches and rugged moorland all nearby. Enjoy our famous 'food run' each morning for the youngsters and young at heart.

Free Colour Brochure:
**St Breward
North Cornwall
PL30 4LZ**

Telephone:
01208 850344

The ROSEMERE *Hotel*

WATERGATE BAY,
Nr NEWQUAY, CORNWALL TR8 4AB

AA

A treat for both you and your pet in the friendly atmosphere of our family run hotel. The breathtaking seaviews and coastal walks, combined with our reputation for fine foods and wines, create the ideal holiday.

- *Dogs welcome free of charge and sleep with you in your room.*
- *Groundfloor seaview rooms with second exterior door giving immediate access to the front of the hotel.*
- *Overlooking the beautiful 2 mile long Watergate beach, just 100yds from the coastal footpath.*
- *Friendly licensed bar.*
- *36 en suite rooms most with seaviews.*

OPEN CHRISTMAS & NEW YEAR
Tel: 01637 860238 Fax:01637 860438

Rosemundy House Hotel

St Agnes, Cornwall
TR5 0UP

ETB
Commended

Rosemundy House Hotel is an elegant Queen Anne residence set in its own informal garden and woodland, sheltered and secluded, in the pretty, unspoilt village of St Agnes, and within easy reach of spectacular North Cornish coast with its magnificent sandy beaches.

Rosemundy offers the perfect combination for a holiday with your pet. Our comfortable bedrooms have their own individual charm and all are centrally heated and provided with colour TV and tea and coffee making facilities. Our 45ft heated swimming pool, games room, badminton court, putting and croquet lawn are here for your pleasure.

There is much to do and much to see in beautiful Cornwall. There are magnificent walks along cliff tops, historic houses and gardens to visit, and many quaint fishing villages with their stone-built harbours to explore.

From only £180 per week for dinner, bed and breakfast in April to £265 in August.

Why not come and see for yourself? Write or phone for your full colour brochure and tariff.

Tel: (01872) 552101

FREE and REDUCED RATE Holiday Visits!
Don't miss our Readers' Offer Vouchers on pages 5 to 18

NOTE

All the information in this book is given in good faith in the belief that it is correct. However, the publishers cannot guarantee the facts given in these pages, neither are they responsible for changes in policy, ownership or terms that may take place after the date of going to press. Readers should always satisfy themselves that the facilities they require are available and that the terms, if quoted, still apply.

CORNISH TRADITIONAL COTTAGES, LOSTWITHEL PL22 0HT (01208 872559). A fine selection of self-catering cottages on both coasts of Cornwall and on Scilly. Write or telephone for free brochure. [Pets £10 per week.]

WELCOME COTTAGE HOLIDAYS. Hundreds of properties in wonderful locations at welcoming low prices. Pets, linen and fuel mostly included. For FREE colour brochure telephone 01756 702209.

CLASSIC COTTAGES (25), HELSTON, CORNWALL TR13 8NA (24 HOUR DIAL-A-BROCHURE 01326 565555). Choose your cottage from 300 of the finest coastal and country cottages throughout the West Country. [Pets £9 weekly.]

POWELLS COTTAGE HOLIDAYS. Your choice of Cottage in Cornwall, Devon, Somerset,Cotswolds, Wye Valley, Gower and Pembrokeshire in our full colour brochure. [Pets £10 per week] FREEPHONE 0800 378771 or apply: 61 High Street, Saundersfoot, Pembrokeshire SA69 9EJ or (24hrs) 01834 813232.

Bodmin

Quaint county town of Cornwall, standing steeply on the edge of Bodmin moor. Pretty market town and touring centre. Plymouth 31 miles, Newquay 20, Wadebridge 7.

COOMBE MILL, ST. BREWARD, BODMIN PL30 4LZ (01208 850344). Superb cottages and beautiful log cabins set in an idyllic 30 acre farm park. Barbecues, fishing, woodland walks, gardens. All cottages have log burners. Free colour brochure. [Pets £10 per week.]

Boscastle

Picturesque village in tiny harbour, with rocky beach, some sand, and fine scenery. Tintagel 4 miles.

Boscastle/Crackington-Haven area. Modern bungalow sleeping 2–6, heating; microwave; ETB 3 Keys Approved. Near sandy beaches, cliff and valley walks. Beautiful scenery, walking distance local store and Inn. Spring and Autumn £80-£180 per week. Pets welcome. MRS PROUT (01840 250289).

MRS M. CONGDON, TREMORLE, BOSCASTLE PL35 0BU (01840 250233). Peaceful, spacious self-catering bungalow in own grounds with views. Comfortable, heated and well-equipped for 2–8. Lovely cliff, valley walks. Spring and autumn £80-£225 per week. Short breaks from £70. ETB 3 Keys Approved. [pw! 🐾]

THE WELLINGTON HOTEL, THE HARBOUR, BOSCASTLE (01840 250202). Historic 16th-century coaching inn by Elizabethan harbour and National Trust countryside. Fine Anglo-French restaurant, specialising in regional cuisine and seafood. Freehouse with real ales, pub grub, open fires and beams. 10 acres of private woodland walks. [🐾]

Bude

Popular seaside resort overlooking a wide bay of golden sand and flanked by spectacular cliffs. Ideal for surfing; sea water swimming pool for safe bathing.

4 Apartments & Cottage sleeping 2/6 in old country house situated in 4 acres grounds. Tremendous views and only 7 miles from beaches. Ideal for families and quiet breaks; children's play area; friendly animals. Well-behaved pets welcome. Open all year. For brochure please contact: ANNE AND DAVID OLIVANT, BENNETTS, WHITSTONE, HOLSWORTHY EX22 6UD (01288 341322).

JOHN AND JULIA HILDER, MORNISH HOTEL, 20 SUMMERLEAZE CRESCENT, BUDE EX23 8HL (01288 352972). Homely and friendly with comfortable, well-equipped rooms. All en suite with tea/coffee making facilities and television. Central heating. Residents' bar. [Pets £2 per day.]

HEDLEY WOOD CARAVAN AND CAMPING PARK, BRIDGERULE, NEAR BUDE EX22 7ED (Tel/Fax: 01288 381404). Superb 16-acre site amidst lovely countryside, 10 minutes from sandy beaches. All modern facilities. Licensed bar, club room, separate children's play area. [🐾 pw!]

JOHN AND ANN CONNELL, "GUNNEDAH", CRACKINGTON HAVEN, NEAR BUDE EX23 0JZ (01840 230265; Fax: 01840 230452)). Self-contained Bungalows and Cottages. All with fully equipped kitchens, bathrooms. Launderette. Pets by prior arrangement. [Pets £5 per week.]

HENTERVENE PINE LODGE CARAVAN AND CAMPING PARK, CRACKINGTON HAVEN, NEAR BUDE EX23 0LF (01840 230365, Fax: 01840 230514). 11/2 miles unspoilt sandy beach. Area of outstanding natural beauty. Luxury caravans to let. First-class facilities for families and pets. Caravans for sale. Open all year. AA 3 Pennants. Short breaks. [pw! Pets £10 per week, 70p per night camping.]

Superbly situated behind beautiful beaches and spectacular coastal scenery overlooking nature reserve, Brightlands offers you the perfect setting. Twelve self - catering apartments are available depending on your needs. All equipped to a high standard. Large lawns, children's playhouse, barbecue facilities. PROPRIETORS: TIM & SIMONE PRINGLE, BRIGHTLAND HOUSE, MAER LANE, BUDE EX23 9EE (01288 352738). [Pets £9.00 per week].

STAMFORD HILL HOTEL, STRATTON, NEAR BUDE EX23 9AY (01288 352709). Elegant Georgian manor, 5 mins from beaches, 15 en suite rooms, all with colour TV, tea/coffee makers. Heated pool, tennis court, badminton etc. Ideal for golf, fishing, walking. ETB 3 Crowns. [pw! £2 per night.]

Two cottages in an area of outstanding natural beauty. Sleep 6 and 8. 100 yards from unspoilt beach. Open all year. Pets and children welcome. APPLY – MR AND MRS H. CUMMINS, MINESHOP, CRACKINGTON HAVEN, BUDE EX23 0NR (01840 230338). [£9 per pet per week.]

Cawsand

Quaint fishing village with bathing beach; sand at low tide. Ideal for watersports. Plymouth (car ferry) 11 miles, (foot ferry) 3.

FRIARY MANOR HOTEL & RESTAURANT, MAKER HEIGHTS, CAWSAND PL10 1JB (Tel/Fax: 01752 822112) On the Rame Peninsula, surrounded by excellent beaches. Spacious en suite rooms have TV, tea/coffee and hairdryers. Restaurant; vegetarian and special diets catered for. Secure parking. Pets welcome.

MR AND MRS A. FIDLER, RAME BARTON GUEST HOUSE, RAME, CAWSAND PL10 1LG (01752 822789). Old Country House standing in own grounds on beautiful Rame Peninsula. Lovely coastline/beaches. Pets, children very welcome. Bed and Breakfast. Licensed. Extensive exercise area. SAE please.[pw! Pets 30p nightly.]

Crackington Haven

Small coastal village in North Cornwall set amidst fine cliff scenery. Small sandy beach. Launceston 18 miles, Bude 10, Camelford 10.

5 beautiful cottages in lovely rural setting 5 miles from Crackington Haven. Log fires, every comfort, furnished and equipped to a very high standard. Dogs welcome by arrangement. Open all year. 3 Keys Commended. APPLY: JANE AND KEITH BERRY, TRENANNICK COTTAGES, TRENANNICK, WARBSTOW, LAUNCESTON PL15 8RP (01566 781443).[🐾].

Crafthole

Village near sea at Portwrinkle. Fine views over Whitsand Bay and River Lynner. Golf course nearby. Torpoint 6 miles.

THE LISCAWN INN, CRAFTHOLE, NEAR TORPOINT PL11 3BD (01503 230863). Charming, family-run 14th century Hotel. Close to Coastal Path in the forgotten corner of Cornwall. En suite accommodation; bar meals available; cask ales a speciality. Open all year. [🐾]

Crantock

Separated from Newquay by the River Gannel. Sandy surging beach backed by dunes. Newquay 4 miles.

FAIRBANK HOTEL, WEST PENTIRE ROAD, CRANTOCK, NEWQUAY TR8 5SA (01637 830424). Licensed family hotel. Superb uninterrupted sea views across sandy bay. Quaint village location. Four-posters available. A la carte menu. B&B from £13. National Trust walks. Dogs welcome. 10% discount May and June on weekly bookings.

Falmouth

Well-known port and resort on Fal estuary, ideal for boating, sailing and fishing; safe bathing from sandy beaches. Of interest is Pendennis Castle (16th century). Newquay 26, Penzance 26, Truro 11.

MRS J. GOODWIN, "GOOD WINDS" GUEST HOUSE, 13 STRATTON TERRACE, FALMOUTH TR11 2SY (01326 313200). Large Georgian house situated on the water's edge with panoramic views over Flushing and Falmouth Harbour. Licensed. En suite rooms available with colour TV. Self Catering available. [🐕]

Ideally situated for touring Cornwall. 3 bedrooms, lounge with colour TV, kitchen/diner; bathroom, shower room with toilet. Hot water, electricity, bed linen incl. Garden. Open all year. MRS B. NEWING, GLENGARTH, BURNTHOUSE, ST GLUVIAS, PENRYN TR10 9AS (01872 863209).[🐕]

Ideally situated, spacious self-catering bungalow with garden. Full heating. Ample parking. Children and dogs welcome. Sleeps 1–6. Low Season: £115 to £165; High Season: £190 to £265. Apply MRS J.A. SIMMONS, 215A PERRY STREET, BILLERICAY, ESSEX CM12 0NZ (01277 654425). [Pets £5 weekly.]

Fowey

Historic town, now a busy harbour. Regatta and Carnival Week in August.

CLASSY COTTAGES – Three superb coastal cottages, locations between Polperro and Fowey. Willy Wilcox cottage is just 11 feet from beach over smugglers' cave. Log fires, dishwashers, washing machines etc. Indoor Private Swimming Pool. Contact FIONA & MARTIN NICOLLE (01720 423000).

Gorran Haven

Coastal village, 3 miles from Mevagissey.

Self catering apartments sleeping 2–7. Beautiful rural area, 600 yards from sandy beach and harbour. Colour TV, cooker, microwave, fridge freezer. Secluded garden, private parking. Open all year. KEN AND SALLY PIKE, TREGILLAN, TREWOLLOCK LANE, GORRAN HAVEN PL26 6NT (01726 842452 24 hours). [pw! Pets £12 per week]

Hayle

Resort, shopping centre and seaport with excellent sands and dunes. Helston 10 miles, Redruth 10, Penzance 8, Cambourne 5.

MR A. JAMES, ST IVES BAY HOLIDAY PARK, 73 LOGGANS ROAD, UPTON TOWANS, HAYLE TR27 5BH (24hr Brochure Line 0800 317713). Park in sand dunes adjoining huge sandy beach. Choice of bars, free entertainment. Chalets, Caravan and Camping. Large indoor pool. [Pets £14 per week.]

Helston

Ancient Stannary town and excellent touring centre, noted for the annual "Furry Dance". Nearby is Loe Pool, separated from the sea by a bar. Truro 17 miles, St Ives 15, Redruth 11.

Family-run Cornish farmstead, converted into fully equipped holiday cottages. Two acres of naturally beautiful gardens, indoor swimming pool, sauna and solarium. For brochure contact SHARON DARLING, "HALWYN", MANACCAN, NEAR HELSTON TR12 6ER (01326 280359).[🐕]

TRENANCE FARM COTTAGES, MULLION, NEAR HELSTON TR12 7HB (01326 240639). ETB 4 Keys Commended Cottages situated midway between the village and Mullion Cove; half-mile from beach. Footpath to cliff top and lovely coastal walks; field to exercise dogs. Summer swimming pool; games room.

MRS A.G. FARQUHAR, PORTHPRADNACK, MULLION, HELSTON TR12 7EX (01326 240226) Well built house with two flats, accommodating 4–6 persons. Fully equipped kitchens, colour TV. Car essential. Weekly terms from £100 – £275. Pets permitted by arrangement.

MRS MARCIA WILLIAMS, POLKANUGGA FARM, ST. MARTIN-IN-MENEAGE, HELSTON TR12 6DU (01326 280322). Bed and Breakfast in period Farmhouse in peaceful location. Ideal for exploring Helford River and Lizard coastline. WI Member. Cooked breakfast £17.50, Continental £15.00. [🐕].

Holywell Bay

Faces west with extensive sands, cliffs, rocks. 51/2 miles Newquay.

Two self-catering Bungalows 2 minutes from beach. Colour TV, private gardens. Pets welcome. £100-£290 per week. APPLY – M. DEVONSHIRE, WHITE SURF, PENTIRE, NEWQUAY TR7 1PP (01637 871862). [🐕]

Lamorna

Village beside steep-sided valley running down to Lamorna Cove, 4 miles south of Penzance.

TREMENETH HOTEL, LAMORNA, PENZANCE TR19 6XL (01736 731367). Situated in an area of outstanding natural beauty, a short walk from the cove, Merry Maidens and the coastal path. Most rooms en suite with central heating and tea/coffee; colour TV. Brochure on request. [🐕]

Land's End

Westernmost part of English mainland with Heritage Centre and England's last post box.

CARDINNEY CARAVAN AND CAMPING PARK, NEAR CROWS-AN-WRA, LAND'S END TR19 6HX (01736 810880 February to November). Peaceful family-run site situated in picturesque countryside. Ideal for touring South West peninsula. 105 pitches, 50 electric hook-ups. Shop and licensed cafe. Laundry, games and TV rooms. Children and pets welcome. ETB 4 ticks, AA 3 Pennants. [🐕]

Launceston

Formally county capital. Situated above R. Kensey valley, 20 miles NW of Plymouth. Remains of Norman castle.

MRS A. STROUT, BRADRIDGE FARM, BOYTON, LAUNCESTON PL15 9RL (01409 271264) Working farm of 400 acres, on border of Cornwall and Devon, ideal for touring. Good farmhouse cooking with home-grown produce. Hot and cold water in bedrooms, tea/coffee facilities. Guests' own bathroom. Beach, golf course, fishing nearby. B&B from £14, evening meals extra.

Liskeard

Pleasant market town and good centre for exploring East Cornwall. Bodmin Moor and the quaint fishing villages of Looe and Polperro are near at hand. Plymouth 19 miles, St Austell 19, Launceston 16, Fowey (via ferry) 15, Bodmin 13, Looe 9.

MRS V.M. NORTHCOTT, "PENDOWER", EAST TAPHOUSE, LISKEARD PL14 4NH (01579 320332). All comforts. Open all year. Main road, Good food. Moderate terms. Ground floor suite available. [🐕]

MRS L.F. ARTHUR, ROSECRADDOC LODGE, LISKEARD PL14 5BU (TEL OR FAX:01579 346768). Modern two/three bedroom bungalows set in lawned gardens and woodland, in countryside at the foot of Bodmin Moor. Many have microwave ovens and videos. Suitable for disabled visitors. From £120-£340 per week. [Pets £10 per week.]

B. WRIGHT, TREWORGEY COTTAGES, DULOE, LISKEARD, CORNWALL PL14 4PP (01503 262730). Old World Country Cottages. Private garden. Heated summer swimming pool. Full linen. Home cooking. Colour TV, videos, dishwashers, microwaves and log fires. Golf, riding and fishing nearby. Looe 3 miles. Colour brochure available. [pw! £11 per week.]

Gorgeous old world country cottages dating back to 15th century. Open all year. Log fires, antiques and lovely country furnishings, fresh linen, flowers and all comforts of home. Heated pool, meals service, private garden, plenty of country walks. A paradise for dogs and their owners. O. SLAUGHTER, TREFANNY HILL, DULOE, LISKEARD PL14 4QF (01503 220622). [One pet free, others £10 weekly.]

MR AND MRS M. BARKER, RIVERMEAD FARM, TWOWATERSFOOT, LISKEARD PL14 6HT (01208 821464). Self-catering Apartments and Farm Cottages convenient for both coasts and moors. Fishing on River Fowey. Pets welcome![🐾]

MRS E. COLES, CUTKIVE WOOD CHALETS, ST. IVE, LISKEARD PL14 3ND (01579 362216). Self-catering chalets in 41 acres of woodland. 2/3 bedrooms; fully equipped inc. linen, colour TV, fridge, cooker and microwave. On site shop. Pets corner for children. Dogs welcome. [🐾]

Lizard

The most southerly point in England, with fine coastal scenery and secluded coves. Sandy beach at Housel Bay. Truro 28 miles, Helston 11.

Helford River area and Lizard Village. A selection of cottages with charm and comfort in village locations. Some spectacular sea views. Sleep 2–9 people. Enclosed gardens. Unrivalled beaches, boating, walking. LIZARD COTTAGES, ROSUICK CHAPEL HOUSE, ST MARTIN, HELSTON TR12 6EA [Pets £10 per week].

PARC BRAWSE HOUSE, PENMENNER ROAD, THE LIZARD TR12 7NR (01326 290466). Lovely old Cornish house overlooking Lizard Point. Comfortable rooms with sea views, colour TV and teamakers; some en suite. Home cooking (including vegetarian). Licensed. Open all year. ETB 2 Crowns Commended, RAC Acclaimed. [Pets £1 per night.]

Looe

Twin towns linked by a bridge over the River Looe. Capital of the shark fishing industry; nearby Monkey Sanctuary is well worth a visit.

TRADITIONAL CORNISH HOLIDAY COTTAGES for 2, 4, 6, 8. 250 yards Polperro harbour, 5 miles Looe. Either magnificently situated directly overlooking harbour, fabulous outlook, 14 miles sea views; or nicely positioned in the quaint old village centre, by river, gardens, parking, 2 minutes shops, beach, cliff walks. GRAHAM WRIGHT, THE MILL, POLPERRO, CORNWALL PL13 2RP (01579 344080).

CARTOLE COTTAGES, PELYNT, LOOE PL13 2QH (01503 220956). Self contained stone cottages sleeping 2–6. Children and pets welcome. Bed linen, central heating, colour TV, cots and high chairs, laundry. Set in 6 acres of gardens and grounds surrounded by countryside. 2 miles Talland Bay, 4 miles Looe and Polperro. [Dogs £12 weekly].

HENDRA FARM COTTAGES, PELYNT, LOOE PL13 2LU (01503 220701). Three quality cottages peacefully set in 120 acres of beautiful countryside on working farm. A hidden retreat only four miles Looe, Polperro, Coastal Path and coves. Excellent locality for walking. Cottages sleep 2 to 5 persons. Heating, electricity and bed linen included in price. 4 Keys Highly Commended.

ALLHAYS COUNTRY HOUSE, TALLAND BAY, LOOE PL13 2JB (01503 272434; Fax: 01503 272929). Come and discover what makes a perfect holiday for you and your pet. En suite rooms (ground floor available). Award-winning food; 2 acres of secluded gardens; coastal paths nearby. ETB 3 Crowns Commended. [pw!🐕]

TRENANT PARK COTTAGES. Four delightful cottages sleep from 2 to 7 persons. Each has spacious lounge with colour TV, fully equipped kitchen, private garden. Ample room to relax. APPLY: MRS E. CHAPMAN, TRENANT LODGE, SANDPLACE, LOOE PL13 1PH (01503 263639/262241).[Pets £15 per week.]

MRS JOY RYDING, APPLE TREES, PORTUAN ROAD, HANNAFORE, LOOE PL13 2DN (01503 262626). Well-furnished, self-contained bungalow flat. Sleeps 2/4. 150 yards sea. Dogs welcome, no charge. Open all year. SAE please. [🐕]

CLASSY COTTAGES – Three superb coastal cottages, locations between Polperro and Fowey. Willy Wilcox cottage is just 11 feet from beach over smugglers' cave. Log fires, dishwashers, washing machines etc. Indoor Private Swimming Pool. Contact FIONA & MARTIN NICOLLE (01720 423000).

TALLAND BARTON CARAVAN PARK, TALLAND BAY, LOOE PL13 2JA (01503 272429). Caravans with electricity and running water, some with showers, flush toilets on family-run farm site close to beaches. Some available from Friday to Friday. Site has shop, licensed club, toilet and shower block, swimming pool, laundry-room. Ideal touring centre. Pets welcome. SAE for colour brochure.

Gorgeous old world country cottages dating back to 15th century. Open all year. Log fires, antiques and lovely country furnishings, fresh linen, flowers and all comforts of home. Heated pool, meals service, private garden, plenty of country walks. A paradise for dogs and their owners. O. SLAUGHTER, TREFANNY HILL, DULOE, LISKEARD PL14 4QF (01503 220622). [One pet free, others £10 weekly.]

Mawgan Porth

Modern village on small sandy bay. Good surfing. Inland stretches the beautiful Vale of Lanherne. Rock formation of Bedruthan Steps is nearby. Newquay 6 miles west.

THE MALMAR HOTEL, TRENANCE, MAWGAN PORTH, NEWQUAY TR8 4DA (01637 860324). Small licensed hotel. Reputable sea-fishing coast. Two good golf courses nearby. Good English cooking. Rooms with tea-making facilities, some en suite. [🐕]

WHITE LODGE HOTEL, MAWGAN PORTH BAY, NEAR NEWQUAY TR8 4BN (01637 860512). Give yourselves and your dogs a quality holiday break at this family-run hotel overlooking beautiful Mawgan Porth Bay. Bedrooms en suite, all rooms with washbasins, shaver points, heaters etc. Lounge bar, games room, sun patio, dining room. Car phone. Phone for free brochure. 2 Crowns Approved. AA. RAC. [🐕 pw!]

Mousehole

Picturesque fishing village with sand and shingle beach. Penzance 3 miles.

Four s/c flats, two with full sea view, at entrance to unspoilt fishing village. Fully equipped, bedding supplied, colour TV. Open all year. From £70.00 per week. Pets welcome. MR A.G. WRIGHT, 100 WENSLEY ROAD, WOODTHORPE, NOTTINGHAM NG5 4JU (Tel and Fax: 0115 963 9279 or 01736 731563). [🐾]

Newquay

Popular family holiday resort surrounded by miles of golden beaches. Semi-tropical gardens, zoo and museum. Ideal for exploring all of Cornwall.

ROSEMERE HOTEL, WATERGATE BAY, NEAR NEWQUAY TR8 4AB (01637 860238). Relaxed, informal, family-run Hotel; large grassed area, beach and Coastal footpath all within 100 yards. 44 rooms, 36 en suite. Licensed bar, entertainment. Open all year. [🐾]

WHITE LODGE HOTEL, MAWGAN PORTH BAY, NEAR NEWQUAY TR8 4BN (01637 860512). Give yourselves and your dogs a quality holiday break at this family-run hotel overlooking beautiful Mawgan Porth Bay. Bedrooms en suite, all rooms with washbasins, shaver points, heaters etc. Lounge bar, games room, sun patio, dining room. Car park. Phone for free brochure. 2 Crowns Approved. AA. RAC. [🐾 pw!]

CORISANDE MANOR HOTEL, PENTIRE, NEWQUAY TR7 1PL (01637 872042). A Hotel of unique turreted Austrian design, quietly situated and commanding an unrivalled position in three-acre secluded landscaped gardens. Private foreshore. 17 en suite bedrooms with TV, tea-making facilities. Chef proprietors. DB&B weekly £199-£250 pp inc. VAT. For brochure and menus telephone David and Chris Grant. AA**RAC, ETB Three Crowns Commended, Les Routiers.[🐾]

PARADISE BEACH HOTEL, WATERGATE BAY, NEWQUAY (01637 860273). Superb location 200 yards from beach (dogs allowed); beautiful cliff walks. En suite rooms; sauna, solarium. Excellent choice meals. Licensed. [🐾]

CY AND BARBARA MOORE, THE RANCH HOUSE, TRENCREEK, NEWQUAY TR8 4NR (01637 875419). Detached bungalow with lovely gardens and superb views. Shower rooms; lounge. Parking. Children and pets welcome. DB&B from £119 per week, B&B from £91 per week. [Pets £2.50 per night, £15 per week.]

Padstow

Bright little resort with pretty harbour on Camel estuary. Extensive sands. Nearby is Elizabethan Prideaux Place. Newquay 15 miles, Wadebridge 8.

Pleasant Victorian House. Well converted to 3 fully equipped apartments. Sleeps 4/6. Large garden. Car park. Dogs love us! MRS WATTS, "WHISTLERS", TREYARNON BAY, PADSTOW PL28 8JR (Tel and Fax: 01841 520228). [🐾]

RAINTREE HOUSE HOLIDAYS, WHISTLERS, TREYARNON BAY, PADSTOW PL28 8JR (Tel and Fax: 01841 520228). We have a varied selection of accommodation. Small or large, houses and apartments, some by the sea. All in easy reach of our lovely beaches. Please write or phone for brochure. [🛏]

Penzance

Well-known resort and port for Scilly Isles, with sand and shingle beaches. Truro 27 miles, Helston 13, Land's End 10, St Ives 8.

EDNOVEAN HOUSE, PERRANUTHNOE, PENZANCE TR20 9LZ (01736 711071). Small friendly 9-bedroomed hotel situated in one acre of gardens. Lovely views overlooking Mount's Bay. Car park. 9-hole putting green. ETB 3 Crowns, AA QQQ. Phone for brochure.[🛏]

GLENCREE PRIVATE HOTEL, 2 MENNAYE ROAD, PENZANCE TR18 4NG (01736 62026). Just off seafront with comfortable friendly atmosphere. Spacious rooms with colour TV and tea-making. Most rooms are en suite, some with good sea views. Unrestricted parking. Good home cooking. All well-behaved pets welcome and their owners too! WCTB 2 Crowns. B&B from £12 nightly, £72 weekly. [🛏]

MRS HOOD, TRENANT PRIVATE HOTEL, ALEXANDRA ROAD, PENZANCE TR18 4LX (01736 62005). Comfortable, friendly Hotel near seafront. Colour TV, teamaker, B&B from £15 nightly, £100 weekly. En suite, four-poster bedrooms and ground floor twin available. Dinner optional. Licensed. Early Breakfasts. All welcome from stick insects to elephants! AA Recommended QQQ, Cornwall Tourist Board.[🛏]

Polperro

Picturesque and quaint little fishing village and harbour. Of interest is the "House of the Props". Fowey 9 miles, Looe 5.

POLPERRO. 250 yards harbour, holiday cottages sleeping 2,4, 6 or 8. Spectacularly situated either overlooking Harbour, fabulous outlook, 15 miles sea views and terraced gardens giving Mediterranean setting or nicely positioned by river in old part of village. Gardens, private parking, 2 minutes shops, beach, quay, NT cliff walks. Well furnished, colour TV. Open all year. Competitive rates. Children Welcome. Ring or write NOW: GRAHAM WRIGHT, THE MILL, POLPERRO, CORNWALL PL13 2RP (01579 344080). [🛏]

CLAREMONT HOTEL, THE COOMBES, POLPERRO PL13 2RG (01503 272241). All rooms en suite with colour TV and tea-making facilities. Bar. Restaurant. Ideally located for walking and touring Cornwall. Short breaks. Open all year. ETB 3 Crowns, AA/RAC 1 Star, Logis.[🛏]

PENRYN HOUSE HOTEL, THE COOMBES, POLPERRO PL13 2RG (01503 272157). Charming family-run hotel in village centre. En suite rooms with colour TV, central heating, phones, courtesy trays. Variety of excellent dishes prepared by speciality chef using local produce and fresh fish, served in our candlelit restaurant. Parking. Bargain Breaks. Murder Mystery Weekends. 3 Crowns. B&B from £19-£26. [pw!]

CLASSY COTTAGES – Three superb coastal cottages, locations between Polperro and Fowey. Willy Wilcox cottage is just 11 feet from beach over smugglers' cave. Log fires, dishwashers, washing machines etc. Indoor Private Swimming Pool. Contact FIONA & MARTIN NICOLLE (01720 423000).

Port Gaverne

Hamlet on east side of Port Isaac, near Camel Estuary.

Homes from home around our peaceful courtyard garden 100 yds from sea in bygone fishing hamlet. Each sleeps six and has full CH, fridge-freezer, washer-dryer, dishwasher, microwave, video. £140 (February) £520 (August) weekly. Daily rates off-season. Resident owners APPLY:- CAROLE & MALCOLM LEE, GULLROCK, PORT GAVERNE, PORT ISAAC PL29 3SQ (01208 880106).[🐾]

Port Isaac

Attractive fishing village with harbour. Much of the attractive coastline is protected by the National Trust. Camelford 9 miles, Wadebridge 9.

Cottages sleep 6/8. Central location. Approximately 4 miles beautiful beaches, moors, golf course and bike trails. Brochure. MRS S. STEPHENS, CASTLE GOFF, LANTEGLOS, CAMELFORD PL32 9RQ (01840 213535).

CHIMNEYS, PORT GAVERNE, PORT ISAAC PL29 3SQ (Tel & Fax: 01208 880254). A charming 18th century cottage only 10 metres from beach. Four bedrooms, two bathrooms, lounge, dining room and kitchen. Good size garden. Brochure from Mrs. Holmes.

LONG CROSS HOTEL & VICTORIAN GARDENS, TRELIGHTS, PORT ISAAC PL29 3TF (01208 880243). Set in magnificent public gardens with tavern in the grounds. Pets' corner. Perfect base for touring. Excellent food served all day. Bargain Spring/Autumn Breaks. [Pets £1 per night.]

Portscatho

Tiny cliff-top resort on Roseland Peninsula overlooking beach of rocks and sand. Harbour and splendid views. Falmouth 5 miles.

ROSEVINE HOTEL, PORTHCURNICK BEACH, PORTSCATHO, TRURO TR2 5EW (01872 580206; Fax: 01872 580230). A friendly, family-managed country house hotel in a peaceful setting with delightful sea views. Top class cuisine, fresh local fish a speciality. Four Crowns Highly Commended. AA/RAC***, Ashley Courtenay Highly Recommended. [pw! Pets £3 per night.]

PETER AND LIZ HEYWOOD, TREWINCE MANOR, PORTSCATHO, NEAR TRURO TR2 5ET (FREEPHONE 0500 657861). Georgian Manor house estate with luxury lodges, cedarwood cabins, cottage, small touring site. Lounge bar and restaurant; launderette. Superb walking and sailing. Dogs welcome. [Pets £16 per week]

Praa Sands

Magnificent stretch of sands and dunes. Nearby is picturesque Prussia Cove. Penzance 7 1/2 miles, Helston 6.

Superb Bungalows sleeping 6 and 8, plus cot. One overlooking sea at Praa Sands. One 2 miles Praa Sands, secluded situation. Well furnished and large gardens all round. All breeds welcome. Terms from £100. APPLY – MRS J. LAITY, CHYRASE FARM, GOLDSITHNEY, PENZANCE TR20 9JD (01736 763301). [Pets £10 per week.]

Redruth

Market town 8 miles west of Truro.

GLOBE VALE HOLIDAY PARK, RADNOR, REDRUTH TR16 4BH (01209 891183). "In the Countryside, near the Sea." Perfect for pets and owners, with unlimited trails to explore and near "Dogs Allowed" beaches. Shop, play area, launderette, bar and games room. Caravans, tourers and tents welcome. [Pets £7.50 per week]

Ruan High Lanes

Picturesque hamlet convenient for Veryan and Philleigh. Beautiful surrounding countryside.

POLSUE MANOR, RUAN HIGH LANES, NEAR TRURO TR2 5LU (Tel/Fax: 01872 501270). Tranquil secluded manor house in 4 acres. All rooms en suite. Close to sandy coves, coastal paths and country walks. Pets very welcome. [Pets £2.50 per night]

St Agnes

Patchwork of fields dotted with remains of local mining industry. Watch for grey seals swimming off St. Agnes Head.

SUNHOLME HOTEL, GOONVREA ROAD, ST AGNES TR5 0NW (01872 552318). Enjoy some of the finest views in the South West. Ideal for touring; cliff walks and beaches. Good food and service. All bedrooms en suite. Write or phone for brochure. [Pets £1.50 per night.]

ROSEMUNDY HOUSE HOTEL, ST AGNES TR5 0UF (01872 552101). An elegant Queen Anne residence set in 4 acres of informal garden and woodland. Swimming pool, games room, croquet, putting. Half board from £180. Send or telephone for colour brochure.[🐾]

THE DRIFTWOOD SPARS HOTEL, TREVAUNANCE COVE, ST AGNES TR5 0RT (01872 552428). Take a deep breath of Cornish fresh air at this comfortable Hotel ideally situated for a perfect seaside holiday. Wonderful food, traditional Cornish home cooking. Children and pets welcome.

MARC WATTS, TREVAUNANCE POINT HOTEL, ST AGNES TR5 0RZ (01872 553235; Fax: 01872 553874). Old world clifftop Hotel, ships timbered rooms, sea views, candlelight cuisine. Sea-food specialities. Open all year. Winter breaks. [🐾 pw!]

St Austell

Old Cornish town and china clay centre with small port at Charlestown (1$^1/_2$ miles). Excellent touring centre. Newquay 16 miles, Truro 14, Bodmin 12, Fowey 9, Mevagissey 6.

ST MARGARET'S HOLIDAY PARK, POLGOOTH, ST AUSTELL PL26 7AX (01726 74283; Fax: 01726 71680). Family-run 27 Bungalows and Chalets in sunny wooded valley. Village Inn, shop, golf 500 yards. Children and pets welcome. From £90 per week. [pw! £8 per week.]

P. W. MILLN, BOSINVER FARM, ST AUSTELL PL26 7DT (01726 72128). Quality self-catering Cottages and Bungalows on small estate. Sleep 2, 3, 4, 5, 6, 11 – one suitable for a wheelchair. Children and dogs welcome. Personally supervised by owners. Colour brochure.[pw! £7 per week.]

St Austell Bay

Near town of same name, extending from Gribbin Head to Black Head.

"SANDWAYS". Detached bungalow surrounded by own gardens. Pleasant coastal situation 5 minutes' walk from dog-friendly large sandy beach and conservation lake. One well-behaved dog welcome. MRS A. BUCKINGHAM, 16 HADDON WAY, CARLYON BAY, ST AUSTELL PL25 3QG (01726 815566). [🐾]

St Ives

Picturesque resort, popular with artists, with cobbled streets and intriguing little shops. Wide stretches of sand.

CARLYON GUEST HOUSE, 18 THE TERRACE, ST IVES TR26 2BP (01736 795317). Warm, friendly atmosphere with good English cooking. All bedrooms with TV and tea/coffee facilities; most with showers. Bed and Breakfast, with Evening Meal optional.

THE LINKS HOLIDAY FLATS, CHURCH LANE, LELANT, ST IVES TR26 3HY (01736 753326). Self-catering Holiday Flats on 2-acre site 5 minutes from beach, dogs allowed. All flats are self-contained with colour TV. Write or phone for brochure.[🐾]

Country Cottages at Hellesveor, one mile St Ives Harbour. Sleep 4–6. Luxuriously equipped; sheets, central heating; garden; parking; farm views, cliff walks. Children welcome. Available all year. Terms £210-£410; includes sheets and heating. Tourist Board Category 3. APPLY: MRS P. H. SEABROOK, 30 NEWCOMBE STREET, MARKET HARBOUROUGH, LEICESTERSHIRE LE16 9PB (01858 463723).

HOTEL ROTORUA, TRENCROM LANE, CARBIS BAY, ST. IVES TR26 2TD (01736 795419). Situated in quiet wooded lane, extensive gardens and heated swimming pool. All rooms en suite, central heating, colour TV, hair dryer, tea/coffee facilities. ETB 3 Crowns Commended, AA One Star. [🐾]

Family holiday Bungalows, each sleeping 4-6 persons. Magnificent views of St Ives Bay. Private parking. Colour TV. Children and pets very welcome. Brochure. Available April to October. Contact: MAUREEN RICHARDS, SPRINGFIELD, LELANT DOWNS, NEAR HAYLE TR27 6LL (01736 753625).

St Just-in-Roseland

Historic town which retains many traces of its mining, farming and fishing past. Land's End 6 miles.

MRS LILLEY, ROSE-DA-MAR HOTEL, ST. JUST-IN-ROSELAND, TRURO TR2 5JB (01326 270 450). Small hotel in heart of the beautiful Roseland. Ideal location for walking, sailing and relaxing. Close to St. Mawes and King Harry ferry. Easy access to all parts of Cornwall. Dogs welcome.

St Mawgan

Delightful village in a wooded river valley. Ancient church has fine carvings.

DALSWINTON COUNTRY HOUSE HOTEL, ST MAWGAN, NEAR NEWQUAY TR8 4EZ (01637 860385). Old Cornish house standing in nine and a half acres of secluded grounds. All rooms en suite, colour TV, tea/coffee facilities. Heated swimming pool. Open for Christmas and New Year. ETB 3 Crowns, AA 2 Stars. [🐾]

St Mellion

Village 3 miles south east of Callington.

KERNOCK COTTAGES. Three traditional stone cottages for 2/6/8 set in 28 acres between Bodmin Moor and Dartmoor. Safe and quiet for pets and the family. Personal attention from resident owners. For brochure call/fax RICHARD STEEL on 01579 350435.[🐾]

Tintagel

Attractively situated amidst fine cliff scenery; small rocky beach with some sand. Famous for associations with King Arthur, whose ruined castle on Tintagel Head is of interest. Bude 19 miles, Camelford 6.

BOSSINEY FARM CARAVAN AND CAMPING PARK, TINTAGEL PL34 0AY (01840 770481). BGHP 4 ticks. Family-run park. 19 luxury letting vans; fully serviced, H&C with shower, room heater, TV. On the coast at Tintagel. Colour brochure available. [🐾]

THE PENALLICK HOTEL, TREKNOW, TINTAGEL PL34 0EJ (01840 770296). Comfortable, family-run licensed hotel, magnificent cliff top position. All rooms colour TV, tea-makers; most en suite/sea views. Open all year. Children over 12 years welcome. [🐕]

MRS M. LEEDS, WILLAPARK MANOR HOTEL, BOSSINEY, TINTAGEL PL34 0BA (01840 770782). Beautiful character house amidst 14 acres and only minutes from the beach. All en suite rooms. Children and pets welcome. Open all year. SAE for brochure. ETB 3 Crowns Commended. [🐕]

MILL HOUSE INN, TREBARWITH STRAND, TINTAGEL PL34 0HD (01840 770200/770932). Picturesque 17th century inn set in 7 acres of woodland with stream running alongside. Ideal for walking, quarter-mile from beach. Seven letting bedrooms, mostly en suite. TV, tea/coffee making facilities, hairdryers. Restaurant, ample parking. Friendly atmosphere. Pets welcome.[Pets £2 per night.]

MRS R. DE BOYER, ROSEBUD COTTAGE, BOSSINEY, TINTAGEL PL34 0AX (01840 770861). Picturesque stone cottage, secluded garden, within walking distance of beautiful headland. Friendly atmosphere, comfortable rooms. Optional evening meals. Private car parking. Pets welcome. [🐕]

Torpoint

Busy and pleasant little town on the Hamoaze facing Devonport from and to which runs a car ferry. Plymouth (via ferry) 3 miles.

WHITSAND BAY HOTEL, PORTWRINKLE, BY TORPOINT, PLYMOUTH PL11 3BU (01503 230276; Fax: 01503 230297). Magnificent Country Manor Hotel on cliff top at edge of beach. Own 18 hole golf course, indoor heated swimming pool. Family-sized en suite rooms. AA 2 Stars, ETB 3 Crowns. [Pets £5.50 per night]

Trebetherick

Village on Padstow Bay, 5 miles north west of Wadebridge.

MRS C. ORD, 14 TREHANNICK CLOSE, ST. TEATH, BODMIN PL30 3LF (01208 850032). Family home, sleeps 10. Close to golf course and Daymer Bay. Very large garden, ideal for children. Parking. Available all year. Bed linen provided. [🐕]

Treknow

Village near north coast of Trebarwith Strand. Camelford 4 miles.

MRS S. M. ORME, "HILLSCROFT", TREKNOW, TINTAGEL (01840 770551). Comfortable accommodation near surfing beach in beautiful National Trust countryside. Walks, riding, sea-fishing all nearby. Car parking. All rooms tea/coffee facilities. Pets welcome. Bed and Breakfast. Non smoking. [🐕]

Truro

Pleasant cathedral city. An excellent touring centre with both north and south coasts within easy reach. Many tourist attractions include fine shops. There are numerous creeks to explore and boat trips may be made across the estuary to Falmouth. Penzance 27 miles, Bodmin 25, Helston 17, St. Austell 14, Falmouth 11, Redruth 8.

IVY COTTAGE, BISSOE, CORNWALL. 200-year-old country cottage 5 miles from Truro. Kitchen/dining room, lounge, 2 bedrooms. All facilities incl. TV and microwave. Terms £108-£295. For brochure phone 01872 863352.

MRS TRESEDAR, MARCORRIE HOTEL, 20 FALMOUTH ROAD, TRURO TR1 2HX (01872 77374 or Fax: 01872 41666). Victorian town house, five minutes' walk from city centre. Ideal touring base. All rooms en suite with central heating, colour TV, telephone, tea-making facilities. Ample parking. Outdoor swimming pool. Major credit cards accepted. Open all year. Bed and Breakfast from £19.50 per person per night. 3 Crowns Approved. [Pets £2.50 per night]

Whitsand Bay

Bay running north-west from Rame Head on south coast to the Long Stone between Downderry and Portwrinkle.

MRS KATHY RIDPATH, FIR COTTAGE, LOWER TREGANTLE, ANTONY, TORPOINT PL11 3AL (01752 822626). On coastal path between Rame Head and Looe. Warm, comfortable accommodation. H&C, colour TV in each room. Surrounded by beautiful countryside. Beach and golf close by. [Pets £5 per week.]

HOLIDAY ACCOMMODATION CLASSIFICATION
in England, Scotland and Wales.

The National Tourist Boards for England, Scotland and Wales have agreed a common 'Crown Classification' scheme for serviced (Board) accommodation. All establishments are inspected regularly and are given a classification indicating their level of facilities and service.

There are six grades ranging from 'Listed' to 'Five Crowns'. The higher the classification, the more facilities and services offered. Crown classification is a measure of facilities, not quality. A common quality grading scheme grades the quality of establishments as 'Approved', 'Commended', 'Highly Commended' or 'Deluxe' according to the accommodation, welcome and service they provide.

For **Self Catering**, holiday homes in England are awarded 'Keys' after inspection and can also be 'Approved', 'Commended', 'Highly Commended' or 'Deluxe' according to the facilities available. In Scotland the Crown scheme includes self-catering accommodation and Wales also has a voluntary inspection scheme for self-catering grading from '1(Standard)' to '5 (Excellent)'.

Caravan and Camping Parks can participate in the British Holiday Parks grading scheme from 'Approved (✓), to 'Excellent (✓✓✓✓); in addition, each National Tourist Board has an annual award for high-quality caravan accommodation in England – Rose Awards; in Scotland – Thistle Commendation; in Wales – Dragon Awards.

When advertisers supply us with information, FHG Publications show Crowns and other awards or gradings, including AA,RAC, Egon Ronay etc. We also award a small number of Farm Holiday Guide Diplomas every year, based on readers' recommendations.

CUMBRIA

KINGSWOOD

OLD LAKE ROAD
AMBLESIDE. TEL: 015394 34081

Near town centre yet off main road. Ample car parking. Comfortable, well-equipped bedrooms with washbasins, tea/coffee making facilities. Colour TV. Central heating. Non-smoking. Pets welcome. Bargain Breaks off season. Phone for rates and details.

IVY HOUSE

Hawkshead, Nr Ambleside, Cumbria LA22 0HS.

Commended — Freephone 0500 657876

Family-run Listed Georgian hotel, full of great charm and character, 11 en suite bedrooms with central heating and equipped with hot drink trays. Contact David or Jane Vaughan for Brochure.

Wanslea Guest House

Lake Road, Ambleside LA22 0DB Tel: 015394 33884

Spacious family-run guest house just a stroll from village and lake. We offer a friendly welcome and comfortable rooms, most en suite. Relax in our licensed residents' lounge with a real fire on winter evenings. B&B from £16pp; Evening Meal also available. Pets welcome by arrangement (please bring bedding).

A Luxury Break in Cumbria at Superb Value Prices!

When you fancy pampering yourself and your pet with a touch of luxury, enjoy the relaxing comfort and superb value of the highly-commended Appleby Manor Country House Hotel. Excellent restaurant, relaxing lounges, indoor leisure club and breathtaking scenery all around.

Phone now for a full-colour brochure and prices: 017683 51571

MILBURN GRANGE

KNOCK, APPLEBY-IN-WESTMORLAND CA16 6DR
TEL/FAX: 017683 61867. MOBILE: 0836 547130

Tiny hamlet nestling at the foot of the Pennines enjoying extensive views over Lakeland Hills. Six quality cottages equipped to highest standards set within two acres. Linen included free of charge. Babysitting available. Children's safe play area. Well behaved pets welcome at £10 per week each. Two other cottages available in nearby idyllic villages. Open all year. Off season bargain breaks from November to March (Excluding Christmas and New Year). Terms from £80 to £350. SAE please for brochure.

STAKIS LODORE SWISS HOTEL

Borrowdale, Near Keswick, Cumbria CA12 5UX
Tel: 017687 77285 Fax: 017687 77343 4 Crowns Highly Commended

Luxury Hotel with fabulous views overlooking Derwentwater and fells beyond. Facilities include 75 bedrooms, magnificent gardens, restaurant and lounge with views, bar, nursery (under sixes), leisure club with pool, sauna, sunbed and gym, tennis, squash and outdoor pool. There is also a hairdresser, games room, shop and outdoor play area.

All the advertisers in PETS WELCOME! have an entry in the appropriate classified section and each classified entry may carry one or more of the following symbols:

🛏   This symbol indicates that pets are welcome free of charge.

£   The £ indicates that a charge is made for pets. We quote the amount where possible, either per night or per week.

pw!   This symbol shows that the establishment has some special provision for pets; perhaps an exercise facility or some special feeding or accommodation arrangements.

⌂   Indicates separate pets accommodation.

PLEASE NOTE that all the advertisers in PETS WELCOME! extend a welcome to pets and their owners but they may attach conditions. The interests of other guests have to be considered and it is usually assumed that pets will be well trained, obedient and under the control of their owner.

NOTE

All the information in this book is given in good faith in the belief that it is correct. However, the publishers cannot guarantee the facts given in these pages, neither are they responsible for changes in policy, ownership or terms that may take place after the date of going to press. Readers should always satisfy themselves that the facilities they require are available and that the terms, if quoted, still apply.

FHG PUBLICATIONS LIMITED publish a large range of well-known accommodation guides. We will be happy to send you details or you can use the order form at the back of this book.

IN THE HEART OF THE LAKES
THE BURNSIDE HOTEL

FOR HOTEL ENQUIRIES RING FREE ON (0800) 220688

THE LAKE DISTRICT'S COMPLETE RESORT
Where we welcome pets – FREE!

Set in mature gardens overlooking Lake Windermere, yet only 300 yards from the Promenade, Steamer Pier and bustling village centre, the Burnside offers you one of the finest holiday locations.

BURNSIDE HOTEL Enjoy a wide choice of en suite bedrooms and lake view suites. Spacious lounges, two widely acclaimed restaurants, a well stocked bar and the incomparable Parklands Country Club all combine to make your stay in Lakeland a truly memorable one.

Full conference facilities. Licenced for Civil Wedding Ceremonies.

★ Christmas and New Year Programmes available ★

BURNSIDE PARK SELF CATERING COTTAGES

For those who like the freedom of self-catering whilst still maintaining the very highest standards of their accommodation. Sleeps 2-6 guests.

PARKLANDS COUNTRY CLUB

Guests and members enjoy access to our all weather leisure centre, incorporating swimming pool with children's area, spa bath, sauna and steam room, badminton and squash courts, trimnasium, beauty salon and solarium, and a children's soft play area. The club lounge and bar offers two full size snooker tables.

For those pets wishing to accompany their owners, you are most welcome throughout the resort, excepting of course the restaurant and leisure club. There are many walks around the area where you may take your owners for their daily exercise!

**THE BURNSIDE HOTEL
BOWNESS ON WINDERMERE
CUMBRIA, LA23 3EP. FREEPHONE : 0800 220688**

TEL: Hotel: (015394) 42211 Cottages: (015394) 46624

FAX: (015394) 43824

English Tourist Board
England for Excellence
National Award Winner

HOST

AA ★★★

HIGHLY COMMENDED

RAC ★★★

ETB ACCESSIBLE
GRADE 1

DENE CREST GUEST HOUSE
Woodland Road, Windermere LA23 2AE
Tel: 015394 44979

ETB Listed.
Proprietors: Anne & Peter Watson

Guests are welcomed to a comfortable, tastefully decorated Guesthouse. All rooms are fully en suite and have colour TV, shaver points , central heating and tea/coffee making facilities. Double, twin and multi-bedded rooms available. There is a choice of Full English, Continental or Vegetarian breakfast. Packed lunch is offered as an alternative or can be purchased for a small fee. Only two minutes away from Bus and Rail Station, very close to town centre and amenities, yet surprisingly quiet. Drying room for walkers and fishermen. Discounts on long stays. Pets Welcome. Terms from £12.50 pp per night, depending on month. Open all year. Short Break terms available.

CUMBRIAN COTTAGES. 180 Luxury cottages and apartments throughout the Lake District and Cumbria. Many properties make pets welcome. All ETB inspected. For FREE Brochure and telephone bookings – 01228 599960 (24hrs). [Pets £15 per week]

BOWNESS HOLIDAYS. A selection of self catering properties in the Lake District and The Yorkshire Dales. For details telephone 01564 771150.

DALES HOLIDAY COTTAGES offer a selection of superb, self catering holiday properties in beautiful rural and coastal locations from the Lakes and Fells that inspired Wordsworth and Beatrix Potter to Cumbria's Borders. Cosy cottages for 2, to a country house for 15, many open all year. For FREE Brochure contact Dales Holiday Cottages, Carleton Business Park, Skipton, North Yorkshire BD23 2DG (01756 799821 & 790919).

LAKELAND LEISURE (015395 58556). Gateway to the Lake District. Luxury Holiday Homes for 2–8 people. Heated indoor and outdoor swimming pools. Bowls, Putting, Tennis and Horse riding on park. Restaurant – Bars. Live family Evening Entertainment. Call now for free colour brochure. [Pets £2.50 p.n.]

WELCOME COTTAGE HOLIDAYS. Hundreds of properties in wonderful locations at welcoming low prices. Pets, linen and fuel mostly included. For FREE colour brochure telephone 01756 702209.

Allonby

Small coastal resort with sand and shingle beach, 5 miles north-east of Maryport across Allonby Bay.

EAST HOUSE GUEST HOUSE, ALLONBY, MARYPORT CA15 6PQ (01900 881264 or 881276). Overlooking Solway Firth, two minutes sea. Central Lakes. Riding, tennis, golf near. Bed & Breakfast from £12 nightly, en suite Bed and Breakfast £15 nightly; EM, Bed and Breakfast £15 nightly, £95 weekly; en suite EM, Bed and Breakfast £18 nightly, £110 weekly.

Ambleside

Popular centre for exploring Lake District at northern end of Lake Windermere. Picturesque Stock Ghyll waterfall nearby, lovely walks. Associations with Wordsworth. Penrith 30 miles, Keswick 17, Windermere 5.

BRANTFELL HOUSE, ROTHAY ROAD, AMBLESIDE LA22 0EE (015394 32239). Chris and Jane welcome you with your well-behaved owners. Great "walkies", breakfasts and dinners. Free sausage per dog each day. En suite rooms, parking; non-smoking. Telephone for information. 2 Crowns Approved.

NANNY BROW COUNTRY HOUSE HOTEL & RESTAURANT, AMBLESIDE LA22 9NF (Tel: 015394 32036; Fax: 015394 32450). Set in five acres of gardens and woodland with stunning views over the Fells and the River Brathay, you can access the local fells and woodlands from the hotel grounds and walk dogs in safety. For full brochure telephone. [Pets £4.50 per night.]

NEW DUNGEON GHYLL HOTEL, GREAT LANGDALE , AMBLESIDE LA22 9JY (015394 37213; Fax: 015394 37666) Situated at head of famed Langdale Valley. Breathtaking views and friendly, relaxed atmosphere. All bedrooms en suite, colour TV and tea/coffee making facilities. Johansens. CTB 3 Crowns. [🐾]

MR E.M.C. SCOTT, CROW HOW HOTEL, RYDAL ROAD, AMBLESIDE LA22 9PN (015394 32193). Country house with 2 acre garden, wonderful Fell views. Ideal walking/touring. Half mile from Ambleside. Spacious rooms, private parking. Special breaks, also S/C apartment. AA 2 Stars, ETB 3 Crowns Commended.[🐾]

THE OLD VICARAGE, VICARAGE ROAD, AMBLESIDE LA22 9DH (015394 33364). "Rest awhile in style." Tranquil wooded grounds in heart of village. Car park. All rooms en suite. Kettle, clock/radio, TV, hairdryer. Quality B&B from £19pp/pn (low season). Reductions for longer stays. Friendly service where your pets are welcome. Phone Ian or Helen Burt.

WANSLEA GUEST HOUSE, LAKE ROAD, AMBLESIDE LA22 0DB (015394 33884). Spacious family-run guest house with walks beginning at the door. Comfortable rooms, mostly en suite. Licensed lounge. B&B from £16; Evening Meal available. Pets welcome by arrangement. 3 Crowns. [Pets £1 per night.]

IVY HOUSE, HAWKSHEAD, NEAR AMBLESIDE LA22 0NS (FREEPHONE 0500 657876). Family-run listed Georgian hotel. 11 en suite bedrooms with central heating and equipped with hot drinks trays. No charge for dogs. Children most welcome. Write or telephone David or Jane Vaughan for brochure .

MRS RUSS, CROYDEN HOUSE, CHURCH ST, AMBLESIDE LA22 0BU (015394 32209). Croyden House offers a warm friendly welcome - comfortable, tastefully furnished rooms (all en suite), all with colour TV, tea/coffee tray and washbasin. Central location. Private car park. Open all year. B&B from £16.50–£21pppn. Special rates for children.

KIRKSTONE FOOT HOTEL, KIRKSTONE PASS ROAD, AMBLESIDE, CUMBRIA LA22 9EH (015394 32232). Country house hotel with luxury self-catering Cottages and Apartments sleeping 2/7. Set in peaceful and secluded grounds. Adjoining lovely Lakeland fells, great for walking. Special winter breaks. [pw/ Pets £2.50 per night.]

THE RED LION INN, HAWKSHEAD, AMBLESIDE LA22 0NS (015394 36213; Fax: 015394 36747). 15th Century Coaching Inn in a picturesque village in the heart of Lakeland. All bedrooms are en suite, with TV and tea/coffee facilities. All the comforts of home. [🐕]

"KINGSWOOD", OLD LAKE ROAD, AMBLESIDE LA22 0AE (015394 34081). Near town centre yet off main road. Ample parking. Rooms have washbasins, tea/coffee making facilities. Colour TV; central heating. Pets welcome. Phone for rates and details. [Pets £1/£1.50 per night.]

THE GABLES HOTEL, AMBLESIDE (015394 33272). Friendly atmosphere, pretty en suite rooms, most with views. B&B from £19; Dinner by prior arrangement £11. 3 Crowns Commended.

Appleby

Pleasant touring centre on River Eden, between Pennines and Lake District. Castle and Moot Hall of historic interest. Trout fishing, swimming pool, tennis, bowls. Kendal 24 miles, Penrith 13.

"JUBILEE COTTAGE", Sleeps 6/7. 18th century cottage situated between North Lakes and Pennines. Car essential; off road parking for two cars. Open all year round. Well-behaved pets welcome. Terms £140–£220. MISS L.I. BASTEN, DAYMER COTTAGE, LEE, NEAR ILFRACOMBE, DEVON (01271 863769).

APPLEBY MANOR COUNTRY HOUSE HOTEL, ROMAN ROAD, APPLEBY-IN-WESTMORLAND CA16 6JB (Tel: 017683 51571; Fax: 017683 52888). Enjoy the comfort of Cumbria's highly commended Country House Hotel with superb meals, relaxing lounges, indoor leisure club and breathtaking scenery all around. Phone for a full colour brochure. [🐕 pw!]

MILBURN GRANGE. 6 quality cottages equipped to the highest standards in tiny hamlet enjoying extensive views over Lakeland Hills. Open all year. Bargain breaks from November to March (excl. Christmas and New Year). Well behaved pets welcome at £10 per week each. Contact: MARGARET BURKE, MILBURN GRANGE, APPLEBY-IN-WESTMORLAND CA16 6DR (Tel/Fax: 017683 61867).

Askam-in-Furness

Coastal village on the Cartmel and Furness peninsula. ETB "Holiday Destination of the Year" Award 1994. Fine sandy beaches and many tourist attractions. Ulverston 4 miles.

MRS C. DOWLE, 1 FRIARS GROUND, KIRKBY-IN-FURNESS LA17 7YB (01229 889601). "Owl Cottage." Self catering. Two bedrooms. Sleeps 4/6. Garden. Garage. 5 minutes sea/sandy beaches. Coniston/Windermere within easy reach. Ideal fell walking. Open all year. [🐕]

Borrowdale

Scenic valley of River Derwent, splendid walking and climbing country.

MARY MOUNT HOTEL, BORROWDALE, NEAR KESWICK CA12 5UU (017687 77223). Set in 4$^1/_2$ acres of gardens and woodlands on the shores of Derwentwater. 2$^1/_2$ miles from Keswick in picturesque Borrowdale. Superb walking and touring. All rooms en suite with colour TV and tea/coffee making facilities. Licensed. Brochure on request. 3 Crowns. [🐾]

STAKIS LODORE SWISS HOTEL, BORROWDALE, NEAR KESWICK CA12 5UX (017687 77285; Fax: 017687 77343). Luxury Hotel with fabulous views overlooking Derwentwater and fells. Facilities include 75 bedrooms, restaurant and lounge, bar and leisure club. 4 Crowns Highly Commended. [Pets £2 per night.]

Buttermere

Between lake of same name and Crummock Water. Magnificent scenery. Of special note is Sour Milk Ghyll waterfall and steep and impressive Honister Pass. Keswick 15 miles, Cockermouth 10.

BRIDGE HOTEL, BUTTERMERE CA13 9UZ (Tel & Fax: 017687 70252). 22 bedrooms, all with private bathrooms; four-posters available. Daily freshly prepared menus, large selection wines; real ales. Superb walking and fishing. Dogs welcome. Self catering apartments available. [Pets £3.20 per night.]

Carlisle

Important Border city and former Roman station on River Eden. The Cathedral (12-14th cent.) has famous east window. 12th cent. Castle is of historic interest, also Tullie House Museum and Art Gallery. Good sports facilities inc. football and racecourse. Kendal 45 miles, Dumfries 33, Penrith 18.

MRS SHEELAGH POTTER, LAKESHORE LODGES, THE LOUGH TROUT FISHERY, THURSTONFIELD CA5 6HB (01228 576552; Fax: 01228 576761). Scandinavian pine Bungalows with verandahs overlooking 30 acre lake surrounded by unspoilt English woodland. 3 Keys. Dream location for fishing holiday. Boats and tackle available. [Pets £20 per week.]

MRS JANE LAWSON, CRAIGBURN FARM, CATLOWDY, PENTON, CARLISLE CA6 5QP (Tel & Fax: 01228 577214). Beautiful countryside, superb food, friendly atmosphere. All bedrooms en suite with tea making facilities and colour TV. Residential licence. Games room. Pets most welcome. 3 Crowns Commended. [🐾]

NEWPALLYARDS, HETHERSGILL, CARLISLE CA6 6HZ (01228 577308). ETB 4 KEYS COMMENDED. Relax and see beautiful North Cumbria and the Borders. Self-catering accommodation in one Bungalow, 3/4 bedrooms; two lovely Cottages on farm. Also Bed and Breakfast or Half Board - en suite rooms. [🐾]

GREEN VIEW LODGES, WELTON, NEAR DALSTON, CARLISLE CA5 7ES. Luxury self-catering lodges and cottages, sleeping 2/7 - two/three bedroomed. Peaceful setting. Central heating, microwave, telephone, linen and towels, bath/shower. Lake Ullswater, Keswick, Gretna Green nearby; golf 5 miles. Terms £145–£480 per week. 4/5 Keys (up to Highly Commended). Telephone: MRS IVINSON (016974 76230). [Pets £15 per week.]

In an undiscovered corner of Cumbria two lovely cottages with 320 tranquil acres of flora and fauna to explore (maps provided). Use of swimming pool from May to September. Central for Hadrian's Wall and Gretna Green. 5 Keys Highly Commended. Apply: MRS J. JAMES, MIDTODHILLS FARM, ROADHEAD, CARLISLE CA6 6PF (016977 48213). [Pets £10.00 per week.]

DALSTON HALL CARAVAN PARK, DALSTON HALL, DALSTON, NEAR CARLISLE CA5 7JX (01228 710165).✓✓✓ Exit 42 off M6, follow signs for Dalston. Small family-run park set in peaceful surroundings. Electric hook-ups, shops, playground, launderette, fly-fishing, nine-hole golf course. [pw!🐾]

Cockermouth

Market town and popular touring centre for Lake District and quiet Cumbrian coast. On Rivers Derwent and Cocker. Fine fell scenery to the east. Birthplace of Wordsworth. The ruined Norman Castle is of interest. Penrith 30 miles, Carlisle 26, Whitehaven 14, Keswick 12, Workington 8, Maryport 7.

HUNDITH HILL HOTEL, LORTON, COCKERMOUTH CA13 9TH (01900 822092; Fax: 01900 828215). Comfortable, quiet family Hotel. Ideal centre for Lakes. We can accommodate disabled/wheelchair users. Dogs welcome. Bed & Breakfast from £20.[Pets £2.00 each per night.]

Coniston

Village 6 miles south-west of Ambleside, dominated by Old Man of Coniston (2635ft).

MRS ANNE HALL, DOW CRAG HOUSE, CONISTON LA21 8AT (015394 41558; Fax: 015394 41911). Two chalet bungalows to let, sleeping two/six. Quiet location. Superb views across lake. Surrounded by gardens, farm fields. Well equipped. Owner maintained. [🐾]

THURSTON HOUSE. Lakeland stone house converted into self-contained, spacious, clean, comfortable apartments sleeping 2/6. Fully equipped including colour TV. Quiet location yet only a short walk to village centre and Lake. Private parking. Open all year. Enquiries to: MR & MRS JEFFERSON, 21 CHALEGREEN, HARWOOD, BOLTON BL2 3NJ (01204 419261). [🐾].

Eskdale

Lakeless valley, noted for waterfalls and ascended by a light-gauge railway. Tremendous views, Roman fort. Keswick 35 miles, Broughton-in-Furness 10 miles.

MRS J.P. HALL, FISHERGROUND FARM, ESKDALE CA19 1TF (01946 723319). Self-catering to suit everyone. Scandinavian Pine Lodges and Cottages – on a delightful traditional farm. Adventure playground. Sports Hall and games room. Pets' and children's paradise. Brochures available. ETB 4 Keys Commended. [🐾]

Grange-over-Sands

Quiet resort at the north of Morecambe Bay, convenient centre for Lake District. Fine gardens; golf, boating, fishing, tennis and bowls. Lancaster 25 miles, Windermere 16.

HAMPSFELL HOUSE HOTEL, HAMPSFELL ROAD, GRANGE-OVER-SANDS LA11 6BG (015395 32567). 3 Crowns Commended, AA**, Ashley Courtney Recommended. Peaceful country house hotel in two wooded acres close to sea and fells. Ideal for walking dogs. All rooms en suite with colour TV and tea/coffee making facilities. Ample safe parking. [🐾]

Grasmere

Village famous for Wordsworth associations; the poet lived in Dove Cottage (preserved as it was), and is buried in the churchyard. Museum has manuscripts and relics.

GRASMERE HOTEL, GRASMERE, NEAR AMBLESIDE LA22 9TA (015394 35277). 12-bedroomed licensed Hotel set in the centre of the Lakes. Ideal for walking or sightseeing. All rooms have en suite facilities, TV etc. Gourmet food and interesting wines. [🐾]

Hawkshead

Quaint village in Lake District between Coniston Water and Windermere. The 16th century Church and Grammar School, which Wordsworth attended, and the Old Court House (N.T.) are of interest. Ambleside 5 miles

BETTY FOLD GUEST HOUSE, HAWKSHEAD HILL, AMBLESIDE LA22 0PS (015394 36611). Self-catering Flat and Cottage. Set in peaceful and spacious grounds. Ideal for the walker and dog. Open all year. 3 Keys Approved. [Pets £2 per night.]

Ireby

Quiet Cumbrian village between the fells and the sea. Good centre for the northern Lake District. Cockermouth 11 miles, Bassenthwaite 6.

WOODLANDS COUNTRY HOUSE AND COTTAGE, IREBY CA5 1EX (016973 71791). In private wooded grounds four miles from Bassenthwaite, ideal for Lakes and Borders. All bedrooms en suite with tea making facilities. Children welcome. Residential licence. B&B from £22.50. 3 Crowns Highly Commended.[🐾]

Kendal

Market town and popular centre for touring the Lake District. Of historic interest is the Norman castle, birthplace of Catherine Parr. Penrith 25 miles, Lancaster 22, Ambleside 13.

ANNE TAYLOR, RUSSELL FARM, BURTON-IN-KENDAL, CARNFORTH, LANCS. LA6 1NN (01524 781334). Bed, Breakfast & Evening Meal offered. Ideal centre for touring Lakes and Yorkshire Dales. Good food, friendly atmosphere on working dairy farm. Modernised farmhouse. Guests' own lounge. [🐾]

MRS HELEN JONES, PRIMROSE COTTAGE, ORTON ROAD, TEBAY CA10 3TL (015396 24791). Excellent rural location for North Lakes and Yorkshire Dales. Superb facilities include jacuzzi bath and four-poster bed. Pets welcome, very friendly. One acre garden. Self contained ground flor flat available. ETB Listed Commended.

Keswick

Famous Lake District resort at north end of Derwentwater with Pencil Museum and Cars of the Stars Motor Museum. Carlisle 30 miles, Ambleside 17, Cockermouth 12.

THE COTTAGE IN THE WOOD, WHINLATTER PASS, KESWICK CA12 5TW (017687 78409). Small comfortable Hotel, once a 17th century coaching inn, in a remote and beautiful situation with superb views. All rooms en suite, with central heating and tea/coffee facilities. Excellent traditional food. No Smoking. 3 Crowns Highly Commended.

OVERWATER HALL, OVERWATER, NEAR IREBY, KESWICK CA5 1HH (017687 76566). Elegant Country House Hotel in spacious grounds. Dogs very welcome in your room. Any 4 nights from £170 per person, inclusive of Dinner, Room and Breakfast. Mini breaks also available all year. 2 AA Rosettes for excellent food. [🐾 pw!]

MARION AND IAN ROBINSON, THELMLEA COUNTRY GUEST HOUSE, BRAITHWAITE, KESWICK CA12 5TD (017687 78305). Set in 13/4 acre grounds with private parking and garden area for guests' use. Ideal base for touring / walking. Superb views. Bedrooms have full facilities including tea / coffee, TV & radio alarm. Full central heating, drying facilities. Bed and Breakfast from £15 to £19.50. Reductions weekly bookings. Brochure. [pw!]

JOHN & JEAN MITCHELL, 35 MAIN STREET, KESWICK (Tel & Fax: 017687 72790; Home Tel No: 016973 20220). Luxurious Lakeland flats and cottages located in one of Keswick's most desirable areas. All gas central heating. Some with two bathrooms (one en suite). From £99 weekly.

SWINSIDE INN, NEWLANDS, KESWICK CA12 5UE (017687 78253). Ideal for fell walking, climbing, sailing etc. Extensive bar menu; eight comfortable bedrooms (some en suite), all with satellite TV and tea making. Reductions for children. [Pets £1 per night].

ROYAL OAK HOTEL, ROSTHWAITE, KESWICK CA12 5XB (017687 77214). Traditional Lakeland hotel with friendly atmosphere. Home cooking, cosy bar and comfortable lounge. Winter and Summer discount rates. Brochure and Tariff available. ETB 3 Crowns Commended. [🐾]

J.A. GRANGE, LAKELAND COTTAGE HOLIDAYS, KESWICK CA12 5ES (017687 71071; Fax: 017687 75036). Warm, comfortable homes welcoming your dog, in Keswick and beautiful Borrowdale. ETB inspected and quality graded.

THRELKELD VILLAGE (KESWICK 4 MILES). Tourist Board 4 Keys Commended. Delightful Bungalows. Sleep 4/6. All amenities, fridge, electric cooker, night storage heaters, colour TV, telephone. Laundry room. Own grounds with ample parking. £170 minimum to £395 maximum. Bargain breaks low season. Children and pets welcome. APPLY – MRS F. WALKER, THE PARK, RICKERBY, CARLISLE CA3 9AA (01228 24848). [pw! 🐾]

AYSGARTH, CROSTHWAITE ROAD, KESWICK. Situated on the outskirts of Keswick 10 minutes from town centre. Furnished to high standard with 3 bedrooms sleeping up to 6. Garden and private parking. APPLY: MRS J. HALL, FISHERGROUND FARM, ESKDALE CA19 1TF (019467 23319). [🐾]

GORDON AND MARIAN TURNBULL, RICKERBY GRANGE, PORTINSCALE, KESWICK CA12 5RH (017687 72344). Delightfully situated in quiet village. Licensed. Imaginative home-cooked food, attractively served. Open almost all year. [Pets £1 per night.]

A traditional 17th-century farmhouse, one acre grounds with lovely garden. Ideal for numerous walks. Good home cooking. Pets and children welcome and catered for. Open all year. 3 Crowns Approved. MURIEL BOND, THORNTHWAITE HALL, THORNTHWAITE, NEAR KESWICK CA12 5SA (Tel and Fax: 017687 78424).[🐾]

HARNEY PEAK, PORTINSCALE, NEAR KESWICK. We offer you the best in S/C accommodation in our spacious, well equipped apartments in the quiet village of Portinscale. Glorious lake views. Ideal for disabled. [Pets £10 per week.] Apply: MRS J. SMITH, 55 BLYTHWOOD ROAD, PINNER, MIDDLESEX HA5 3QW (0181-429 0402 or 0860 721270).

ALLAN AND VIVIENNE CAIRNS, SWAN HOTEL, THORNTHWAITE, KESWICK CA12 5SQ (017687 78256). Bed, Breakfast and Evening Meal in quiet country hotel in beautiful surroundings. Keswick 4 miles. Fully licensed. Pets welcome. RAC Merit Award. [pw! £1.25 per night.]

LOW BRIERY RIVERSIDE HOLIDAY VILLAGE, KESWICK CA12 4RN (017687 72044). Cottages, flats, lodges and caravans; superb amenities and leisure facilities. On eastern outskirts of Keswick.

Kirkby Lonsdale

Small town on River Lune, 14 miles north-east of Lancaster. Of interest – the motte and bailey castle, mid 19th century Market House and the 16th century Abbots Hall.

MRS PAT NICHOLSON, GREEN LANE END FARM, LUPTON, KIRKBY LONSDALE, CARNFORTH LA6 2PP (015395 67236). Bed and Breakfast from £14 per person in 17th-century farmhouse with oak beams, fine old staircase. In peaceful area of Lakeland ideal for touring Lakes and Dales. Pets by arrangement. Self catering accommodation in Kirkby Lonsdale also available.

Kirkby Stephen near (Mallerstang)

5 miles south on B6259 Kirkby Stephen to Hawes road.

COCKLAKE HOUSE, MALLERSTANG CA17 4JT (017683 72080). Charming, High Pennine Country House B&B in unique position above Pendragon Castle in Upper Mallerstang Dale offering good food and exceptional comfort to a small number of guests. Two double rooms with large private bathrooms. Three acres riverside grounds. Dogs welcome.

Kirkoswald

Village in the Cumbrian hills, lying north west of the Lake District. Ideal for touring. Penrith 7 miles.

SECLUDED COTTAGES AND LEISURE FISHING, KIRKOSWALD CA10 1EU (24 hr brochure line 01768 898711 manned most Saturdays). Tranquilly secluded quality cottages, guaranteed clean, well equipped and well maintained. Centrally located for Lakes, Pennines, Hadrian's Wall, Borderland. Enjoy the Good Life in comfort. Pets welcome . Bookings/enquiries 01768 896275. [Pets £2 per night].

Little Langdale

Hamlet 2 miles west of Skelwith Bridge. To west is Little Langdale Tarn, a small lake.

HIGHFOLD COTTAGE, LITTLE LANGDALE. A well-equipped cottage, ideally situated for walking and touring. Superb mountain views. Sleeps 5. ETB 3 Keys Commended. Pets and children welcome. Weekly £175–£295. MRS C.E. BLAIR, 8 THE GLEBE, CHAPEL STILE, AMBLESIDE LA22 9JT (015394 37686).[🐾]

Lorton

Village 4 miles south east of Cockermouth.

NEW HOUSE FARM, LORTON, COCKERMOUTH CA13 9UU (Tel and Fax: 01900 85404). New House Farm has 15 acres of fields, woods, streams and ponds which guests and dogs can wander around. Comfortable en suite accommodation and fine traditional food. Off season breaks. ETB 3 Crowns Highly Commended.[🐾 🏠]

Loweswater

Hamlet at end of Lake Loweswater (owned by National Trust). Beautiful hilly scenery.

LOWESWATER HOLIDAY COTTAGES, LOWESWATER, COCKERMOUTH CA13 9UX (01900 85232). Nestling among the magnificent Loweswater/Buttermere fells, our luxury cottages are available all year. They have open fires, colour TV, central heating, a four poster and gardens. Colour Brochure. [🐾 🏠]

Lowick

Delightful small village in Lake District National Park, 3 miles from Coniston Water and ideal for exploring the Southern and Western Lakes.

MRS JENNY WICKENS, GARTH ROW, LOWICK GREEN, ULVERSTON LA12 8EB (01229 885633). Traditional cottage standing alone amidst farmland and common. Quality accommodation, good food, excellent walking, no smoking. Ideal for children and pets. B&B from £14.00. Brochure. [🐾]

Mungrisdale

Small village ideal for touring. Keswick 8 miles.

NEAR HOWE FARM HOTEL AND COTTAGES, MUNGRISDALE, PENRITH CA11 0SH (Tel or Fax: 017687 79678). Quiet, away from it all. Within easy reach of Lakes walking. Good food. Bar, log fire in cold weather. 5 Bedrooms en suite. B&B from £17. [Pets – Hotel £1 per day, in Cottages £10 per week.]

Near Sawrey

This beautiful village on the west side of Windermere has many old cottages set among trees and beautiful gardens with flowers. The world-famous writer Beatrix Potter lived at Hill Top Farm. A ferry travels across the lake to Hawkshead (2 miles), Far Sawrey ¹/₂ mile.

SAWREY HOUSE COUNTRY HOTEL, NEAR SAWREY, HAWKSHEAD LA22 0LF (015394 36387; Fax: 015394 36010). Elegant family-run hotel in three acres of peaceful gardens with magnificent views across Esthwaite Water. Excellent food, warm friendly atmosphere. Lounge, separate bar. Children and pets welcome. 3 Crowns Highly Commended. RAC Highly Acclaimed. [Pets £3 per night.]

Newby Bridge

Village at southern end of Lake Windermere, 8 miles from Ulverston.

NEWBY BRIDGE HOTEL, NEAR ULVERSTON LA12 8NA (015395 31222). Overlooking Lake Windermere. 3 night breaks from £89 per person Dinner, Bed and Breakfast. All rooms en suite with two movie channels. Bar and restaurant.

Penrith

Historic market town and centre for touring Lake District. Of interest are ruined 14th century castle, Gloucester Arms (1477) and Tudor House, believed to have been school attended by Wordsworth. Excellent sporting facilities. Windermere 27 miles, Keswick 18.

MRS MARY TEASDALE, LISCO, TROUTBECK, PENRITH CA11 0SY (017687 79645). Open all year for Bed and Breakfast, optional Evening Meal. Good Home Cooking. All rooms tea/coffee facilities. Lounge, Dining room, TV. Children welcome. Ideally placed for Lake District. Moderate terms. [pw!]

SECLUDED COTTAGES AND LEISURE FISHING, KIRKOSWALD, PENRITH CA10 1EU (01768 896275; Fax available. 24 hr brochure line 01768 898711 – manned most Saturdays). Tranquilly secluded quality cottages, guaranteed clean, well equipped and well maintained. Centrally located for Lakes, Pennines, Hadrian's Wall, Borderland. Enjoy the Good Life in comfort. Pets welcome. [Pets £2 per night].

LOW GARTH GUEST HOUSE, PENRUDDOCK, PENRITH CA11 0QU (017684 83492). Tastefully converted 18th century barn in peaceful surroundings with magnificent views, offering a warm welcome and Aga-cooked meals. En suite facilities. [🐕]

MRS BARBARA PEARSON, FAR HOWE FARM, TROUTBECK, PENRITH CA11 0SH (017687 79245). Secluded working farm, one mile from main road with beautiful views. Three double rooms. DB&B. Home cooking. Central heating. Log fires in cold weather.

Ravenglass

Village 4 miles south-east of Seascale. Miniature railway takes tourists on 7 mile trip up Eskdale.

ESKMEALS HOUSE, ESKMEALS, NEAR RAVENGLASS LA19 5YA (01229 717151). Lovely old listed Georgian house in idyllic wooded setting, close to estuary and beach. Delightful bedrooms. Excellent Cumbrian breakfast and evening meals. Self catering cottage available.

Silloth

Solway Firth resort with harbour and fine sandy beach. Mountain views. Golf, fishing. Penrith 33 miles, Carlisle 23, Cockermouth 17.

MR AND MRS G.E. BOWMAN, TANGLEWOOD CARAVAN PARK, CAUSEWAY HEAD, SILLOTH CA5 4PG (016973 31253). Friendly country site, excellent toilet and laundry facilities. Tourers welcome or hire a luxury caravan. Telephone or send stamp for colour brochure. [🐕]

Windermere

Famous resort on lake of same name, the largest in England. Magnificent scenery. Car ferry from Bowness, one mile distant. Kendal 9 miles.

Many attractive self-catering holiday homes in a variety of good locations, all well equipped and managed by our caring staff. Pets welcome. For brochure, contact: LAKELOVERS, THE TOFFEE LOFT, ASH STREET, WINDERMERE LA23 3RA (015394 88855; Fax: 015394 88857). [Pets £12.50 per week.]

WYN AND IAN CAPPER, UPPER OAKMERE, 3 UPPER OAK STREET, WINDERMERE LA23 2LB (015394 45649). Built in traditional Lakeland stone and situated close to park. Warm, clean and very friendly. Single people welcome. Pets preferred to people. B&B £14.50 per person per night, en suite family rooms £15.50; children half price. Dinner optional. [🐕]

GREENRIGGS GUEST HOUSE, 8 UPPER OAK STREET, WINDERMERE LA23 2LB (015394 42265). Small, family-run guest house situated in a quiet cul de sac close to a park, with easy access to shops, lake and all transport. B&B from £15.00. [🐕]

BURNSIDE HOTEL, KENDAL ROAD, BOWNESS ON WINDERMERE LA23 3EP (015394 42211). The Lake District's Complete Resort, set in mature gardens overlooking Lake Windermere. Pets welcome – FREE! Choose either luxurious hotel or one of our self catering cottages and relax in our on-site leisure club. FREEPHONE 0800 220688 for bookings. [🐕]

FIRGARTH PRIVATE HOTEL, AMBLESIDE ROAD, WINDERMERE LA23 1EU (015394 46974). Elegant Victorian house close to Lake viewpoint on outskirts of Windermere village. Individually designed en suite rooms with colour TV, tea/coffee facilities. Private parking. Good dog walks nearby. Bed and Breakfast from £16.50 per person. ETB 2 Crowns. [🐕]

YORKSHIRE HOUSE, 1 UPPER OAK STREET, WINDERMERE LA23 2LB (015394 44689). A warm Scottish welcome, good food and clean, comfortable rooms. En suite rooms available. Licensed. B&B from £12, DB&B from £21. Short breaks available [🐕]

QUARRY GARTH COUNTRY HOUSE HOTEL, TROUTBECK BRIDGE, WINDERMERE LA23 1LF (015394 88282; Fax: 015394 46584). Elegant and tranquil country house hotel set in 8 acres of gardens. 2 AA Rosette Awards. Superb six course meals. Log fires, warm comfort. All rooms en suite.

HILLTHWAITE HOUSE HOTEL, THORNBARROW ROAD, WINDERMERE LA23 2DF (015394 43636; Fax: 015394 88660). Set in 3 acres of secluded gardens. All bedrooms en suite with satellite TV; some with personal jacuzzi. Superb leisure facilities including indoor pool. Pets welcome.

ANNE & PETER WATSON, DENE CREST GUEST HOUSE, WOODLAND ROAD, WINDERMERE LA23 2AE (015394 44979). Comfortable, tastefully furnished Guesthouse. All rooms en suite, colour TV, central heating, tea/coffee making. Open all year. Short Break terms available. Pets Welcome. [Pets £2 per stay]

LOW SPRINGWOOD HOTEL, THORNBARROW ROAD, WINDERMERE LA23 2DF (015394 46383). Fashion and Twiggy (Boxers) and Treacle (Heinz 57) would like to welcome you to their peaceful Hotel in its own secluded gardens. Lovely views of the Lakes and Fells. All rooms en suite with colour TV etc. Some four-posters. Brochure available. ETB 3 Crowns. [pw! 🐕]

KIRKWOOD, PRINCE'S ROAD, WINDERMERE LA23 2DD (015394 43907). A warm friendly atmosphere with individual personal service. En suite rooms with colour TV and tea/coffee making. Hosts pleased to help plan tours and walks. Two Crowns, RAC Highly Acclaimed, AA QQQQ. [🐕]

APPLEGARTH HOTEL, COLLEGE ROAD, WINDERMERE LA23 1BU (015394 43206; Fax: 015394 46636). An elegant Victorian mansion house, with individually designed bedrooms and four-poster rooms. All rooms with private facilities, most with Lake and Fell views. Lounge bar and car park. Restaurant (please pre-book). Ideally situated for shops, restaurants, walking and touring. Free use of private leisure club. Close to bus and rail stations. ETB 3 Crowns. AA [🐕]**

DERBYSHIRE

DERBYSHIRE *Ashbourne*

DERBYSHIRE *Ashbourne, Biggin, Buxton, Matlock*

BERESFORD ARMS HOTEL
Station Road, Ashbourne, Derbyshire DE6 1AA
Tel: 01335 300035 Fax: 01335 300065

Situated in the centre of Ashbourne, Gateway to the Peak District, The Beresford offers a warm welcome
in a pleasant environment of 'Olde Worlde' charm and character, with pets and children being
especially catered for. It makes a perfect starting point to explore the area or visit Alton Towers
which is only 10 miles away. Open Christmas and New Year.   ETB ♛ ♛ ♛

IVY HOUSE   EMTB ♛ ♛

Newhaven, Biggin by Hartington, Buxton, Derbyshire SK17 0DT

Recently renovated Georgian Grade II Listed Guest House maintaining many original features – log fires
and flagstone floors. Luxury en suite accommodation. Near Tissington and High Peak Trails and Dovedale.
Ideal for walking, cycling and touring. Non-smoking. Dogs welcome.
Proprietor: Patricia Flint Tel: 01298 84709

PRIORY LEA HOLIDAY FLATS

Beautiful situation adjoining woodland walks and own meadows. Cleanliness assured; comfortably furnished
and well equipped. Colour TV. Bed linen available. Sleep 2/8. Ample private parking. Close to Poole's
Cavern Country Park. Brochure available from resident owner. Open all year. 1997 terms from £80 to £210.
Short Breaks available. ꕯꕯ/ꕯꕯꕯ Approved.

Mrs Gill Taylor, 50 White Knowle Road, Buxton SK17 9NH. Tel: 01298 23737

THE CHARLES COTTON HOTEL
Hartington, Near Buxton SK17 0AL

The Charles Cotton is a small comfortable hotel with a starred rating for the AA and RAC. The hotel lies in the heart of the Derbyshire
Dales, pleasantly situated in the village square of Hartington, with nearby shops catering for all needs. It is renowned throughout the
area for its hospitality and good home cooking. Pets and children are wlecome; special diets catered for. The Charles Cotton makes
the perfect centre to relax and explore the area, whether walking, cycling, brass rubbing, pony trekking or even hang gliding. Open
Christmas and New Year   **TEL: 01298 84229**

LANE END HOUSE, GREEN LANE, TANSLEY,
near MATLOCK DE4 5FJ   Tel & Fax: 01629 583981
A non-smoking Georgian Farmhouse close to Chatsworth, Haddon, Hardwick, Kedleston and
Dovedale. Lovingly refurbished by caring owners who serve delicious food at yesterday's
prices. Walk in nearby fields or explore the wonderful countryside of the Peak District.
ETB ♛ ♛ Highly Commended. AA Selected QQQQ and RAC Highly Acclaimed.
- Bargain Breaks - Brochure Available - Marion and David Smith. Pets £2.50 per night.

WELCOME COTTAGE HOLIDAYS. Hundreds of properties in wonderful
locations at welcoming low prices. Pets, linen and fuel mostly included. For
FREE colour brochure telephone 01756 702209.

Ashbourne

Market town on River Henmore, close to its junction with River Dove. Several interesting old
buildings. Birmingham 42 miles, Nottingham 29, Derby 13.

MRS M.A. RICHARDSON, THROWLEY HALL FARM, ILAM, ASHBOURNE DE6
2BB (01538 308202/308243). Self-catering accommodation in farmhouse for up
to 12 and cottage for seven people. Also Bed and Breakfast in farmhouse.
Central heating, washbasins, tea/coffee facilities in rooms. Children and pets
welcome. Near Alton Towers and stately homes. Tourist Board 2 Crowns/4 Keys
Commended.

MRS A.M. WHITTLE, STONE COTTAGE, GREEN LANE, CLIFTON, ASHBOURNE, DE6 2BL (01335 343377). Charming 19th Century cottage near quiet village of Clifton. Ideal touring base. Reductions for children under 10. Bed and Breakfast from £18.00, Dinner £9. Pets by arrangement.

MRS M.M. STELFOX, DOG AND PARTRIDGE, SWINSCOE, ASHBOURNE DE6 2HS (01335 343183). 17th century Inn offering ideal holiday accommodation. Many leisure activities available. All bedrooms with washbasins, colour TV, telephone and private facilities. [pw! 🐕]

DERBYSHIRE COTTAGES. In the grounds of a 17th century Inn, close to Peak District, Alton Towers and Ashbourne. Each has own patio, fully fitted kitchen, colour TV. Children and pets welcome. Phone MARY (01335 300202) for further details.

BERESFORD ARMS HOTEL, STATION ROAD, ASHBOURNE DE6 1AA (01335 300035; Fax: 01335 300065). Situated in the centre of Ashbourne and offering a warm welcome, especially to pets and children. It makes a perfect starting point to explore the area or visit Alton Towers. 3 Crowns. [🐕]

Biggin

Situated 8 miles north of Ashbourne

PATRICIA FLINT, IVY HOUSE, NEWHAVEN, BIGGIN BY HARTINGTON, BUXTON, SK17 0DT (01298 84709) Recently renovated Georgian Grade II Listed Guest House maintaining many original features. Luxury en suite accommodation. Near Tissington, High Peak Trails and Dovedale. Non-smoking. Dogs welcome. [🐕]

Buxton

Well-known spa and centre for the Peak District. Beautiful scenery and good sporting amenities. Leeds 50 miles, Matlock 20, Macclesfield 12.

BUXTON VIEW, 74 CORBAR ROAD, BUXTON SK17 6RJ (01298 79222). Attractive house very near moors and 10 minutes from town centre. En suite rooms. Bed and Breakfast from £16 pppn; Evening Meal available. Pets very welcome. ETB 3 Crowns Commended, AA QQQ Recommended.

WHEELDON TREES FARM, EARL STERNDALE, BUXTON SK17 0AA (01298 83219). Eighteenth century barn convertion offers seven cosy self-catering holiday cottages. Sleep 2-6. Laundry, payphone and games room. 4 Keys Commended. [🐕]

PRIORY LEA HOLIDAY FLATS. Close to Poole's Cavern Country Park. Fully equipped. Sleep 2/8. Cleanliness assured. Terms £80 - £210. Open all year. Short Breaks available. 2-3 Keys Approved. MRS GILL TAYLOR, 50 WHITE KNOWLE ROAD, BUXTON SK17 9NH (01298 23737). [Pets £1 per night.]

THE CHARLES COTTON HOTEL, HARTINGTON, NEAR BUXTON SK17 0AL (01298 84229). Small hotel, AA & RAC star rated. Good home cooking and hospitality. In heart of Derbyshire Dales. Special diets catered for. Ideal for relaxing, walking, cycling, hang gliding. [🐕]

MRS LYNNE P. FEARNS, HEATH FARM, SMALLDALE, BUXTON SK17 8EB (01298 24431). Farm in Peak District, 4½ miles from Buxton. Quiet location. Many activities locally. Cot and babysitting available. Car essential. Bed and Breakfast from £14.50, reductions children and weekly stays.

Matlock

Inland resort and spa in the Derwent Valley. Chesterfield 9 miles.

TUCKERS GUEST HOUSE, 48 DALE ROAD, MATLOCK DE4 3NB (01629 583018). Victorian home in central but secluded position. Spacious, well-equipped, cosy rooms. Wonderful scenery and walks; lots to see and do. Pets welcome to stay in rooms. Bed and English/Vegetarian Breakfast from £17.00. Evening Meals by arrangement. Open all year. [pw! 🐕]

MRS G. PARKINSON, DIMPLE HOUSE, DIMPLE ROAD, MATLOCK DE4 3JX (01629 583228). 19th Century house close to Matlock. Large garden. Ideal for visiting Chatsworth and Peak Park. TV and teamaking in all rooms. EMTB Listed/Approved. B&B from £16. [🐕]

LANE END HOUSE, GREEN LANE, TANSLEY DE4 5 FJ (01629 583981). A non-smoking Georgian farmhouse close to Chatsworth and Haddon. Lovingly refurbished by caring owners who serve delicious food at yesterday's prices. Walk in nearby fields or explore the wonderful countryside that surrounds us. ETB 2 Crowns Highly Commended, AA Selected QQQQ Award and RAC Highly Acclaimed. [Pets £2.50 per night]

Peak District National Park

A green and unspoilt area at the southern end of the Pennines, covering 555 square miles.

BIGGIN HALL, PEAK PARK (01298 84451). Close Dove Dale. 17th Century hall sympathetically restored. Baths en suite, log fires, C/H comfort, warmth and quiet. Fresh home cooking. Beautiful uncrowded footpaths. Brochure on request.

Winster

Charming village 4 miles west of Matlock, steeped in history.

MRS D. MACBAIN, BRAE COTTAGE, EAST BANK, WINSTER DE4 2DT (01629 650375). Spacious B&B detached cottage annexe. En suite, TV, tea/coffee facilities. Breakfast area. Garage. Patio. Picturesque Peak village. Double/twin, family. £16 per person. 1 Crown Commended. [🐕 pw!]

APPLEDORE   OTTER COTTAGE

Traditional fisherman's cottage with panoramic estuary views, 50 yards to slipway. Garden. Totally equipped – two TVs and VCR; microwave, autowasher, etc. Also unique harbourside apartments and modern bungalow. Brochure:

B.H. SMITH, 26 MARKET STREET, APPLEDORE, DEVON EX39 1PP
Tel: 01237 476154 (or if no personal reply 01271 78907)

Mariners Cottage
Irsha Street, Appledore
View from garden

Elizabethan fisherman's cottage right at the sea edge — the high tide laps below the garden wall. Extensive open sea and estuary view of ships, lighthouses, fishing and sailing boats. The quayside, beach, shops, restaurants and fishing trips are all close by. Riding, sailing, tennis, golf, sandy beaches, historic houses, beautiful coastal walks, and the Country Park are all near. Mariners Cottage (a historic listed building) sleeps six, plus baby, in three bedrooms, and has a modern bathroom, fitted kitchen, children's play house, washing machine, dining room and large lounge with colour TV, own parking. Gas central heating makes Mariners good for winter holidays from £95 per week. Dog welcome. Picture shows view from enclosed garden. SAE please for brochure of this and other cottages to:

Mrs P.A. Barnes, Boat Hyde, Northam, Bideford EX39 1NX
or phone (01237) 473801 for prices and vacancies only.

SEA BIRDS

Sea edge, pretty Georgian cottage facing directly out to the open sea. **Sea Birds** is a spacious cottage with large lounge, colour TV, dining room with french windows onto garden, modern fitted kitchen, 3 double bedrooms, bathroom, second WC downstairs. Lawned garden at back with garden furniture overlooking the sea. Sea views from most rooms and the garden are magnificent; views of the open sea, boats entering the estuary, sunset, sea birds, own parking. Appledore is still a fishing village; fishing trips from the quay, restaurants by the water. Area has good cliff and coastal walks, stately homes, riding, swimming, golf, surfing, excellent beaches. Off peak heating. Winter prices from £95 weekly. Other cottages available.

Ring 01237 473801 for prices and vacancies *only* or send SAE for brochure to
P.S. BARNES, Boat Hyde, Northam, Bideford, Devon EX39 1NX

Mrs Angela Bell
Wooder Manor
Widecombe in the Moor
Near Ashburton TQ13 7TR
Tel: (01364) 621391

Modernised granite cottages and converted coach house on 108-acre working family farm nestled in the picturesque valley of Widecombe, surrounded by unspoilt woodland moors and granite tors. Half a mile from village with post office, general stores, inn with dining room, church and National Trust Information Centre. Excellent centre for touring Devon with a variety of places to visit and exploring Dartmoor by foot or on horseback. Accommodation is clean and well-equipped with colour TV, central heating, laundry room. Children welcome. Large gardens and courtyard for easy parking. Open all year, so take advantage of off-season reduced rates. Short Breaks also available. Two properties suitable for disabled visitors. Brochure available.
¥ ¥ ¥ *Commended*.

SYMBOLS

🐾 Indicates no charge for pets. are welcome free of charge.
£   Indicates that a charge is made for pets: nightly or weekly.
pw! Shows some special provision for pets; exercise facility, feeding or accommodationarrangement.
⌂   Indicates separate pets accommodation.

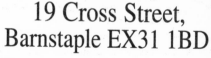

NOTE

All the information in this book is given in good faith in the belief that it is correct. However, the publishers cannot guarantee the facts given in these pages, neither are they responsible for changes in policy, ownership or terms that may take place after the date of going to press. Readers should always satisfy themselves that the facilities they require are available and that the terms, if quoted, still apply.

PETS STAY FREE

Sandy Cove Hotel stands in 20 acres of cliff, coast and garden. The Hotel Restaurant overlooks the sea and cliffs with spectacular views of the bay. You will probably wonder how we can do it for the price when we offer a FIVE-COURSE MEAL including seafood platters with lobster, smoked salmon and steak. Every Saturday a Swedish Smorgasbord and Carvery carved by the Chef, and followed by dancing till late. Live entertainment weekly from Whitsun until September. All bedrooms have colour TV, telephone, teamaking and are en suite. The cocktail bar overlooks the bay and you have the use of the hotel's 80° heated indoor pool and recreation centre with sauna, sunbed, gym equipment and whirlpool, ALL FREE OF CHARGE.

Please return this advertisement to qualify for "Pets Stay Free" offer. Bargain Breaks and weekly rates available all year.

Includes 5-course Evening Meal and coffee. Children— free accommodation. Please send for free brochure pack. Children under 8 years completely free, including meals.

Sandy Cove Hotel
Combe Martin Bay,
Devon EX34 9SR
Tel: (01271) 882243 & 882888

Indoor pool heated to 80°F with roll-back sides to enjoy the sun

Brixham

HOLIDAY PARK

Spend this years holiday in Brixham. Take time
to explore the crooked streets and quaint shops
that surround Brixham's nearby Harbour. Make
your holiday one to remember. Relax under the palm
trees or laze by the Pool with it's spectacular views over Torbay.

Explore the nearby beach with lovely walks through the woods beyond, or stroll along
the seafront into Brixham.

In the evening you can enjoy a meal and entertainment in the Bayview Club.

YOUR ACCOMMODATION

Choice of a chalet or caravan. Our lapwing and
Albatross accommodations are cosy 1 bedroomed
chalets. Avocet, Fulmar and Sanderling are the more
spacious two bedroomed chalets. Then, to complete the
range our 2 & 3 bedroom caravans - the Petrel,
Cormorant & Shearwater's.

★ Indoor Htd Swimming Pool ★ 150 yards from Beach
★ Heated Toddlers Pool ★ Free Club Membership
★ Beautiful Scenery ★ Comfortable Bar offering Meals &
　Take-away Service ★ Well Stocked Shop ★ Launderette
★ 10 Minutes Walk from Brixham Harbour & Centre
★ Childrens Play Area ★ Free Bed Linen ★ *Pets Welcome*

01803 853324

FISHCOMBE COVE · BRIXHAM · SOUTH DEVON

WEST AISH FARM
MORCHARD BISHOP, NR CREDITON, DEVON EX17 6RX
Tel/Fax: 01363 877427   Molly and Jeff Kingaby

Wake up to the sounds of the countryside in our stone cottages.
Enjoy the peaceful setting of this former cobbled farmyard.
Drink in the delightful views across the valley and after a day's touring, walking or riding,
Relax by a log fire or light the barbecue.

Exeter 13 miles   *Rosemoor Gardens (RHS) 21 miles*
Castle Drogo (NT) 20 miles   *Killerton House (NT) 16 miles*
Knight Hayes (NT) 15 miles

Two self catering cottages sleep 5 (suitable for partially disabled)
Prices: £110 - £260. **Open all year.** Short Breaks: 3 nights £90.

| Welcome Host | COMMENDED ♦ ♦ ♦ |

AA ★★ RAC *CROYDE BAY HOUSE HOTEL*   ♛♛♛ HIGHLY COMMENDED

A small friendly Hotel in unique position beside the beach at Croyde Bay.
Situated on the Coastal Footpath with miles of beautiful walks on the
doorstep. All rooms are en-suite with TV and tea/coffee making facilities and
command views of the beach. Our good food and friendly atmosphere will
make your stay here a holiday to remember. Please phone or write

MRS JENNIFER PENNY, CROYDE BAY HOUSE HOTEL,
CROYDE BAY, NORTH DEVON EX33 1PA
TEL: 01271 890270

WEST WINDS GUEST HOUSE
Moor Lane, Croyde Bay EX33 1PA
Tel/Fax: 01271 890489. Mobile: 0831 211247

Small guest house located picturesquely by the water's edge overlooking
Croyde Bay beach adjacent to Baggy Point National Trust coastal path.
Private steps to the beach. En suite rooms available, all with TV, radio,
tea/coffee making facilities; some rooms have sea view. Dogs welcomed. Ample car parking.
Residential bar and separate sun lounge overlooking sea. Situated in an ideal position for surfing,
touring Exmoor National Park and surrounding countryside. Comfortable and relaxing atmosphere.
Open all year. Bed and Breakfast from £23 per person. Write or telephone for brochure.

♛♛♛ Commended   AA QQQ Recommended

Mrs B. Hill   **SUNNYSIDE FARM**   Tel: 01884 855322
Butterleigh, Near Cullompton EX15 1PP

Enjoy the picturesque countryside in mid Devon only $3\frac{1}{2}$ miles from M5 Junction 28.
Central for touring. Bedrooms with en suite, tea/coffee making facilities. Lounge with
TV. Short Breaks. B&B from £16 daily. Evening meal optional.

FHG PUBLICATIONS LIMITED publish a large range of well-
known accommodation guides. We will be happy to send you
details or you can use the order form at the back of this book.

The

Warmest  *in the West !*

One of the finest choices for your holiday in South Devon, *Welcome Family* offers all the facilities and atmosphere of a large holiday centre, but with the personal service of a small park. Situated in a very

picturesque part of South Devon, only a short level walk to the famous safe sandy dunes and wildlife areas. Only 15 minutes from the M5, a half hour drive from a host of attractions, including Dartmoor, Torbay or Exeter.

WELCOME FAMILY HOLIDAY PARK
DAWLISH WARREN, SOUTH DEVON EX7 0PH
Reservations 01626 862070 - Dial a Brochure 01626 888323

- Stylish **DOLPHIN CLUB** & Entertainment Centre
- Super indoor heated **NEPTUNE TROPICANA** Water Leisure Complex – four Feature-packed Pools, Solarium, Sauna, spectator viewing
- New **CRUISERS** adult Cocktail Bar
- Children's **JOLLY ROGER** club with Disco, Cinema & large Games arcade
- Short, level walk to safe sandy beach
- Great **Value-for-money** prices

- **FREE** Electricity, Linen, Colour TV
- Welcome TV – great films, local attractions, and more
- 2 Shops
- Cafe
- 2 Takeaways
- Crazy Golf
- Adventure playground
- Launderette
- Hire Service with computer games
- Pets *Welcome* (at small charge)
- Choose from economy 4-berth to luxury 8-berth caravans

TORCROSS APARTMENT HOTEL

ETB

♟ ♟ ♟

Commended

At the Water's Edge on Slapton Sands

Close to Dartmouth in the lush unspoilt countryside of the South Hams and adjoining Slapton Ley Nature Reserve. 18 superb self-catering Apartments. Sea and lake views. Some ground floor apartments and lifts to all floors. Central heating. Waterside Restaurant and Village Inn. Apartment "Takeaway" food service. Brochure with pleasure.

Torcross Apartment Hotel (Ref PW), Torcross, Near Kingsbridge, South Devon TQ7 2TQ
Tel: 01548 580206

TEIGN VALLEY FOREST
HALDON LODGE FARM, KENNFORD
NEAR EXETER, DEVON EX6 7YG Tel: 01392 832312

Delightful modern 34ft Caravan only five miles from Exeter and short distance Dawlish, Teignmouth and Torbay, from £70 per week. Lounge (TV), 2 bedrooms, kitchen, bathroom (H&C) and toilet. *Attractive private grounds in peaceful surroundings. Famous village inns, two beautiful Coarse Fishing Lakes and farm shop.* Small private camping site. Pony trekking available. Special welcome to less experienced riders.

Pets Welcome ● Open all year ● Enquiries to D.L. Salter

All the advertisers in PETS WELCOME! have an entry in the appropriate classified section and each classified entry may carry one or more of the following symbols:

♟   This symbol indicates that pets are welcome free of charge.

£   The £ indicates that a charge is made for pets. We quote the amount where possible, either per night or per week.

pw!   This symbol shows that the establishment has some special provision for pets; perhaps an exercise facility or some special feeding or accommodation arrangements.

⌂   Indicates separate pets accommodation.

PLEASE NOTE that all the advertisers in PETS WELCOME! extend a welcome to pets and their owners but they may attach conditions. The interests of other guests have to be considered and it is usually assumed that pets will be well trained, obedient and under the control of their owner.

Readers are requested to mention this guidebook when seeking accommodation (and please enclose a stamped addressed envelope).

Hedley Wood Caravan & Camping Park
Bridgerule, Holsworthy, Devon EX22 7ED
Tel & Fax: 01288 381404

16 acre woodland family-run site with outstanding views, where you can enjoy a totally relaxing holiday with a "laid-back" atmosphere, sheltered and open camping areas. Just 10 minutes' drive from the beaches, golf courses, riding stables and shops.

On-site facilities include: Children's adventure areas, Bar, Clubroom, Shop, Laundry, Meals and all amenities. Free hot showers and water. Nice dogs/pets are welcome. Daily kennelling facility. Dog walks/Nature trail. Clay pigeon shoot. Static caravans for hire, **caravan storage** available.
Open all year.

RAC Selected Site

The Belfry Country Hotel
Yarcombe, Near Honiton, East Devon EX14 9BD

Victorian village school converted to a small luxury Hotel. Beautifully appointed en suite rooms. Lovely views over Blackdown Hills and Yarty Valley. Cosy Bar/Restaurant serving AA Rosette-awarded scrumptious home cooking. Log fire, comfy lounge. Ideal walking and touring area. Free entry for hotel guests to local Classic Gardens and heated swimming pool. Phone **Jackie & Tony Rees** on:

01404 861234 or Fax 01404 861579 for brochure and information

AA ★★ 75% Rosette   ETB 👑👑👑👑 Commended

Lower Luxton Farm, Upottery, Honiton, Devon EX14 9PB

Get away from the toil of everyday life at Lower Luxton Farm, where a warm welcome awaits you in an area of outstanding natural beauty. Peaceful walks; ideal base for touring. Carp fishing. Good home cooking using fresh farm produce. Reductions early and late season. Pets welcome. *Weekly terms from £120, 6 Dinners and Bed and Breakfast.*

SAE for brochure and terms Mrs Elizabeth Tucker Tel: 01823 601269

TANFIELD HOTEL

Hope Cove, Near Kingsbridge, South Devon
Tel: 01548 561268

A warm welcome awaits you from John and Pauline Ward at this Ashley Courtenay recommended licensed hotel overlooking the tiny fishing village of Hope Cove. A peaceful place, quiet and uncrowded, Hope Cove is ideal for a relaxing holiday. The spectacular coastal path over miles of National Trust property offers an ideal situation for dog owners. All rooms are centrally heated, en suite and all have colour TV, hairdryers, tea and coffee making facilities. Colour brochure available on request. Mid-week bookings accepted. Bargain breaks available.

FREE and REDUCED RATE Holiday Visits!
Don't miss our Readers' Offer Vouchers
on pages 5 to 18

The Darnley Private Hotel

Belmont Road, Ilfracombe EX34 8DR

Approved

The Darnley Hotel is an elegant Victorian residence set in its own informal garden, complete with nature walk to the town centre and seafront. Within easy reach of The Torrs and South West Coastal Walk with its spectacular scenery. Exmoor National Park and the sandy beaches of Woolacombe and Croyde are only a short drive away.

The Darnley has the perfect atmosphere for a holiday with your pet. Our comfortable bedrooms are all centrally heated and have colour TV and tea and coffee making facilities.

- **Personal Service and friendly atmosphere.**
- **Pets sleep in your room with you.**
- **Parking in grounds.**
- **Varied Menu and excellent wine list.**
- **Cosy bar.**
- **Most major credit cards accepted.**

There is much to see and do in beautiful North Devon, with wonderful walks, historic houses, and gardens to visit and explore. Weekly terms from £189 - £200 Bed , Breakfast & Evening Meal Special 5 night break £130 - £150.

Christmas Festivities
4 nights Full Board - £200

New Year Celebrations
4 nights Half Board - £160

For colour brochure telephone
Reg or Val on 01271 863955

The Old Coach House
SELF CATERING HOLIDAYS

Architect conversion of the old coach houses of Watermouth Castle into 8 apartments of character. A select courtyard complex with gardens, situated in a quiet and secluded valley just 200 yards from the sea and picturesque Watermouth Cove.
Enjoying a reputation for many repeat bookings, the apartments are independent, charmingly furnished and fully equipped including night storage heaters, colour TV, etc.
A perfect North Devon holiday base for wide family interests – the sea, Exmoor countryside, riding, coast walking, 18-hole golf course within 1 mile, plus the many facilities of nearby Ilfracombe and Combe Martin.

★ Accommodation for 2 -6 people ★ Dogs welcome ★ Private parking ★ Proprietor managed

Colour brochure and price list from:

Peggy Dobson, The Old Coach House, Watermouth, Ilfracombe, Devon EX34 9SJ
Telephone : 01271 867340

Instow Beach Haven Cottage

View from garden

Seafront cottage overlooking the sandy beach. Instow is a quiet yachting village with soft yellow sands and a pretty promenade of shops, old houses, pubs & cafés serving drinks and meals. Beach Haven has extensive beach & sea views from the house and garden, sleeps 5, own garage and parking, gas fired central heating, colour TV, washing machine. Lawned garden overlooking sea with terrace & garden furniture. Coastal walks & cycle trails, boat to Lundy Island. Dog welcome.

Please send SAE for colour brochure of this and other cottages to:
P.I.BARNES, Boat Hyde. Northam, Bideford EX39 1NX (01237 473801)

Midships, Lane End, Instow
Sleeps 6 plus cot

45 yards from sandy beach, pretty cottage with gas central heating. Double bedded room, twin bedded room with washbasin; modern bathroom, lounge with colour TV and convertible sofa, dining room. Fitted kitchen with fridge/freezer, cooker, washing machine and tumble dryer. Children and pets welcome. SAE for brochure of this and two other properties to:

Mrs P. Baxter, Huish Moor Farmhouse, Instow, Bideford, Devon EX39 4LT or phone (01271) 861146

Beachdown

CHALLABOROUGH BAY,
KINGSBRIDGE,
SOUTH DEVON TQ7 4JB
TEL: KINGSBRIDGE (01548) 810089

Delightful cedarwood chalets just 250 yards from a safe, sandy beach. Gardens and children's play areas on peaceful 2-acre site. Experience stunning cliff walks on South Devon's Heritage Coast. A haven for surfing, windsurfing and diving enthusiasts. Heated pool and golf nearby; Dartmoor National Park 30 mins. Pets welcome. Colour brochure available.

Contact NICKY FAULKNER for details.

ETB 3 KEYS APPROVED

Gara Mill

Slapton, Kingsbridge, Devon TQ 2RE
SELF CATERING in comfortable detached lodges or flats within the 16th century mill. Peaceful riverside setting, woodland walks on your doorstep. TV's, laundry, play area, games room.
Children and pets welcome. Please ring for brochure.
Tel: 01803 770295   **Allan and Marcia Green.**

BLACKWELL PARK, LODDISWELL, KINGSBRIDGE

Bed, Breakfast and Evening Meal is offered in Blackwell Park, a 17th century farmhouse situated 5 miles from Kingsbridge. Seven bedrooms, some en suite, and all with washbasins

and tea-making facilities. Games room; large garden, also adjoining 54 acres of woodland/Nature Reserve. Ample food with a choice of menu. CHILDREN AND PETS ESPECIALLY WELCOME; babysitting. Pets welcome FREE of charge. Dartmoor, Plymouth, Torbay, Dartmouth and many beaches lie within easy reach. ETB 2 Crowns.
Bed, Breakfast and Evening Meal
Proprietress: Mrs B. Kelly Tel: 01548 821230
Blackwell Park, Loddiswell TQ7 4EA

HALLSANDS HOTEL,
North Hallsands, Kingsbridge, Devon
Tel: Chivelstone (01548) 511264
Family Hotel on the sea edge. Children and doggie terms.
Bed, Breakfast and Evening Meal. Fully licensed. Good food.
Fishing and bathing. Compressed air available.

PETS STAY FREE

Your pets are welcome to stay free if you return this advert with your booking

THE EXMOOR SANDPIPER INN

A fine old coaching Inn, reputedly dating in part from the 13th and 15th centuries. It is in a beautiful setting amidst rolling moors, high above Lynmouth on the coastal road with the dramatic backdrop of Exmoor. Let us spoil you on arrival with a **free cream tea** and then be shown up to a beautiful character bedroom with tea making, colour TV and bathroom en suite, designed for your every comfort. A warm bath then a 5-course dinner including smoked salmon, seafood platters with lobster, steaks and a delicious selection of sweets. Sit in the character bars and sample our real ales or watch the late film in your bedroom. After a traditional English breakfast set off to discover the magic of Exmoor whether in the car or on foot, along Doone Valley following the River to the majestic Watersmeet, or further to the Valley of the Rocks and up over to Glenthorne and beyond to the Devon/Somerset Borders. We have 7 circular walks around the area and the Inn can provide a packed lunch.

Please write or ring for FREE colour brochure to:-

The Exmoor Sandpiper Inn, Countisbury, Lynmouth, N. Devon EX35 6NE Tel: 01598 741263

Self-contained holiday flat at
LYNTON AND LYNMOUTH RAILWAY STATION
Sleeps up to six in two bedrooms (cot available). Sitting room. Bathroom
and separate WC. Kitchen/dining room. Children and pets welcome.

SAE to MRS PRYOR, STATION HOUSE, LYNTON, DEVON Tel: (01598) 752275 or 752381 Fax: (01598) 752475

Sylvia House Hotel
ETB ♛♛♛
COMMENDED

"A DELIGHTFUL GEORGIAN ENGLISH HERITAGE LISTED
HOUSE IN THE LITTLE SWITZERLAND OF ENGLAND"
Offering delightful rooms, most en suite, some with four-poster beds
at no extra cost. All rooms with TV and tea and coffee making
facilities. Scrumptious home-cooked dinner served by candlelight in
our elegant dining room. Pets are very welcome free of charge. Bed
and Breakfast from £15 to £18 per person; Dinner with choice of
menu £10. Special weekly rates and Bargain Breaks. Open all year.

**LYDIATE LANE, LYNTON, NORTH DEVON EX35 6HE
TEL: (01598) 752391**

COMBE PARK HOTEL, originally a 17th century Hunting Lodge, is a
comfortable Hotel uniquely situated within National Trust parkland.

9 bedrooms with
private bath/shower
rooms. Licensed
with well furnished
lounges. Fresh
seasonal produce.

ASHLEY COURTENAY & AA
A haven for walking,
riding and fishing.
Dogs welcome.
Open mid-March to
end October.

Combe Park Hotel, Hillsford Bridges, Lynton EX35 6LE Tel: (01598) 752356

THE TURRET
♛♛
33 Lee Road, Lynton, Devon EX35 6BS

Delightful, family-run Victorian hotel situated in the centre of this picturesque
village, ideal for exploring Exmoor and its magnificent coastline.
*All of our rooms have colour TV and beverage making facilities;
most are en suite. Superb home cooking; vegetarians catered for.
Licensed. Open all year.*
Bed and Breakfast from £15 to £21;
Reductions for Short Breaks and weekly bookings.
TELEPHONE FOR FREE BROCHURE 01598 753284

SYMBOLS
🐴 Indicates no charge for pets. are welcome free of charge.

£ Indicates that a charge is made for pets: nightly or weekly.

pw! Shows some special provision for pets; exercise facility, feeding or accommodation arrangement.

⌂ Indicates separate pets accommodation.

Hotel, Restaurant & Inn
THE PORT LIGHT

Doggies' Heaven, Walkers' Paradise, Romantics' Dream
A totally unique location, set amidst acres of National Trust
coastal countryside with panoramic views towards
Cornwall, Dartmoor and France.

WE ARE REALLY TOTALLY PET FRIENDLY

- Luxury en suite rooms, some with access straight onto the gardens
- Close to secluded sandy cove (dogs permitted) 15 minutes' walk
- No charge for pets which are most welcome throughout the hotel
- Outstanding reputation for superb home-cooked fayre specialising in fresh sea food
- Set alongside the famous National Trust Salcombe to Hope Cove coastal walk
- Fully licensed bar - log burner - real ale
- BARGAIN BREAKS THROUGHOUT THE YEAR
- Large free car park

**The size of our advert shows our dedication
to pets and their owners**

**Bolberry Down, Malborough, Near Salcombe,
South Devon Tel: (01548) 561384 or (0831) 218047**
"Where the Locals and Tourists Wine and Dine"
Sean and Sonya Hassall

NOTE

All the information in this book is given in good faith in the
belief that it is correct. However, the publishers cannot
guarantee the facts given in these pages, neither are they
responsible for changes in policy, ownership or terms that may
take place after the date of going to press. Readers should
always satisfy themselves that the facilities they require are
available and that the terms, if quoted, still apply.

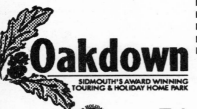

WELCOME COTTAGE HOLIDAYS. Hundreds of properties in wonderful locations at welcoming low prices. Pets, linen and fuel mostly included. For FREE colour brochure telephone 01756 702209.

TOAD HALL COTTAGES. 100 outstanding waterside and rural properties in truly beautiful locations in Devon. Call for our highly acclaimed brochure. Video also available. TEL: 01548 853089.

CLASSIC COTTAGES (25), HELSTON, CORNWALL TR13 8NA (24 HOUR DIAL-A-BROCHURE 01326 565555). Choose your cottage from 300 of the finest coastal and country cottages throughout the West Country. [Pets £9 weekly.]

COASTAL COTTAGES of North Devon. Croyde, Woolacombe Bay, Saunton Sands. Superb selection of self catering holiday homes conveniently located for superb sandy beaches and unspoilt coastline. For Colour Brochure : DAVIDS HILL, GEORGEHAM, NORTH DEVON EX33 1QF (01271 890040/890057)

POWELLS COTTAGE HOLIDAYS. Your choice of Cottage in Cornwall, Devon, Somerset, Cotswolds, Wye Valley, Gower and Pembrokeshire in our full colour brochure. [Pets £10 per week] FREEPHONE 0800 378771 or apply: 61 High Street, Saundersfoot, Pembrokeshire SA69 9EJ or (24hrs) 01834 813232.

WEST COUNTRY COTTAGES. From Land's End to the New Forest, from South Hams to the Cotswolds. ETB Graded and Commended Cottages; video available. For free brochure apply: WEST COUNTRY COTTAGES, THE GEMINIDS (PW), ABBOTSKERSWELL, DEVON TQ12 5PP (01626 333679). [£9 per pet per week]

MARSDENS COTTAGE HOLIDAYS, DEPT 14, 2 THE SQUARE, BRAUNTON EX33 2JB (01271 813777; Fax: 01271 813664)). Experience the charms of a North Devon holiday from the comfort and luxury of a Marsdens holiday cottage. Write or phone today for your free colour brochure.

Appledore

Unspoilt resort and small port on estuaries of Taw and Torridge. Sandy beach, good bathing. Bideford 3 miles.

OTTER COTTAGE. Traditional fisherman's cottage. Totally equipped – 2 TVs, VCR, microwave, autowasher etc. Also unique harbourside apartments and bungalow. Brochure from B.H. SMITH, 26 MARKET STREET, APPLEDORE EX39 1PP. Tel: 01237 476154 (or if no personal reply 01271 78907). [Pets £8 per week.]

SEA BIRDS, pretty Georgian cottage facing directly out to the open sea. Spacious cottage with large lounge, colour TV, dining room, modern fitted kitchen and 3 double bedrooms, own parking. Other cottages available. SAE to P.S. BARNES, BOAT HYDE, NORTHAM, BIDEFORD, DEVON EX39 1NX (01237 473801). [pw! Dog £5 per week.]

MARINERS COTTAGE, IRSHA STREET, APPLEDORE. Elizabethan fisherman's Cottage at sea edge. Extensive views of sea and boats. Enclosed garden. Sleeps 6: three bedrooms, lounge, dining room, children's play house, own parking. Good fishing, coastal walks. SAE please to MRS P.A. BARNES, BOAT HYDE, NORTHAM, BIDEFORD EX39 1NX or phone 01237 473801 for prices and vacancies only. [pw! Dog £5 per week.]

Ashburton

Delightful little town on southern fringe of Dartmoor. Centrally placed for touring and the Torbay resorts. Plymouth 24 miles, Exeter 20, Kingsbridge 20, Tavistock 20, Teignmouth 14, Torquay 14, Totnes 8, Newton Abbot 7.

PARKERS FARM HOLIDAYS, HIGHER MEAD FARM, ASHBURTON, NEWTON ABBOT TQ13 7LJ (01364 652598; Fax: 01364 654004). Farm Cottages and Caravans to let, also level touring site with toilet/shower block and electric hook-ups. Central for touring; 12 miles Torquay. Pets welcome. [Pets £12 per week in cottage/caravan]

MRS A. BELL, WOODER MANOR, WIDECOMBE-IN-THE-MOOR, NEAR ASHBURTON TQ13 7TR (01364 621391). Cottages on family farm. Surrounded by unspoilt woodland and moors. Clean and well equipped, colour TV, central heating, laundry room. Two properties suitable for disabled visitors. Brochure available. 4 Keys Commended. [Pets £10 per week.]

Axminster

Agricultural town in the Axe river valley, famous for carpets. Cattle and street market.

LILAC COTTAGE. A beautifully renovated cottage. Oil-fired central heating. All electric kitchen. Inglenook fireplace; beamed ceiling. Sleeps six plus cot. Colour TV. Garden. Garage. SAE please. APPLY – MRS J.M. STUART, HUNSCOTE HOUSE, WELLESBOURNE, WARWICKSHIRE CV35 9EX (Tel/Fax: 01789 840228) or Mrs Young (01769 573788). [Pets £5 per week.]

Aylesbeare

Quiet village set in beautiful countryside within easy reach of M5 motorway, Exeter and South East Devon resorts. Exeter 8 miles, Sidmouth 8, Ottery St Mary 5.

MRS H. BALE, GREAT HOUNDBEARE FARM, AYLESBEARE, EXETER EX5 2DB (01404 822771). In the heart of the countryside yet only minutes from Exeter, M5 and coast. B&B: all rooms en suite, colour TV, tea/coffee; or self-catering: cottage sleeps up to 14. Secure stabling/grazing and kennels if required. 2 Crowns Commended. [Pets £2.50 per night ⌂]

Barnstaple

The largest town in Devon, once an important centre for the wool trade, now a lively shopping centre with thrice weekly market, modern leisure centre etc.

COASTAL EXMOOR HIDEAWAYS. House with indoor pool and jacuzzi; house on beach; riverside cottages in 80-acre valley; plus many more properties. Dogs welcome. Breaks from £98. TELEPHONE 01598 763339.

BEACH AND BRACKEN EXMOOR HOLIDAYS, BRATTON FLEMING, BARNSTAPLE EX32 7TL (01598 710702). Comfortable self-catering cottages; farmhouse accommodation with food. Short notice all-season breaks. Telephone anytime.

MRS C.M. WRIGHT, FRIENDSHIP FARM, BRATTON FLEMING, BARNSTAPLE EX31 4SQ (01598 763291 evenings). Comfortable three-bedroom Bungalow, sleeps 6 plus cot. Linen provided. Situated on edge of Exmoor, near coast (Combe Martin). From £100 Low Season, £220 High Season. [🐕 pw!]

NORTH DEVON HOLIDAY HOMES, 19 CROSS STREET, BARNSTAPLE EX31 1BD (01271 76322 (24 hours); Fax: 01271 46544). Send for guide to 500 of best value Cottages around Devon's National Trust coast. All regularly inspected and guaranteed to offer first class value. [Pets £10 per week.]

MRS V.M. CHUGG, VALLEY VIEW, MARWOOD, BARNSTAPLE EX31 4EA (01271 43458). Bungalow on 300 acre farm. Bed and Breakfast accommodation. Near Marwood Hill Gardens and Arlington Court. Children most welcome, free baby-sitting. Dogs by arrangement. Terms from £13. [pw!]

Berrynarbor

This peaceful village overlooking the beautiful Sterridge valley, has a 17th cent. pub and even older church and is a half-mile from the coast road between Combe Martin (1 1/2 miles) and Ilfracombe (3 miles).

SANDY COVE HOTEL, BERRYNARBOR EX34 9SR (01271 882243 or 882888). Hotel set amidst acres of gardens and woods. Heated swimming pool. Children and pets welcome. A la carte restaurant. All rooms en suite with colour TV, tea-making. Free colour brochure on application. [🐕]

Bideford

Neat port and resort on River Torridge. Attractive, many-arched stone bridge, wooded hills. Boat trips from quay. The sea is 3 miles distant at Westward Ho! Exeter 43 miles, Launceston 32, Bude 26, Ilfracombe 21, Barnstaple 9, Torrington 7.

JENNY AND BARRY JONES, THE PINES AT EASTLEIGH, NEAR BIDEFORD, NORTH DEVON EX39 4PA (01271 860561, e-mail Barry@barpines.demon.co.uk). A warm welcome and a peaceful relaxing time. En suite rooms. Generous farmhouse style cooking. Open all year. Licensed. Children welcome. B&B from £29. No Smoking. ETB 3 Crowns Highly Commended. [pw! Pets £2 per night]

Bigbury-on-Sea

A scattered village overlooking superb coastal scenery and wide expanses of sand.

MR SCARTERFIELD, HENLEY HOTEL, FOLLY HILL, BIGBURY-ON-SEA TQ7 4AR (01548 810240). Edwardian cottage-style hotel, spectacular sea views. Near good beach, dog walking. en suite rooms with telephone, tea making, TV etc. Home cooking. No smoking establishment. Licensed. 3 Crowns Commended. AA 1 Star. [Pets £1.00 per night.]

PAT CHADWICK, "MARINERS", RINGMORE DRIVE, BIGBURY-ON-SEA, KINGSBRIDGE TQ7 4AU (01548 810454). Two large flats with extensive sea views. Sandy beaches within yards. Golf nearby. Dogs welcome. [🐾]

MRS J. TUCKER, MOUNT FOLLY FARM, BIGBURY-ON-SEA, KINGSBRIDGE TQ7 4AR (01548810267). Cliff top position, with outstanding views of Bigbury Bay. Spacious, self catering wing of farmhouse, attractively furnished. Farm adjoins golf course and River Avon. Lovely coastal walks, ideal centre for South Hams and Dartmoor. Always a warm welcome, pets too!

Bovey Tracey

Little town nestling on southern fringe of Dartmoor. Fine scenery including Haytor Rocks (4 miles) and Becky Falls (3 1/2 miles). The 14th cent. Church is of interest. Exeter 14 miles, Torquay 13, Teignmouth 12, Ashburton 8, Newton Abbot 6, Chudleigh 4.

BLENHEIM COUNTRY HOUSE HOTEL, BOVEY TRACEY TQ13 9DH (01626 832422). Family Hotel on edge of Dartmoor National Park. RSPCA member. Open all year. All pets free. 2 Crowns. [🐾]

SELF CATERING. Modern , three-bedroomed traditionally built bungalow. Fenced garden, pets welcome. Bed linen provided. ETB 3 Keys. Terms from £200-£360 per week all inclusive. Enquiries: MR P. J. MOUNTFORD, CHURCH MEADOW, COOMBE CROSS, BOVEY TRACEY TQ13 9EP (01626 832824).

Brixham

Lively resort and fishing port, with quaint houses and narrow winding streets. Ample opportunities for fishing and boat trips.

HOLIDAYS TORBAY, 26 COTMORE CLOSE, BRIXHAM TQ5 0EF (01803 854708). Harbourside cottages, houses, flats. Sea views and close to beaches, town and coastal walks. Colour TV, clean and comfortable. [🐾]

DEVONCOURT HOLIDAY FLATS, BERRYHEAD ROAD, BRIXHAM TQ5 9AB (01803 853748 24 hours). 24 self-contained flats with private balcony, colour television, heating, private car park, all-electric kitchenette, separate bathroom and toilet. Open all year. [Pets £10 per week.]

BRIXHAM HOLIDAY PARK, FISHCOMBE COVE, BRIXHAM (01803 853324). Chalets and caravans 10 minutes' walk from Brixham harbour and centre. Indoor heated pool, club, bar, shop, launderette. Pets welcome.

Buck's Mills

Picturesque hamlet in steeply descending coombe above Barnstaple Bay. Clovelly 3 miles.

ROSEMARY & RAY NEWPORT, THE OLD MILL, BUCK'S MILLS, BIDEFORD EX39 5DY (01237 431701). Comfortable 17th century cottage/tea rooms. Warm and friendly atmosphere, good home cooking, log fires. In quiet coastal village with beach and woodland walks. Open all year. [🐾]

Budleigh Salterton

South Devon resort of dignified charm. Attractive sea-front, shingle beach, pleasant walks in vicinity. Good fishing in sea and River Otter. Facilities for tennis, bowls, croquet, golf. Hayes Barton, birthplace of Sir Walter Raleigh, is 3 miles distant. Taunton 16 miles, Exeter 14, Sidmouth 7, Exmouth 5.

TIDWELL HOUSE COUNTRY HOTEL, KNOWLE, BUDLEIGH SALTERTON EX9 7AG (01395 442444). Come and unwind at this Listed Georgian house of great character set in 3 acres of gardens. Ideal centre for walking, touring, playing golf etc. Large en suite rooms. Pets and children welcome. [Pets £1 per night.]

Chagford

Unspoilt little town on the edge of Dartmoor in an area rich in prehistoric remains. Noted for 16th-century bridge, and Tudor and Georgian houses.

I. SATOW, WEEKE BROOK, CHAGFORD TQ13 8JQ (01647 433345). Away from the tumult of the world. One mile charming small Dartmoor town. Lovely ancient thatched house. Pets welcome. Bed and Breakfast £11.00 to £15.00.

A wonderful variety of over 450 cottages, houses and apartments all over the West Country, ideal for self catering holidays. Many accept pets. Free colour brochure from HELPFUL HOLIDAYS, COOMBE 49, CHAGFORD, DEVON TQ13 8DF (01647 433535 24hrs).

Chittlehamholt

Standing in beautiful countryside in the Taw Valley and just off the B3227. Barnstaple 9 miles, South Molton 5.

SNAPDOWN FARM CARAVANS, CHITTLEHAMHOLT, UMBERLEIGH, NORTH DEVON EX37 9PF (01769 540708). 12 only – 6 berth caravans with flush toilets, showers, colour TV, fridges, cookers and fires. Laundry room. Picnic tables. Unspoilt countryside – field and woodland walks. Terms £80 to £220 inc. gas and electricity in caravans. [Pets £8.75 per week.]

Chulmleigh

Mid-Devon village set in lovely countryside, just off A377 Exeter to Barnstaple road. Exeter 23 miles, Tiverton 19, Barnstaple 18.

THE FOX AND HOUNDS, EGGESFORD HOUSE HOTEL, EGGESFORD, NEAR CHULMLEIGH EX18 7JZ (01769580345; Fax: 01769 580262). 30 acres of countryside and forest. 7 miles River Taw salmon/trout fishing. Ideal touring centre for Dartmoor, Exmoor coasts. 20 en suite bedrooms. B&B from £31.50. [Pets £3.50 per night.]

Combe Martin

Coastal village with harbour set in sandy bay. Good cliff and rock scenery. Of interest is the Church and "Pack of Cards" Inn. Barnstaple 14 miles, Lynton 12, Ilfracombe 6.

RONE HOUSE HOTEL, KING STREET, COMBE MARTIN EX34 0AD (01271 883428). Small, comfortable family-run Hotel, close to sea. Central heating. TV and private facilities in most bedrooms. Heated swimming pool. Pets and children welcome. [🐕]

MODERN BUNGALOWS on a choice of two attractive sites. Sleep 2, 4,6, or 8 people. Adjacent to safe beach. Lounge with free colour television. Heated swimming pool, crazy golf course. Free entertainment and dancing. JOHN FOWLER HOLIDAYS, DEPARTMENT PW, MARLBOROUGH ROAD, ILFRACOMBE EX34 8PF (01271 866766). [Pets £12 per week.]

SAFFRON HOUSE HOTEL, KING STREET, COMBE MARTIN EX34 0BX (01271 883521). Charming farmhouse hotel in picturesque coastal village on Exmoor. Ideal for touring, lovely views. Heated swimming pool and pretty gardens. ETB 3 Crowns Commended. [🐕]

MR M.J. HUGHES, MANLEIGH HOLIDAY PARK, RECTORY ROAD, COMBE MARTIN EX34 0NS (01271 883353). Holiday Chalets, accommodate 4/6 persons. In 6 acres. Free use of swimming pool. Dogs welcome provided they are kept under control. Also 12 luxury Caravans to let. Graded 4 ticks. [Pets £14 per week. pw!]

Crediton

Ancient small town. Chapter house with Cromwellian relics. Cidermaking. Cathedral-type church. 7 miles from Exeter.

WEST AISH FARM, MORCHARD BISHOP, NEAR CREDITON EX17 6RX (Tel/Fax: 01363 877427). Relax by a log fire after a day's touring, walking or riding. Self catering cottages situated in the peaceful setting of a former cobbled farmyard. Two cottages, sleep 5. £110-£260. Short Breaks: 3 nights £90. [🐕]

Croyde

Village 7 miles south-west of Ilfracombe on the Golden Coast. Gem, rock and shell museum includes giant clams from the South Pacific.

JOHN AND DIANA WOODINGTON, FIG TREE FARMHOUSE, ST MARY'S ROAD, CROYDE EX33 1PJ (Tel & Fax: 01271 890204). Bed and Breakfast in 400 year old thatched Devon Longhouse. Friendly welcome and very comfortable en suite available. Pets particularly welcome. Acre garden. Accommodation for dogs on site. Kennelling available. Dog sitting, feeding or walking by arrangement. 2 Crowns Commended. [pw! Pets £1 per night 🏠]

MR AND MRS G. PADDISON, MANOR COTTAGE, 11 ST MARY'S ROAD, CROYDE EX33 1PE (Tel/Fax: 01271 890324). Comfortable bungalow, sleeps 5. Enclosed garden and car space. Easy walking distance to beach and village. Coastal footpath and golf course nearby. Available all year.

Croyde Bay

Charming village nestling in a sheltered combe behind Croyde Bay.

MRS J. RABEY, "SON-GAL", ASH LANE, BRAUNTON EX33 2EF (01271 816835). Self-catering detached house – luxury accommodation in unspoilt village near sheltered, flat, sandy beach.Three bedrooms, one en suite; lounge with TV and video; dining room; kitchen with electric cooker, microwave, fridge and dishwasher. Garage, patio, enclosed garden. Pets welcome - No Charge. Short breaks available. [🐕]

MRS JENNIFER PENNY, CROYDE BAY HOUSE HOTEL, CROYDE BAY, NORTH DEVON EX33 1PA (01271 890270). Small hotel beside beach at Croyde Bay. All rooms en suite with tea/coffee making facilities. Good food and friendly atmosphere. AA and RAC 2 Stars, 3 Crowns Highly Commended. [🐕]

MR A. BENNETT, 11 WEST CROYDE, CROYDE EX33 1QA (01271 890321). 2 bedroomed bungalow (sleeps 4). Beautifully equipped with TV, video, washing machine etc. Large enclosed rear garden and patio within earshot of sea. Close to Devon Coastal Path and Tarka Trail. Village location near to local surfing, golf, cycling.

WEST WINDS GUEST HOUSE, MOOR LANE, CROYDE BAY EX33 1PA (Tel/Fax: 01271 890489). Small guest house by water's edge overlooking beach. Comfortable, relaxing atmosphere. En suite rooms available. Dogs welcome. Open all year. Write or telephone for brochure. [Pets £2 per night]

Cullompton

Small market town off the main A38 Taunton - Exeter road. Good touring centre. Noted for apple orchards which supply the local cider industry. Taunton 19 miles, Exeter 13, Honiton 11, Tiverton 9.

MRS J.M. HILL, SUNNYSIDE FARM, BUTTERLEIGH, NEAR CULLOMPTON, TIVERTON EX15 1PP (01884 855322). 130-acre mixed farm, central for touring Dartmoor and Exmoor. En suite bedrooms with tea/coffee facilities. Bed and Breakfast; Evening Meal optional. Children welcome. [🐕]

FOREST GLADE HOLIDAY PARK (PW), KENTISBEARE, CULLOMPTON EX15 2DT (01404 841381). Country estate with deluxe 2/4/6 berth caravans. All superbly equipped. Many amenities on site. Mother and Baby Room. Campers and tourers welcome. SAE for free colour brochure. AA Four Pennants; 5 ticks ✓✓✓✓ [Pets 50p per night.]

Dartmoor

365 square miles of National Park with spectacular unspoiled scenery, fringed by picturesque villages.

MRS SUSAN BOOTY, "ROGUES ROOST", POUNDSGATE, NEWTON ABBOT TQ13 7PS (01364 631223). Dartmoor National Park. Two self-catering moorland properties sleeping 4 and 7. Children and dogs welcome. Off beaten track. [🐕]

MRS PIPER, DARTMOOR LADYMEDE, THROWLEIGH, NEAR OKEHAMPTON EX20 2HU (01647 231492) Delightful bungalow situated on edge of village of Throwleigh. Children and pets welcome. Local pub serves Evening Meals. Bed & Breakfast from £16 per person. ETB Registered. [Pets £1 per night]

DARTMOOR COUNTRY HOLIDAYS, MAGPIE LEISURE PARK, DEPT PW, BEDFORD BRIDGE, HORRABRIDGE, YELVERTON PL20 7RY (01822 852651). Purpose-built pine lodges in peaceful woodland setting. Sleep 2–7. Furnished to very high standard (microwave, dishwasher etc.) Easy walk to village and shops. Launderette. Dogs permitted. [Pets £12.50 per week.]

DEVONSHIRE INN, STICKLEPATH, OKEHAMPTON EX20 2NW (01837 840626). A real country pub! Out the back door past the water wheels, cross the river by ford or footbridge and up through the woods onto the north edge of Dartmoor proper. Dogs and horses always welcome, fed and watered. 1994 Winner National Beta Petfood Golden Bowl Competition for most dog-friendly pub!

P. WILKENS, POLTIMORE, RAMSLEY, SOUTH ZEAL EX20 2PD (01837 840209). Dartmoor National Park. Self catering accommodation consisting of summer chalet, granite barn conversion and superb detached bungalow. Also pretty thatched guest house. All with direct access to the Moor. Write or phone for details. [1st pet free, 2nd or more £7.50 each per week.]

TWO BRIDGES HOTEL, TWO BRIDGES, DARTMOOR PL20 6SW (01822 890581; Fax: 01822 890575). Famous Olde World riverside Inn. Centre Dartmoor. Log fires, very comfortable, friendly, own brewed beer, excellent food. Ideal walking, touring, fishing, riding, golf. Warning – Addictive. [🐾]

CHERRYBROOK HOTEL, TWO BRIDGES, YELVERTON PL20 6SP (01822 880260). Set in the heart of Dartmoor National Park. Seven comfortably furnished en suite bedrooms. Good quality home-cooked food with menu choice. Ideal for touring. 3 Crowns Commended. [🐾]

MRS J. COLTON, PEEK HILL FARM, DOUSLAND, YELVERTON PL20 6PD (Tel & Fax: 01822 854808). The gateway to Dartmoor. Sunny, en suite rooms. The biggest breakfast. Packed lunches. Evening meal. Spectacular views. All pets welcomed. 2 Crowns Commended. [🐾]

PRINCE HALL HOTEL, TWO BRIDGES, DARTMOOR PL20 6SA (01822 890403; Fax: 01822 890676). Small, friendly, relaxed country house hotel with glorious views onto open moorland. Walks in all directions. Eight en suite bedrooms. Log fires. Gourmet cooking by French owner/chef. Excellent wine list. Fishing, riding, golf nearby. 3 Crowns Commended. [🐾]

MOORLAND HALL HOTEL, BRENTOR ROAD, MARY TAVY, NEAR TAVISTOCK PL19 9PY (01822 810466). Small Victorian country house hotel with direct access onto Dartmoor. All rooms en suite. Children and pets welcome. Riding, fishing, golf nearby. AA Rosette. Vegetarians catered for. [Pets £1.50 per night.]

Dartmouth

Historic port and resort on the estuary of the River Dart, with sandy coves and pleasure boat trips up the river. Car ferry to Kingswear.

DARTSIDE HOLIDAYS, RIVERSIDE COURT, SOUTH EMBANKMENT, DARTMOUTH TQ6 9BH (01803 832093; Fax: 01803 835135). Comfortable holiday apartments with private balconies and superb river and harbour views. Available all year with colour TV, linen and parking. From £79-£625 per week. Free Colour Brochure on request. [Pets £10 per week.]

MRS S.R. RIDALLS, THE OLD BAKEHOUSE, 4 BROADSTONE, DARTMOUTH TQ6 9NR (01803 832109). Three Cottages (one with four-poster bed). Sleep 2–6. Near river, shops, restaurant. Blackpool Sands 15 minutes' drive. TV, linen hire, baby-sitting. Open all year. ETB 3 Keys up to Commended. [🐕]

TORCROSS APARTMENT HOTEL, TORCROSS, NEAR KINGSBRIDGE TQ7 2TQ (015485 80206). Family self-catering in our luxury apartment hotel; accommodation available in a wide range of sizes. Equipped to highest standards. Inn, Waterside Family Restaurant. Pets welcome. Brochure on request. [Pets £7-£24 per week]

Dawlish

Bright resort with sandy beach and sandstone cliffs. Lovely gardens with streams, waterfalls and famous black swans. Exeter 13 miles, Torquay 12.

MRS P. KITSON, 3 CLEVELAND PLACE, DAWLISH EX7 9HZ (01626 865053). Town cottages – brand new comfortable accommodation for 2/5. Parking. Three minutes' walk beaches. 2–3 bedrooms, downstairs cloakroom. Enclosed patio garden. Special terms for couples. Also 6-bedroom family town house sleeping up to 10. [🐕]

MRS F.E WINSTON, "STURWOOD", 1 OAK PARK VILLAS, DAWLISH EX7 0DE (01626 862660). Holiday flats. Comfortable, self-contained, accommodating 2-6. Own bathroom, 1/2 bedrooms. Colour television. Garden. Parking. Full Fire Certificate. Leisure centre and beach close by. Pets welcome. [pw!]

Dawlish Warren

A 500 acre nature reserve with a sandy spit at the mouth of the River Exe.

WELCOME FAMILY HOLIDAY PARK, DAWLISH WARREN, SOUTH DEVON EX7 0PH (Reservations: 01626 862070, Dial a brochure: 01626 888323). Activities include the Dolphin Club and entertainment centre, indoor heated swimming pool, sauna and Jolly Roger club with disco and cinema. Free electricity, linen and colour TV. [Pets £20 per week.]

Dunsford

Attractive village in upper Teign valley with Dartmoor to the west. Plymouth 35 miles, Okehampton 16, Newton Abbot 13, Crediton 9, Exeter 8.

M.I. HARRISON, ROYAL OAK INN, DUNSFORD, NEAR EXETER EX6 7DA (01647 252256). Welcome to our Victorian country inn. We specialise in real ales and home-made food. All en suite rooms are in a 300-year-old converted barn. B&B from £20. Each room has its own front door opening into a beautiful walled courtyard. WCTB Approved. [🐾]

Exeter

Chief city of the South-West with a cathedral and university. Ample shopping, sports and leisure facilities.

MR CHRIS MORRIS, CLOCK TOWER HOTEL, 16 NEW NORTH ROAD, EXETER EX4 4HF (01392 424545). English Tourist Board 2 Crowns. Listed building of character in city centre 10 minutes' level walk stations, shops and Cathedral. All modern facilities including en suite rooms with baths and satellite TV. Licensed. Credit cards. Rates from £12.50 B&B. Colour brochure available. [🐾]

MRS D.L. SALTER, HALDON LODGE FARM, KENNFORD, NEAR EXETER EX6 7YG (01392 832312). Modern Holiday Caravan. Two bedrooms, kitchen, lounge, bathroom/toilet. TV. Farm shop, famous village Inns. Sea short distance. Private grounds near Teign Valley Forest with two Coarse Fishing lakes. Pets welcome. [pw! 🐾]

MRS SALLY GLANVILL, RYDON FARM, WOODBURY, EXETER EX5 1LB (Tel and Fax: 01395 232341). 16th Century Devon Longhouse on working dairy farm. Bedrooms with private or en suite bathrooms, hairdryers, tea/coffee facilities. Romantic 4-poster. Open all year. ETB 2 Crowns Highly Commended, AA QQQQ Selected. From £18 to £24. [🐾]

Exmoor

265 square miles of unspoiled heather moorland with deep wooded valleys and rivers, ideal for a walking, pony trekking or fishing holiday.

MR AND MRS D. HILLIER, BRENDON HOUSE HOTEL, BRENDON, LYNTON EX35 6PS (01598 741206). Small comfortable country hotel in beautiful Lyn Valley. Licensed. Good Devon cooking. Fishing permits sold. Dogs very welcome. B&B from £17, DB &B from £28. [🐾]

Exmouth

Resort on the estuary of the River Exe with excellent sands and bathing.

MARGARET GRAY, "NORTHLEIGH", WEST DOWN FARM, SANDY BAY, EXMOUTH EX8 5BU (01395 271141). Modernised three-bedroomed farm cottage ideally situated close to the coastal path and sandy beach. Exeter 10 miles (M5). The four berth accommodation is equipped with washing machine, fridge/freezer and microwave. Enclosed patio garden. Garage and parking. Children welcome.

CARLTON GUEST HOUSE, 110 ST ANDREWS ROAD, EXMOUTH EX8 1AT (01395 265940). Small family guest house close to town centre, 100 yards from sandy beach. Front door keys, access to rooms at all times. All rooms washbasins, shaver points, colour TV, tea-making. Full English Breakfast. Fire Certificate. Car park. B&B from £14.

Harberton

Small picturesque village two miles from Totnes.

M.H. & J.S. GRIFFITHS, "OLD HAZARD", HIGHER PLYMOUTH ROAD, HARBERTON, TOTNES TQ9 7LN (01803 862495). 3 miles Totnes. Attractive well-equipped cottage and spacious self contained farmhouse flat. Convenient rural location. Open all year. Dogs welcome. Brochure on request. [Pets £7.00 per week.]

Heddon's Mouth

Secluded cove beneath towering cliffs, where River Heddon meets the sea.

HEDDON'S GATE HOTEL, HEDDON'S MOUTH, PARRACOMBE, BARNSTAPLE EX31 4PZ (01598 763313; Fax: 01598 763363). Victorian Country Hotel overlooking the beautiful Heddon Valley, 7 miles from Lynton. 2 acre field for exclusive use by hotel guests and their dogs! 3 Crowns Highly Commended. [pw! 🐾]

Holsworthy

Town 9 miles east of Bude

HEDLEY WOOD CARAVAN AND CAMPING PARK, BRIDGERULE, NEAR BUDE EX22 7ED (Tel/Fax: 01288 381404). Superb 16-acre site amidst lovely countryside, 10 minutes from sandy beaches. All modern facilities. Licensed bar, club room, separate children's play area. [🐾 pw!]

Honiton

Busy South Devon town now happily by-passed. Noted for lace and pottery. Excellent touring centre. Newton Abbot 31 miles, Exmouth 18, Taunton 18, Exeter 17, Budleigh Salterton 16, Lyme Regis 15, Chard 13, Sidmouth 10.

THE BELFRY COUNTRY HOTEL, YARCOMBE, NEAR HONITON EX14 9BD (01404 861234; Fax: 01404 861579). Small luxury hotel with lovely views over Blackdown Hills and Yarty Valley. Cosy bar/restaurant serving home cooking. Log fire, comfy lounge. Ideal walking and touring area. ETB 4 Crowns Commended, AA Two Stars and Rosette. [🐾]

MRS E. TUCKER, LOWER LUXTON FARM, UPOTTERY, HONITON EX14 9PB (01823 601269). Olde worlde Farmhouse in area of outstanding natural beauty. Ideal for touring. Carp fishing. Good home cooking. Children welcome. B&B or D,B&B. Weekly terms from £120, 6 Dinners and Bed and Breakfast. [🐾]

MRS J.C. HAYES, ROLLS HAYES FARM, LUPPITT, NEAR HONITON (01481 37546). Large thatched self-catering farmhouse. Five acres of grounds, two lounges, games room, massive fully equipped kitchen with Rayburn, open fires, central heating, many extras. Available all year, including short breaks. ETB 5 Keys Commended.

Hope Cove

Attractive fishing village, flat sandy beach and safe bathing. Fine views towards Rame Head; cliffs. Kingsbridge 6 miles.

TANFIELD HOTEL, HOPE COVE, NEAR KINGSBRIDGE TQ7 3HF (01548 561268). A warm welcome awaits you at this Ashley Courtenay recommended, licensed Hotel. Ideal for a relaxing holiday. All rooms have central heating, en suite facilities, hairdryers, colour TV, tea/coffee making. Colour brochure. Bargain breaks available. [Pets £1.50 per night.]

MR AND MRS P.G. PEDRICK, HOPE BEACH HOUSE, HOPE COVE, NEAR KINGSBRIDGE TQ7 3HH (01548 560151). Seven luxury 2 and 3 bedroom Apartments, all facilities, equipped to highest standards: ETB 4 Keys Commended. Linen supplied free. Open all year. Children/pets welcome. [Pets £12 weekly.]

Ilfracombe

This popular seaside resort clusters round a busy harbour. The surrounding area is ideal for coastal walks.

ST BRANNOCKS HOUSE HOTEL, ST BRANNOCKS ROAD, ILFRACOMBE EX34 8EQ (01271863873). Good food and excellent accommodation guaranteed at this friendly seaside Hotel. All rooms TV, tea making; most en suite. Licensed bar. Parking. Children and pets welcome. RAC Acclaimed [🐕]

COMBE LODGE HOTEL, CHAMBERCOMBE PARK, ILFRACOMBE EX34 9QW (01271 864518). Pets and their owners will enjoy holidays at our licensed Hotel. en suite rooms available, good food, total freedom and walks galore. Dogs sleep in your bedroom. [pw! 🐕]

THE OLD COACH HOUSE, WATERMOUTH, ILFRACOMBE EX34 8SJ (01271 862340). Accommodation for 2 to 6 persons in converted courtyard complex. Fully equipped, colour TV etc. Terms from £80 to £310. Colour brochure from **Peggy Dobson.**

JOHN FOWLER HOLIDAYS, DEPARTMENT PW, MARLBOROUGH ROAD, ILFRACOMBE EX34 8PF (01271 866766). Modern Bungalows to sleep 2, 4, 6 or 8 people. Lounge with free colour television. Heated swimming pool, crazy golf course. Free entertainment and dancing. Sea and shops are close. [Pets £12 per week.]

THE DARNLEY PRIVATE HOTEL, BELMONT ROAD, ILFRACOMBE EX34 8DR (01271 863955). Enjoy a holiday in the tranquil setting of this hotel, only five minutes' walk from main shopping area. All rooms have central heating and en suite rooms are available. Pets welcome. [🐕]

WESTWELL HALL HOTEL, TORRS PARK, ILFRACOMBE EX34 8AZ (01271 862792, FREEPHONE 0500 607006). Elegant Victorian hotel in own grounds, adjacent to National Trust coastal walks. All spacious rooms en suite with colour TV and tea/coffee facilities. AA Recommended, RAC Acclaimed, ETB 3 Crowns. [🐕]

CAIRN HOUSE HOTEL, ST BRANNOCKS ROAD, ILFRACOMBE EX34 8EH (01271 863911). Set in own grounds 5 minutes from all amenities. Good food and comfort. Choice of menu. Any day arrival. RAC One Star. [🐕]

Instow

On estuaries of Taw and Torridge, very popular with boating enthusiasts. Barnstaple 6 miles, Bideford 3.

BEACH HAVEN COTTAGE, INSTOW. Seafront cottage overlooking sandy beach. Extensive beach and sea views. Sleeps 5, own garage and parking. Central heating, colour TV, coastal walks. Dog welcome. For colour brochure send SAE to P. I. BARNES, BOAT HYDE, NORTHAM, BIDEFORD EX39 1NX (01237 473801). [Pets £5 per week]

Modern cottage-style house next to beach. Excellent views. Sleeps six people plus cot. Full central heating. Pets and children welcome. For brochure apply – MRS P.W. BAXTER, HUISH MOOR FARMHOUSE, INSTOW, BIDEFORD EX39 4LT (01271 861146). [🐕]

Kingsbridge

Pleasant town at head of picturesque Kingsbridge estuary. Centre for South Hams district with its lush scenery and quiet coves. Plymouth 21 miles, Dartmouth 15, Totnes 13.

WOODLAND VIEW GUEST HOUSE, KILN LANE, STOKENHAM, KINGSBRIDGE TQ7 2SQ (01548 580542). In picturesque village one mile sea. Superb walking. Comfortable rooms. Pets very welcome. No guard dogs. [Pets 95p nightly.]

BEACHDOWN, CHALLABOROUGH BAY, KINGSBRIDGE TQ7 4JB (01548 810089). Self catering holidays for families in pleasant cedarwood bungalows 200 yards from quiet, sandy beach. Children's playground. Local shopping. Pets welcome. Fully furnished and equipped. ETB Approved 3 Keys. Contact NICKY FAULKNER for details. [pw! £15 per week.]

HALLSANDS HOTEL, NORTH HALLSANDS, KINGSBRIDGE 01548 511264). Fully licensed family Hotel offering Bed, Breakfast and Evening Meal. Good food. Fishing, bathing and compressed air available.

MRS B. KELLY, BLACKWELL PARK, LODDISWELL, KINGSBRIDGE TQ7 4EA (01548 821230). 17th century Farmhouse, 5 miles from Kingsbridge. Ideal centre for Dartmoor, Plymouth, Torbay, Dartmouth and many beaches. Some bedrooms en suite. Bed, Breakfast and Evening Meal or Bed and Breakfast. Pets welcome free of charge. ETB 2 Crowns. [🐾]

GARA MILL. Self catering in comfortable detached lodges or flats in 16th century mill. TVs, laundry, play area, games room. Woodland walks. Ring for brochure. ALLAN AND MARCIA GREEN, GARA MILL HOUSE, SLAPTON, KINGSBRIDGE TQ7 2RE (01803 770295). [Pets £10 per week.]

LIPTON FARM, EAST ALLINGTON, NEAR TOTNES TQ9 7RN (01548 521252). Luxury 30ft, six-berth caravan on organic farm in quiet valley. Outdoor swimming pool. Kingsbridge 5 miles. Ideal centre for beautiful beaches, coastal walks, touring Dartmoor. From £150 per week. [Pets £5 per week.]

MR & MRS H.D. IDE, FAIRFIELD, WALLINGFORD ROAD, KINGSBRIDGE TQ7 1NF (01548 852441). "Garden Flat" sleeps 2–5, £140 to £190 per week. Direct access to garden, ideal for children (8 years and over) and/or dogs. Colour TV. Bed linen provided. Parking space. A friendly welcome and cream tea await you.

JOURNEYS END INN, RINGMORE, NEAR KINGSBRIDGE TQ7 4HL (01548 810205). Historic inn in unspoilt setting. Extensive food menu served in bar and dining room; wide range of real ales. Comfortable en suite bedrooms with colour TV. Golf, fishing nearby. [Pets £2.50 per night]

Lynton/Lynmouth

Picturesque twin villages joined by a unique cliff railway (vertical height 500ft). Lynmouth has a quaint harbour and Lynton enjoys superb views over the rugged coastline.

THE EXMOOR SANDPIPER INN, COUNTISBURY, NEAR LYNMOUTH EX35 6NE (01598 741263). This fine old coaching inn is in a beautiful setting with good food and hotel facilities for complete comfort. All 16 rooms en suite with colour TV, tea/coffee making. [🐾]

THE HEATHERVILLE HOTEL, TORS PARK, LYNMOUTH EX35 6NB (01598 752327). Country house hotel in peaceful setting with magnificent river and woodland views. Tea and coffee making in all rooms. Some en suite rooms with colour TV. Traditional English cooking. Licensed. Four minutes' walk to village. Parking. Bargain Breaks. Pets very welcome free of charge.[🐾]

SHELLEY'S COTTAGE HOTEL, WATERSMEET ROAD, LYNMOUTH EX35 6EP (01598 753219). Small family-run hotel, overlooking village and sea. All rooms en suite, double or twin, with colour TV and tea/coffee facilities. Write or phone for brochure. [🐾]

GABLE LODGE, LEE ROAD, LYNTON EX35 6BS (01598 752367). Grade II Listed building. Friendly and homely atmosphere. En suite rooms with TV and beverage trays. Licensed. Good home cooking. Car park and garden. Non smoking. [🐾]

DAVID BARNES AND JOHN WALLEY, COMBE PARK HOTEL, HILLSFORD BRIDGES, LYNTON EX35 6LE (01598 752356). Exmoor. Comfortable exquisite Country House Hotel near Lynton within National Trust parkland. Bedrooms with all facilities. Dogs welcome. Bargain Breaks. [pw! £1 per night.]

SYLVIA HOUSE HOTEL, LYDIATE LANE, LYNTON EX35 6HE (01598 752391). A charming Georgian Hotel offering delightful rooms, most en suite, some with four-poster beds, all with colour TV and tea/coffee making facilities. Freshly prepared and cooked cuisine. [🐾]

MRS W. PRYOR, STATION HOUSE, LYNTON (01598 752275/752381 Fax: 01598 752475). Holiday Flat situated in the former narrow gauge railway station closed in 1935, overlooking the West Lyn Valley. Centrally placed for Doone Valley and Exmoor. Parking available. [🐾]

R.S. BINGHAM, NEW MILL FARM, BARBROOK, LYNTON EX35 6JR (01598 753341). Exmoor Valley. Two delightful genuine modernised XVII century cottages by stream on 100-acre farm with A.B.R.S. Approved riding stables. Free fishing. SAE for brochure. [pw! Pets £15 per week.]

COUNTISBURY LODGE HOTEL, TORS PARK, LYNMOUTH EX35 6NB (01598 752388; Freephone 0500 0600729). Former Victorian vicarage, peacefully secluded yet only 5 minutes to Lynmouth village. En suite rooms with tea/coffee facilities, central heating, and choice of menu. Log fires. Parking. Spring/Autumn Breaks. [🐾]

EAST LYN HOUSE, WATERSMEET ROAD, LYNMOUTH EX35 6EP (01598 752540). Large Victorian residence just 3 minutes' walk from the harbour. All bedrooms en suite bath or shower, colour TV, clock radio. RAC Highly Acclaimed.

THE TURRET, 33 LEE ROAD, LYNTON EX35 6BS (01598 753284). Delightful, family-run Victorian hotel, ideal for exploring Exmoor and magnificent coastline. All rooms have colour TV and beverage making facilities; most en suite. Superb home cooking; Licensed. Open all year. [🐾]

Moretonhampstead

Small market town on the east side of Dartmoor containing 17th-century Almhouses.

WHITE HART HOTEL, THE SQUARE, MORETONHAMPSTEAD, SOUTH DEVON (01647 440406). This historic Coaching Inn has stood in the town square for over 350 years and now has 20 De-Luxe bedrooms en suite with colour televisions. Traditional dishes served in the Restaurant. ETB 4 Crowns Highly Commended. [🐾]

Mortehoe

Adjoining Woolacombe with cliffs and wide sands. Intresting rock scenery beyond Morte Point. Barnstaple 15 miles, Ilfracombe

LUNDY HOUSE HOTEL, MORTEHOE, WOOLACOMBE EX34 7DZ (01271 870372). Quality en suite accommodation in small, friendly hotel. Superb food, licensed bar lounge, à la carte restaurant. Write or phone for full details. Also holiday cottage, sleeps 6. [🐕]

Newton Abbot

Known as the Gateway to Dartmoor and the coast, this lively market town has many fine buildings, parks and a racecourse.

MRS E. V. WHALE, ROSELANDS, TOTNES ROAD, IPPLEPEN, NEWTON ABBOT TQ12 5TD (01803 812701). Three detached chalets, set in peaceful private garden within easy reach of all South Devon attractions and Dartmoor. Self contained accommodation for 2/4 adults or 2 adults and 2/3 children. PETS MOST WELCOME. Safe parking. [1st pet free, additional pets £5 per week]

Ottery St Mary

Pleasant little town in East Devon, within easy reach of the sea. Many interesting buildings including 11th-century parish Church. Birthplace of the poet Coleridge.

MR AND MRS M. FORTH, FLUXTON FARM HOTEL, OTTERY ST MARY EX11 1RJ (01404 812818). Charming 16th-century farmhouse with large garden. Good food superbly cooked, log fires. Peace and quiet, all modern conveniences. Teasmaids. Licensed. ETB Three Crowns, AA Listed. [🐕 pw!]

Paignton

Popular family resort on Torbay with long, safe sandy beaches and small harbour. Exeter 25 miles, Newton Abbot 9, Torquay 3.

AMBER HOUSE HOTEL, 6 ROUNDHAM ROAD, PAIGNTON TQ4 6EZ (01803 558372). Family-run licensed hotel. En suite facilities and ground floor rooms. Good food. Highly recommended. A warm welcome assured to pets and their families. 3 Crowns. [🐕 pw!]

MRS J. SMERDON, THE MAISONETTE, GLENSIDE, MOLES CROSS, MARLDON, PAIGNTON TQ3 1SY (01803 873222) Self contained modern property. Three bedrooms, lounge/dining room with colour TV. Fitted kitchen. Fully equipped for up to 7 persons. Terms £120 to £260 inc electricity. Open all year. [🐕]

ELBERRY FARM, BROADSANDS, PAIGNTON TQ4 6HJ (01803 842939). 400 yards from Broadsands beach, set in own grounds of 55 acres. 3 family rooms, 1 twin-bedded room; tea making facilities. Reductions for children. Pets by arrangement. Telephone for brochure. [Pets £1 per night]

J. AND E. BALL, DEPARTMENT P.W., HIGHER WELL FARM HOLIDAY PARK, STOKE GABRIEL, TOTNES TQ9 6RN (01803 782289). Within 4 miles Torbay beaches and 1 mile of River Dart. Central for touring. Dogs on leads. Tourist Board graded park, 3 Ticks. [Pets £9 per week in statics, free in tents and tourers.]

Plymouth

Historic port and resort, impressively rebuilt after severe war damage. Large naval docks at Devonport. Beach of pebble and sand.

PATRICIA STEER, "ROOKERY NOOK", NOSS MAYO, PLYMOUTH PL8 1EJ (01752 872296). Quiet village 10 miles from Plymouth on picturesque River Yealm Estuary. River and coastal walks. TV lounge, tea/coffee facilities. Also self catering accommodation. B&B from £15.00. Dogs free. [🐾]

CRANBOURNE HOTEL, 282 CITADEL ROAD, THE HOE, PLYMOUTH PL1 2PZ (01752 263858/661400; Fax: 01752 263858). Convenient for Ferry Terminal and City Centre. All bedrooms with colour TV and tea/coffee. Ample parking. Keys provided for access at all times. Under personal supervision. Pets by arrangement. ETB 2 Crowns. [🐾]

CARSONS, FREEPOST (SWB 40021), 5 REGENT STREET, PLYMOUTH PL4 8BR (01752 254425/263753). Superb self-contained apartments. Sleep 2–6 persons . 20 yards from seafront. Colour TV. Available all year. Pets welcome. [🐾]

HEADLAND HOTEL, RADFORD ROAD, WEST HOE, PLYMOUTH PL1 3BY (01752 660866). Licensed. Very friendly atmosphere. Pets welcome. Rooms with bath en suite. Two lounges. Spacious restaurant. 150 yards sea front.

LAMPLIGHTER HOTEL, 103 CITADEL ROAD, THE HOE, PLYMOUTH PL1 2RN (01752 663855; Tel/Fax: 01752 228139). Family-run hotel situated close to seafront, Barbican and city centre. All rooms with tea/coffee and Sky TV/video. Car park. Pets by arrangement. Access and Visa accepted. 2 Crowns Commended.

CHURCHWOOD VALLEY, DEPT PW, WEMBURY BAY, NEAR PLYMOUTH PL9 0DZ (01752 862382). Relax in luxury log cabins with own patio & BBQ. In wooded valley leading to beach. Licensed shop, launderette, riding stables. Two family pets welcome free of charge. ✓✓✓✓ [🐾]

Salcombe

Fishing and sailing centre in a sheltered position. Fine beaches and coastal walks nearby.

THE SALCOMBE BOAT COMPANY, WHITESTRAND, SALCOMBE TQ8 8ET (01548 843730/844224). A holiday with a difference. Unwind with a houseboat holiday on Salcombe's tranquil estuary. Write or phone for brochure. [Pets £15 weekly.]

GRAFTON TOWERS HOTEL, MOULT ROAD, SALCOMBE TQ8 8LG (01548 842882). Small luxury Hotel with wonderful views. Convenient for ferry, town. Magnificent walks. Speciality local seafood. Homemade desserts. 2 Stars AA, RAC. [Pets £2.50 per night.]

SEAMARK HOLIDAY APARTMENTS, THURLESTONE SANDS, NEAR SALCOMBE TQ7 3JY (01548561300). 5 lovely apartments adjoining coastal path. Beach 500 yards, golf one mile. Indoor heated pool, sauna and games room. Laundry room. Pay phone. Colour brochure. [Pets £10 per week.]

A.R. AND J.A. FERRIS, ROCK HOUSE MARINE, THURLESTONE SANDS, NEAR SALCOMBE TQ17 3JY (01548 561285). Sample a touch of luxury in Hotel apartments in secluded bay. Heated pool, games room, waterside bar. Full Hotel facilities except Breakfast. Restaurant serves fresh food, bar snacks. [Pets £5 per week.]

THE PORT LIGHT, BOLBERRY DOWN, MALBOROUGH, NEAR SALCOMBE TQ7 3DY (01548561384 or 0831 218047). A totally unique location set amidst acres of National Trust coastline. Luxury en suite rooms. Superb home-cooked fare, specialising in local seafood. Licensed bar. Pets welcome throughout the hotel. Bargain Breaks throughout the year. [🐕]

MRS E.J. LONSDALE, FERN LODGE, HOPE COVE, KINGSBRIDGE TQ7 3HF (01548 561326). PETS FREE OF CHARGE. Fern Lodge offers comfort, good food and personal attention. Five rooms en suite. Three minutes from sea. All pets accepted. ETB Two Crowns. [🐕]

Seaton

Bright East Devon resort near Axe estuary. Shingle beach and chalk cliffs; good bathing, many lovely walks in vicinity. Exeter 23 miles, Sidmouth 11.

MILKBERE HOLIDAYS, MILKBERE HOUSE, 14 FORE STREET, SEATON EX12 2LA (01297 22925). Attractive self-catering Cottages, Bungalows, Apartments. Coast and Country on Devon/Dorset border. Free colour brochure. Pets welcome. [£15 per week.]

SEATON. Self-contained Holiday Bungalows. ETB 2 Keys Approved, rural site. Fully equipped, accommodate six plus cot. Optional linen hire. Parking. Adjacent filling station and shop. Pets, children welcome. Contact: NETHERHAY HOLIDAYS, NETHERHAY, NEAR BEAMINSTER, DORSET DT8 3RH (Tel. and Fax: 01308 868872 [24 hours]). [Pets £10 per week.]

Shaldon

Delightful little resort facing Teignmouth across the Teign estuary. Sheltered by the lofty prominence of Shaldon Ness, beach side activities are largely concerned with boats and sailing; beaches are mainly of sand. Mini-golf course. The attractions of Teignmouth are reached by a long road bridge or passenger ferry.

JOHN & EILEEN PILE, "BEAULIEU", COMMONS OLD ROAD, SHALDON TQ14 0EF (01626 872331). Two comfortable self-catering apartments each sleeping 6 (can be combined). Parking for cars, boat (river mooring available). River and harbour views. Minutes from village centre and beach. Pets welcome. [🐕]

GLENSIDE HOTEL, RINGMOOR ROAD, SHALDON TQ14 0EP (01626 872448). Charming, waterside, cottage hotel. Level river walks to beach. En suite available. Garden, car park. B&B from £18.00; D, B&B from £27.00. Telephone for brochure. [Pets £1.50 per night.]

MRS P. O'DONNELL, THE ROUND HOUSE, MARINE PARADE, SHALDON TQ14 0DP (01626 873328). Situated right on the beach with glorious views from all apartments in this pretty, olde worlde village. Full central heating. Parking. [£5 weekly per dog.]

EAST CLIFF HOLIDAY APARTMENTS, MARINE PARADE, SHALDON TQ14 0DP (01626 872334). Beautifully furnished, self-contained Apartments with modern kitchen and bathroom. Prices include bed linen, colour television, central heating, parking, laundry facilities, telephone. No smoking. [pw! Pets £5 weekly.]

Sidmouth

Sheltered resort, winner of many awards for its floral displays. Good sands at Jacob's Ladder beach.

SWEETCOMBE COTTAGE HOLIDAYS. ROSEMARY COTTAGE, WESTON, NEAR SIDMOUTH EX10 0PH (01395 512130; Fax: 01395 515680). Selection Cottages, Farmhouses and Flats in Sidmouth and East Devon. Televisions, gardens. Colour video available on request. Pets welcome. Please ask for our illustrated brochure. [🐕]

ENID & BERT CARR, BARRINGTON VILLA GUEST HOUSE, SALCOMBE ROAD, SIDMOUTH EX10 8PU (01395 514252). A Regency Villa in beautiful gardens on the River Sid. Dog-walk riverside park nearby. Ample forecourt parking. Dogs with house trained owners most welcome. ETB 2 Crowns Commended. [🐕]

OAKDOWN CARAVAN PARKS, WESTON, SIDMOUTH EX10 0PH (01297 680387; Fax: 01395 513731). Two privately owned parks set in the East Devon Heritage Coast. Level, well drained and closely mown. Luxury Holiday Homes for hire, pitches for touring units. Colour brochure. AA Three Pennants; BGHP ✓✓✓✓ [pw! Pets from £1.00 per night.]

LOWER KNAPP FARM, SIDBURY, SIDMOUTH EX10 0QN (01404 871438). Luxury self catering cottages sleeping 2/8 set in 16 acres. Indoor heated pool, sauna, solarium. All cottages with fully fitted kitchens; colour TV etc. Linen supplied. Colour brochure on request. Three Keys. [Pets £15 per week.]

South Brent

Just off the busy A38 Plymouth to Exeter road, this is a good centre on the River Avon for Dartmoor and the South Devon resorts. Plymouth 15 miles, Ashburton 8.

EDESWELL FARM COUNTRY CARAVAN PARK, RATTERY, SOUTH BRENT TQ10 9LN (01364 72177). Picturesque Park in 21 acres wooded hillside. Ideally situated for Dartmoor, Torbay, South Devon. 18 static caravans, 46 touring pitches. Indoor pool, games room; bar, shop, launderette. [pw! £7.00 weekly static, 50p per night touring.]

Enchanting, select site for those seeking a quiet restful holiday amidst beautiful surroundings, overlooking the Dartmoor Hills. Fully serviced luxury caravans, with colour TV, fridge, heater and shower. Separate low density site for tents/tourers. Several acres for carefree exercising. ✓✓✓. APPLY – TREVOR AND JILL HORNE, WEBLAND FARM HOLIDAY PARK, AVONWICK, NEAR SOUTH BRENT TQ10 9EX (01364 73273). [pw! Pets £1 nightly.]

Southleigh

Village situated 3 miles north-west of Seaton.

WISCOMBE PARK, SOUTHLEIGH, NEAR COLYTON EX13 6JE (01404 871474). Nature lovers' and children's paradise. Working farm. Beautiful walks. Trout and coarse fishing. Near Coast. Comfortable self-contained accommodation. Free brochure. [🐾]

South Molton

On the southern edge of Exmoor, 12 miles east of Barnstaple, this busy market town is noted for its antiques and elegant Georgian buildings.

NORTH LEE HOLIDAY LETS, NORTH LEE FARM, SOUTH MOLTON, NORTH DEVON EX36 3EH (Tel and Fax: 01598 740248). Southern edge of Exmoor. One and two bedroomed new barn conversions. Fully equipped, bed linen and towels included. Courtyard setting. Pets welcome. Easy reach of Exmoor and Coast. Open all year. Weekend and short breaks available. [🐾 pw!]

MR & MRS JONES, YEO FARM, MOLLAND, NEAR SOUTH MOLTON EX36 3NW (01769 550312). Pets welcome including horses. Beautiful comfortable 18th century farmhouse, peaceful yet accessible. Ideal riding, hiking, fishing. Further details on request.

Tavistock

Birthplace of Sir Francis Drake and site of a fine ruined Benedictine Abbey. On edge of Dartmoor, 13 miles north of Plymouth.

MRS P.G.C. QUINTON, HIGHER QUITHER, MILTON ABBOT, TAVISTOCK PL19 0PZ (01822 860284). Modern self-contained barn conversion. Own private garden. Terms from £195 inc. linen, coal and logs. Electricity metered. [🐾]

Teign Valley

Picturesque area on edge of Dartmoor. The River Teign flows into the English Channel at Teignmouth.

S. & G. HARRISON-CRAWFORD, SILVER BIRCHES, TEIGN VALLEY, TRUSHAM, NEWTON ABBOT TQ13 0NJ (01626 852172). Comfortable bungalow on the edge of Dartmoor. Good centre for birdwatching, forest walks, golf, riding; fishing nearby. All rooms en suite. Self catering caravans also available. B&B from £23.00 nightly.

Teignmouth

Resort at mouth of River Teign. Bridge connects with Shaldon on south side of estuary.

LYME BAY HOUSE HOTEL, DEN PROMENADE, TEIGNMOUTH TQ14 8SZ (01626 772953). Near rail and coach stations and shops. En suite facilities available. Licensed. Lift – no steps. Bed and Breakfast. [🐕]

Tiverton

Market town on River Exe 12 miles north of Exeter, centrally located for touring both North and South coasts.

MRS PRATT, MOOR BARTON, NOMANSLAND, TIVERTON EX16 8NN (01884 860325). 18th-century superior farmhouse on a 250-acre mixed farm, situated equidistant from North and South coasts. Four double, four family and one twin-bedded rooms. Children welcome. B&B from £15 per night; DB&B £120 per week inclusive.

PALFREYS BARTON, COVE, TIVERTON EX16 7RZ (01398 331456). Four six-berth caravans on a 235 acre working dairy farm, beautifully sited adjacent to farmhouse with marvellous views. All caravans fully equipped. Available March to October.

Torbay

Bay which extends from Hope's Nose in the north to Berry Head in the south — the location of three of Devon's most popular resorts: Torquay, Paignton and Brixham.

THE SMUGGLERS HAUNT HOTEL, CHURCH HILL, BRIXHAM TQ5 8HH (01803 853050; Fax: 01803 858738). Friendly, private 300-year-old hotel situated in the centre of old Brixham. Quality bar and à la carte menus. Vegetarian choice; children's menu. Fully equipped en suite rooms. Children and pets welcome. ETB 3 Crowns, AA 2 Stars. [🐕]

Torquay

Popular resort on the English Riviera with a wide range of attractions and entertainments. Yachting and watersports centre with 10 superb beaches and coves.

MR AND MRS D.G. MAISEY, CROSSWAYS AND SEA VIEW HOLIDAY FLATS, MAIDENCOMBE, TORQUAY TQ1 4TH (01803 328369). Modern self-contained flats set in one-acre grounds. Sleep 2/5. Colour TV. Pets welcome – exercise field adjacent. Children's play area. [🐕 pw!]

SOUTH SANDS APARTMENTS, TORBAY ROAD, LIVERMEAD, TORQUAY TQ2 6RG (01803 293521; Fax: 01803 293502). 18 superior self-contained ground and first floor Apartments for 1–5 persons. Central heating. Open all year. Parking. Beach 100 yards. Convenient Riviera Centre, theatre, marina. Mini Breaks except Summer season. [pw! £1 per night.]

CLEVEDON HOTEL, MEADFOOT SEA ROAD, TORQUAY TQ1 2LQ (01803 294260). Set in its own peaceful grounds 300 yards from beach and woods. En suite rooms with TV, radio/alarm and tea/coffee. Licensed bar and traditional home cooked meals. [🐕]

MRS M.A. TOLKIEN, FAIRMOUNT HOUSE HOTEL, HERBERT ROAD, CHELSTON, TORQUAY TQ2 6RW (01803 605446). Somewhere special - a small licensed hotel with comfortable en suite bedrooms, cosy bar, delicious home cooking. Peaceful setting. One mile town centre. B&B from £23 per person. Bargain Breaks available. [Pets £2 per night.]

LORNA DOONE APARTMENTS, TORWOOD GARDENS ROAD, TORQUAY (RESERVATIONS: 01694 722244) Situated 500 yards from town centre shops and seafront. Luxury apartments with colour TV, microwave, modern bathroom and kitchen. Families and dogs welcome. From £172 per week for 2 persons. [Pets £15 per week].

RED HOUSE HOTEL AND MAXTON LODGE HOLIDAY APARTMENTS, ROUSDOWN ROAD, CHELSTON, TORQUAY TQ2 6PB (01803 607811). Choose either the friendly service and facilities of a hotel or the privacy and freedom of self-catering apartments. The best of both worlds! 4 Keys/3 Crowns Commended. [🐕 or £3 per night in hotel.]

MR AND MRS T.H. FISH AND FAMILY, FAIRLAWNS HALL, ST MICHAEL'S ROAD, TORQUAY TQ1 4DD (01803 328904). Delightful self-contained holiday apartments and mews cottages. Central heating available. Pets welcome. Large woods nearby, gardens and parking. Stamp for brochure. [Pets £10 weekly.]

Torrington

Pleasant market town on River Torridge. Good centre for moors and sea. Exeter 36 miles, Okehampton 20, Barnstaple 12, Bideford 7.

SALLY MILSOM, STOWFORD LODGE, LANGTREE, NEAR TORRINGTON EX38 8NU (01805 601540). Away from the crowds. Four luxury cottages with heated indoor pool, and two secluded period farm cottages. Sleep 4/6. Peaceful countryside, convenient North Devon coast and moors. Magnificent views and walks. ETB 4 Keys Highly Commended. Phone for brochure. [pw! Pets £10 per week.]

Umberleigh

Village on River Taw, 7 miles from Barnstaple.

8 Country Cottages sleeping from 2 to 12 in rural area; lovely views, private patios and gardens. Well furnished and equipped. Heated pool, tennis court, BHS approved riding school. Laundry room. Open all year ETB 4 Keys Commended. APPLY: TERRY & JANE SHERAR, COLLACOTT FARM, KING'S NYMPTON, UMBERLEIGH, NORTH DEVON EX37 9TP. (01769 572491)

Westward Ho!

Charming village named after the novel by Charles Kingsley. Good sands; two-mile long pebble ridge to the north west.

Self-catering Bungalows, almost adjoining three miles of glorious sand. Fully carpeted, with free colour TV, bathroom, WC, H&C, electric cooker, fridge. Free colour brochure on request. APPLY – JOHN FOWLER HOLIDAYS, DEPARTMENT PW, MARLBOROUGH ROAD, ILFRACOMBE EX34 8PF (01271 866766). [Pets £12 per week.]

Woolacombe

A favourite resort for children, with long, wide stretches of sand. Barnstaple 15 miles, Ilfracombe 6.

WOOLACOMBE BAY HOLIDAY PARCS. Two fantastic holiday parks in sunny Woolacombe. Superb fun for all the family. Extensive sporting and leisure facilities. Phone now for brochure and bookings (01271 870343).

PAT AND TONY WORTHINGTON, COMBE RIDGE HOTEL, THE SEA FRONT, WOOLACOMBE EX34 7DJ (01271 870321). 7 bedroomed detached hotel facing Combesgate Beach. Open February to end October. 3 Crowns. Ample private parking. [Pets £1 per night/£5 per week.]

PEBBLES HOTEL, COMBESGATE BEACH, WOOLACOMBE EX34 7EA (01271 870426). Family-run Hotel overlooking sea and beaches. All rooms en suite, with colour TV, tea/coffee making etc. Special Short Break packages. Write or phone for colour brochure. [🐕]

CROSSWAYS HOTEL, SEAFRONT, WOOLACOMBE EX34 7DJ (01271 870395). Homely, family-run licensed Hotel surrounded by National Trust land. Children and pets welcome. ETB 3 Crowns Commended. [🐕]

MRS JOYCE BAGNALL, CHICHESTER HOUSE, THE ESPLANADE, WOOLACOMBE EX34 7DJ (01271 870761). Holiday apartments on sea front. Fully furnished, sea and coastal views. Watch the sun go down from your balcony. Open all year. SAE Resident Proprietor. [Pets £8 per week.]

EUROPA PARK, STATION ROAD, WOOLACOMBE (01271 870159). Luxury bungalows, superb views. Touring caravans and tents. Full facilities. Pets welcome, 6-acre dog park. Indoor heated swimming pool. [Pets £5 per week.]

FHG PUBLICATIONS LIMITED publish a large range of well-known accommodation guides. We will be happy to send you details or you can use the order form at the back of this book.

DORSET

MILLMEAD COUNTRY HOTEL

ᵃᵃᵃ Commended

Goose Hill, Portesham DT3 4HE Tel/Fax: 01305 871432

Two star country hotel in an area of unspoilt beauty, close to Swannery, sub tropical gardens. All rooms en suite, ground floor rooms. Excellent home prepared cuisine.

ᑫᑫᑫ *Tamarisk Farm*

West Bexington, Dorchester DT2 9DF

On slope overlooking Chesil beach, two secluded CHALETS and one large and two smaller BUNGALOWS on farm with beef cows, sheep and horses and organic market garden. Good centre for touring, sightseeing, walking. Pets and children welcome. Terms from £105-£450.

SELF CATERING   **Mrs Josephine Pearse Tel: 01308 897784**

ANVIL HOTEL & RESTAURANT

Salisbury Road, Pimperne, Blandford, Dorset DT11 8UQ Tel: 01258 453431/480182

A long, low thatched building set in a tiny village deep in the Dorset countryside — what could be more English? This typical old English hostelry offers good old-fashioned hospitality, a mouth-watering full à la carte menu in the charming beamed restaurant, and a wide selection of bar meals in the attractive bar. All bedrooms have private facilities. Ample parking.

ᵃᵃᵃ Commended, Les Routiers. From £45 single, £70 double; £110 for two persons for 2 nights.

SURREY DENE
SELF-CONTAINED HOLIDAY FLATS

Beautifully situated adjoining Bournemouth Upper Gardens
in which you may exercise your pet.

Convenient shopping centre

Flats are comfortable, with separate kitchen, own private bathroom, colour television, at no extra charge. 2–7 persons. Free private parking. NO VAT.

Pets welcome. Open all year round.

Send SAE for brochure, stating details of party and dates required to:
**Resident Proprietors Mr & Mrs E.A. Murray and Mrs B. Ector, Surrey Dene,
33 Surrey Road, Bournemouth, Dorset BH4 9HR Telephone 01202 763950.**

OVERCLIFF HOTEL

3 MINS TO LOVELY BEACH — THRU' CHINE WALKS — PETS WELCOME FREE!
Small comfortable, licensed hotel. Friendly atmosphere, home cooking,
TV lounge. En suite available. Teamakers. B&B from £15 daily; BB&EM £100-£150
weekly. OPEN ALL YEAR

**29 Beaulieu Road, Alum Chine, BOURNEMOUTH BH4 8HY
Tel: 01202 761030**

Readers are requested to mention this guidebook when seeking accommodation (and please enclose a stamped addressed envelope).

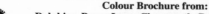

The Stables   Hyde Crook, Frampton, Dorchester, DT2 9NW Tel: 01300 320075

The Stables is a large equestrian property which sits in a small area of woodland off the A37 which provides easy travelling to Dorchester from a location which enjoys uninterrupted views of open Dorset countryside. We are a registered small holding of approximately 20 acres, with sheep, ducks and horses, and specialise in providing accommodation and livery for cross country riding. Pets, particularly dogs, are always welcome.

Providence House
Lyme Road, Uplyme,
Lyme Regis DT7 3TH
Tel: 01297 445704

Set in the lovely village of Uplyme, one mile from Lyme Regis, our small Regency guest house has been beautifully renovated and welcomes you as do we, Clem and Jean Ansell. The meals are special and the beds very comfortable. We have a small cat but your dog is welcome. All rooms are freshly decorated and are either en suite or have private facilities. Bed and Breakfast from £15.50; four-course Dinner and coffee £8.00

The Old Bakehouse Hotel   Piddletrenthide, Dorchester, Dorset DT2 7QR

Family-run country B&B Hotel ideal for visiting Dorset's beauty spots. All bedrooms en suite with colour TV. Garden and heated outdoor swimming pool. Parking. Several good (and safe) walks locally and plenty of good eating places nearby.
Write or phone 01300 348305 for prices and brochure

Commended   AA QQQ

AA QQQ   ETB Commended

The Poachers Inn

Special Offer
1st November
to 31st March
2 Nights
DB&B
£66pp
Third Night
FREE

10%
Discount
7 Days or
more

Piddletrenthide, Dorset DT2 7QX Tel: 01300 348358

Country Inn, set in the heart of the lovely Piddle Valley. Within easy reach of all Dorset's attractions. All rooms en suite, colour TV, tea/coffee, telephone, swimming pool, riverside garden, restaurant, half board guests choose from our A la carte menu at no extra cost.

All rooms have own front door leading to good dog walks.

Terms from Bed and Breakfast £23-25 DB&B £33-£35.
Send for brochure

WHISPERING PINES
Self-contained holiday flat near Canford Cliffs
*Fully furnished and equipped except linen *Kitchen with electric cooker, fridge *Colour TV *Good location within easy reach of beaches, entertainment and places of interest *Parking space *Non-smokers only *Sleeps 2/3 adults.
Terms: Low Season from £85.50 per week; High Season from £149.50 per week.
Please send SAE for brochure to: Mrs H. Lee, 9 Spur Hill Avenue, Lower Parkstone, Poole BH14 9PH.
Tel: 01202 740585

HOLIDAY ACCOMMODATION CLASSIFICATION
in England, Scotland and Wales.

The National Tourist Boards for England, Scotland and Wales have agreed a common 'Crown Classification' scheme for serviced (Board) accommodation. All establishments are inspected regularly and are given a classification indicating their level of facilities and service.

There are six grades ranging from 'Listed' to 'Five Crowns'. The higher the classification, the more facilities and services offered. Crown classification is a measure of facilities, not quality. A common quality grading scheme grades the quality of establishments as 'Approved', 'Commended', 'Highly Commended' or 'Deluxe' according to the accommodation, welcome and service they provide.

For **Self Catering**, holiday homes in England are awarded 'Keys' after inspection and can also be 'Approved', 'Commended', 'Highly Commended' or 'Deluxe' according to the facilities available. In Scotland the Crown scheme includes self-catering accommodation and Wales also has a voluntary inspection scheme for self-catering grading from '1(Standard)' to '5 (Excellent)'.

Caravan and Camping Parks can participate in the British Holiday Parks grading scheme from 'Approved' (✓), to 'Excellent (✓✓✓✓); in addition, each National Tourist Board has an annual award for high-quality caravan accommodation in England – Rose Awards; in Scotland – Thistle Commendation; in Wales – Dragon Awards.

When advertisers supply us with information, FHG Publications show Crowns and other awards or gradings, including AA,RAC, Egon Ronay etc. We also award a small number of Farm Holiday Guide Diplomas every year, based on readers' recommendations.

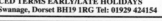

TOLPUDDLE HALL
TOLPUDDLE, NR DORCHESTER. DT2 7EW

An historic house in the village centre in an area of outstanding natural beauty, not far from the coast. Centre for local interests; e.g. birdwatching, walking, local history, Thomas Hardy, the Tolpuddle Martyrs, etc. Two double, one twin, one family and two single bedrooms. Tea/coffee making, TV sitting room. Terms from £15 per person. Weekly rate available. Pets welcome except high season. Open all year. *Tel: Mr Paul Wright (01305 848986)*

BLOXWORTH HOLIDAY COTTAGES

Large Georgian Farmhouse and thatched cottages in quiet village. Sleep 2/12. Purbeck beauty spots and beaches along the Dorset Coast easily accessible. Pleasant walks. Beautiful Poole Harbour 10 miles. Comfortably furnished and equipped except linen and towels. Dogs welcome. Open all year. Ideal for winter weekends.
SAE to:
Mr and Mrs P.G. Macdonald-Smith, Bloxworth Estate, Nr Wareham, Dorset BH20 7EF
Tel/Fax: 01929 459442

Gorselands Caravan Park
"Peaceful and Pretty"

*Fully Serviced
  caravans
*Shop
*Launderette
*Games room

*Self contained flats
*Village Pub
  100 yards
*Beach car park
  3 mins by car

Attractive secluded park set in coastal valley overlooking Chesil Beach. Tourist Board graded. Glorious sea views. Country and seaside walks. An ideal base for discovering Dorsets's charming villages and Heritage coastline. The beach is a mile either by car or through the meadows, and the fishing is excellent. Pets are most welcome

Colour brochure Dept. PW
Gorselands Caravan Park
West Bexington-on-Sea, Dorset DT2 9DJ
Tel: 01308 897232   Fax: 01308 897239

NOTE

All the information in this book is given in good faith in the belief that it is correct. However, the publishers cannot guarantee the facts given in these pages, neither are they responsible for changes in policy, ownership or terms that may take place after the date of going to press. Readers should always satisfy themselves that the facilities they require are available and that the terms, if quoted, still apply.

WELCOME COTTAGE HOLIDAYS. Hundreds of properties in wonderful locations at welcoming low prices. Pets, linen and fuel mostly included. For FREE colour brochure telephone 01756 702209.

Abbotsbury

Village of thatched cottages in sheltered green valley. Benedictine monks created the famous Abbotsbury Swannery.

MRS JOSEPHINE PEARSE, TAMARISK FARM, WEST BEXINGTON, DORCHESTER DT2 9DF (01308 897784). Self Catering. Overlooking Chesil Beach: two secluded Chalets and one large and two smaller Bungalows on mixed organic farm with arable, sheep, cattle, horses and market garden with vegetables on sale. Good centre for touring, sightseeing, all sports. Pets and children welcome. ETB 3 Keys. Terms from £105 to £450. [🦮]

MILLMEAD COUNTRY HOTEL, GOOSE HILL, PORTESHAM DT3 4HE (Tel/Fax: 01305 871432). Two star country hotel in an area of unspoilt beauty, close to Swannery, sub tropical gardens. All rooms en suite, ground floor rooms. Excellent home prepared cuisine.

Blandford

Handsome Georgian town that rose from the ashes of 1731 fire; rebuilt with chequered brick and stone. Also known as Blandford Forum.

ANVIL HOTEL & RESTAURANT, PIMPERNE, BLANDFORD DT11 8UQ (01258 453431/480182). A typical Old English hostelry offering good old-fashioned English hospitality. A la carte menu and bar meals. All bedrooms with private facilities. Ample parking. 3 Crowns Commended, AA and RAC **. [Pets £2.50 per night]

Bournemouth

One of Britain's premier holiday resorts with miles of golden sand, excellent shopping and leisure facilities. Lively entertainments include Festival of Lights at the beginning of September.

SEAWAY HOLIDAY FLATS. Self contained holiday flats with exercise area in garden. Three minutes' level walk between shops and cliffs, with lift to fine sandy "Pets Allowed" beach. Most reasonable terms early and late season. , 41 GRAND AVENUE, SOUTHBOURNE, BOURNEMOUTH BH6 3SY (01202 300351). [🦮 pw!]

CORRA LINN, 13 KNYVETON ROAD, BOURNEMOUTH BH1 3QG (01202 558003). Self catering holiday flatlets. Situated on the East Cliff within easy reach of sea, shops and entertainments. Fully equipped with central heating, TV, linen and refrigerator. Children and pets welcome. Free parking. Terms from £35 pp. [Pets £5 per week.]

ALUM GRANGE HOTEL, 1 BURNABY ROAD, ALUM CHINE, BOURNEMOUTH BH4 8JF (01202 761195). Pets and owners are assured of a warm welcome at this superbly furnished hotel, 250 yards from the beach. All rooms with colour TV and tea/coffee making. [🦮]

CAIRNSMORE PRIVATE HOTEL, 37 BEAULIEU ROAD, BOURNEMOUTH BH4 8HY (01202 763705). 4 minutes' walk through wooded glades to sea. Colour TV in all bedrooms, all en suite. Parking. B, B & ED from £22 per person per day. Residential licence. Special diets catered for. No charge for pets. 3 Crowns Commended. [🐕 pw!]

CRAVEN GRANGE HOLIDAY FLATS, 17 BODORGAN ROAD, BOURNEMOUTH BH2 6JY (01202 296234). Self-contained flats and cottage, 2–6 persons. Town centre, golf and parks nearby. Car parking. Free Welcome Pack. Pets welcome. Telephone or SAE for details. [🐕]

MIKE AND LYN LAMBERT, AARON, 16 FLORENCE ROAD, BOURNEMOUTH BH5 1HF (01202 304925/01425 474007). Modern Holiday Apartments sleeping one to 10 persons, close to sea and shops. Recently extensively renovated with new kitchens and bathrooms. Clean well-equipped flats. Car park and garages. Write or phone for colour brochure and terms. [Pets £14 weekly]

St George's Holiday Flats are near sea and shops; Questors overlooks quiet, wooded Pleasure Gardens; superb for you and your dog. Both properties have good car parks; pay-phones, laundry, TV, fridges in all units. Clean and fully equipped. We like dogs. Apply: SANDRA & BARRY GLENARD, 45 BRANKSOME WOOD ROAD, BOURNEMOUTH BH4 9JT (01202 763262). [Pets £12 per dog, per week]

CONISTON HOTEL, 27 STUDLAND ROAD, ALUM CHINE, BOURNEMOUTH BH4 8HZ (01202 765386). Three minutes to lovely beach through Chine walks. Pets welcome free. Small, comfortable hotel. Home cooking, licensed bar, friendly atmosphere. B&B from £15 pppn. [🐕]

BILL AND MARJORIE TITCHEN, WHITE TOPPS HOTEL, 45 CHURCH ROAD, SOUTHBOURNE, BOURNEMOUTH BH6 4BB (01202 428868). Situated in quiet position close to lovely walks and beach. Dogs welcome. Free parking. Residential licence. [🐕]

SUE AND CLIFF LOGGEY, ASHDALE HOTEL 35 BEAULIEU ROAD, ALUM CHINE, BOURNEMOUTH BH4 8HY (01202 761947). Recommended for our warm, friendly atmosphere and good, plentiful food. Delightful situation by Alum Chine. Clean, well-equipped bedrooms. Licensed. [🐕]

OVERCLIFF HOTEL, 29 BEAULIEU ROAD, ALUM CHINE, BOURNEMOUTH BH4 8HY (01202 761030). Small comfortable licensed Hotel, en suite available. Home cooking. TV lounge. Three minutes to beach. B&B from £15, BB&EM from £100-£150 weekly. Open all year. [🐕]

MRS W. HOLLAND, 12 AVONCLIFFE ROAD, SOUTHBOURNE, BOURNEMOUTH BH6 3NR (01202 426650). Self catering flatlet on Southbourne cliff top. Fully equipped, close shops, buses; car parking available. Small dogs welcome. Open all year. Rates from £75 to £95. SAE Mrs W. Holland.[🐕]

SEA BREEZE, 32 ST CATHERINE'S ROAD, SOUTHBOURNE, BOURNEMOUTH BH6 4AB (01202 433888). Small peaceful Hotel, opposite beach where dogs allowed. All rooms en suite, TV, teamakers. Parking. Pets welcome. B&B from £17; Evening Meal £8.50. [Pets £2.50 per night]

THE STUDLAND DENE HOTEL, ALUM CHINE, WEST CLIFF, BOURNEMOUTH BH4 8JA (01202 765445). Overlooking the beach, marvellous walks. All rooms with TV, direct-dial phone; all en suite. A la carte restaurant, carvery. [Pets £2 per night]

MR AND MRS E. A. MURRAY AND MRS B. ECTOR, "SURREY DENE", 33 SURREY ROAD, BOURNEMOUTH BH4 9HR (01202 763950). Comfortable self contained Flats, beautifully situated adjoining Bournemouth Upper Gardens. Free private parking. SAE for brochure. [🐾]

THE EMBASSY HOTEL, MEYRICK ROAD, EAST CLIFF, BOURNEMOUTH BH1 3DW (01202 290751; Fax: 01202 557459). 3 star rated Hotel, with easy walking distance of the beaches and town centre. En suite bedrooms, heated outdoor pool and games room. Superb service and excellent cuisine. Free car parking. B&B from £22 per night. [Pets £3 per night]

MR AND MRS J. JENKINS, THE VINE HOTEL, 22 SOUTHERN ROAD, SOUTHBOURNE, BOURNEMOUTH BA6 3SR (01202 428309). Small family Hotel only 3 minutes' walk from sea and shops. All rooms en suite. Residential licence. Pets welcome. No smoking in bedrooms and dining room. [🐾]

3 self-contained apartments in quiet avenue, one minute from clean, sandy beaches and 5 minutes from shops. Sleep 3/6. Fully equipped including linen. All have fridge, toilet and shower room, fitted carpets, colour TV, central heating, electric meter. Parking. Terms from £75. Contact: MRS HAMMOND, STOURCLIFFE COURT, 56 STOURCLIFFE AVENUE, SOUTHBOURNE, BOURNEMOUTH BH6 3PX (01202 420698). [Pets £5 weekly]

MRS JENNIE STARLING, STELLA MARIS GUEST HOUSE, 88 SOUTHBOURNE ROAD, BOURNEMOUTH BH6 3QQ (01202 426874). Friendly guest house near sea and shops. Clean and comfortable. Plenty of good home cooking; menu choice. All bedrooms with tea/coffee, colour TV, washbasins; some en suite. Guest lounge with Sky TV. Car park. Sensible prices; generous Senior Citizen and child discounts. [🐾]

Bridport

Market town of Saxon origin noted for rope and net making. Harbour at West Bay has sheer cliffs rising from the beach.

MRS S. NORMAN, FROGMORE FARM, CHIDEOCK, BRIDPORT DT6 6HT (01308 456159). The choice is yours – Bed and Breakfast, optional Evening Meal, in charming farmhouse, OR self-catering Cottage equipped for six plus cot, pets welcome. Brochure and terms free on request [🐾]

Super Self Catering Bungalows in old smugglers' haunt of Eype, near market town of Bridport. Beach 5 minutes' walk. Accommodation suitable for the wheelchair user. No club or disco. CONTACT: MR SPEED, GOLDEN ACRE, EYPE, NEAR BRIDPORT DT6 6AL (01308 421521)

MR F. LOOSMORE, MANOR FARM HOLIDAY CENTRE, CHARMOUTH, BRIDPORT DT6 6QL (01297 560226). All units for 6 people, 10 minutes' level walk to beach, many fine local walks. Swimming pools, licensed bar with family room, shops, launderette. Sporting facilities nearby. Children and pets welcome. SAE. [Pets £15 per week]

MRS CAROL MANSFIELD, LANCOMBES HOUSE, WEST MILTON, BRIDPORT DT6 3TN (01308 485375). 4 Keys Approved. Pretty cottages in converted barns. Panoramic views to sea four miles away. Set in 10 acres, some have fenced gardens. Many walks from our land. [Pets £10.00 per week]

BRIDPORT ARMS HOTEL, WEST BAY, BRIDPORT DT6 4EN (01308 422994). Thatched Hotel on edge of beach in picturesque West Bay. Two character bars, real ale, wide range bar meals. A la carte Restaurant featuring local fish. 2 Crowns Approved. AA/RAC One Star [🐕]

Charmouth

Small resort on Lyme Bay, 3 miles Lyme Regis. Sandy beach backed by undulating cliffs where many fossils are found. Good walks.

DOLPHINS RIVER PARK, BERNE LANE, CHARMOUTH DT6 6RD (012975 60022). Luxury 4 and 6 berth Caravans on small, peaceful park. Licensed shop, coin-op laundry; children's play area. One mile from beach. Colour brochure available. [Pets £8.50 per week]

Christchurch

Residential town near coast. Yachting based on Christchurch harbour, with outlet into Christchurch Bay.

Country Holiday Chalet near woods and sea. Dogs welcome, SAE. APPLY – MRS L. M. BOWLING, OWLPEN, 148 BURLEY ROAD, BRANSGORE, DORSET BH23 8DB (01425 672875). [pw! 🐕]

Crewkerne

Market town on a sheltered slope of the Blackdown Hills, 8 miles south-west of Yeovil.

MRS G. SWANN, BROADVIEW GARDENS, 43 EAST STREET, CREWKERNE TA18 7AG (01460 73424). Unusual Colonial bungalow built in an era of quality. En suite rooms with colour TV, C/H, Tea/Fac. Non-Smoking. Bed and Breakfast £23-£27. [🐕 pw!]

Dorchester

Busy market town steeped in history. Home of Thomas Hardy. Roman remains include Amphitheatre and villa.

LAMPERT'S COTTAGE, SYDLING ST. NICHOLAS, CERNE ABBAS DT2 9NU (01300 341659; Fax: 01300 341699). Bed and Breakfast in unique 16th century thatched cottage. Three double bedrooms. Dining room with inglenook fireplace and original beams. Open all year. Terms on request. [🐕]

MRS JACOBINA LANGLEY, THE STABLES, HYDE CROOK (ON A37), FRAMPTON, DORCHESTER DT2 9NW (01300 320075). A comfortable equestrian property in some 20 acres grounds. Well situated for bridleways/footpaths. Guests' TV lounge, three bedrooms with en suite and private facilities. Tourist Board 2 Crowns. [pw! £1.50 per dog per night.]

CHURCHVIEW GUEST HOUSE, WINTERBOURNE ABBAS, DORCHESTER DT2 9LS (01305 889296). Beautiful 17th Century Licensed Guest House set in the heart of West Dorset, character bedrooms, delightful period dining room, two lounges and bar. Non-smoking. B&B £18.50-£25pp. B&BEM £29.50-£37. Three Crowns, AA QQQ. [🐕]

MRS RITA BOWN, LAMPERTS FARMHOUSE AND COTTAGE, 11 DORCHESTER ROAD, SYDLING ST NICHOLAS, DORCHESTER DT2 9NU (01300 341 790). 17th Century thatched listed farmhouse nestling in the Sydling valley. Choose self catering in our well-equipped farm cottage or B&B in our tastefully decorated en suite bedrooms. [🐕]

Lyme Regis

Picturesque little resort with harbour, once the haunt of smugglers. Shingle beach with sand at low tide. Fishing, sailing and water ski-ing in Lyme Bay. Taunton 28 miles, Dorcheter 24, Honiton 15, Seaton 8.

PROVIDENCE HOUSE, LYME ROAD, UPLYME, LYME REGIS DT7 3TH (01297 445704). Small Regency guest house in lovely village of Uplyme, one mile from Lyme Regis. All rooms freshly decorated, either en suite or private facilities. [🐕]

Piddletrenthide

Village 6 miles north of Dorchester.

THE OLD BAKEHOUSE HOTEL, PIDDLETRENTHIDE, DORCHESTER DT2 7QR (01300 348305). Family-run B&B hotel ideal for visiting Dorset's beauty spots. All bedrooms en suite. Several good walks nearby. Write or phone for brochure. Two Crowns Commended. AA QQQ. [Pets £2 per stay]

THE POACHERS INN, PIDDLETRENTHIDE DT2 7QX (01300 348358). On B3143 in lovely Piddle Valley, this delightful Inn offers en suite rooms with colour TV, tea/coffee making, phones. Swimming pool; residents' lounge. Restaurant or Bar meals available. Garden – good dog walks! B&B from £23.00. 3 Crowns. AA QQQ. [Pets £1 per night]

Poole

Popular resort, yachting and watersports centre with large harbour and many creeks. Sand and shingle beaches. Salisbury 30 miles, Dorchester 23, Blandford 14, Wareham 9, Bournemouth 5.

WHISPERING PINES. Self-contained holiday flat. Fully equipped except linen. Colour TV. Within easy reach of beaches and entertainments. SAE for brochure to MRS H. LEE, 9 SPUR HILL AVENUE, LOWER PARKSTONE, POOLE BH14 9PH (01202 740585). [🐕]

"SEA-WITCH", 47 HAVEN ROAD, CANFORD CLIFFS, POOLE BH13 7LH (01202 707697). Small licensed Hotel, clean, comfortable, fully en suite. B&B from £23-£33; Evening Meals. Convenient for ferries. Own car park. Open all year. [🐕]

Shaftesbury

Small town on hillside overlooking Blackmoor Vale, 18 miles west of Salisbury.

KINGTON MANOR FARM, CHURCH HILL, KINGTON MAGNA, NEAR GILLINGHAM, SHAFTESBURY SP8 5EG (01747 838371). Attractive farmhouse situated in quiet, pretty village. Double/family room with shower and WC, twin-bedded room with/without private bathroom. Tea/coffee making facilities. Excellent pub food nearby. Bed and hearty Breakfast from £16 per person per night. [🐾]

Studland

Unspoilt seaside village at south-western end of Poole Bay 3 miles north of Swanage.

KNOLL HOUSE HOTEL, STUDLAND BN19 3AW (01929 450450; Fax: 01929 450423) Country House Hotel within National Trust reserve. Golden beach.100 acre grounds. Family suites, six lounges. Tennis, golf, swimming, games rooms, health spa. Full board terms £58-£86 daily. See also our full-page advertisement under Studland Bay. [Pets £3.50 nightly]

THE MANOR HOUSE, STUDLAND BAY (01929 450288) An 18th century Manor House, nestling in 20 acres of secluded grounds. All bedrooms en suite with central heating, colour TV, direct dial telephone, tea/coffee making facilities. [Pets £2.75 per night.]

Sturminster Newton

Small town on River Stour edged by Blackmoor Vale. Blandford Forum 8 miles.

MRS S. SOFIELD, THE OLD POST OFFICE, HINTON ST MARY, STURMINSTER NEWTON DT10 1NG (01258 472366; Fax: 01258 472173). Comfortable, homely and convenient for exploring the beautiful, varied scenery of unspoilt Dorset. Hearty, traditional home cooking, lounge, large garden, car park. Sociable pub in village. Footpaths and river walks. Optional Evening meals £7. B&B £16. Brochure. "The Friendly Place". [🐾]

Swanage

Traditional family holiday resort set in a sheltered bay ideal for water sports. Good base for a walking holiday.

LIMES HOTEL, 48 PARK ROAD, SWANAGE BH19 2AE (01929 422664). Small friendly Hotel. En suite rooms, tea/coffee facilities. Licensed bar. Central heating. Children and pets welcome. Telephone or SAE for brochure.

MRS GILLIAN MACDERMOTT, THE LITTLE MANOR, 389 HIGH STREET, SWANAGE BH19 2NP (Tel & Fax: 01929 422948). A friendly small Guest House open all year round where pets and children are welcome. Television, tea and coffee making facilities in all rooms. [🐾]

MRS M SMITH, 35 PROSPECT CRESCENT, SWANAGE BH19 1BD (01929 423441). Comfortable Guest House. Quiet, level position. Good food. Bed and Breakfast. TV Lounge. Pets welcome. Parking. [🐾]

MRS M. STOCKLEY, SWANAGE CARAVAN SITE, 17 MOOR ROAD, SWANAGE BH19 1RG (01929 424154). 4/5/6-berth Caravans. Pets welcome. Easter to October. Colour TV. Shop. Parking space. Rose Award Park ✓✓✓✓ [🐕]

Tolpuddle

Small village 4 miles west of Bere Regis, famous for "Tolpuddle Martyrs", agricultural labourers transported to Australia for opposing a drop in wages.

TOLPUDDLE HALL, TOLPUDDLE, NEAR DORCHESTER DT2 7EW (01305 848986). An historic house in village centre. 2 double, 1 twin, 1 family and 2 single bedrooms. Tea/coffee making. Pets welcome except High Season. Open all year.

Wareham

Picturesque riverside town almost surrounded by earthworks, considered pre-Roman. Nature reserves of great beauty nearby. Weymouth 19 miles, Bournemouth 14, Swanage 10, Poole 6.

MRS L. S. BARNES, LUCKFORD WOOD HOUSE, EAST STOKE, WAREHAM BH20 6AW (01929 463098; Fax: 01929 405715). Spacious, peaceful surroundings. B&B in luxurious farmhouse. Camping facilities include showers and toilets. Near Lulworth Cove, Tank Museum and Studland Monkey World. Open all year. LISTED. AA QQ [🐕]

Bloxworth Holiday Cottages. Large Georgian farmhouse and thatched cottages sleeping 2/12. Well furnished and equipped except linen and towels. Quiet village in country estate. Open all year. Dogs welcome. SAE to MR & MRS P. G. MACDONALD-SMITH, BLOXWORTH ESTATE, NEAR WAREHAM, DORSET BH20 7EF (Tel/Fax: 01929 459442). [🐕]

West Bexington

Seaside village with pebble beach. Chesil beach stretches eastwards. Nearby is Abbotsbury with its Benedictine Abbey and famous Swannery. Dorchester 13 miles, Weymouth 13, Bridport 6.

GORSELANDS CARAVAN PARK, DEPT PW, WEST BEXINGTON-ON-SEA DT2 9DJ (01308 897232; Fax: 01308 897239). Quality graded "very good" park. Fully serviced and equipped 4/6 berth caravans. Shop and launderette on site. Glorious sea views. Good country and seaside walks. One mile to beach. Personal attention. Holiday apartments with sea views and private garden. Pets most welcome. Colour brochure on request. [🐕]

Weymouth

Set in a beautiful bay with fine beaches and a picturesque 17th-century harbour, Weymouth has a wide range of entertainment and leisure amenities.

ACE HOLIDAY FLATS, 48-50 SPA ROAD, WEYMOUTH DT3 5EW (01305 779393). Clean, comfy self-contained Flats. 2–8 persons and dogs. Ample car park and garden. Near local shops, pub, Radipole Lake. Easy access town and sea. [Pets £12 weekly]

WEYMOUTH BAY HOLIDAY PARK, PRESTON. One 6-berth Caravan. Near sea. Dogs welcome. APPLY – MRS D. W. CANNON, 151 SANDSTONE ROAD, GROVE PARK, LONDON SE12 0UT (0181–857 7586) [🐕]

CO. DURHAM

ASH HOUSE

Ideally situated on Village Green. Beautifully appointed Victorian home, lovingly restored. The elegant rooms are spacious, one with Traditional Four Poster. Adjacent A1M Motorway. 10 minutes historic Durham. Well placed between York and Edinburgh. Excellent value.

24 The Green, Cornforth, Durham DL17 9JH. Tel: 01740 654654

Ivesley Equestrian Centre, Waterhouses, Durham DH7 9HB
Elegantly furnished, comfortable country house set in 220 scenic acres.
Near Durham but quiet and very rural. En suite bedrooms. Excellent food.
Licensed. Equestrian facilities available. Contact Mrs P. A. Booth for details.
Tel: 0191 373 4324 Fax: 0191 373 4757 ❦❦❦ *Highly Commended*

Castleside

A suburb 2 miles south-west of Consett.

LIZ LAWSON, BEE COTTAGE FARM, CASTLESIDE, CONSETT DH8 9HW (01207 508224). Working farm in lovely surroundings. Visitors welcome to participate in all farm activities. Ideal for Metro Centre, Durham Cathedral, Beamish Museum etc. Bed and Breakfast; Evening Meal available. ETB 2 Crowns Highly Commended. [🐾]

Cornforth

Village 4 miles north-west of Sedgefield.

ASH HOUSE, 24 THE GREEN, CORNFORTH, DURHAM DL17 9JH. (01740 654654). Ideally situated Victorian home, lovingly restored. The elegant rooms are spacious. Adjacent A1M Motorway. 10 minutes historic Durham. Excellent value. [🐾]

Waterhouses

6 miles west of Durham

MRS P.A. BOOTH, IVESLEY EQUESTRIAN CENTRE, WATERHOUSES, DURHAM DH7 9HB (0191 373 4324; Fax: 0191 373 4757). Elegantly furnished comfortable country house set in 220 acres. Near Durham but quiet and rural. En suite bedrooms. Excellent food. Licensed. Equestrian facilities available.

FHG PUBLICATIONS LIMITED publish a large range of well-known accommodation guides. We will be happy to send you details or you can use the order form at the back of this book.

ESSEX

Saffron Walden

Unspoilt town dominated by 193ft spire of Essex's largest church. Timber-framed 15th and 16th century buildings with elaborate plasterwork.

MRS D. FORSTER, PARSONAGE FARM, ARKESDEN, SAFFRON WALDEN CB11 4HB (01799 550306). Lovely Victorian farmhouse on busy arable farm with some resident pets; lots of "walkies" on "set aside" and footpaths for pets. For owners, en suite facilities available; coffee/tea making and TV in rooms. Tennis and relaxing in large garden. Bed and Breakfast from £15 – £20 per person. One Crown. [🐕]

GLOUCESTERSHIRE

All the advertisers in PETS WELCOME! have an entry in the appropriate classified section and each classified entry may carry one or more of the following symbols:

🐕   This symbol indicates that pets are welcome free of charge.

£   The £ indicates that a charge is made for pets. We quote the amount where possible, either per night or per week.

pw!   This symbol shows that the establishment has some special provision for pets; perhaps an exercise facility or some special feeding or accommodation arrangements.

⌂   Indicates separate pets accommodation.

PLEASE NOTE that all the advertisers in PETS WELCOME! extend a welcome to pets and their owners but they may attach conditions. The interests of other guests have to be considered and it is usually assumed that pets will be well trained, obedient and under the control of their owner.

175

CHARLTON KINGS HOTEL

Cheltenham, Gloucestershire GL52 6UU
Tel: 01242 231061 / Fax: 01242 241900

ETB 🏵🏵🏵🏵 Highly Commended

The ideal venue for Cheltenham and the Cotswolds situated in an acre of garden in an area of outstanding natural beauty on the edge of town. All rooms (some reserved for non-smokers) have views of the Cotswold Hills, which are easily reached on foot – there is a footpath right alongside the hotel leading onto the famous Cotswold Way. There is plenty to do and see, or simply watch the world go by from the conservatory. During your stay you will be tempted to try our cosy restaurant offering an imaginative and varied menu. Above all, we offer a standard of service only a small hotel can provide.

Johansens Recommended.

🏵🏵🏵 **HALLERY HOUSE HOTEL & RESTAURANT** **AA**
48 Shurdington Road, Cheltenham, Gloucestershire. GL53 0JE. QQQ
Tel: (01242) 578450 Fax: (01242) 529730

All Pets with well behaved owners are welcome to our friendly hotel. 🚲
Logis of All facilities, together with good food, good fun and good friends. **RAC**
Great Britain **Brochure Available** Acclaimed

PARKEND HOUSE HOTEL

Parkend, Near Lydney, Gloucestershire GL15 4HL Tel: 01594 563666

Small country house hotel situated in the heart of the Royal Forest of Dean. All rooms en suite, TV etc. Ideal centre for touring Forest and Wye Valley. Horse riding, golf, walking and cycling. Dinner, Bed and Breakfast from £33 pppn. Pets and children welcome.

Write or ring for brochure, sample menu and details of local places of interest.

Established 22 years 🏵🏵 AA and RAC Listed

Large Country House with attractive garden, overlooking fields. Four minutes to town centre. One four-poster bedroom; double, twin or family rooms, some en suite. Tea/coffee making facilities, colour TV in all rooms. TV lounge. Central heating. Children and pets welcome. Car park. Bed and Full English Breakfast from £16.00 to £19.50. Open all year except Christmas. **Evesham Road, Stow-on-the-Wold**

THE LIMES
GL54 1EN Tel: 01451 830034/831056

DOWNFIELD HOTEL
134 CAINSCROSS RD, STROUD GL5 4HN
(01453 764496)

Bed and Breakfast, Evening Meal optional. Hot and cold all rooms, some with private baths. Central heating. TV lounge. Colour TV in most rooms, tea/coffee facilities all rooms. Some with telephones. Residents' bar. Ideal for touring Cotswolds and as a stopover for travel to Devon/Cornwall. 5 miles from Junction 13, M5. Ample parking. Families and pets welcome. Personal supervision by proprietors. All major credit cards accepted.

AA QQQ ETB 🏵🏵🏵 RAC Acclaimed.

Court Farm Randwick, Stroud GL6 6HH. Tel: 01453 764210 Fax: 01453 766428

A 17th century beamed farmhouse, centre of hillside village of Randwick. Beautiful views over Stroud Valleys. Much of our food produced organically on seven acres of meadowland. A stream divides the sloping fields, haven for wildlife. Large garden for guests to enjoy, village pub food. Tourist attractions nearby include Wildfowl Trust, Gloucester Waterways, Prinknash Abbey, Berkeley Castle. Bed and Breakfast from £15 to £17; Evening Meal can be provided. Children and pets welcome.

SYMONDS YAT ROCK MOTEL   **Hillersland, Near Coleford GL16 7NY**
Telephone: Dean (01594) 836191

Small family run Motel. All rooms en suite with colour TV and central heating.
Licensed restaurant. Situated near Symonds Yat East and the Wye Valley in a
beautiful area of the Royal Forest of Dean. Dogs welcome. Brochure on request.
Tourist Board Listed.

WELCOME COTTAGE HOLIDAYS. Hundreds of properties in wonderful
locations at welcoming low prices. Pets, linen and fuel mostly included. For
FREE colour brochure telephone 01756 702209.

POWELLS COTTAGE HOLIDAYS. Your choice of Cottage in Cornwall, Devon,
Somerset, Cotswolds, Wye Valley, Gower and Pembrokeshire in our full colour
brochure. [Pets £10 per week.] FREEPHONE 0800 378771 for apply: 61 High
Street, Saundersfoot, Pembrokeshire SA69 9EJ or (24hrs) 01834 813232.

Bourton-on-the-Water

Delightfully situated on the River Windrush which is crossed by miniature stone bridges. Stow-on-the-Wold 4 miles.

CHESTER HOUSE HOTEL, VICTORIA STREET, BOURTON-ON-THE-WATER GL54
2BU (01451 820286; FREEPHONE 0500 131291). Personally supervised by
proprietor Mr Julian Davies. All rooms en suite, all with central heating, colour
TV, radio, phone, tea/coffee making facilities. Ideal for touring Cotswolds. [🐾]

Bristol

Busy University city on River Avon (spanned by Brunel's famous suspension bridge). SS Great Britain, Brunel's iron ship, is moored in the old docks. Gloucester 35 miles, Bath 13.

MRS C. B. PERRY, CLEVE HILL FARM, UBLEY, NEAR BRISTOL BS18 6PG (01761
462410). Family-run dairy farm in beautiful countryside. Self-catering
accommodation in "The Cider House". Fully equipped except towels and linen.
£1 electricity meter. One double, one twin room, one double bed settee. Terms
from £95 to £200 per week. Obedient pets welcome. [🐾]

ALANDALE HOTEL, 4 TYNDALL'S PARK ROAD, CLIFTON, BRISTOL BS8 1PG
(0117 973 5407). An elegant, warm and friendly hotel, centrally situated with
car park. Colour TV, telephone and tea/coffee making facilities in all the
bedrooms. All pets welcome. ETB 2 Crowns. [🐾]

Cheltenham

Anglo-Saxon market town transformed into elegant Regency resort with the discovery of medicinal springs. 8 miles east of Gloucester.

HALLERY HOUSE HOTEL AND RESTAURANT, 48 SHURDINGTON ROAD,
CHELTENHAM GL53 0JE (01242 578450 Fax: 01242 529730). All pets with well
behaved owners are welcome to our friendly hotel. All facilities, together with
good food, good fun and good friends. Brochure available.[pw! 🐾]

CHARLTON KINGS HOTEL, CHELTENHAM, GLOUCESTER GL52 6UU (01242 231061; Fax: 01242 241900). Ideal venue for Cheltenham and the Cotswolds. All rooms have views of the Cotswold Hills. We offer a standard of service only a small hotel can provide. ETB 4 Crowns Highly Commended. [🛏]

Coleford

Small town in Forest of Dean 3 miles River Wye. Gloucester 19 miles, Chepstow 13, Monmouth 6.

MR L. E. CAPELL, SYMONDS YAT ROCK MOTEL, HILLERSLAND, NEAR COLEFORD GL16 7NY (01594 836191). Family-run Motel in Royal Forest of Dean near Wye Valley. All rooms en suite, colour TV, central heating. Licensed restaurant. Dogs welcome. Brochure on request. [🛏]

Lydney

Small town 8 miles north-east of Chepstow. Nearby Lydney Park has ruined 12th-century castle and remains of Roman temple set amongst woodland, lakes, fine shrubs and trees.

PARKEND HOUSE HOTEL, PARKEND, NEAR LYDNEY GL15 4HL (01594 563666). Small country hotel surrounded by parkland. All rooms en suite. Good food and friendly service. Pets and children welcome. Ideal for Cheltenham, Bath and Bristol. [Pets £1.50 per night.]

Nailsworth

Hilly town 4 miles south of Stroud.

LESLEY WILLIAMS-ALLEN, THE LAURELS, INCHBROOK, NAILSWORTH GL5 5HA (01453 834021; Fax: 01453 834004). 18th century house. en suite bedrooms. Secure garden and parking. Swimming pool. Snooker. Licensed. Excellent food. No smoking. Three commons and excellent walks nearby. 3 Crowns. Brochure available. [🛏]

Painswick

Beautiful little Cotswold town with characteristic stone-built houses.

MISS E. COLLETT, HAMBUTTS MYND, EDGE ROAD, PAINSWICK GL6 6UP (01452 812352). Bed and Breakfast. Old Cotswold house, very quiet. Close to village. Central heating and open fire in winter months. One double room, one twin, one single, all with TV. From £21.50 to £41.00 per night. RAC Acclaimed. [🛏]

Stow-on-the-Wold

Charming Cotswold hill-top market town with several old inns and interesting buildings including the church in which hundreds of prisoners were confined after a Civil War battle in 1646. Birmingham 45 miles, Gloucester 26, Stratford-upon-Avon 21, Cheltenham 18, Evesham 16, Chipping Norton 9.

"THE LIMES", EVESHAM ROAD, STOW-ON-THE-WOLD GL54 1EN (01451 830034/831056). Large country house. Attractive garden, overlooking fields, 4 minutes town centre. Television lounge. Central heating. Car park. Bed and Breakfast from £16 to £19.50. Children and pets welcome. AA, RAC. Twin, double or family rooms, some en suite.

Stroud

Cotswold town on River Frome below picturesque Stroudwater Hills, formerly renowned for cloth-making. Bristol 32 miles, Bath 29, Chippenham 25, Cheltenham 14, Gloucester 9.

COURT FARM, RANDWICK, STROUD GL6 6HH (01453 764210; Fax: 01453 766428). A 17th century beamed farmhouse on working farm. Much of our food produced organically. Large garden. Abundant wildlife. Children and Pets welcome.

DOWNFIELD HOTEL, CAINSCROSS ROAD, STROUD GL5 4HN (01453 764496). Washbasins in all rooms, central heating. Residents' bar. Ideal for touring Cotswolds. Personal supervision, 5 miles M5. Ample parking. Children and pets welcome. Evening Meal optional. ETB 3 Crowns; AA QQQ; RAC Acclaimed. [🐕]

HAMPSHIRE

HAMPSHIRE   *Hayling Island, Lymington*

NOTE

All the information in this book is given in good faith in the belief that it is correct. However, the publishers cannot guarantee the facts given in these pages, neither are they responsible for changes in policy, ownership or terms that may take place after the date of going to press. Readers should always satisfy themselves that the facilities they require are available and that the terms, if quoted, still apply.

Ashurst

Three miles north-east of Lyndhurst.

WOODLANDS LODGE HOTEL, BARTLEY ROAD, WOODLANDS, NEW FOREST S04 2GN (01703 292257). Luxury Hotel offering peace and tranquillity. 18 bedrooms, all en suite, with TV, hairdryer, telephone etc. Modestly priced dinner menu and wine list offering excellent value. ETB 4 Crowns Highly Commended.

Bramshaw

New Forest village surrounded by National Trust land. Golf course nearby. Southampton 10 miles, Lyndhurst 6.

BRAMBLE HILL HOTEL, BRAMSHAW, NEAR LYNDHURST S043 7JG (01703 813165). Fully licensed country house hotel with own livery stables. Unique seclusion amidst glorious surroundings. Unlimited riding and walking territory. Dogs welcome. [Pets £4 per night.] DIY livery for horses.

Brockenhurst

Popular village attractively situated in New Forest. Golf course. Bournemouth 18 miles, Southampton 13, Lymington 5, Lyndhurst 4.

BALMER LAWN HOTEL, LYNDHURST ROAD, BROCKENHURST S042 7ZB (01590 623116; Fax: 01590 623864). Country House Hotel set in the heart of the New Forest. Ideal for country walking. Indoor and outdoor leisure facilities. 55 bedrooms, all en suite. Excellent cuisine. AA***, RAC. [🐾].

Hayling Island

Family resort with sandy beaches. Ferry to Portsmouth and Southsea. Linked by bridge to Havant (5 miles).

HAYLING HOLIDAYS LTD, 44A EASTOKE AVENUE, HAYLING ISLAND PO11 9QP (01705 467271). Book with confidence. Holiday homes and caravans all close to sea. Superbly equipped and very clean. Personal service. Telephone now for free colour brochure. [Pets £10 per week.]

Lymington

Residential town and yachting centre 15 miles east of Bournemouth.

MRS P.J. ELLIS, EFFORD COTTAGE, EVERTON, LYMINGTON SO41 0JD (Tel and Fax: 01590 642315). Friendly family home in an acre of garden. Excellent centre for New Forest and South Coast. All rooms with colour TV, tea/coffee facilities. Evening meals if required. B&B from £19pp. 3 Crowns Commended, AA QQQQ Selected, RAC Acclaimed. [Pets £2 per night]

Lyndhurst

Good base for enjoying the fascinating New Forest as well as the Hampshire coastal resorts. Bournemouth 20 miles, Southampton 9.

ORMONDE HOUSE, SOUTHAMPTON ROAD, LYNDHURST SO43 7BT (01703 282806, Fax: 01703 282004). Elegant luxury at affordable prices. Pretty en suite rooms, bar and lounge. All rooms CTV, phone and beverage making. Situated opposite the open forest for you and Rover to discover together. AA QQQQ. [Pets £2.50 per night]

Middle Wallop

Village 7 miles south-west of Andover.

FIFEHEAD MANOR HOTEL RESTAURANT, MIDDLE WALLOP, STOCKBRIDGE SO20 8EG (01264 781565; Fax: 01264 781400). Beautiful historic manor house surrounded by three acres of lovely gardens. Divine food. Wonderful welcome for you and your dog. 4 Crowns Highly Commended, 3 Star RAC/AA, Egon Ronay, Good Hotel Guide. [🐾 pw!]

New Forest

Area of heath and woodland of nearly 150 square miles, formerly Royal hunting grounds. Home of ponies which roam freely through unspoilt countryside.

NEW FOREST. Luxury 2-bedroomed residential-type caravan, (sleeps 4/6). Maintained to high standard, full kitchen, bathroom, sitting/dining room, own garden. Idyllic setting in heart of New Forest. Non-smoking, ample parking. Well behaved dogs welcome. £195-£235 including electricity (May-Sept). MRS E. MATTHEWS, THE ACORNS, OGDENS, NEAR FORDINGBRIDGE SP6 2PY (01425 655552)

JUDY HARRISON, LITTLE FOREST LODGE, POULNER HILL, RINGWOOD BH24 3HS (01425 478848; Fax: 01425 473564). Comfortable country house hotel set in 2 acres. All bedrooms en suite. Riding, golf and fishing nearby. Children and dogs are very welcome. AA QQQQQ Premier Selected. [Pets £3 per night]

Modern six-berth Caravan – two bedrooms, shower, toilet, colour TV. Indoor and outdoor pools, jacuzzi, sauna, bars, entertainment, restaurant, takeaway, supermarket on site. Phone 01256 55009 (01256 355009 after April 97) or SAE to MRS L. A. WESTON, 19 KNIGHT STREET, BASINGSTOKE RG21 1AX. [🐾]

THE CROWN HOTEL, LYNDHURST, NEW FOREST SO43 7NF (01703 282922). Privately-owned, in lively village, mellow "Listed" building, very English. 39 en suite bedrooms. Such food for owners, such walks for dogs! Garden with dog loo. [Pets £5 per night]

WHITLEY RIDGE COUNTRY HOUSE HOTEL, BEAULIEU ROAD, BROCKENHURST SO42 7QL (01590 622354; Fax: 01590 622856). Georgian Hotel set in 5 acres of secluded grounds. Twelve bedrooms, all en suite, cosy bar and splendid dining room. Superb cuisine, friendly and efficient service. Ideally located for the New Forest. [🐾]

MRS J. PEARCE, ST.URSULA, 30 HOBART ROAD, NEW MILTON BH25 6EG (01425 613515). Excellent facilities and warm welcome for well behaved pets and owners! Ground floor suite suitable for disabled guests, plus single and twin rooms. Bed & Breakfast from £17. [🐾]

Ringwood

Busy market town on the River Avon, and a centre for trout fishing, trekking and rambling. There are some attractive old houses and inns and a pretty Early English church. Bournemouth 13 miles, Lyndhurst 12.

MS S. P. STREET AND MS M. D. JENKINS, SUNEST PARK, 126 RINGWOOD ROAD, ST IVES, RINGWOOD BH24 2NT (01425 473750). New Forest: Bungalow / Chalets, fully equipped, sleep 2/6. Small park, fenced gardens. Pets welcome. Local fishing, riding, walking, golf, sailing, coast 8 miles. [Pets £10 per week.]

MR AND MRS D. C. HAYLES, BURBUSH FARM, POUND LANE, BURLEY, NEAR RINGWOOD BE24 4EF (01425 403238). Character cottage delightfully situated in the heart of the New Forest close to Burley village. Equipped to highest standard with central heating. Each sleeps five. From £150 per week. [Pets £10 per week.]

Sway

Village in southern part of New Forest and within easy reach of sea. Lymington 4 miles south east.

MRS THELMA ROWE, 9 CRUSE CLOSE, SWAY SO41 6AY (01590 683092). Ground floor accommodation. Bedroom, private bathroom and sitting room. Tea making facilities. TV. 3 minutes from open Forest. 4 miles from coast. Bed and Breakfast from £16. [🐾]

Winchester

Site of an old Roman town. Ancient capital of Wessex and of England. Notable Cathedral, famous boys' public school, a wealth of old and historic buildings.

ROYAL HOTEL, ST PETER STREET, WINCHESTER SO23 8BS (01962 840840; Fax: 01962 841582). Quality hotel of character quietly located in the heart of England's ancient capital. All rooms en suite with satellite TV, tea and coffee and telephone. ETB 5 Crowns Commended. [🐾]

HEREFORD & WORCESTER

HEREFORD & WORCESTER *Bromyard*

Cowarne Hall Cottages 🛈🛈🛈🛈 Highly Commended
A splendid historic Gothic Hall with beams, open fireplaces, arched windows and doorways has been sensitively converted to provide luxurious holiday cottage accommodation. Situated in a quiet country lane with meadow, orchards and woods, within easy reach of the historic towns of Malvern, Bromyard, Hereford and Worcester. The cottages are centrally heated and have a patio, garden and parking. Details supplied of the area's attractions including a working farm and Hop Trail. Situated on an extensive network of country lanes, ideal for dog walks. Free colour brochure.

Mr & Mrs R.M. Bradbury, Cowarne Hall Cottages, Much Cowarne, Bromyard HR7 4JQ Tel: 01432 820317; Fax: 01432 820093.

Bromyard

Medieval market town 12 miles west of Worcester; the streets are lined with half-timbered buildings.

MR & MRS R.M. BRADBURY, COWARNE HALL COTTAGES, MUCH COWARNE, BROMYARD HR7 4JQ (01432 820317; Fax: 01452 820093). Luxurious holiday cottage accommodation, centrally heated, with patio, garden and parking. Within easy reach of Malvern, Bromyard, Hereford and Worcester. Ideal for dog walks. [£10 per week per pet].

Great Malvern

Fashionable spa town in last century with echoes of that period. Greatest treasure is the 11th-century church with 15th-century stained glass.

MR AND MRS D. BERISFORD, WHITEWELLS FARM COTTAGES, RIDGWAY CROSS, NEAR MALVERN WR13 5JS (01886 880607). Charming converted Cottages, sleep 2–6. Fully equipped with colour TV, fridge, iron, etc. Linen, towels also supplied. One cottage suitable for disabled guests. ETB 4 Keys Highly Commended. [Pets £12 per week.]

MALVERN HILLS HOTEL, WYNDS POINT, MALVERN WR13 6DW (01684 540237). Enchanting Hotel sitting atop the Malvern Hills. Magnificent views, prettily decorated en suite rooms, oak-panelled lounge; friendly and efficient staff. Excellent walking country. Water dishes provided. Great animal lovers. [🐾]

ANN AND BRIAN PORTER, CROFT GUEST HOUSE, BRANSFORD, WORCESTER WR6 5JD (01886 832227). 16th-18th century country house, 10 minutes from Worcester, Malvern and M5. En suite rooms, tea coffee trays, central heating. Dinners available; residential licence. Sauna and family jacuzzi. Dogs and children welcome; cot and baby listening service; family room. 2 Crowns. AA QQ. [🐾]

Hay-on-Wye

Paradise for book-lovers in a peaceful market town which has become a world famous second-hand book centre.

In a tranquil setting poised between two cultures. Full modern facilities – remote-control TV, fully fitted kitchens and gas fired central heating. Private garden patio. Call us now for a colour brochure: BRONYDD HOLIDAY COTTAGES, BRONYDD, HAY-ON-WYE HR3 5RX (01497 820766). [pw! 🐾]

Hereford

Well-known touring centre on River Wye with several interesting old buildings including Cathedral. Good sport and entertainment facilities including steeple-chasing. Cheltenham 37 miles, Gloucester 28, Ross-on-Wye 15.

NEW PRIORY HOTEL, STRETTON SUGWAS, HEREFORD (01432 760264; Fax: 01432 761809). The New Priory Hotel is situated just a short distance from the Hereford city limits in 3½ acre grounds. 10 bedrooms all with private bath or shower except for single rooms which have an adjacent shower. 3 Crowns. [🐾]

MARJORIE AND BRIAN ROBY, FELTON HOUSE, FELTON, NEAR HEREFORD HR1 3PH (01432 820366). Period-furnished Country House in tranquil setting. Double, single, twin-bedded rooms. Bed and Breakfast from £18.50. Vegetarian choice. Good Inns nearby for evening meals. Ideal locality for touring. [🐾]

THE STEPPES, ULLINGSWICK, NEAR HEREFORD HR1 3JG (01432 820424; Fax: 01432 820042). Award-winning hotel with intimate atmosphere. Large luxury en suite bedrooms. Set in Wye Valley within easy reach of Malverns and Black Mountains. Ashley Courteney, AA 2 Stars, 2 Food Rosettes, Good Hotel Guide, Johansens, ETB 4 Crowns Highly Commended. [🐾]

MRS R. T. ANDREWS, WEBTON COURT, KINGSTONE, HEREFORD HR2 9NF (01981 250220). Georgian black and white farmhouse in heart of beautiful Wye Valley. All bedrooms with washbasins. Children and pets welcome. B&B or Evening Dinner, B&B. Large parties catered for. Long-term accommodation at reduced rates. Riding and riding lessons available.

DIANA SINCLAIR, HOLLY HOUSE FARM, ALLENSMORE, HEREFORD HR2 9BH (01432 277294, Mobile 0589 830 223). Escape with your horse or dog to our spacious luxury farmhouse. Bed and Breakfast from £16.

Kington

Town on River Arrow, close to Welsh border, 12 miles north of Leominster.

MRS C. D. WILLIAMS, RADNOR'S END, HUNTINGTON, KINGTON HR5 3NZ (01544 370289). Detached cottage (sleeps 5) in lovely unspoiled Welsh border countryside, where rolling hills are home to Buzzard, Kestrel, Red Kite and a rich variety of other birds and wild flowers. Offa's Dyke footpath and Kilvert's Country nearby. Ample parking, lawn. [🐾]

Ledbury

Pleasant town ideally situated for Cotswolds and Wye Valley. Buildings of note include Almshouses, Black and White Houses and Church. Good centre for bowls, fishing, riding and tennis. Monmouth 23 miles, Leominster 22, Gloucester 17, Tewkesbury 14, Malvern 8.

MRS JANE WEST, CHURCH FARM, CODDINGTON, LEDBURY HR8 IJJ (01531 640271). Black and white 16th-century Farmhouse on a working farm close to the Malvern Hills — ideal for touring and walking. Three double bedrooms. Excellent home cooking. Warm welcome assured. Bed and Breakfast from £19.50. Open all year. [🐾]

Leominster

Old wool town among rivers, hop-yards and orchards. Many lovely timbered buildings. Five miles north west is Croft Castle. Birmingham 45 miles, Gloucester 37, Hereford 13, Ludlow 11.

MRS P. W. BROOKE, NICHOLSON FARM, LEOMINSTER HR6 0SL (01568 760269). Cottage and two Bungalows sleeping 2–5. Open Easter to early October. Linen hire available. Attractive, peaceful area, good walking. Convenient Hereford and Worcester Cathedral Cities and for visits to Elan Valley Lakes north of A44. [🐾]

Much Birch

Village six miles south of Hereford.

POOLSPRINGE FARM COTTAGES. 5 delightfully converted cottages on secluded farm. Ideal for touring. Use of indoor heated swimming pool, sauna and solarium. Fully equipped incl. colour TV. Linen for hire on request. Four Keys. APPLY: DAVID AND VAL BEAUMONT, POOLSPRINGE FARM, MUCH BIRCH, HEREFORD HR2 8JJ (Tel & Fax: 01981 540355). [Pets £15 weekly.]

Ross-on-Wye

An attractive town standing on a hill rising from the left bank on the Wye. Cardiff 47 miles, Gloucester 17.

YE HOSTELRIE, GOODRICH, ROSS-ON-WYE HR9 6HX (01600 890241). Enjoy comfort and good food at this fully centrally heated 17th Century Inn. We have a reputation for quality food at a reasonable price.

THE KING'S HEAD HOTEL, 8 HIGH STREET, ROSS-ON-WYE HR9 5HL (FREEPHONE: 0800 801098). Small coaching inn dating back to the 14th century with all bedrooms offering en suite bathrooms and a full range of modern amenities. A la carte menu offers home-cooked food which is served in a warm and friendly atmosphere. [🐴]

THE ARCHES COUNTRY HOUSE HOTEL, WALFORD ROAD, ROSS-ON-WYE HR9 5PT (01989 563348). Georgian Country House. Lovely rooms with all facilities; en suite available. Centrally heated. Pets welcome. Bed and Breakfast or Half Board, weekly reductions available. AA QQQ, RAC, Les Routiers, Three Crowns.

GRAHAM WILLIAMS, THE SKAKES, GLEWSTONE, ROSS-ON-WYE HR9 6AZ (01989 770456). 18th century farmhouse, orchard and garden setting, with superb views. Stone walls, open fireplace, licensed barn restaurant; well-equipped rooms, central heating. Parking. Bed and Breakfast from £17.00. [🐴]

GEOFFREY AND JOSEPHINE BAKER, BROOKFIELD HOUSE, LEDBURY ROAD, ROSS-ON-WYE HR9 7AT (01989 562188). Early 18th century Listed house only 5 minutes' walk from town centre. Licensed. All bedrooms with TV and tea-making. Ideal for golfers and walkers. 2 Crowns Approved. [🐴]

ISLES OF SCILLY

St. Mary's

Largest of group of granite islands and islets off Cornish Coast. Terminus for air and sea services from mainland. Main income from flower-growing. Seabirds, dolphins and seals abound.

MRS PAMELA MUMFORD, SALLAKEE FARM, ST. MARY'S TR21 0NZ (01720 22391). Self catering farm cottage, available all year round. Sleeps 5. Children and pets welcome. Write or phone for details. Three Keys.

ISLE OF WIGHT

NOTE

All the information in this book is given in good faith in the belief that it is correct. However, the publishers cannot guarantee the facts given in these pages, neither are they responsible for changes in policy, ownership or terms that may take place after the date of going to press. Readers should always satisfy themselves that the facilities they require are available and that the terms, if quoted, still apply.

"A Peaceful Retreat"

Country Garden Hotel
Church Hill, Totland Bay
Isle of Wight PO39 0ET

RAC
★★★

Ashley
Courtenay

Tucked away behind the gentle curve of Totland's golden sands and lovely walks, yet overlooking the sea, this really does offer the best of both worlds. Ashley Courtenay sums it up perfectly as "...A really superb hotel set in beautiful gardens", adding that here too "you will relish the superb cuisine" in one of the island's finest restaurants. All rooms have bath AND shower, TV, radio, fridge, phone, hairdryer and hospitality tray.

Gourmet Dinners.

ANY DAY TO ANY DAY
B&B, HALF BOARD, FULL BOARD

★ Doubles ★ Twins

★ Singles ★ Suites ★ Ground floor rooms
SPECIAL SPRING AND AUTUMN RATES
Prices <u>from</u> £44 per day and £275 per week

Tel: (01983) 754521
Fax: (01983) 754421

For brochure, tariff and sample menu

♨♨♨♨ **COMMENDED**

Readers are requested to mention this guidebook when seeking accommodation (and please enclose a stamped addressed envelope).

Alum Bay

In extreme west of island, one mile from the Needles and lighthouse. Cliffs and multicoloured sands, Newport 13 miles, Yarmouth 5.

MARION SMITH, HEADON HALL, ALUM BAY PO39 0LD (01983 752123). Lovely two bedroom apartments, fully equipped for 4/6, including colour television. Breathtaking views. Dogs welcome. [Pets £10 per week.]

Bonchurch

Formerly a fishing and quarrying hamlet, during the last century Bonchurch became a magnet for many eminent literary figures. Its peace and beauty are as evident today as they were in days gone by.

BONCHURCH MANOR, BONCHURCH PO38 1NU (01983 852868). Bonchurch Manor combines elegance and comfort to provide a perfect setting for a holiday at any time of the year. Tastefully furnished bedrooms all with private facilities. Restaurant is regarded as one of the finest on the island. [🐾]

Chale

Pleasant village with sand and shingle beach. Several picturesque chines in the vicinity. Freshwater 11 miles, Newport 9, Ventnor 7.

JOHN AND JEAN BRADSHAW, THE CLARENDON HOTEL, CHALE PO38 2HA (01983 730431). 17th Century Coaching Inn overlooking magnificent West Wight coast. Television lounge. First-class restaurant. Live entertainment nightly all year round. [Pets £4 per night, £20 per week]

Colwell Bay

Small resort at western extremity of the island, excellent sands, cliff walks. Totland 2 miles, Yarmouth 2.

ONTARIO PRIVATE HOTEL, COLWELL COMMON ROAD, COLWELL BAY PO39 0DD (01983 753237). Family-run Hotel. Home cooking. En suite bedrooms, licensed bar, private parking. Only four minutes' walk to the beach. Three Crowns.

Cowes

Yachting centre with yearly regatta since 1814. Home of Royal Yacht Squadron. Victorian and Edwardian shops line narrow streets behind wide esplanade. Newport 4 miles.

SUNNYCOTT CARAVAN PARK, COWES PO31 8NN (01983 292859). 20 Deluxe and Luxury 4 and 6 berth caravans on quiet country park in rural surroundings. Laundry room and shop on site. Bring your pet for a holiday too! [🐾]

Freshwater

Pleasant and quiet resort on Freshwater Bay, near the start of the Tennyson Trail, Sandown 20 miles, Cowes 15, Newport 11, Yarmouth 4.

THE ROBERTS FAMILY, MOUNTFIELD HOLIDAY PARK, NORTON GREEN, FRESHWATER (01983 752993). 2/6-berth Bungalows, Chalets and Caravans, all set in beautiful countryside. Licensed bar. Television. Good food. ETB 3 ticks. [Pets £15 per week.]

Niton

Delightful village near sea at the southernmost part of the island. Several secluded chines nearby, clifgwalks. Ventnor 5 miles.

MR AND MRS D. A. HERON, WINDCLIFFE MANOR, SANDROCK ROAD, NITON UNDERCLIFFE PO38 2NG (Tel & Fax: 01983 730215). Bed, Breakfast and Evening Meal in a historic Manor House set in wooded gardens. Heated pool. Colour television. Games room. Children and dogs welcome. 3 Crowns Highly Commended. [pw!]

Ryde

Popular resort and yachting centre, fine sands, pier. Shanklin 9 miles, Newport 7, Sandown 6.

HILLGROVE PARK, FIELD LANE, ST HELENS, NEAR RYDE PO33 1UT (01983 872802). Select site 10 minutes sea, 3 minutes bus stop. Self-service shop, heated swimming pool. Pets welcome. Phone for brochure. [Pets £10.00 per week]

Sandown

Traditional seaside resort nestling beside Shanklin within the largest bay on the island. Zoo and Pier Theatre.

ISLAND COTTAGE HOLIDAYS. Charming cottages in rural surroundings and close to the sea. Beautiful views - attractive gardens - delightful walks. All properties have Tourist Board quality classifications. £100 - £400. For brochure please contact: HONOR VASS, THE OLD VICARAGE, KINGSTON, WAREHAM, DORSET BH20 5LH (01929 480080). [🐾]

Shanklin

Safe sandy beaches and traditional entertainments make this a family favourite. Cliff lift connects the beach to the cliff top.

ALAN AND LYN AYLOTT, HARROW LODGE HOTEL, EASTCLIFF PROMENADE, SHANKLIN (01983 862800; Fax: 01983 868889). Family-run hotel, all rooms en suite with colour TV. Licensed bar, varied menu. Open all year. ETB 3 Crowns Commended. [🐾]

THE CRESCENT HOTEL, HOPE ROAD, SHANKLIN, ISLE OF WIGHT PO37 6EA (01983 863140). This comfortable hotel now offers dog owners a walking package – IOW Strollers. This includes advance information and maps tailored to suit your interests and abilities. See our advertisement for hotel details. [Pets £1.50 per night, £9 per week.]

Totland

Little resort with good sands, safe bathing and high cliffs. Newport 13 miles, Yarmouth 3, Freshwater 2.

COUNTRY GARDEN HOTEL, CHURCH HILL, TOTLAND BAY PO39 OET (01983 754521: Fax: 01983 754421). Overlooking the sea, superb hotel; all rooms with bath and shower, TV, telephone, fridge, hairdryer etc. Telephone for brochure, tariff. Special spring and autumn rates. [pw! pets £2 per day]

SENTRY MEAD HOTEL, MADEIRA ROAD, TOTLAND BAY PO39 OBJ (01983 753212; Freephone 0500 131277). Get away from it all at this friendly and comfortable haven, just two minutes from sandy beach. Bedrooms have en suite bath or shower, colour TV and radio. Delicious table d'hôte dinners; lunchtime bar menu. [Pets £1 per night]

Ventnor

Well-known resort with good sands, downs, popular as a winter holiday resort. Nearby is St Boniface Down, the highest point on the island. Ryde 13 miles, Newport 12, Sandown 7, Shanklin 4.

A. EVANS, "THE WATERFALL", SHORE ROAD, BONCHURCH, VENTNOR PO38 1RN (01983 852246). Spacious, self-contained Flats. Sleep up to 4. Colour TV. Sun verandah and garden. The beach, the sea and the downs nearby. [🐾]

RAVENSCOURT HOLIDAY BUNGALOWS, OCEAN VIEW ROAD, VENTNOR PO38 1AA (01983 852555). For self catering holidays for you and your pet on England's Sunshine Isle. Attractive bungalows, each accommodates up to six. Adjoins National Trust downland overlooking Ventnor. SAE or phone for brochure. [🐾]

SEAGULLS HOTEL, BELLEVUE ROAD, VENTNOR PO38 1DB (01983 852085). en suite, centrally heated rooms with colour TV. Excellent home cooked menu. Hotel overlooks sea in quiet location. Close to Botanical Gardens, coastal paths and downs. Parking. Licensed. ETB 3 Crowns Commended, AA QQQ. Colour brochure. [🐾]

WOODLYNCH HOLIDAY APARTMENTS, SHORE ROAD, BONCHURCH, VENTNOR PO38 1RF (01983 852513). Comfortable self-contained holiday apartments in picturesque seaside village from £80 per week. Pleasant seaside and country walks, gardens and private parking. Dogs welcome. Tourist Board Member. Please write or phone for brochure and tariff. [🐾]

Yarmouth

Coastal resort situated 9 miles west of Newport. Castle built by Henry VIII for coastal defence.

THE ORCHARDS HOLIDAY CARAVAN & CAMPING PARK, NEWBRIDGE, YARMOUTH, ISLE OF WIGHT PO41 OTS (Tel: 01983 531 331; Fax: 01983 531 666). Luxury caravans. Excellent camping facilities. Heated outdoor swimming pool, self service shop. Takeaway food bar. Coarse fishing. Complete ferry booking service. Five ticks. Rose Award. [Pets £1 per night, pw!]

"TUCKAWAY" – Holiday Chalet in private, secluded position. Sleeps six. swimming pool. Dogs welcome. Large grassed area. Tourist Board Approved. APPLY – R. STEDMAN, FURZEBREAK, CRANMORE AVENUE, YARMOUTH PO41 OXR (01983 760082). [🐾]

SILVERGLADES CARAVAN PARK, SOLENT ROAD, CRANMORE, YARMOUTH PO41 0XZ (01983 760172). 6-berth caravans on small family-run site in picturesque West Wight.

Broadstairs

Quiet resort, once a favourite of Charles Dickens. Good sands and promenades.

CASTLEMERE HOTEL, WESTERN ESPLANADE, BROADSTAIRS CT10 1TD (01843 861566; Fax: 01843 866379). 40 bedrooms, 31 with private bathrooms. Telephone and colour television in bedrooms. Television lounge. Licensed. Selective menus. Near beach, on seafront. Diets and children catered for. Dogs welcome. ETB 3 Crowns Commended, AA, RAC. [Pets £2.00 per night].

TREVOR AND JEAN WEBB, HANSON HOTEL, 41 BELVEDERE ROAD, BROADSTAIRS (01843 868936). Small, friendly licensed Georgian Hotel. Home comforts; babies, children and pets welcome. Attractive bar. SAE. [pw! Pets 50p per night.]

Folkestone

Important cross-Channel port with good sandy beach and narrow old streets winding down to the harbour.

ABBEY HOUSE HOTEL, 5-6 WESTBOURNE GARDENS, OFF SANDGATE ROAD, FOLKESTONE CT20 2JA (01303 255514; Fax: 01303 245098). Friendly, Two Crown licensed Hotel, five minutes from Leas Promenade and Country Park. Convenient for Tunnel and Ferry. Bed and Breakfast from £18.00. [Pets £1 per night.]

THE HORSESHOE HOTEL, 29 WESTBOURNE GARDENS, FOLKESTONE CT20 2HY (01303 243433). Spacious Private Hotel close Promenade and town centre. All rooms colour TV, washbasins, tea/coffee making facilities; some en suite. Parking. Friendly hospitality and good home cooking. Mini Breaks. Details on request. Hotel and Catering Reg. ETB 2 Crowns. [🐾]

Herne Bay

Homely family resort on North Kent coast. Shingle beach with sand at low tide. Maidstone 32 miles, Faversham 13, Canterbury 9, Whitstable 5.

MR AND MRS N. EVANS, 156 BELTINGE ROAD, HERNE BAY CT6 6JE (01227 375750). A fully furnished detached bungalow for three people (double and single bedrooms). Car parking space and enclosed rear garden. Brochure on request. [🐕]

Hythe

Village on west bank of Southampton Water. Ferry connection for pedestrians. Urban expansion inland.

STADE COURT HOTEL, HYTHE CT21 6DT (01303 268263; Fax: 01303 261803). Situated on the seafront close to parks and the beach, the hotel has comfortable well-equipped bedrooms with en suite facilities. Leisure and golf facilities available at our sister hotel close by. Phone for brochure and tariff. Pets "Doggie Dinner" £7.50 per night.

LANCASHIRE

LANCASHIRE *Blackpool*

HAMPSON HOUSE
Hotel & Restaurant
AA**   RAC**   ETB ♕♕♕
Hampson Lane, Hampson Green, Nr. Lancaster
Tel: 01524 751158 Fax: 01524 751779

A family-run, fully licensed hotel with 14 bedrooms all with private facilities, radio, telephone, TV, and welcome tray. Set in two acres of mature gardens, the original house was built circa 1600 A.D. and was the home of the Welsh family from 1666 until 1973 when it was sold and converted into a hotel. Situated in an area known as "The Gateway to the Lakes" it is also an ideal base for the leisure traveller to use while touring the North West of England or halfway house for the traveller on his way North or South.

*   Manchester 40 miles * Blackpool 16 miles * The Lakes 30 miles *
* Morecambe 8 miles * Lancaster 4 miles * Glasson Park 4 miles *

CRIMOND HOTEL   ♕♕♕♕
Knowsley Road, Southport PR9 0HN Tel: 01704 536456 Fax: 01704 548643
The Crimond Hotel is situated close to the promenade and town centre. The 12 bedroom
hotel has an indoor pool, sauna and jacuzzi. Open all year.
All bedrooms en suite with colour TV, radio, hair dryer and direct-dial telephone.
Large car park.

Blackpool

Famous resort with fine sands and many attractions and vast variety of entertainments. Blackpool Tower (500ft). Three piers. Manchester 47 miles, Lancaster 26, Preston 17, Fleetwood 9.

ASH-LEA GUEST HOUSE, 76 LORD STREET, BLACKPOOL FY1 2DG (01253 28161). Good food and comfort assured. All rooms TV, some rooms toilet en suite. Free showers. Close to all amenities. B&B from £11.00, Evening Meal optional extra. No charge for pets. [🐾]

THE BRAYTON HOTEL, 7-8 FINCHLEY ROAD, GYNN SQUARE, BLACKPOOL FY1 2LP. The small hotel with the BIG reputation. A family-run hotel overlooking Gynn gardens and the promenade offering quality food from a varied menu. Comfortable rooms and a licensed bar, easy parking. Open all year. For tariff and brochure ring 01253 351645. [🐾]

MRS C. MOORE, COTSWOLD HOLIDAY FLATLETS, 2A HADDON ROAD, NORBRECK, BLACKPOOL FY2 9AH (01253 352227). Holiday Flatlets fully equipped. Cross road to beach and trams. Select area. Open all year. Short Breaks early season and Illuminations. SAE. [🐕]

Carnforth

Small town 6 miles north of Lancaster. Steamtown Railway Centre offers train rides, model and minature railways and other memorabilia.

MRS MARGARET HOLMES, KILN CROFT, MAIN STREET, WARTON, CARNFORTH LA5 9NR (01524 735788). Small, family-run hotel where you can relax by a log fire or wander round the animal garden. Licensed restaurant serving home-produced organic vegetables and own meat when available. Walks up beautiful Warton Crag from house and many to the picturesque villages around. Five minutes from J35 M6. B&B £18.50 en suite.

Quality Cottages on Lakes/Dales border set in tranquil countryside. Converted from old stone barns. Well-equipped, TV, central heating; own gardens, patio, picnic tables, BBQ. Indoor/outdoor play areas. Indoor heated pool May/September. 4 Keys Commended. Apply MR & MRS MORPHY, MANSERGH FARMHOUSE COTTAGES, BORWICK, NEAR CARNFORTH LA6 1JS (01524 732586).

Clitheroe

Pleasant market town, with ruined Norman keep standing on limestone cliff above grey roofs. Pendle Hill 4 miles to the east, from where there are spectacular views of the Forest of Bowland.

THE INN AT WHITEWELL, FOREST OF BOWLAND, NEAR CLITHEROE BB7 3AT (01200 448222; Fax: 01200 448298). Beautiful riverside setting. Log fires and antique furniture throughout. Six miles of salmon and trout fishing. Shooting by arrangement. 3 Crowns. [🐕 pw!].

MRS FRANCES OLIVER, WYTHA FARM, RIMINGTON, CLITHEROE BB7 4EQ (01200 445295). Farmhouse accommodation in heart of countryside. Panoramic views. Warm welcome. Double and family rooms. Ideal touring centre. Bed and Breakfast from £14. Evening Meal £8. [pw! Pets £1 per day]

Lancaster

For centuries the county town of Lancashire. Lancaster canal, which runs to north of Kendal, crosses the Lune on a fine aqueduct built in 1797 by Rennie. An impressive Norman Castle and fine Georgian houses around the area. Preston 20 miles.

HAMPSON HOUSE, HAMPSON LANE, HAMPSON GREEN, LANCASTER (Tel: 01524 751158 Fax: 01524 751779). A family-run fully licensed hotel with 14 bedrooms all with private facilities, radio, telephone, TV and welcome tray. Set in two acres of mature gardens and situated in an area known as "The Gateway to the Lakes", it is also an ideal base for the leisure traveller.

Southport

Attractive and well-planned resort with sands and dunes. Many family atttractions. Blackpool 34 miles, Liverpool 20.

CRIMOND HOTEL & RESTAURANT KNOWSLEY ROAD, SOUTHPORT PR9 OHN (Tel: 01704 536456; Fax: 01704 548643). Situated close to the town centre this 19 bedroom hotel can cater for all your needs with the luxury of an indoor Leisure Centre. Open all year. Table d'hôte service. Full central heating. [🐾]

St Annes

Very poular family resort with good sands. Good shopping centre. Preston 15 miles, Blackpool 5 miles.

MRS M. MACKOON, ORCHARD COURT, 50/52 ORCHARD ROAD, ST ANNES FY8 1PJ (01253 712653). Self-catering flats with en suite facilities and large gardens. 2 minutes to shops, cafes, beach. Linen provided. Car park. Open all year, Short Breaks available. [🐾 pw!]

LEICESTERSHIRE

LEICESTERSHIRE   *Melton Mowbray*

SYSONBY KNOLL HOTEL **ASFORDBY ROAD** **MELTON MOWBRAY** **LEICESTERSHIRE LE13 OHP** **Tel: 01664 63563** **Fax: 01664 410364**	Traditional family-run hotel on outskirts of market town. The newly refurbished bar and restaurant overlook the gardens and paddock to the river. A la carte, table d'hôte and bar menus served until 9pm. All bedrooms, some ground floor, en suite with TV and hospitality tray. Outdoor swimming pool. ♛ ♛ ♛ ♛ Commended RAC ★★★ AA ★★ Les Routiers

Melton Mowbray

Old market town, centre of hunting country. Noted for Stilton cheese and pork pies. Large cattle market. Church and Anne of Cleves' House are of interest. Kettering 29 miles, Market Harborough 22, Notttingham 18, Grantham 16, Leicester 15.

SYSONBY KNOLL HOTEL, ASFORDBY ROAD, MELTON MOWBRAY LE13 OHP (01664 63563; Fax: 01664 410364.). Traditional family-run hotel; all bedrooms (some ground floor) en suite with TV and hospitality tray. Outdoor swimming pool; bar and restaurant. 4 Crowns Commended, AA**, RAC ***. [🐾]

Redmile

Village 7 miles west of Grantham.

PEACOCK FARM GUESTHOUSE & COUNTRY RESTAURANT, VALE OF BELVOIR, REDMILE NG13 0GQ (01949 842475 Fax: 01949 843127). Professional service combined with old fashioned hospitality. Ideal for touring, walking or relaxing. B&B and self catering bungalow. Open Christmas. All pets by arrangement. 2 Crowns. [Pets £2 per night/£10 per week].

LINCOLNSHIRE

KIRTON LODGE HOTEL

13 DUNSTAN HILL, KIRTON IN LINDSEY, DN21 4DU. Tel: 01652 648994.
Small, friendly Hotel with 'doggie mad' owners. Ideally situated for a multitude of 'doggie & human' activities. All rooms en suite with the usual creature comforts. Excellent restaurant holding 'A.C.E.' award.

Special D.B.B rates for 2 nights or more.   ☞☞☞ Commended

Kirkstead Mill Old Cottage   WOODHALL SPA.   ♔♔♔♔ Highly Commended

Sleeps 7–10 plus baby. Non-smokers only. Very well equipped, three bedrooms – colour TV, video, washing machine, fridge/freezer, microwave etc. £99-£440 per week. Membership of local leisure club. Beside river; rowing boat provided.

**Apply: Mrs Barbara Hodgkinson, "Hodge's Lodges," 52 Kelso Close,
Worth, Crawley, West Sussex RH10 7XH. Tel: 01293 882008; Fax: 01293 442008.**

Kirton in Lindsey

A small town 8 miles south of Scunthorpe, with an airfield to the south east.

KIRTON LODGE HOTEL, 13 DUNSTAN HILL, KIRTON IN LINDSEY DN21 4DU (01652 648994). Small, friendly Hotel, "Dog Mad" owners, all dogs welcome. Ideally situated for a multitude of "doggie" activities, i.e., beaches, woods, lakes. All rooms en suite with full services. Three Crowns Commended. [🐾]

Market Rasen

Market town and agricultural centre 14 miles north-east of Lincoln

MRS M. E. DAWSON-MARGRAVE, THE WAVENEY GUEST HOUSE, WILLINGHAM ROAD, MARKET RASEN LN8 3DN (01673 843236). Very comfortable, smoke-free accommodation in small market town surrounded by woodland and close to Lincolnshire Wolds; golf and race courses. All rooms with private facilities, colour TV, tea-making equipment. Guests' own lounge and dining room. Excellent food. Private parking. Brochure available. 2 Crowns Commended. [🐾]

Woodhall

Spa town 6 miles south-west of Horncastle.

KIRKSTEAD MILL OLD COTTAGE, WOODHALL SPA. Sleeps 7+3 plus baby. Non-smokers only. Very well equipped; three bedrooms; – colour TV, washing machine, fridge/freezer, microwave etc. 4 Keys Highly Commended. £99 -£440 per week. Beside river; rowing boat provided. Apply: MRS BARBARA HODGKINSON, "HODGE'S LODGES," 52 KELSO CLOSE, WORTH, CRAWLEY, WEST SUSSEX RH10 7XH (01293 882008; Fax: 01293 442008). [Pets £10 per week]

LONDON

Kingston upon Thames

Market town, Royal borough, and administrative centre of Surrey, Kingston is ideally placed for London and environs.

CHASE LODGE GUEST HOUSE, 10 PARK ROAD, HAMPTON WICK, KINGSTON-UPON-THAMES KT1 4AS (0181 943 1862). Charming Guest House, recently refurbished, situated in a quiet area close to Hampton Court and Bushy Park. All rooms have telephone, TV, fridge, teamaking. Some four-poster rooms. Bed and Breakfast, Evening Meals, Supper Trays. 4 Crowns. [🐾].

London

Legislative Capital of UK and major port. Theatres, shops, museums, places of historic interest. Airports at Heathrow and Gatwick.

ST ATHANS HOTEL, 20 TAVISTOCK PLACE, RUSSELL SQUARE, LONDON WC1H 9RE (0171 837 9140, Fax: 0171 833 8352). Family Bed and Breakfast near British Museum, shops, parks and theatres. Russell Square two blocks away, Euston and King's Cross stations ten minutes. LTB LISTED. [🐾]

FHG PUBLICATIONS LIMITED publish a large range of well-known accommodation guides. We will be happy to send you details or you can use the order form at the back of this book.

NORFOLK

East Norwich Inn,
Old Road, Acle, Norwich NR13 3QN

Midway between Great Yarmouth and Norwich, we are ideally situated for visiting all Heritage, National Trust and holiday attractions. The inn is situated on a quiet residential road and has a full "on" licence with a good local bar trade. All rooms are situated well away from the bar area and comprise 2 twin rooms, 4 double rooms and 3 family rooms. All en suite, with colour Sky TV and tea/coffee making facilities. Ample car parking. Pets welcome by arrangement.

👑 👑 👑

Tel: 01493 751112

Bed and Breakfast from £17 per person per night. Three night break prices available.

CASTAWAYS HOLIDAY PARK

BGHP ✓✓✓✓

Set in the quiet, peaceful village of Bacton, with direct access to fine, sandy beach, and ideal for touring Norfolk and The Broads. Modern Caravans with all amenities. Licensed Club, Entertainment, Amusement Arcade, Children's Play Area. PETS WELCOME.

Enquiries and Bookings to: Roger and Beccy Fitches, Castaways Holiday Park, Paston Road, Bacton-on-Sea, Norfolk NR12 0JB Tel: (01692) 650436 and 650418

Readers are requested to mention this guidebook when seeking accommodation (and please enclose a stamped addressed envelope).

COME TO BEAUTIFUL NORFOLK
With Blue Riband Holidays

Go *Blue Riband* For Quality Inexpensive Self Catering Holidays

Where your dog is welcome, choice of location – all in the borough of Great Yarmouth

* **Detached 3 bedroom Bungalows for all seasons** set in a delightful Parkland at Hemsby Village as featured in the picture above, with Satellite TV, miniature railway and children's playground. *All bungalows now have a fridge/freezer.*
* **Seafront Bungalows** at Caister with enclosed rear gardens leading directly onto a sandy beach and promenade. **Sand Dunes Cottages** close to the beach in Caister Village.
* **Detached 2 & 3 bedroom Bungalows** at Scratby with enclosed gardens.
* **Detached Sea-Dell Chalets,** Beach Road, Hemsby, a lovely quiet location.
* **Belle Aire Park,** Hemsby, 2 & 3 bedrooms, free electricity, Cabaret Clubhouse.
* **Choice of Holiday Parks:-** Hemsby, Scratby, California and Caister. Some parks have a swimming pool and clubhouse.
* **Modern Seafront Caravans** at Caister Beach Park, unrivalled position, 4-8 berth all mains services, Cabaret Clubhouse, electricity and gas included. Swimming pool available at small extra charge. Park adjoins the beach, no roads to cross.

Excellent facilities to exercise your dog at all the above locations.
Your dog is allowed on local beaches.

Special Features:- Safe car parking beside your bungalow, colour TV, heating, bath with shower or shower room, duvets and microwave ovens in all bungalows and most chalets. Cots, baby chairs & linen hire.

Bungalows have electric nightstore heating available all year round, for Christmas, Easter and Winter Breaks this is now included in the holiday price.

Reasonable Prices from £75 per week. **DOGS** £6 per week. **Discounts** for small family and Senior Citizens on early and late holidays. **Bargain Short Breaks** during Spring and Autumn, 4/5 days Friday – Monday or Monday – Friday, up to 4 persons £50, dogs £1 per night. Short Breaks subject to availability during June and early July. Prices on request (normally 50% of weekly charge).

Free Colour Brochure:- DON WITHERIDGE, BLUE RIBAND HOUSE, PARKLANDS, HEMSBY, GREAT YARMOUTH NR29 4HA

Dial-a-brochure 7 days a week **01493 730445;** all calls personally answered.

All the advertisers in PETS WELCOME! have an entry in the appropriate classified section and each classified entry may carry one or more of the following symbols:

🐾   This symbol indicates that pets are welcome free of charge.

£   The £ indicates that a charge is made for pets. We quote the amount where possible, either per night or per week.

pw!   This symbol shows that the establishment has some special provision for pets; perhaps an exercise facility or some special feeding or accommodation arrangements.

⌂   Indicates separate pets accommodation.

PLEASE NOTE that all the advertisers in PETS WELCOME! extend a welcome to pets and their owners but they may attach conditions. The interests of other guests have to be considered and it is usually assumed that pets will be well trained, obedient and under the control of their owner.

Acle

Small town 8 miles west of Great Yarmouth.

Bacton-on-Sea

Village on coast, 5 miles from North Walsham.

RED HOUSE CHALET AND CARAVAN PARK, PASTON ROAD, BACTON-ON-SEA NR12 0JB (01692 650815). Small family-run site, ideal for touring Broads. Chalets, caravans and flats all with showers, fridges and colour TV. Some with sea views. Licensed. Open March–January. [Pets £10 weekly.]

Beeston

Small village with shop and public house mid way King's Lynn, Norwich and the coast. C

MR & MRS KINNAIRD, BIRCH COTTAGE, DEREHAM ROAD, BEESTON, KING'S LYNN PE32 2NQ (01328 701659). 300 year old beamed cottage with log burner and central heating. Sleeps 6-8 people in 3/4 bedrooms. Fenced garden and parking area. From £200 - £300 Easter - October. All fuel inclusive. Use of kennel if required – dog and babysitting available. [🐾 pw!]

Beetley

Village 4 miles/6 km north of East Dereham, which is notable for old buildings, inc. parish church, early 16c Cottages now Museum of local history.

MRS JENNY BELL, PEACOCK HOUSE, PEACOCK LANE, OLD BEETLEY, DEREHAM NR20 4DG (01362 860371). Old farmhouse in lovely countryside. All rooms en suite, tea / coffee facilities. Own lounge, B&B from £17/18 pp. Open all year. ETB 2 Crowns Highly Commended. Children and dogs welcome. [pw! 🐾]

Brooke

Attractive small village 8 miles south of Norwich; Lowestoft 20 miles, Great Yarmouth 25.

MRS D. VIVIAN-NEAL, WELBECK HOUSE, BROOKE, NEAR NORWICH NR15 1AT (01508 550292). Peaceful 300-year-old former farmhouse with wooded garden. Tea/coffee making. All diets catered for. Ample parking. Local coarse fishing. Dogs welcome. Non-smoking house. [🐾].

Bunwell

Hamlet situated 6 miles south of Wymondham.

BUNWELL MANOR, BUNWELL STREET, BUNWELL, NEAR NORWICH NR16 1QU (01953 788304). Peaceful setting - 2 acres mature garden with ponds. Friendly, homely atmosphere, traditional freshly prepared food. Log fire in winter. Central to all attractions. Children and pets welcome. AA/RAC 2 Star. ETB 3 Crowns Commended.

Burnham Market

Village five miles west of Wells-next-the-Sea.

THE HOSTE ARMS, THE GREEN, BURNHAM MARKET PE31 8HD (01328 738257). 17th century Hotel overlooking village green. 21 bedrooms, elegantly furnished, all en suite with colour TV and telephone. Bar and restaurant menus, AA 2 Rosettes. [🐾]

Cromer

Attractive resort built round old fishing village. Norwich 21 miles.

KINGS CHALET PARK. Comfortable well-equipped chalets on quiet site; ideally placed for woodland and beach walks. 10 minutes' walk to town, shops nearby. Details from MRS I. SCOLTOCK, SHANGRI-LA, LITTLE CAMBRIDGE, DUTON HILL, DUNMOW, ESSEX (01371 870482). [🐕]

ROSEACRE COUNTRY HOUSE, WEST RUNTON, NEAR CROMER NR27 9QS. Self-catering apartments sleeping 2/8. Private gardens, car park. Few minutes sea, shops, golf, riding. Woodland walks nearby. Short breaks out of season. Open all year. Brochure. JOAN AND RODNEY SANDERS (01263 837221).

All-electric Holiday Cottages accommodating 4 to 6 persons in beautiful surroundings. Sandy beaches, sports facilities, Cinema and Pier (live shows). Parking. Children and pets welcome. Brochure: NORTHREPPS HOLIDAY PROPERTIES, CROMER, NORFOLK NR27 OJW (01263 578196 or 512236).[Pets £12 weekly].

Diss

Twisting streets with Tudor, Georgian and Victorian architecture. 12th century St. Mary's Church and 6 acre mere, haven for wildfowl.

BRENDA WEBB, STRENNETH, AIRFIELD ROAD, FERSFIELD, DISS IP22 2BP (01379 688182, Fax: 01379 699260). 17th Century former farmhouse, fully renovated, full central heating. All rooms en suite, colour TV, tea/coffee; some non-smoking, most on ground floor. Extensive breakfast menu. Licensed. 2 Crowns Commended. [🐕]

Downham Market

Market town and agricultural centre on River Ouse, 10 miles south of King's Lynn.

CROSSKEYS RIVERSIDE HOTEL, BRIDGE STREET, HILGAY, NEAR DOWNHAM MARKET PE38 0LD (01366 387777). A small country hotel beside the River Wissey. Restaurant offering table d'hôte and à la carte menus. All bedrooms en suite, with colour TV, coffee/tea making facilities. Pets most welcome. [Pets £3 per week]

East Dereham

Situated 16 miles west of Norwich. St Nicholas Church has 16th century bell tower.

SCARNING DALE, SCARNING, EAST DEREHAM NR19 2QN (01362 887269). Self catering cottages (not commercialised) in grounds of owner's house. On-site indoor heated swimming pool and full-size snooker table. B&B for six also available in house (sorry no pets).

Foxley

Village 6 miles east of East Dereham.

Self Catering Chalets (2/3 bedrooms) on working farm. All fully equipped, with central heating. 20 miles from coast, 15 from Broads. Mature woodland nearby. Ideal for walking. Three Keys Approved. MOOR FARM HOLIDAYS (PW), FOXLEY NR20 4QN (01362 688523). [Pets £10 per week]

Gimingham

Village 4 miles north of North Walsham.

MR & MRS J.A. HARRIS, BRIDGE FARM STABLES, WINDMILL ROAD, GIMINGHAM, NEAR MUNDESLEY NR11 8HL (01263 720028). Working stables situated on outskirts of Gimingham village. Rural views, central heating, TV/clock radios in 2 of 3 bedrooms (sleep 6). Dogs welcome.

Great Yarmouth

Traditional lively seaside resort with a wide range of amusements, including the Marina Centre and Sealife Centre.

Go BLUE RIBAND for quality inexpensive self-catering holidays where your dog is welcome – choice of locations all in the borough of Great Yarmouth. Detached 3 bedroom bungalows, seafront bungalows, detached Sea-Dell chalets and modern sea front caravans. Free colour brochure: DON WITHERIDGE, BLUE RIBAND HOUSE, PARKLANDS, HEMSBY, GREAT YARMOUTH NR29 4HA (01493 730445). [Pets £6 per week].

MRS J. S. COOPER, SILVERLEA, MILE ROAD, CARLETON RODE, NORWICH NR16 1 NE (01953 789 407). Modern holiday chalets at Winterton-on-Sea. Sleep six. Grassed site close to beach with marvellous sea views. A pets' paradise! [Pets £8 per week.]

CAREFREE HOLIDAYS, SOLITAIRE, PARKLAND ESTATE, NORTH ROAD, HEMSBY, GREAT YARMOUTH NR29 4HE (01493 732176). A wide selection of superior chalets for live-as-you-please holidays near Great Yarmouth and Norfolk Broads. All amenities on site. Sports facilities, parking. Children and pets welcome. [pw! 1st pet free.]

MRS PAULINE SMITH, "ANCHOR", 21 NORTH DENES ROAD, GREAT YARMOUTH NR30 4LW (01493 844339). Completely self-contained Flats with own shower and toilet. Fully equipped at no extra cost. Reduced terms early and late season. Close by public amenities. Children and pets welcome. [pw!]

ANGLIA COASTAL HOLIDAYS, WINTERTON VALLEY CHALET ESTATE, 'POPPYLANDS', 2 BUSH ROAD SOUTH, WINTERTON-ON-SEA, GREAT YARMOUTH NR29 4BZ (01708 723063). Superior modern chalets in peaceful surroundings. All enjoying panoramic coastal views with direct access to dunes and uncrowded sandy beaches. Fully equipped and furnished to high standards. [Pets £15 per week].

The way holidays used to be. SAND DUNE COTTAGES, TAN LANE, CAISTER-ON-SEA, GREAT YARMOUTH NR30 5DT (01493 667786 / 03855 61363). Established 1982. Adjacent to golf course; dunes and sea 200 yards. Great Yarmouth 10 minutes' drive. 2 and 4 night breaks early / late season. Open Christmas. Pets welcome. SAE for brochure.

Horning

Lovely riverside village ideally placed for exploring the Broads. Great Yarmouth 17 miles.

SILVER BIRCHES HOLIDAYS, GREBE ISLAND, LOWER STREET, HORNING NR12 8PF (Tel/Fax: 01692 630858). Five well-equipped houseboats and seven all-weather motor day launches. All the comforts of a caravan afloat! Surrounded by lawns, adjacent parking. Ideal for families, fishermen and their pets. [Pets £15 per stay]

Hunstanton

Neat little resort which faces west across The Wash. Norwich 47 miles, Cromer 38.

MRS BROWN, MARINE HOTEL, HUNSTANTON PE36 5EH (01485 533310). Overlooking sea and green. Pets welcome, free of charge. Colour televisions. Open all year except Christmas period. SAE for terms and brochure. [🐕]

COBBLERS COTTAGE, 3 WODEHOUSE ROAD, OLD HUNSTANTON PE36 6JD (01485 534036). Near Royal Sandringham/Norfolk Lavender. All en suite twin/double rooms. Colour TV and tea-making. Near the beach, golf, birdwatching, pubs and restaurants. Sauna and jacuzzi. Also self catering annexe. [🐕]

King's Lynn

Ancient market town and port on the Wash with many beautiful medieval and Georgian buildings.

MRS JOAN BASTONE, MARANATHA GUEST HOUSE, 115 GAYWOOD ROAD, KING'S LYNN PE30 2PU (01553 774596). Large house, 10 minutes' walk from town centre. Direct road to Sandringham and the coast. Animal lovers and their pets welcomed. B&B from £14 per person. 2 Crowns Approved, AA QQ, RAC. [pw! Pets £1 per night]

Mundesley-on-Sea

Small resort backed by low cliffs. Good sands and bathing. Norwich 20 miles, Cromer 7.

"WHINCLIFF", CROMER ROAD, MUNDESLEY NR11 8DU (01263 720961). Clifftop house, sea views and sandy beaches. Rooms with colour TV and tea-making. En suite family/twin room. Evening Meal optional. An abundance of coastal and woodland walks; many places of interest and local crafts. Well-behaved dogs welcome. [🐕]

JULIA GILBURT, OVERCLIFF LODGE, MUNDESLEY, NORWICH NR11 8DB. (Tel/Fax: 01263 720016). Victorian Guest House. Quiet coastal location. En suite rooms. Excellent food. Ideal base for North Norfolk and Broads. Open all year. Private car park. Non smoking. [🐕]

KILN CLIFFS CARAVAN PARK, CROMER ROAD, MUNDESLEY NR11 8DF (01263 720449). Peaceful family-run site situated around an historic brick kiln. Six-berth caravans for hire, standing on ten acres of grassy cliff top. All caravans fully equipped (except linen) and price includes all gas and electricity.

Neatishead

Ideal for touring East Anglia. Close to Norwich. Aylsham 14 miles, Norwich 10, Wroxham 3.

ALAN AND SUE WRIGLEY, REGENCY GUEST HOUSE, THE STREET, NEATISHEAD, NORFOLK BROADS NR12 8AD (01692 630233). 17th century five-bedroom guest house renowned for generous English breakfasts. Ideal East Anglian touring base. Accent on personal service. Tourist Board 2 Crowns Commended, AA QQQ. Dogs welcome. [Pets £1.50 per night.]

North Walsham

Market town 14 miles north of Norwich, traditional centre of the Norfolk reed thatching industry.

MRS V. O'HARA, GEOFFREY THE DYER'S HOUSE, CHURCH PLAIN, WORSTEAD, NORTH WALSHAM NR28 9AL (01692 536562). 17th century Listed weaver's house in centre of conservation village. Close to Broads, Coast, Norwich. Good walking and touring. All rooms en suite. Wholesome, well-cooked food. Dogs welcome. ETB 2 Crowns. [🐕]

HILL HOUSE COUNTRY HOTEL, SCARBOROUGH HILL, OLD YARMOUTH ROAD, NORTH WALSHAM NR28 9NA (01692 402151; Fax: 01692 406686). Dogs, bring your master and missus to this charming country hotel. All rooms en suite; licensed bar and dining room. Self catering cottage also available.[Pets £2 per night]

Nominated for prestigious B&B awards, the en suite guest lodges at the 18th century Toll Barn have every modern amenity, adjacent paddocks for dog walking. Ideal for walking, coast, Norfolk Broads, North Norfolk and Norwich. ETB Listed Highly Commended, AA QQQQ. ANNETTE TOFTS, THE TOLL BARN, OFF NORWICH ROAD, NORTH WALSHAM NR28 0JB (01692 403063; Fax: 01692 406582). [Pets £1.50 per night.].

Norwich

County town and Cathedral city with a daily open air market, medieval streets, a Norman castle and good shopping and leisure facilities.

SOUTHREPPS HOLIDAY COTTAGES. Five delightful cottages situated in the village of Southrepps, just 3 miles from the coast and safe, sandy beaches. 3 cottages with two bedrooms and 2 with three rooms. Each has a lounge with double bed settee and colour TV. Apply: MR CODLING, CHURCH FARM GUEST HOUSE, SOUTH REPPS, NORWICH NR11 8NP (01263 833248). [pw! 🐕]

THE GEORGIAN HOUSE HOTEL, 32/34 UNTHANK ROAD, NORWICH NR2 2RB (01603 615655 – 4 lines; Fax: 01603 765689). Ideal for sightseeing in Norwich or touring East Anglia. 27 bedrooms, all en suite, with colour TV, radio, tea/coffee making facilities. Licensed. ETB 3 Crowns Commended. [🐕]

Sheringham

Small, traditional resort which has grown around a flint-built fishing village. Sandy beaches and amusements.

ACHIMOTA, 31 NORTH STREET, SHERINGHAM NR26 8LW (01263 822379). Award-winning small guest house in quiet part of Sheringham. Cliff, heath and woodland walks galore in this "Area of Outstanding Natural Beauty". Tourist Board rating "Two Crowns Commended". Council "Heartbeat Award". En suite rooms. NO SMOKING. Brochure on request. [🐾].

Swaffham

Old market town. 15th-century church, Palladian market cross. Norwich 28 miles, King's Lynn 15.

Nar Valley Holiday Cottage, Norfolk. Charming cottage in the unspoilt Nar Valley. Winter weekends or Summer holidays. Telephone for brochure. NAR VALLEY HOLIDAYS, ESTATE OFFICE, WESTACRE, KING'S LYNN PE32 1UB (01760 755254; Fax: 01760 755444).[🐾]

MRS GREEN, PAGET, MAIN ROAD, NARBOROUGH, KING'S LYNN PE32 1TE (01760 337734). Private house offering B&B. Lounge available, log fire. Televisions in bedrooms. Ample parking. Trout and coarse fishing, lakes, pleasant rural walks. Situated between the old market town of Swaffham and King's Lynn. SAE please. [🐾].

Thetford

Town at confluence of River Thet and Little Ouse River, 12 miles north of Bury St Edmunds.

KEVIN AND YVONNE FICKLING, ROSE COTTAGE, BUTTERS HALL LANE, THOMPSON, THETFORD IP24 1QQ (01953 488104). Comfortable flint-walled house, situated in acre of garden, 3 miles south of Watton (off A1075). Colour TV, tea making facilities in spacious bedrooms. Delicious breakfasts served in oak beamed dining room. Very peaceful, wonderful walks. Sorry, no smoking. EATB Listed Commended. £35 per couple per night.

Wells-next-the-Sea

Lovely little resort with interesting harbour, famous for its cockles, whelks and shrimps. A winding creek leads to a beach of fine sands with dunes. Norwich 31 miles, King's Lynn 27, Cromer 19.

MRS J. M. COURT, EASTDENE, NORTHFIELD LANE, WELLS-NEXT-THE-SEA NR23 1LH (01328 710381). Homely Guest House offers warm welcome. Bed and Breakfast from £18. Two double, one twin bedded rooms, all en suite; colour television lounge. Private parking. Les Routiers recommended. Tourist Board 2 Crowns Approved. [Pets £1 per night].

Winterton-on-Sea

Good sands and bathing. Great Yarmouth 8 miles.

WINTERTON VALLEY HOLIDAYS. A selection of modern superior fully appointed holiday chalets sleeping 2-6 persons. Duvets and colour TV in all chalets. Panoramic views of the sea from this quiet 35-acre estate. 5 minutes beach, 8 miles Great Yarmouth. Pets very welcome. For colour brochure: 15 KINGSTON AVENUE, CAISTER-ON-SEA NR30 5ET (01493 377175). [Pets £15 per week.].

Self-contained ground floor of cottage in quiet seaside village. Broad sandy beach and pleasant walks. Close to Norfolk Broads. Secluded garden. Double, twin and single bedrooms, sleep 5 plus cot. Bed linen provided. Fully equipped for self-catering family holiday. £140-£300 per week. Full details from MR M. J. ISHERWOOD, 79 OAKLEIGH AVENUE, LONDON N20 9JG (0181-445 2192). [Pets £5 per week.]

Wroxham

Village 7 miles north east of Norwich.

THE BROADS HOTEL, STATION ROAD, WROXHAM, NORWICH NR12 8UR (01603 782869; Fax: 01603 784066). Comfortable hotel owned and run by dog-loving family. Ideally situated for boating, fishing and exploring the beautiful Norfolk countryside and coastline. All rooms fully en suite. [🐾]

NORTHAMPTONSHIRE

NORTHAMPTONSHIRE   *Weedon*

The Globe Hotel

High Street, Weedon, Northampton NN7 4QD

🏆🏆🏆🏆 **Commended**   RAC★★

While retaining its historic character, The Globe has been completely refurbished to a most comfortable standard. 18 en suite bedrooms. Within easy touring distance of Warwick, Leamington Spa, Stratford, Naseby Battlefield and Silverstone. Close to Grand Union Canal. Comprehensive food operation OPEN ALL DAY features home fayre bar meals and à la carte menu. Special weekend Giveaway Breaks.

A Countryside Inn

Tel: 01327 340336   Fax: 01327 349058

Weedon

Village 4 miles south east of Daventry.

THE GLOBE HOTEL, HIGH STREET, WEEDON, NORTHAMPTON NN7 4QD (01327 340336; Fax: 01327 349058). Set in countryside close to Grand Union Canal. 18 en suite bedrooms. Comprehensive food operation. Convenient for Warwick, Stratford, Silverstone. Special Weekend Giveaway Breaks. Four Crowns Commended. [pw! 🐾]

NORTHUMBERLAND

NORTHUMBERLAND *Alnmouth, Alnwick, Belford, Corbridge, Ninebanks*

Sheila and Gordon Inkster

MARINE HOUSE PRIVATE HOTEL
Marine Road, Alnmouth NE66 2RW
Tel: 01665 830349

Charming hotel in fine sea front location. 10 individually appointed en suite bedrooms, four course gourmet candlelit dinner, cocktail bar, games room, sea views, children and pets very welcome.ETB 3 Crowns Commended. AA Selected QQQQ, RAC Highly Acclaimed, Hospitality Awards. D, B&B Daily per person – high season £39-£42; Northumbrian Log Fire Beaks; Oct/Apr £36.00.

NORTHUMBRIA COAST AND COUNTRY COTTAGES LTD
Self Catering Holiday Cottage Agency. ETB Reg.
A superb selection of cottages in beautiful Northumberland
FREE COLOUR BROCHURE: 01665 830783 (24HRS)

VILLAGE FARM SELF CATERING
Town Foot Farm, Shilbottle, Alnwick, Northumberland NE66 2HG Tel and Fax: 01665 575591

Top-quality accommodation with a choice of 17th Century farmhouse or Scandinavian lodges and cottages. Indoor pool, sauna, solarium, games room, riding, tennis court, trout pond and award-winning beaches within 3 miles. Castles and Hills close by. Open all year. Short Breaks Autumn/Winter. Comprehensive brochure.

3-5 keys up to Highly Commended

Comfortable cottage situated on the the A1 in the village of Warenford, 12 miles north of Alnwick. Four bedrooms (2 family/twin, 2 double), all with washbasins, central heating, tea/coffee. All rooms ground level with use of gardens and car park. Ideal base for exploring coast or countryside. Golf courses nearby. Pets welcome. Terms from £12 to £17; Evening Meal optional. ☎ Commended
Jan and David Thompson, The Cott, Belford NE70 7HZ (01668 213233)

LOVELY NORTHUMBERLAND – CORBRIDGE
Matthews, Hayes House, Newcastle Road, Corbridge NE45 5LP (01434 632010)

B&B – Spacious, attractive, stone-built Guest House set in seven acres of grounds. Single, Double, Twin,
Family Bedrooms: 2 with showers, all with tea-making facilities. Lounge, dining rooms. Open 12 months of the year.
B&B £16, children's reductions. **Stairlift for disabled.** Self catering - 3 Cottages, Flat, Caravan.
Awarded three Farm Holiday Guide Diplomas. Car Parking. Brochure/booking send SAE. ETB ☎

Taylor Burn, Ninebanks, Hexham, Northumberland NE47 8DE
Warm welcome and good food on quiet working hill farm with spectacular views. Large comfortable farmhouse with spacious bedrooms; guests' lounge and bathroom; beamed dining room. No Smoking. Guests can join in farm activities; excellent for walkers and country lovers.
Special weekend breaks; 10% reduction for weekly stays
Mrs Mavis Ostler   **Tel: 01434 345343**

DALES HOLIDAY COTTAGES offer a selection of superb, self catering, holiday properties in beautiful rural and coastal locations from Durham's Land of the Prince Bishops, through Cookson country to the Scottish Borders. Cosy cottages for 2, to a country house for 12, many open all year. For FREE Brochure contact Dales Holiday Cottages, Carleton Business Park, Skipton, North Yorkshire BD23 2DG (01756 799821 & 790919).

Alnmouth

Quiet little resort with wide sands. Alnwick with its impressive Norman Castle is 5 miles north west.

NORTHUMBRIA COAST AND COUNTRY COTTAGES LTD. Selected self catering holiday cottages. ETB Registered Agency. Discover beautiful unspoilt Northumberland in one of our personally selected properties — over 130 to choose from – pets welcome in many. Colour brochure: 01665 830783. [Pets £3.00 per week.]

G. A. SWEET, THE HOPE & ANCHOR HOTEL, 44 NORTHUMBERLAND STREET, ALNMOUTH, ALNWICK NE66 2RA (01665 830363). Three Crowns Approved. "Sam" our chihuahua says: "Great for pets, close to the seaside yet on the edge of Northumberland's magnificent countryside, you can't go wrong, come along!" [🐾]

SHEILA AND GORDON INKSTER, MARINE HOUSE PRIVATE HOTEL, 1 MARINE ROAD, ALNMOUTH NE66 2RW (01665 830349). Charming hotel in fine seafront location. Home cooking, cocktail bar, games room. Sea views. Children and pets very welcome. ETB 3 Crowns Commended. AA Selected QQQQ. RAC Highly Acclaimed. Runners up – Best Family Holiday 1984. Selected Guesthouses 1988. Northumberland TB Holiday Host award. [🐾]

MRS A. STANTON, MOUNT PLEASANT FARM, ALNMOUTH, ALNWICK NE66 3BY (01665 830215). Situated at top of hill on outskirts of village; convenient for castles and Holy Island. Self-contained annexe sleeps 2 adults and one child; open-plan kitchen, shower room. From £120 to £155 per week.

Alnwick

Situated in a historic area. Amongst the attractions are the Norman castle, Dunstanburgh Castle and Warkworth Castle. Nine-hole golf course, fishing, riding, tennis. Newcastle-upon-Tyne 34 miles, Berwick-upon-Tweed 30, Morpeth 19, Wooler 18.

VILLAGE FARM SELF CATERING, TOWN FOOT FARM, SHILBOTTLE, ALNWICK NE66 2HG (Tel/Fax: 01665 575591). Top quality accommodation with a choice of 17th century farmhouse or Scandinavian lodges and cottages. Indoor pool, games room, tennis court and award-winning beaches within 3 miles. Open all year. Short Breaks Autumn/Winter. Comprehensive brochure. [🐾]

Belford

Village 14 miles south east of Berwick-upon-Tweed

JAN AND DAVID THOMPSON, THE COTT, BELFORD NE70 7HZ (01668 213233). On A1 12 miles north of Alnwick. Two family/twin and two double bedrooms, all with washbasins, tea/coffee. Garden and car park. Ideal base for coast and countryside. Pets welcome.

Belsay

Village five miles north west of Ponteland. Belsay Hall is a Neo-Classical building resembling a Greek temple, has extensive gardens. 14th century castle.

MRS KATH FEARNS, BOUNDER HOUSE, BELSAY, NEWCASTLE-UPON-TYNE NE20 OJR (01661 881267). Stone farmhouse in beautiful Northumberland countryside, off A696 road. Two double (en suite), one family and one twin room from £18 p.p.p.n. Also self catering annexe cottage, sleeps 4. ETB 4 Keys Highly Commended. Full central heating. Linen supplied. From £120 per week. Telephone for brochure.

Berwick-upon-Tweed

Historic border town on River Tweed encompassed by massive 13th century walls. Three great bridges span the river on which sailing, canoeing, water ski-ing and fishing are popular pastimes. North Berwick 42 miles, Alnwick 29, Kelso 23, Wooler 17, Coldstream 14.

MRS M. J. MARTIN, FELKINGTON FARM, BERWICK-UPON-TWEED TD15 2NR (01289 387220). Comfortable cottages - ideal base to explore the coast and Border country. Visit historic homes or tempting craft shops, walk in the Cheviots or fish the Tweed. Playground, games room, woodland walk. Children and pets welcome. 3 Keys Commended. Brochure available.

Corbridge

Small town on north bank of River Tyne, 3 miles east of Hexham. Nearby are remains of Roman military town of Corstopitum.

THE HAYES, NEWCASTLE ROAD, CORBRIDGE NE45 5LP (01434 632010). Superior flat for 4/5 and 3 ground floor cottages for 2/5 persons available all year. Colour TV. Also luxury 6-berth caravan. Children and pets welcome. All properties, except flat, suitable for disabled. For details send SAE (ref. FHG).[🐴]

Derwent Reservoir

3¹/₂ miles long, set in heather-covered moorland. Picnic tables; fishing permits available.

ANNA WARD, SHOTLEY BRIDGE, NEAR DERWENT RESERVOIR, CONSETT DH8 9TS (01207 255216). Accommodation is in the farmhouse cottage with central heating, washbasins in every room, bathroom, shower and toilet; outside washbasin and toilet. Lounge for guests with tea/coffee making facilities and TV. Meals are served if required in the farmhouse which is within a few yards. One Crown Approved. [Pets £1 per night].

Haltwhistle

Small market town about 1 mile south of Hadrian's Wall.

MRS CAROLINE CLAYTON, HOLE HOUSE, BLENKINSOPP, NEAR HALTWHISTLE NE49 0LQ (016977 47383). Labrador Nell thoroughly recommends Stable Cottage – luxurious stone byre with log burning stove. Excellent walking – Hadrian's Wall / North Pennines. ETB 4 Keys Highly Commended (and 4 Paws!).

Hexham

Market town on bank of River Tyne, with medieval priory church. Racecourse 2 miles, Newcastle upon Tyne 20 miles.

RYE HILL FARM, SLALEY, NEAR HEXHAM NE47 OAH (01434 673259). Pleasant family atmosphere in cosy farmhouse. Bed and Breakfast and optional Evening Meal. Bedrooms with TV and tea/coffee facilities. All en suite. Laundry facilities. Table licence. 3 Crowns Commended. [pw! Pets £1 per night.]

Ninebanks

Hamlet four miles south-west of Allendale.

MRS MAVIS OSTLER, TAYLOR BURN, NINEBANKS, HEXHAM NE47 8DE (01434 345343). Warm welcome and good food on quiet working hill farm. Large comfortable farmhouse with spacious bedrooms; guests' lounge and bathroom. No smoking. Join in farm activities. [pw! Pets £1 per night]

Rothbury

Market town on steep bank of River Coquet, 11 miles south-west of Alnwick.

TERRY AND JANET CLUBLEY, WHITTON FARMHOUSE HOTEL, ROTHBURY, MORPETH NE65 7RL (Tel/Fax: 01669 620811). Charming country hotel in open country with en suite rooms (TV and hospitality tray), licensed lounge. Country house style dinners served each evening in attractive dining room. Riding from hotel's stables. Fishing and golf nearby. 14 miles from spectacular beaches.

Warkworth

Village on River Coquet near North Sea Coast north-west of Amble with several interesting historic remains.

WARKWORTH HOUSE HOTEL, BRIDGE STREET, WARKWORTH NE65 OXB (01665 711276; Fax: 01665 713323). Set in heart of small village, ideal for dog walking. Miles of open uncrowded beaches. Delicious evening meals. Phone for brochure. [🐾]

OXFORDSHIRE

OXFORDSHIRE   *Oxford, Thame*

BRAVALLA GUEST HOUSE

Homely Guest House one mile south-east of centre. Majority of rooms en suite with TV and beverage facilities. Parking. From £20 per person. (Pets £1 per night)

Mrs B. A. Downes, Bravalla Guest House, 242 Iffley Road, Oxford OX4 1SE

♥♥   **Telephone: 01865 241326/250511**   **AA RAC**

Crown and Cushion Hotel and Leisure Centre
High Street, Chipping Norton, Near Oxford OX7 5AD

♥♥♥♥
Commended

500-year old Coaching Inn, tastefully modernised to provide 40 excellent en suite bedrooms; some four-poster suites. "Old World" bar, log fires, real ale, good food, Egon Ronay Recommended. Indoor pool, multi -gym, solarium etc. Modern conference centre. Located in picturesque Cotswolds town midway between Oxford and Stratford-upon-Avon. Convenient London, Heathrow, M40. Blenheim Palace, Bourton-on-the-Water, Stow-on-the-Wold, Shakespeare Country all nearby. Pets welcome.

Price Busters start at £19.50; D,B&B at just £34.50

Tel: 01608 642533 Fax: 01608 642926. Colour brochure Freephone 0800 585251.

LITTLE ACRE
Tetsworth, Nr Thame, Oxford OX9 7AT Tel: 01844 281423

A charming secluded country house retreat with pretty landscaped garden and dining area overlooking spectacular waterfall, offering every comfort in 18 acres of private grounds. Single, twin and double rooms all with central heating, colour TV, tea/coffee making facilities, some en suite. A perfect place to relax and enjoy the local countryside in a quiet location. Pets allowed in bedrooms. Value for money from just £13 per night.

Oxford

Ancient university city on the Thames, here known as the Isis. Apart from the colleges there are many fine buildings, particularly churches and inns. Eights Week is a well-known river spectacle held at the end of May. Numerous entertainment and sporting facilities. London 56 miles, Stratford-upon-Avon 39, Windsor 39, Henley-on-Thames 24, Banbury 23, Chipping Norton 20, Burford 19.

MRS B. A. DOWNES, BRAVALLA GUEST HOUSE, 242 IFFLEY ROAD, OXFORD OX4 1SE (01865 241326 or 250511). Homely Guest House one mile south-east of centre. Majority of rooms en suite with TV and beverage facilities. Parking. From £20 per person. 2 Crowns, AA RAC Listed. [Pets £1 per night]

THE RANDOLPH HOTEL, BEAUMONT STREET, OXFORD OX1 2LN (01865 247481; Fax: 01865 791678). An impressive neo-Gothic hotel in the heart of the city centre. 109 bedrooms, 2 restaurants, Chapters Bar. 24hr room service. Car park. Excellent riverside walks; University parks 5 minutes. 5 Crowns, RAC ****.

CROWN & CUSHION HOTEL AND LEISURE CENTRE, HIGH STREET, CHIPPING NORTON, NEAR OXFORD OX7 5AD (01608 642533; Fax: 01608 642926; Colour Brochure Freephone 0800 585251). 500-year-old coaching inn tastefully modernised. En suite bedrooms; some four-posters. Old World bar; indoor pool, solarium etc. Convenient Stratford, Oxford, London, Shakespeare Country. Price Busters from £19.50.

Stanton Harcourt

Delightful village with thatched cottages spread out along winding country road. Parts of ruined manor date back to 12th century.

MRS MARGARET CLIFTON, STADDLE STONES, LINCH HILL, STANTON HARCOURT OX8 1BB (01865 882256). A welcome for dogs at the Chalet Bungalow with four acres of grounds adjoining bridle paths. Bedrooms with en suite or private bathrooms. Disabled persons and children welcome. Bed and Breakfast from £16.50.

Thame

Town on River Thame 9 miles south west of Aylesbury. Airport at Haddenham.

MS. JULIA TANNER, LITTLE ACRE, TETSWORTH, NEAR THAME OX9 7AT (01844 281423). A charming secluded country house retreat offering every comfort in 20 acres of private grounds nestling under Chilterns escarpment. Single Twin/ Double rooms, majority en suite, colour TV, beverage facilities. A perfect place to relax and enjoy the abundance of footpaths on our doorstep . . . your dog will love it. ONLY 3 mins. Junction 6 M40. [🐕– Bring dog basket with you. ⌂]

Woodstock

Old town 8 miles north-west of Oxford. Home to Oxford City and County Museum.

MRS B. JONES, GORSELANDS FARMHOUSE AUBERGE, NEAR LONG HANBOROUGH, WOODSTOCK OX8 6PU (01993 881895; Fax: 01993 882799). Old Cotswold Stone House with flagstone floors and oak beams situated in peaceful countryside. Convenient for many attractions. B&B from £17 50. En suite rooms. Evening Meals from £10.95. 2 Crowns, RAC Listed. [🐕].

SHROPSHIRE

SHROPSHIRE   *Church Stretton*

The Travellers Rest Inn, Upper Affcot (A49)
Church Stretton SY6 6RL
Telephone: 01694 781275; Fax: 01694 781555

The Travellers Rest Inn is situated on the main A49 between Church Stretton and Craven Arms. You are assured of a good welcome, good food and good accommodation, and good old fashioned service, plus a smile at no extra charge. The accommodation is fully centrally heated with four en suite rooms on the ground floor and six bedrooms on the first floor, all with washbasins and shaver points. Colour TVs in all rooms, together with tea/coffee making facilities. Children and pets welcome.

Bed and Breakfast from £22 to £30; Evening Meal from £5.

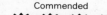

Bishop's Castle

*Small town in hills on Welsh border eight miles north west of Craven Arms. Scanty remains of
12th century castle.*

MRS P. ALLBUARY, THE GREEN FARM, WENTNOR, BISHOP'S CASTLE SY9 5EF
(01588 650394). En suite annexe sleeps two–four. B&B from £15.50. Two inns
within 400 yards. Ideal walking country; riding available (extra). [🐾 pw!]

Church Stretton

Delightful little town and inland resort in lee of Shropshire Hills. Walking and riding country. Facilities for tennis, bowls, gliding and golf. Knighton 22 miles, Bridgnorth 19, Ludlow 15, Shrewsbury 12.

THE LONGMYND HOTEL, CHURCH STRETTON SY6 6AG (01694 722244/8; Fax: 01694 722718). Situated overlooking the beautiful Welsh border this hotel has a subtle mixture of superb modern and period rooms equipped with every refinement demanded by the discerning guest of today. 4 Crowns.

BELVEDERE GUEST HOUSE, BURWAY ROAD, CHURCH STRETTON SY6 6DP (01694 722232). On slopes of Long Mynd, 200 yards from Church Stretton and 6000 acres of National Trust hill country. Central heating. Teasmaids. Two guest lounges. ETB 3 Crowns Commended. AA QQQQ, RAC Acclaimed. Bed and Breakfast £22. Evening Meal £9.50. Reductions children, party, weekly. [🐾]

MYND HOUSE HOTEL, LITTLE STRETTON, CHURCH STRETTON SY6 6RB (01694 722212). Distinguished 8 bedroomed hotel and restaurant in rural hamlet at base of NT Long Mynd. Iron Bridge 15 miles. Award winning food and wine. Dogs free but contribution to Roden NCDL Rescue Centre appreciated. [🐾]

F. & M. ALLISON, TRAVELLERS REST INN, UPPER AFFCOT, NEAR CHURCH STRETTON SY6 6RL (01694 781275; Fax: 01694 781555). RAC Inn. Fully licensed inn on the main A49. Good base for touring. Ample parking space. Children and dogs welcome. 2 Crowns Approved. SAE or phone for further details. [🐾]

Cleobury Mortimer

Charming little town of timbered and Georgian houses, with very little building since the mid-nineteenth century, except Gilbert Scott's restoration of the church. There is fishing on the River Rea, and walking in the Wyre Forest or on Clee Hill, which rises to over 1,600 ft. Ludlow 10 miles.

THE REDFERN HOTEL, CLEOBURY MORTIMER DY14 8AA (01299 270395). Eleven well-equipped bedrooms, all with private facilities and some on the ground floor. Award-winning restaurant noted for fine food. ETB 4 Crowns Commended. No charge for pets to PETS WELCOME! readers. [🐾]

Craven Arms

Attractive little town with some interesting old half-timbered houses. Weekly cattle and sheep sales. Nearby is imposing Stokesay Castle (13th cent.) open regularly. Bridgnorth 21 miles, Shrewsbury 20, Ludlow 8.

SUE TRUEMAN'S "B&B AT THE BELL", LEAMOOR COMMON, CRAVEN ARMS SY7 8DN (01694 781231; Fax: 01694 781461). Guests say "home from home". Quality accommodation in 121/2 acres of natural beauty. Kids, pets, horses welcome. Exquisite countryside, historic towns. ETB Listed. From £15.00. [🐾]

MRS J. WILLIAMS, HURST HILL FARM, CLUN, CRAVEN ARMS SY7 OJA (01588 640224). Comfortable riverside farmhouse. Woodlands, riding ponies. Convenient for Offa's Dyke, Stiperstones. Bed and Breakfast from £17, Dinner, Bed and Breakfast from £24. 2 Crowns Commended. AA Recommended. Winner "Shropshire Breakfast Challenge".

Ironbridge

Situated on side of River Severn gorge and named after bridge spanning it which was cast in 1773 and still used by pedestrians.

VIRGINIA AND ROBERT EVANS, CHURCH FARM, ROWTON, WELLINGTON, TELFORD TF6 6QY (01952 770381). Experience a true country holiday on our working farm in scenic Shropshire. En suite rooms, tea/coffee making, four-poster bed. 2 Crowns. Also 2 self-catering cottages and 2 caravans for hire. 3 Keys Commended. Ideal touring area. [🐕]

Ludlow

Lovely and historic town on Rivers Teme and Corve with numerous old half-timbered houses and inns. Impressive Norman castle; river and woodland walks. Golf, tennis, bowls, steeplechase course. Worcester 29 miles, Shrewsbury 27, Hereford 24, Bridgnorth 19, Church Stretton 16.

MAURICE & GILLIAN PHILLIPS, THE CECIL GUEST HOUSE, SHEET ROAD, LUDLOW SY8 1LR (Tel and Fax: 01584 872442). Comfortable Guest House offers a relaxing atmosphere, freshly cooked food and spotlessly clean surroundings. Some en suite. All rooms have colour TV and tea makers. Licensed. Parking. 10% discount for five nights or more. ETB Two Crowns Commended, AA QQQ, RAC Acclaimed. [🐕].

Oswestry

Borderland Market town. Many old castles and fortifications including 13th century Chirk Castle, Whittington Castle, Oswestry's huge Iron Age hill fort, Offa's Dyke. Wales' highest waterfall close by. Llangollen 10 miles, Shrewsbury 16, Vyrnwy 18, Bala Lake 25.

PEN-Y-DYFFRYN COUNTRY HOUSE HOTEL, NEAR RHYDYCROESAU, OSWESTRY SY10 7DT (Tel. & Fax: 01691 653700). Georgian Rectory set in Shropshire/ Welsh Hills. Seven en suite bedrooms, colour TV. Licensed Restaurant. 5-acre grounds. Very quiet and relaxed. Dinner, Bed and Breakfast from £43.00 per person. Pets free. 3 Crowns Highly Commended. [🐕 pw!]

Shrewsbury

Fine Tudor Town with many beautiful black and white timber buildings, Abbey and Castle. Riverside walks, Quarry Park and Dingle flower garden. 39 miles north-west of Birmingham.

RYTON FARM HOLIDAY COTTAGES, RYTON, DORRINGTON, SHREWSBURY SY5 7LY (01743 718449). Traditional country cottage sleeping 6 or converted barn for 2 or 4 persons. Well-equipped kitchens, colour TV, fitted carpets, towels and linen. Pets especially welcome. 3 Keys Commended. [Pets £17 per week. pw!]

Stiperstones

Situated beneath Stiperstones Ridge (1700 feet), and near to scenic Shropshire Hills and a nature reserve.

ROY AND SYLVIA ANDERSON, TANKERVILLE LODGE, STIPERSTONES, MINSTERLEY, SHREWSBURY SY5 0NB (01743 791401). Country Guest House next to a nature reserve in the dramatic Shropshire hills. Cats and small/medium dogs accepted and may share owners' rooms. Pleasant walks. B&B from £15.95. 1 Crown Commended. AA Recommended QQ. [Pets £1 per night.]

Telford

New town (1963). Ten miles east of Shrewsbury. Includes the south bank of the River Severn above and below Ironbridge, site of the world's first iron bridge (1777).

BOURTON MANOR, BOURTON, MUCH WENLOCK TF13 6QE(01746 785531). Set in small hamlet nestling close to Wenlock Edge. Single, twin and double luxury bedrooms each with radio, colour TV etc. Ideal for walking and riding; Telford, Shrewsbury nearby. Dogs welcome. [pw! Pets £2 per night]

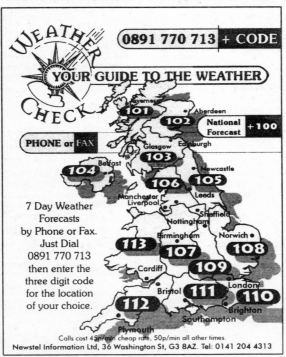

NOTE

All the information in this book is given in good faith in the belief that it is correct. However, the publishers cannot guarantee the facts given in these pages, neither are they responsible for changes in policy, ownership or terms that may take place after the date of going to press. Readers should always satisfy themselves that the facilities they require are available and that the terms, if quoted, still apply.

PETS STAY FREE

THE EXMOOR WHITE HORSE INN

Exford,
West Somerset
TA24 7PY

Tel: 01643 831229
Fax: 01643 831246

♛ ♛ ♛

Managers: Peter and Linda Hendrie

INN: Situated in the delightful Exmoor village of Exford, overlooking the River Exe and surrounded by high moorland on almost every side, this family-run 16th Century Inn is an ideal spot for that well earned break. The public rooms are full of character with beams, log fires (Oct-April) and Exmoor stone throughout. There are 18 bedrooms, all of which have en suite facilities, colour TV, teamaking and central heating, and are furnished in keeping with the character of the Inn.

RESTAURANT: A variety of dishes to excite the palate served, including lobster, seafood platters, local venison & fish, whilst the bar has an extensive snack menu, with home made pies, local dishes and is renowned for its carvery. The menus change regularly with daily specials available.

NEARBY: Excellent walking country with a selection of circular walks from the Inn, plus many other local walks available. The village is also noted for its excellent riding facilities. Hunting, fishing & shooting can be arranged upon request. Open all year. Mini Breaks a speciality.

★ Remember that your pets are free providing that
you return this advert with your booking ★

THE PERFECT RETREAT FOR YOU AND YOUR DOG

241

CLASSIC COTTAGES (25), HELSTON, CORNWALL (24 HOUR DIAL-A-BROCHURE 01326 565555). Choose your cottage from 300 of the finest coastal and country cottages throughout the West Country. [Pets £9 weekly.]

POWELLS COTTAGE HOLIDAYS. Your choice of Cottage in Cornwall, Devon, Somerset, Cotswolds, Wye Valley, Gower and Pembrokeshire in our full colour brochure. [Pets £10 per week.] FREEPHONE 0800 378771 or apply: 61 High Street, Saundersfoot, Pembrokeshire SA69 9EJ or (24hrs) 01834 813232.

Axbridge

Pleasant market town at foot of Mendips. Interesting Tudor houses. Bath 27 miles, Bristol 17, Bridgwater 16, Glastonbury 14, Wells 10, Cheddar 3.

L. F. DIMMOCK, MANOR FARM, CROSS, AXBRIDGE BS26 2ED (01934 732577). A working beef and sheep farm of 250 acres adjoining the beautiful Mendip Hills. Children and pets welcome. All rooms with tea/coffee making. B&B from £12.50 pp pn.

Bath

The best-preserved Georgian city in Britain, Bath has been famous since Roman times for its mineral springs. It is a noted centre for music and the arts, with a wide range of leisure facilities.

THE OLD MALT HOUSE HOTEL, RADFORD, TIMSBURY, NEAR BATH BA3 1QF (01761 470106). A relaxing, comfortable hotel, in beautiful surroundings between Bath and Wells. Gardens, lawns. All bedrooms en suite. Restaurant and bar meals. 3 Crowns Commended. [Pets £1 per night.]

TOWN AND COUNTRY COTTAGES. Wide choice of quality cottages in Bath, Cotswolds, Somerset and Herefordshire. Over 50 welcome pets. Personal attention and free brochure. APPLY – 22 CHARMOUTH ROAD, NEWBRIDGE, BATH BA1 3LJ (01225 481764). [🐾]

MR & MRS G. E. HUNT, THORNWOOD HOUSE, THE LEY, BOX, WILTSHIRE SN13 8EW (01225 743162). Delightful village location with country walks on doorstep, the Georgian city of Bath just 6 miles away and many more West Country attractions nearby. Small comfortable self catering flat with all facilities including its own plant-filled patio. Sleeps 2/4. [🐾]

DAVID & JACKIE BISHOP, TOGHILL HOUSE FARM, FREEZING HILL, WICK, NEAR BATH BS15 5RT (01225 891261; Fax: 01225 892128). Luxury barn conversions on working farm 3 miles north of Bath. Each equipped to very high standard, bed linen provided. Also en suite B&B accommodation in 17th century farmhouse. [pw! Pets £7 per week]

Brean

Coastal village with extensive sands. To the north is the promontory of Brean Down. Weston super-Mare 9 miles, Burnham-on-Sea 5.

EMBELLE HOLIDAY PARK, COAST ROAD, BREAN, BURNHAM-ON-SEA TA8 2QZ (Freephone 0500 400 412). Chalets and holiday homes on quiet park. Direct access to beach. Full facilities. Colour television. Pets welcome. Near entertainments. Club and restaurant. Free brochure. [Pets £15.00 per week].

WESTWARD RISE HOLIDAY PARK, SOUTH ROAD, BREAN, NEAR BURNHAM ON-SEA TA8 2RD (01278 751310). All-electric chalet bungalows on small site adjoining beach. 2 double bedrooms, shower, toilet. Colour TV, fridge, cooker. Shops, restaurants, clubs nearby. SAE for brochure. [Pets £10 per week.]

Bridgwater

Small port on River Parrett, 9 miles north east of Taunton.

MRS. N. THOMPSON, PLAINSFIELD COURT, PLAINSFIELD, OVER STOWEY, BRIDGWATER TA5 1HH (01278 671292; Fax: 01278 671687). B&B and Self Catering in Farmhouse and Granary dating from 15th century, set in the Quantocks. Magnificent riding country. Stabling, turn out. Dogs welcome.

Cheddar

Picturesque little town in the Mendips, famous for its Gorge and unique caves. Cheese-making is a speciality. Good touring centre. Bath 24 miles, Burnham-on-sea 13, Weston-super-Mare 11.

BROADWAY HOUSE HOLIDAY TOURING CARAVAN AND CAMPING PARK, CHEDDAR BS27 3DB (01934 742610; Fax: 01934 744950). Family business specialising in family holidays. Activities include archery, abseiling and shooting. Mountain bike/tandem hire; swimming pool. Pets welcome in some of our holiday homes. Very welcome on camping park.

MARION SHERRINGTON & JILL GREEN, WINSTON MANOR HOTEL, CHURCHILL BS19 5NL (01934 852348). Pets and well-trained owners most welcome! Secluded walled garden for emergency night-time outings! Close to Wells, Glastonbury, Bath and Cheddar. Excellent walking country. Our guests tell us the food is excellent too! Special break rates available. [🐾]

Churchill

Village convenient for the Mendips, the sea and the historic city of Bristol. Associations with the Marlborough family. Bristol 13 miles.

LYNCOMBE LODGE, CHURCHILL BS19 5PQ (01934 852335; Fax: 01934 853314). Set in an area of outstanding natural beauty. A warm welcome assured for you and your pet. Fabulous cooking, most rooms en suite. A multitude of footpaths to explore. [Pets £15 per week]

Crewkerne

Market town on a sheltered slope of the Blackdown Hills 8 miles west of Yeovil.

MRS G. SWANN, BROADVIEW GARDENS, 43 EAST STREET, CREWKERNE TA18 7AG (01460 73424). Unusual Colonial bungalow built in an era of quality. En suite rooms with colour TV, C/H, Tea/Fac. Non-Smoking. Bed and Breakfast £23-£27. [🐾 pw!]

Dulverton

Attractively set between Exmoor and Brendon Hills. Good fishing. In vicinity, prehistoric Tarr Steps (A.M and N.T.). Exeter 27 miles, Taunton 26, Lynton 23, Minehead 19, Tiverton 13.

EXMOOR – LOWER CHILCOTT FARM, DULVERTON TA22 9OQ (01398 323439). Self catering character cottages. Walks, adjacent riding school. Children, pets and mothers-in-law welcome. Sleep 2–9. [🐾]

MRS BRENDA COATES, CHAPPLE FARM, BURY, DULVERTON TA4 2DP (01398 331364). Exmoor working farm with 16th century oak-beamed farmhouse. Three bedrooms with washbasins, tea/coffee making. Traditional farmhouse breakfasts and evening meals. Children and dogs welcome. [🐕]

ABIGAIL HUMPHREY, HIGHERCOMBE FARM, DULVERTON TA22 9PT (01398 323616). A 450 acre farm on Exmoor in peaceful setting. All rooms en suite. Log fires, farmhouse cooking and much more. ETB 1 Crown Commended. Also private self-catering wing of farmhouse. 4 Keys Commended. [🐕]

TARR STEPS HOTEL, HAWKRIDGE, NEAR DULVERTON TA22 9PY (01643 851293). Delightful Country House Hotel nestling against the wooded slopes of the River Barle. A paradise for walking, riding, fishing. Dogs, horses and children welcome! Superb cuisine, very comfortable en suite rooms. [Pets £2.00 nightly, 🏠]

Dunster

Pretty village with interesting features, including Yarn Market, imposing 14th century Castle. Priory Church and old houses and cottages. Minehead 3 miles.

THE YARN MARKET HOTEL, HIGH STREET, DUNSTER TA24 6SF (01643 821425; Fax: 01643 821475). An ideal location for walking and exploring Exmoor. Family-run hotel with a friendly, relaxed atmosphere, home cooking, en suite rooms with colour TV and tea making facilities. Non-smoking preferred. [pw! 🐕]

Exford

Fine touring centre for Exmoor and North Devon, on River Exe. Dulverton 10 miles.

BRYAN & JANE JACKSON, HUNTERS MOON, EXFORD, NEAR MINEHEAD TA24 7PP (01643 831695). Cosy bungalow smallholding in the heart of Exmoor. Good food (optional Evening Meal), glorious views, friendly atmosphere. Pets welcome, free stabling available. Open all year. [🐕]

EXMOOR HOUSE HOTEL, CHAPEL STREET, EXFORD TA24 7PY (01643 831304). Situated in picturesque village (middle of Exmoor). Comfortable accommodation, en suite rooms with colour TV and beverage facilities. B&B from £18.00. [🐕]

Exmoor

One of the country's smaller National Parks, with many beautiful sights and places of interest. Much of the moor remains untouched by modern life.

THE ROYAL OAK INN, WITHYPOOL, EXMOOR NATIONAL PARK TA24 7QP (01643 831506/7; Fax: 01643 831659). The Royal Oak Inn has been renowned for its comfort and food for approximately three centuries and has many awards for the latter. It is an ideal base for riding, fishing or simply to walk and enjoy the calm and beauty of the moors. [🐕 🏠]

THE SHIP INN, HIGH STREET, PORLOCK TA24 8QT (01643 862507). Comfortable accommodation in famous old inn. Excellent English cooking, bar serving real ale and snacks. Car parking. [🐶]

THE CROWN HOTEL, EXFORD TA24 7PP (01643 831554/5; Fax: 01643 831665). Situated in rural England. All bedrooms with bath, colour television, hairdryer. Excellent cuisine and fine wines. Bargain Breaks. Superb dog holiday country. [pw! 🏠]

CUTTHORNE, LUCKWELL BRIDGE, WHEDDON CROSS TA24 7EW (01643 831255). Enjoy a touch of sheer luxury at our 14th century country house in glorious Exmoor. En suite facilities, log fires, candlelit dinners. Children's high teas. Stabling. 3 Crowns Highly Commended. [🐶 in B&B; £11.75 per week S/C]

JANE & BARRY STYLES, WINTERSHEAD FARM, SIMONSBATH TA24 7LF (01643 831222; Fax: 01643 831628). Four tastefully furnished and well equipped cottages plus small flat situated in the midst of beautiful Exmoor. Pets welcome, stables and grazing available. Colour brochure on request. [Dogs £12 per week, horses £7.]

Draydon Cottages, Exmoor. 7 attractive s/c barn conversion cottages situated 2 miles north-west of Dulverton. Well equipped and maintained with heating throughout. Excellent base for exploring Exmoor. KATHARINE HARRIS, 6 CRABB LANE, ALPHINGTON, EXETER, DEVON EX2 9JD (01392 433524). [Dogs £10.50 weekly.]

THE EXMOOR WHITE HORSE INN, EXFORD TA24 7PY (01643 831229; Fax: 01643 831246). Family-run 17th century inn situated in charming Exmoor village. 18 bedrooms all en suite, with colour TV and tea making. Fully licensed. Restaurant with varied menu. [🐶]

MISSES N.&J. FORD, CASTLE FARM, EXFORD, MINEHEAD TA24 7NL (01643 831292). Heart of Exmoor. Peaceful and secluded self-catering farmhouse wing situated on upper reaches of the Exe Valley. Walkers' paradise. £120-£250 per week. Well-behaved dogs welcome free of charge. Stabling. Brochure on request, stamp appreciated. [🐶]

HIGHER TOWN, DULVERTON, EXMOOR TA22 9RX. (01398 341272). Bungalow sleeps 6. Bedding, linen and electricity provided. Separate toilet and bathroom with shower. Colour TV, open fire. Kitchen has electric cooker, fridge/freezer and washer/dryer. Centrally heated and double glazed.

MRS P. EDWARDS, WESTERMILL FARM, EXFORD TA24 7NJ (01643 831238; Fax: 01643 831660). Delightful Scandinavian pine log Cottages and a Cottage attached to farmhouse. Campsite for Tents/Dormobiles. Information centre and small shop. One/Three Keys Commended. 500 acre farm, varied way-marked walks.

Hillfarrance

4 miles west of Taunton with its 12th century castle. Situated in valley of Taunton Deane, famed for its apples and cider.

ANCHOR COTTAGES, THE ANCHOR INN, HILLFARRANCE, TAUNTON TA4 1AW (01823 461334). Three self-catering cottages, each sleeps up to 5. Full central heating, colour TV; tastefully furnished to high standard. Private gardens and ample parking. Anchor Inn renowned for good food. [🐾]

Ilminster

Market town founded in Saxon times, with charming Georgian houses and a 15th century minster.

MRS GRACE BOND, GRADEN, PEASMARSH, NEAR DONYATT, ILMINSTER TA19 OSG (01460 52371). Comfortable home in peaceful location within easy reach M5. Multi-screen cinema, ten-pin bowling, Cricket St Thomas (Crinkley Bottom), coast just 20 miles. Many local attractions, pubs serving good food. Bed and full English Breakfast from £15.00. Weekly terms available.

Minehead

Neat and stylish resort on Bristol Channel under the shelter of wooded North Hill. Small harbour, sandy bathing beach. Attractive gardens, golf course and good facilities for tennis, bowls and horse riding. Within easy reach of the beauties of Exmoor.

16th Century Cottage for two and Cottage with inglenook and beamed ceilings for 7/9. Fully furnished. Pets welcome. APPLY – MR T. STONE, TROYTES FARM STEAD, TIVINGTON TA24 5RP (01643 704531). [🐾]

MERTON HOTEL, WESTERN LANE, THE PARKS, MINEHEAD TA24 8BZ (01643 702375). Pets and their families most welcome at this small, family hotel. 10 en suite rooms. Near town, sea front half a mile. Home cooking. [🐾]

Porlock

Most attractive village beneath the tree-clad slopes of Exmoor. Picturesque cottages, old Ship Inn and interesting church). Good bathing from pebble beach at delightful Porlock Weir (2 miles). Several picture-book villages nearby. Lynton 11 miles, Minehead 6.

MRS CHRISTINE FITZGERALD, "SEAPOINT", UPWAY, PORLOCK TA24 8QE (01643 862289). Spacious Edwardian house overlooking Porlock Bay. Open log fires. Coastal/moorland walks. Excellent traditional or vegetarian food. All bedrooms en suite with tea/coffee facilities. 2 Crowns. [🐾]

CASTLE HOTEL, PORLOCK TA24 8PY (01643 862504). Fully licensed, family-run hotel in centre of lovely Exmoor village. 11 en suite bedrooms, all with colour TV. Bar snacks and meals. Well-behaved children and pets welcome. 4 Crowns.

MR & MRS A. D. HARDICK, PORLOCK CARAVAN PARK, HIGHBANKS, PORLOCK, NEAR MINEHEAD TA24 8NS (01643 862269) Well-equipped Caravans for hire, with main drains and water, electric light, TV, launderette. Dogs welcome. Touring caravans, Dormobiles and tents welcome. Write or phone for a brochure.

MR & MRS ROBINSON, THE SHIP INN, HIGH STREET, PORLOCK TA24 8QT (01643 862507). Thatched 13th cent. Inn with walking distance of sea and moor. 11 bedrooms, most en suite. Local produce supplements traditional English cooking in candlelit restaurant. [🐾]

Shipham

Pleasant village on edge of Mendip Hills, Cheddar 31/2 miles, Axbridge 3.

PENSCOT FARMHOUSE HOTEL, SHIPHAM, WINSCOMBE BS25 1PW (01934 842659). Take a break in Somerset with your pet! Quiet, country Hotel near Cheddar. Large attractive garden. Good farmhouse food. Log fires in winter. [🐾]

Somerton

Small market town .with medieval market place.

SARAH VINCENT, LAVENDER COTTAGE, SUTTON ROAD, SOMERTON TA11 6QL (01458 272501). Bed and Breakfast. Garden, TV room. Ideal holiday venue – walking, fishing, golf, beach. National Trust properties, Theme Park, Clark's Village, museums. Dogs welcome.

Taunton

County town, rich in historical associations. Good touring centre. Many sporting attractions. Notable links with the past include the Castle, part of which is believed to be 12th century. Bristol 43 miles, Exeter 32, Weston-super-Mare 29.

MR & MRS D.A. SMALL, ASHE FARM CARAVAN AND CAMPING SITE, THORNFALCON, TAUNTON TA3 5NW (01823 442567; Fax: 01823 443372). Quiet farm site with 30 touring pitches and two holiday caravans. Showers, toilet, electric hook-ups, shop, games room, tennis court. Ideal for touring coast, Exmoor and Somerset Levels. Fully equipped caravans sleep 6. Open April to October. Pets welcome. AA 3 Pennants.

Watchet

Small port and resort with rocks and sands. Good centre for Exmoor and the Quantocks. Bathing, boating, fishing, rambling. Tiverton 24 miles, Bridgwater 19, Taunton 17, Dunster 6.

LORNA DOONE CARAVAN PARK, WATCHET TA23 0JB (01984 631206). Small quiet park with beautiful views of the coastline and Quantock Hills. Fully equipped luxury caravans. Rose Award Park. [Pets £12 weekly]

SUNNY BANK HOLIDAY CARAVANS, DONIFORD, WATCHET TA23 0UD (01984 632237). Small picturesque family park on coast. All caravans with mains services. Colour TV. Showers. Heated swimming pool. Shop. Launderette. BHHPA 5 ticks. Also caravans for sale. Brochure. [Pets £14 per week.]

WEST BAY CARAVAN PARK, WATCHET TA23 OBJ (Tel/Fax: 01984 631261). Small, quiet park with panoramic sea views. Ideal for relaxing and touring Exmoor and Quantock Hills. Open March-October. ✓✓✓✓✓ Rose Award. Pets welcome. [Pets £12 weekly.]

Weston-Super-Mare

Popular resort on the Bristol Channel with a wide range of entertainments and leisure facilities. An ideal base for touring the West Country.

MR AND MRS C. G. THOMAS, ARDNAVE CARAVAN PARK, KEWSTOKE, WESTON-SUPER-MARE BS22 9XJ (01934 622319). Caravans 4-6 berth, de luxe with colour TV, electric lighting, showers and toilets, 2-3 bedrooms. 4-Star two-bedroom caravans; all facilities, colour TV. Parking. Dogs allowed. Graded 4 ticks. [🐾 pw!]

BRAESIDE HOTEL, 2 VICTORIA PARK, WESTON-SUPER-MARE BS23 2HZ (Tel/Fax: 01934 626642). Delightful, family-run hotel, close to shops and sea front. All rooms en suite, colour TV, tea/coffee making. November to April THIRD NIGHT FREE. See display advertisement. [🐾]

Withypool

Delightful Exmoor village on River Barle. Dulverton 8 miles.

WESTERCLOSE COUNTRY HOUSE HOTEL AND RESTAURANT, WITHYPOOL, EXMOOR TA24 7QR (01643 831302; Fax: 01643 831307). Set in tranquillity of the National Park, ideal for a holiday with your horse and dog. Stabling and kennels available. 10 en suite bedrooms; excellent food and wines. 3 Crowns Highly Commended, AA** [Dogs free, stabling £5 per night per horse. 🏠]

Wootton Courtenay

Nestling in idyllic Exmoor countryside with fine views of Dunkery Beacon. Minehead 5 miles.

DUNKERY BEACON HOTEL, WOOTTON COURTENAY TA24 8RH (01643 841241). Country House Hotel with superb views. Fully en suite rooms, colour TV. Lots of lovely "walkies". Special autumn and spring breaks. Write or phone Kenneth or Daphne Midwood for details.[🐾]

MRS N. E. COBB, BURROW FARM, WOOTTON COURTENAY, NEAR MINEHEAD TA24 7UD (01643 841361). Thatched period farmhouse in glorious countryside, 5 miles from Minehead and the coast. Self catering – weekly lets in summer, long/short lets in winter. Games room; large sheltered garden. Ideal for walkers; fishing, riding and golf locally. Children and pets very welcome. From £120 to £380 per week. [🐾]

FHG PUBLICATIONS LIMITED publish a large range of well-known accommodation guides. We will be happy to send you details or you can use the order form at the back of this book.

STAFFORDSHIRE

Burton-upon-Trent

Historic brewing centre and Shire horse stables are included among 400 years of brewing heritage in Bass Museum.

LITTLE PARK HOLIDAY HOMES, TUTBURY, BURTON-ON-TRENT DE13 9JH (01283 812654). Barn conversion luxury chalets overlooking Dove Valley and Peak District next to medieval castle of Tutbury. Few minutes' walk to numerous shops, pubs, restaurants. [pw! 🐾].

SUFFOLK

Aldeburgh

Coastal town 6 miles south-east of Saxmundham. Medieval Moot Hall now on beach. Annual music festival at Snape Maltings.

WENTWORTH HOTEL, ALDEBURGH IP15 5BD (01728 452312). Country House Hotel overlooking the sea. Immediate access to the beach and walks. Two comfortable lounges with log fires and antique furniture. Refurbished bedrooms with all facilities and many with sea views. Restaurant specialises in fresh produce and sea food.

Bury St. Edmunds

Birthplace of Magna Carta retains its 12th century layout, boasting Norman Tower, Cathedral and Abbey Gate. This prosperous market town on the River Lark lies 28 miles east of Cambridge.

RAVENWOOD HALL COUNTRY HOUSE HOTEL AND RESTAURANT, ROUGHAM, BURY ST EDMUNDS IP30 9JA (01359 270345; Fax: 01359 270788). 16th century heavily beamed Tudor Hall set in seven acres of perfect dog walks. Beautifully furnished en suite bedrooms; renowned restaurant; relaxing inglenook fires. AA***. [pw! 🐕]

BRADFIELD HOUSE, BRADFIELD COMBUST, BURY ST EDMUNDS IP30 0LR (01284 386301; Fax: 01284 386177). Just off the A134. 17th century hotel surrounded by unspoilt countryside and historic villages. Two-acre garden, log fires, restaurant. Well decorated roms with all facilities. Well behaved dogs welcome.

Dunwich

Small village on coast, 4 miles south west of Southwold.

MRS ELIZABETH COLE, MIDDLEGATE COTTAGES, MIDDLEGATE BARN, DUNWICH IP17 3DW (01728 648741). Three cottages situated in quiet, private road 200 yards from the sea. All furnished and equipped to a high standard. Centrally heated; available all year. [🐕]

Hadleigh

Historic town on River Brett with several old buildings of interest including unusual 14th century church. Bury St Edmunds 20 miles, Harwich 20, Colchester 14, Sudbury 11, Ipswich 10.

EDGEHILL HOTEL, 2 HIGH STREET, HADLEIGH IP7 5AP. (01473 822458; Fax: 01473 823848) 16th-century property offering a warm welcome. Comfortable accommodation and good home-cooked food. Licensed. Pets welcome. SAE or telephone for details. ETB 3 Crowns Commended. [🐕]

Henstead

Village in tranquil countryside with the sea only 21/2 miles away. The Broads are nearby and there are local riding facilities. Beccles 6 miles, Lowestoft 6, Southwold 6.

MRS D.K. FARMILOE, HENSTEAD HALL, HENSTEAD, NEAR BECCLES NR34 7LD (01502 740371). Georgian Mansion standing in 12 acres including woodland. Dogs welcome, owners tolerated. Lounge; oak-panelled dining room. Bed and Breakfast only. Write for brochure. [🐕]

Kessingland

Little seaside place with expansive sandy beach, safe bathing, wildlife park, lake fishing. To the south is Benacre Broad, a beauty spot. Norwich 26 miles, Aldeburgh 23, Lowestoft 5.

Quality seaside Bungalows, all with colour television, refrigerator, parking, linen service. Children and pets welcome. Direct access to beach. APPLY—KNIGHTS HOLIDAY HOMES, 198 CHURCH ROAD, KESSINGLAND, SUFFOLK NR33 7SF (FREEPHONE 0800 269067). [Pets £19.50 per week.]

Sudbury

Birthplace of painter, Thomas Gainsborough, with a museum illustrating his career. Colchester 13 miles.

Situated in small, picturesque village within 15 miles of Sudbury, Newmarket Racecourse and historic Bury St Edmunds. Bungalow well equipped to accommodate 4 people. All facilities. Car essential, parking. Children and pets welcome. Terms from £51 to £102 per week. For further details send SAE to MRS M. WINCH, PLOUGH HOUSE, STANSFIELD, SUDBURY CO10 8LT (01284 789253).

SURREY

Lingfield

Village 4 miles north of East Grinstead.

STANTONS HALL FARM, BLINDLEY HEATH RH7 6LG (01342 832401). 18th century farmhouse. Ground floor en suite rooms, with own enclosed patio area and access straight onto 3 acre field, ideal for dog walks etc.

All the advertisers in PETS WELCOME! have an entry in the appropriate classified section and each classified entry may carry one or more of the following symbols:

🐾   This symbol indicates that pets are welcome free of charge.

£   The £ indicates that a charge is made for pets. We quote the amount where possible, either per night or per week.

pw!   This symbol shows that the establishment has some special provision for pets; perhaps an exercise facility or some special feeding or accommodation arrangements.

⌂   Indicates separate pets accommodation.

PLEASE NOTE that all the advertisers in PETS WELCOME! extend a welcome to pets and their owners but they may attach conditions. The interests of other guests have to be considered and it is usually assumed that pets will be well trained, obedient and under the control of their owner.

NOTE

All the information in this book is given in good faith in the belief that it is correct. However, the publishers cannot guarantee the facts given in these pages, neither are they responsible for changes in policy, ownership or terms that may take place after the date of going to press. Readers should always satisfy themselves that the facilities they require are available and that the terms, if quoted, still apply.

EAST SUSSEX

EAST SUSSEX *Arlington, Battle, Brighton*

FHG PUBLICATIONS LIMITED publish a large range of well-known accommodation guides. We will be happy to send you details or you can use the order form at the back of this book.

Chiddingly, East Sussex

Adorable, small, well-equipped cottage in grounds of Tudor Manor

- Full central heating
Two bedrooms • Colour TV
- Fridge/freezer, microwave, dishwasher, laundry facilities, telephone • Use of indoor heated swimming pool, sauna/jacuzzi, tennis and badminton court • Large safe garden

FROM £275 - £515 PER WEEK INCLUSIVE

PETS AND CHILDREN WELCOME

Breaks available £176 - £210   SEETB 4 Keys Commended

Apply: Eva Morris, "Pekes", 124 Elm Park Mansions, Park Walk, London SW10 0AR

Tel: 0171-352 8088 Fax: 0171-352 8125

Fairlight Cottage, Warren Road (via Coastguard Lane), Fairlight, East Sussex TN35 4AG
A warm welcome awaits you at our comfortable country house, delightfully situated alongside Hastings Country Park with cliff-top walks and magnificent coastal views. Bedrooms are tastefully furnished, with central heating, en suite facilities and tea/coffee trays. Large comfortable TV lounge; good home cooking served in the elegant dining room. Evening meals by prior arrangement and guests may bring their own wine. An ideal base for exploring the ancient towns of Rye, Winchelsea, Battle and Hastings. No smoking in the house. Ample parking space and use of garden. Pets always welcome. **Janet & Ray Adams (01424 812545)**

BEAUPORT PARK HOTEL

AA/RAC ★★★

A Georgian Country House Hotel set amid 33 acres of formal gardens and woodland. All rooms have private bath, satellite colour TV, trouser press, hairdryer and auto-dial telephone. Outdoor Swimming Pool, Tennis, Squash, Badminton, Outdoor Chess, French Boules, Croquet Lawn, Putting, Golf and Riding School. Own woodland walks. Special Country House Breaks available all year. Please telephone for Brochure and Tariff.

BEAUPORT PARK HOTEL
Battle Road, Hastings TN38 8EA
Tel: Hastings (01424) 851222

Readers are requested to mention this guidebook when seeking accommodation (and please enclose a stamped addressed envelope).

CLEAVERS LYNG

**16TH CENTURY COUNTRY HOTEL
CHURCH ROAD,HERSTMONCEUX,
EAST SUSSEX BN27 1QJ
TEL: (01323) 833131
FAX: (01323) 833617**

For excellent home cooking in traditional English style, comfort and informality, this small, family-run hotel in the heart of rural East Sussex is well recommended. Peacefully set in beautiful landscaped gardens extending to 1 ½ acres featuring an ornamental rockpool with waterfall. Adjacent to Herstmonceux Castle West Gate, the house dates from 1577 as its oak beams and inglenook fireplace bear witness. This is an ideal retreat for a quiet sojourn away from urban clamour. The castles at Pevensey, Scotney, Bodiam and Hever are all within easy reach, as are Battle Abbey, Kipling's House, Batemans, Michelham Priory and the seaside resorts of Eastbourne, Bexhill and Hastings. The bedrooms are fully en suite, and all have central heating and tea/coffee making facilities, some with separate sitting area with colour TV. On the ground floor there is an oak-beamed restaurant with a fully licensed bar, cosy residents' lounge with television, and an outer hall with telephone and cloakrooms. Cleavers Lyng does not have any single rooms, however at certain times of the year, we offer a reduced single occupancy rate for double/twin bedroom. At Cleavers Lyng we observe a strictly non-smoking policy in our Restaurant and T.V. Lounge. Smoking is permitted in the Lounge Bar. Amex, Visa and Mastercard accepted.

Pets welcome. Peace, tranquillity and a warm welcome await you.
Special Attraction: Badger Watch. Room Rate from £22.50 pp, sharing Double/Twin rooms.

POLHILLS Arlington, Polegate BN26 6SB (01323 870004)

Idyllically situated on shore of reservoir and edge of Sussex Downs within easy reach of the sea. Fully furnished period cottage (approached by own drive along the water's edge) available for self-catering holidays from April to October (inclusive). Fly fishing for trout can be arranged during season. Accommodation consists of two main bedrooms; tiled bathroom. Lounge with colour TV; large well-fitted kitchen with fridge freezer, electric cooker, microwave, washing machine; dining room with put-u-up settee; sun lounge. Central heating. Everything supplied except linen. Most rooms contain a wealth of oak beams. Children and pets welcome. Car essential. Ample parking. Shops two miles. Golf, hill climbing locally. Sea eight miles. Weekly terms from £165 to £210 (electricity included).

JEAKE'S HOUSE

**Mermaid Street, Rye, East Sussex TN31 7ET
Telephone: 01797 222828 Fax: 01797 222623**

Dating from 1689, this beautiful Listed Building stands in one of England's most famous streets. Oak-beamed and panelled bedrooms overlook the marsh to the sea. Brass, mahogany or four-poster beds with linen sheets and lace; honeymoon suite. En suite facilities, TV, radio, telephone. Residential licence. Traditional and vegetarian breakfast served. £20.50-£29.50 per person. *Access, Visa and Mastercard accepted.*

AA ♛♛♛♛♛ PREMIER SELECTED   RAC Highly Acclaimed   César Award
Good Hotel Guide   ETB ♚♚ Highly Commended

Arlington

Village in valley of River Cuckmere below the South Downs. Hailsham 3 miles.

MRS P. BONIFACE, LAKESIDE FARM, ARLINGTON, POLEGATE BN26 6SB (01323 870111). Situated on the edge of Arlington Reservoir. Eastbourne within 15 miles. Accommodation sleeps 4–6 with two double rooms, lounge, dining area, kitchen, bathroom. Open April to October. Weekly from £160. [🐾]

MRS J. HOBDEN, CHILVERBRIDGE FARM, ARLINGTON, POLEGATE BN26 6SB (01323 870349). Caravan on working farm. Double bed, bunk beds, double bed settee in lounge. H/C water, bath/shower, flush toilet. Colour TV. Between Brighton and Eastbourne. Terms £95-£120.

Battle

Site of the famous victory of William the Conqueror; remains of an abbey mark the spot where Harold fell.

LITTLE HEMINGFOLD HOTEL, TELHAM, BATTLE TN33 0TT (01424 774338). In the heart of 1066 Country, 40 acres of bliss for you and your pets. Farmhouse hotel, all facilities. Fishing, boating, swimming, tennis. Special Breaks all year. Discounts for children. FREE accommodation for pets. [🐾]

Brighton

Famous resort with shingle beach and sand at low tide. Varied entertainment and nightlife; excellent shops and restaurants. Portsmouth 48 miles, Hastings 37, Newhaven 9.

BEST OF BRIGHTON & SUSSEX COTTAGES has available a very good selection of houses, flats, apartments and cottages in Brighton and Hove as well as East and West Sussex areas. Town centre / seaside and countryside locations - many taking pets. (01273 308779; Fax: 01273 300266).

GEOFF & MARION BURGESS, DIANA HOUSE, 25 ST GEORGE'S TERRACE, BRIGHTON BN2 1JJ (01273 605797).100 yards seafront, close town, Lanes, marina and conference centre. All rooms with showers, colour TV, tea/coffee, CH, some en suite. [🐕]

KEMPTON HOUSE HOTEL, 33/34 MARINE PARADE, BRIGHTON BN2 1TR (01273 570248). Private seafront Hotel, relaxed and friendly atmosphere, overlooking beach and Pier. En suite rooms available, all modern facilities. Satellite TV. Choice of Breakfasts. Pets and children always welcome. [🐕]

Chiddingly

Charming village, 4 miles north-west of Hailsham. Off the A22 London-Eastbourne road.

Adorable, small, well-equipped cottage in grounds of Tudor Manor. Two bedrooms. Full central heating. Colour TV. Fridge/freezer, laundry facilities. Large safe garden. Use indoor heated swimming pool, sauna/jacuzzi and tennis. From £275 to £515 per week inclusive. 4 Keys Commended. Contact: EVA MORRIS, "PEKES", 124 ELM PARK MANSIONS, PARK WALK, LONDON SW10 OAR (0171–352 8088; Fax: 0171–352 8125). [2 dogs free, extra dog £5 (max. 4) pw!]

Fairlight

Village 3 miles east of Hastings.

JANET & RAY ADAMS, FAIRLIGHT COTTAGE, WARREN ROAD, FAIRLIGHT TN35 4AG (01424 812545). A warm welcome awaits you at our comfortable country house. Tasteful en suite bedrooms with central heating, tea/coffee. TV lounge and good home cooking. No smoking. Ample parking. [🐕]

Hastings

Seaside resort with a famous past — the ruins of William the Conqueror's castle lie above the Old Town. Many places of historic interest in the area, plus entertainments for all the family.

MRS VICKI SAADE, "COPPERBEECHES", 41 CHAPEL PARK ROAD, ST LEONARDS-ON-SEA, HASTINGS TN37 6JB (01424 714026). Lovely Victorian Guest House with friendly, relaxed atmosphere; pets most welcome. Off-road parking; close to Hastings Station. Good walks, ideal for touring 1066 Country. Rooms with colour TV, tea/coffee facilities and central heating £14-£17 per person. Sorry no smokers. ETB 2 Crowns [pw! 🐕].

BEAUPORT PARK HOTEL, BATTLE ROAD, HASTINGS TN38 8EA (01424 851222). Georgian country mansion in 33 acres. All rooms private bath, colour television, trouser press, hairdryer, telephone. Country house breaks available all year. [pw!]

MRS D. BEYNON, c/o HAVELOCK ACCOMMODATION SERVICE, CROSS WING, 72 ALL SAINTS STREET, HASTINGS (01424 436779; evenings and weekends 0181–399 9605). 15th century cottage. New fitted kitchen, colour TV. Sleeps 3. Just off sea front in Old Town and fishing quarter. Well-behaved pets welcome.[🐕]

Herstmonceux

Small village four miles north-east of Hailsham. Royal Observatory at Herstmonceux Castle.

CLEAVERS LYNG 16th-CENTURY COUNTRY HOTEL, CHURCH ROAD, HERSTMONCEUX BN27 1QJ (01323 833131; Fax: 01323 833617). Small family-run Hotel in heart of rural East Sussex. Bedrooms en suite with tea making. Oak-beamed restaurant, bar, residents' lounge. Pets welcome. [🐕]

Polegate

Quiet position, 5 miles from the popular seaside resort of Eastbourne. London 58 miles, Lewes 12.

MRS P. FIELD, 20 ST JOHN'S ROAD, POLEGATE BN26 5BP (01323 482691). Homely private house. Quiet location; large enclosed garden. Parking space. Ideally situated for walking on South Downs and Forestry Commission land. All rooms washbasins and tea coffee facilities. Bed and Breakfast. Pets very welcome. [pw!]

MR & MRS G. BURGESS, POLHILLS, ARLINGTON, POLEGATE BN26 6SB (01323 870004). Fully furnished period cottage available for self catering holidays from April to October (inclusive). Everything supplied except linen.Weekly terms from £165 to £210 (electricity included).

Rye

Picturesque hill town with steep cobbled streets. Many fine buildings of historic interest. Hastings 12 miles, Tunbridge Wells 28.

FIDDLER'S OAST, WATERMILL LANE, BECKLEY, NEAR RYE TN31 6SH (Tel/Fax: 01797 252394). Beautiful wooded setting near Rye and Kent border. Ideal for exploring 1066 country. All rooms en suite. Children, pets and well behaved adults welcome! SETB Listed Commended. [Pets £5 per week]

FLACKLEY ASH HOTEL, PEASMARSH, RYE TN31 6YH (01797 230651; Fax: 01797 230510). Georgian Country House Hotel in beautiful grounds. Indoor swimming pool and Leisure Centre. AA Rosette for our food. Visit Rye and the castles and gardens of East Sussex and Kent. ETB 4 Crowns Highly Commended. [Pets £5 per night.]

MRS D. AVERY, "THACKER", OLD BRICKYARD, RYE TN31 7EE (01797 225870). Quietly situated cottage for two overlooking countryside yet within strolling distance of town centre. Well furnished, fully equipped including linen. Enclosed garden. Dogs very welcome.

JEAKE'S HOUSE, MERMAID STREET, RYE TN31 7ET (01797 222828; Fax: 01797 222623). Dating from 1689, this Listed Building has oak-beamed and panelled bedrooms overlooking the marsh. En suite facilities, TV, radio, telephone. £20.50-£29.50 per person. AA QQQQQ. [🐾]

THE STRAND HOUSE, WINCHELSEA, NEAR RYE TN36 4JT (01797 226276; Fax: 01797 224806). Attractive 15th century house of character. All rooms en suite with colour TV and hot drinks tray. ETB 3 Crowns Commended. AA QQQQ Selected, RAC Acclaimed. [🐾]

Telscombe

Tranquil Downland hamlet close to South Downs Way. 4 miles south of Lewes and 2 miles from coast.

DUCK BARN HOLIDAYS, 51 SCHOOL ROAD, FIRLE, NEAR LEWES BN8 6LF (01273 858221). Beautiful converted Barn, sleeps 8/10; Coach House for 4/5; Cosy Cottage for 2/3. Central heating, woodburners. Exposed beams– pine furniture. Children, dogs and horses welcome. Brochure. [pw! £10 weekly.]

WEST SUSSEX

WEST SUSSEX   *Bognor Regis*

FREE and REDUCED RATE Holiday Visits! Don't miss our Readers' Offer Vouchers on pages 5 to 18

Cavendish Hotel

115 Marine Parade
Worthing BN11 3QG
Tel: 01903 236767
Fax: 01903 823840

The prime sea front location provides an ideal base for touring Sussex villages and the rolling South Downs. Dogs allowed on the beach 1st October until 30th April and on the beach half a mile away all year.
Nearby are Arundel, Chichester and Goodwood House; to the east is Brighton and the Royal Pavilion and the historic town of Lewes.

All rooms at the Cavendish are en suite, have colour television, direct-dial telephone and tea/coffee making facilities. The friendly bar is a popular rendezvous with the locals and offers real ale with a wide range of beers, lagers, wines and spirits.
£80 per person for any two nights Dinner, Bed & Breakfast.
No charge for dogs belonging to readers of Pets Welcome!

Bognor Regis

Renowned for its wide sands and safe bathing, Bognor is ideal for family holidays, with a pier, promenade, gardens and a variety of entertainments.

BLACK MILL HOUSE HOTEL, PRINCESS AVENUE, BOGNOR REGIS (01243 821945). Children and dogs most welcome. Situated in the quieter West End of town, near sea and Marine Gardens, West End shops and bus routes. Attractive cocktail bar. Games room, colour TV, private bathrooms, central heating throughout. Lift. Enclosed garden. Open all year. Mini-Breaks – 2 days D,B&B from £60 (October to March). Own car park. No service charge. Short summer breaks. [Pets £2 per night]

JOAN AND ROGER TANN, ALANCOURT HOTEL, MARINE DRIVE WEST, BOGNOR REGIS (Tel & Fax: 01243 864844). Fully licensed Hotel near Marine Park Gardens. All rooms colour TV, tea/coffee facilities, heating, many en suite. Friendly atmosphere. Children and pets welcome. Goodwood and Fontwell racecourses nearby. [🐕]

Eastergate

Village between the sea and South Downs. Fontwell Park steeplechase course is nearby. Bognor Regis 5 miles S.

WANDLEYS CARAVAN PARK, EASTERGATE PO20 6SE (01903 745831 evenings, weekends; 01243 543235 9am–5pm weekdays). Comfortable holiday caravans in tranquil little country park. All with internal WC and shower. Only 15 minutes from Sussex Downs, Bognor and Chichester. [🐕]

Pulborough

Popular fishing centre on the River Arun. Nearby South Downs Way makes it an ideal centre for walking. Arundel 8 miles.

THE BARN OWLS, LONDON ROAD, COLDWALTHAM, PULBOROUGH RH20 ILR (01798 872498). Small country Hotel specialising in gourmet breaks and holidays. 2 night breaks from £85. Bed and Breakfast (en suite) from £150 weekly. Gourmet Christmas and New Year breaks. Bed and Breakfast from £24 per night. Telephone for brochure. [pw! 🐕]

CHEQUERS HOTEL, PULBOROUGH RH20 IAD (01798 872486). Lovely Queen Anne house in village overlooking Arun Valley. Excellent food. Children and dogs welcome. AA and RAC 2 Star. ETB 4 Crowns Highly Commended. No charge for dogs belonging to readers of Pets Welcome! [pw! 🐕]

Worthing

Residential town and seaside resort with 5-mile seafront. Situated 10 miles west of Brighton.

CAVENDISH HOTEL, 115 MARINE PARADE, WORTHING BN11 3QG (01903 236767; Fax: 01903 823840). Ideal base for touring Sussex villages and the rolling South Downs. All rooms are en suite, have TV, direct-dial telephone and tea/coffee facilities. No charge for dogs belonging to readers of *Pets Welcome!*. [🐕]

WARWICKSHIRE

WARWICKSHIRE   *Stratford-Upon-Avon*

RAYFORD CARAVAN PARK
RIVERSIDE, TIDDINGTON ROAD,
STRATFORD-UPON-AVON CV37 7BE
Tel: (01789) 293964

PETS WELCOME. A HAPPY AND INTERESTING HOLIDAY FOR ALL

River
Launch
Service
to
Stratford

Situated within the town of Stratford-upon-Avon, on the banks of the river, Rayford Park is ideally placed for visiting all Shakespearean attractions and the beautiful Cotswolds. In Stratford itself there is everything you could wish for: shops, pubs, restaurants, swimming pool, sports centre, the Royal Shakespeare Theatre, and a generous helping of history and the Bard! The luxury 12ft wide Caravan Holiday Homes accommodate up to 6 persons in comfort. All have kitchen with full-size cooker, fridge; bathroom with shower/washbasin/WC; two bedrooms, one double-bedded and one with two single beds (cot sides available);double dinette/two single settees in lounge; electric fire, colour TV, carpeted throughout.Also available: TWO COTTAGES, "Sleepy Hollow" and "Kingfisher Cottage", all modern facilities, set on riverside. Private fishing. BROCHURE ON REQUEST.

Stratford-upon-Avon

Historic town famous as Shakespeare's birthplace and home. Many interesting old buildings; rebuilt Shakespeare Memorial Theatre. There is a steeplechase course here. London 91 miles, Birmingham 24, Warwick 8.

JANE WELDON, BRIDGE HOUSE, ALDERMINSTER, NEAR STRATFORD-UPON-AVON CV37 8NY (01789 450521; 0850 065856 mobile). Charming Georgian house convenient for Stratford and the Cotswolds. Some rooms private facilities; all have colour TV and tea/coffee facilities. Fully enclosed garden. Licensed. Bed and Breakfast £20-£24. [🛏 pw!]

MR R.F. EVERETT, NEWBOLD NURSERIES, NEWBOLD-ON-STOUR, STRATFORD-UPON-AVON CV37 8DP (01789 450285). Small farm and hydroponic tomato nursery close to Cotswolds, Stratford-upon-Avon, Warwick and Blenheim. Comfortable rooms with colour TV, tea/coffee. Local pub serves evening meals at budget prices. En suite available. Bed and Breakfast from £15. Children half price. [🛏]

MRS H. J. MELLOR, ARRANDALE, 208 EVESHAM ROAD, STRATFORD-UPON-AVON CV37 9AS (01789 267112). Guest House situated near River Avon, theatre, Shakespeare properties. Washbasins, tea making, TV, central heating, en suite available. Children, pets welcome. Parking. Bed and Breakfast £15-£17.50. Weekly terms £100-£115. Evening Meal £6. [🐾]

RAYFORD CARAVAN PARK, TIDDINGTON ROAD, STRATFORD-UPON-AVON (01789 293964). Luxury Caravans, sleep 6. Fully equipped kitchens, bathroom/shower/WC. Also two riverside Cottages, all modern facilities to first-class standards. Private fishing. On banks of River Avon. [Pets £12 weekly.]

Warwick

Town on the River Avon, 9 miles south-west of Coventry, with medieval castle and many fine old buildings.

WOODSIDE GUEST HOUSE, CLAVERDON, NEAR WARWICK CV35 8PJ (01926 842446). A peaceful family guest house in 22 acres of own gardens and woodland. Lovely views, walks, log fires. Happy to welcome four-legged guests. ETB One Crown. Brochure available. Special Autumn Breaks.

MR & MRS D. CLAPP, THE CROFT, HASELEY KNOB, WARWICK CV35 7NL (Tel & Fax: 01926 484447). Smallholding with a friendly, family atmosphere and situated in picturesque rural surroundings. Very comfortable accommodation. Bedrooms, most en suite, with colour TV, tea/coffee facilities. Ground floor en suite bedrooms available. Bed and Full English Breakfast from £20. Pets welcome. [Pets £1 per night]

WEST MIDLANDS

Birmingham

The second-largest city in Britain, with Art Galleries to rival London. The Bull Ring has been modernised and includes an impressive shopping centre, but there is still plenty of the old town to see; the town hall, the concert hall and the Cathedral Church of St Philip.

ANGELA AND IAN KERR, THE AWENTSBURY HOTEL, 21 SERPENTINE ROAD, SELLY PARK, BIRMINGHAM B29 7HU (0121–472 1258). Victorian Country House. Large gardens. All rooms have colour TV, telephones and tea/coffee making facilities. Some rooms en suite, some with showers. All rooms central heating, wash-basins. Near BBC Pebble Mill, transport, University, city centre. Bed and Breakfast from £25 Single Room, from £39 Twin Room, inclusive of VAT.

WILTSHIRE

Dairy Farm on the Wiltshire/Gloucestershire borders. Malmesbury 3 miles, 15 minutes. M4 (junction 16 or 17). **SELF CATERING**: The Bull Pen and Cow Byre each sleep 2/3 plus cot. Double bedded room, bathroom, kitchen, lounge. 3 KEYS COMMENDED . **B&B** in 15C farmhouse - three comfortable rooms, one en suite. Listed COMMENDED.

John & Edna Edwards, Stonehill Farm, Charlton, Malmesbury SN16 9DY Tel: 01666 823310

Swaynes Firs Farm
Grimsdyke, Coombe Bissett, Salisbury, Wiltshire SP5 5RF

Small working farm with horses, cattle, poultry, geese and duck ponds. Spacious rooms, all en suite with colour TV and country views. Ideal for visiting the many historic sites in the area. Rates: Adults £20 per night B&B. Children £10 sharing adults' room. Dogs - Free.

Mr A. Shering   AA QQ   ☞ Approved   Tel: 01725 519240

CRUDWELL COURT
HOTEL & RESTAURANT
Crudwell, Near Malmesbury,
Wiltshire SN16 9EP
Tel: 01666 577194 Fax: 01666 577853

Restaurant and residential licence; 15 bedrooms, all with private bathrooms; Historic interest; children and dogs welcome; car park (45); Cheltenham 20 miles; Bath 18; Exit 17 M4 7 miles; Cirencester 5; Malmesbury 3; Tetbury 2.

17th century rectory set in three acres of lovely Cotswold walled gardens with lily ponds, outdoor heated swimming pool. Recommended by recognised independent guides. The resident owners have created a relaxed and comfortable atmosphere with excellent cooking and extensive wine lists. The bedrooms have exceptionally good beds, are all individually decorated and have lovely views of the surrounding gardens leading to farm land. All cooking is freshly prepared to order and the panelled diningroom overlooking the walled garden is open to non residents for all meals and snack lunches.

Mini-breaks are available throughout the year by prior arrangement.
Christmas and New Year packages.

Coombe Bissett

Village on River Ebble 3 miles south west of Salisbury.

MR A.SHERING, SWAYNES FIRS FARM, GRIMSDYKE, COOMBE BISSETT, SALISBURY SP5 5RF (01725 519240). Small working farm with horses, poultry, geese and duck ponds. Spacious rooms, all en suite with colour TV. Ideal for visiting the many historic sites in the area. [🐕]

268

Malmesbury

Country town on River Avon with a late medieval market cross. Remains of medieval abbey.

MRS A. HILLIER, LOWER FARM, SHERSTON, MALMESBURY SN16 0PS (01666 840391). Self contained wing of farmhouse. Sleeps 3/5. Working farm. Large lawn and fields. Ideal for pets and children. Fishing. Half mile from shops, pubs/restaurants. Wiltshire/Gloucestershire Borders, ideal for Bath, Cotswolds, etc. £95-£160 per week. Electricity £1 meter. [Pets £5 each per week.]

CRUDWELL COURT HOTEL AND RESTAURANT, CRUDWELL, NEAR MALMESBURY SN16 9EP (01666 577194; Fax: 01666 577853). 17th century rectory in lovely gardens with outdoor heated pool.15 bedrooms, all with private bathrooms. Excellent cooking and extensive wine list. [🐾]

JOHN AND EDNA EDWARDS, STONEHILL FARM, CHARLTON, MALMESBURY SN16 9DY (01666 823310). Family-run dairy farm, ideal for touring. 3 comfortable rooms, one en suite. Also 2 fully equipped bungalow-style barns, each sleeps 2/3 plus cot, self catering. [🐾]

EAST YORKSHIRE

WELCOME COTTAGE HOLIDAYS. Hundreds of properties in wonderful locations at welcoming low prices. Pets, linen and fuel mostly included. For FREE colour brochure telephone 01756 702209.

Bridlington

Traditional family holiday resort with picturesque harbour and a wide range of entertainments and leisure facilities. Ideal for exploring the Heritage coastline and the Wolds.

THE TENNYSON HOTEL, 19 TENNYSON AVENUE, BRIDLINGTON YO15 2EU (Tel & Fax: 01262 604382). 1994 Golden Bowl Award Winner for the Most Pet-Friendly Hotel in Yorkshire. Offering fine cuisine in attractive surroundings. Close to beach and cliff walks. AA QQQ, 3 Crowns Highly Commended.[🐾 pw!]

Readers are requested to mention this guidebook when seeking accommodation (and please enclose a stamped addressed envelope).

274

VALLEY VIEW FARM

Sally Robinson's
Farmhouse Accomodation
BED, BREAKFAST & DINNER
* working farm * home cooking * table licence
* private parking * full central heating * colour TV
* pets welcome * dogs free! * good walking area
* quiet roads * self-catering cottages * kennel & run available
Guests' comfort is our priority • DOGS, bring your owners!

For brochure & further details get in touch with Sally Robinson, at
Valley View Farm, Old Byland, Helmsley, York YO6 5LG Tel: 01439 798221

SYMBOLS

🐕 Indicates no charge for pets. are welcome free of charge.

£ Indicates that a charge is made for pets: nightly or weekly.

pw! Shows some special provision for pets; exercise facility, feeding or accommodationarrangement.

⌂ Indicates separate pets accommodation.

HIGHLY ACCLAIMED

A Premier Location

THE PREMIER
LICENSED HOTEL

The Premier occupies a superb position on Scarborough's famous Esplanade, with breathtaking views of sea and coastline in this beautiful, quiet, elegant, unspoilt area.

This lovely Victorian hotel is privately owned and run, with the advantages of both a **lift** to all the very comfortable en suite bedrooms and a **private car park.** Relax in our sea-view lounge or enjoy a quiet drink in our residents' bar. We specialise in traditional English cuisine of the highest standard, using the very best fresh local produce.

Just cross the road, linger awhile in the beautiful Italian and Rose Gardens, or let the magnificence of the sea enthral you.

DOGS VERY WELCOME.

Full details from:

**MAUREEN AND RON JACQUES
66 ESPLANADE, SCARBOROUGH,
NORTH YORKSHIRE YO11 2UZ
TEL: 01723 501062**

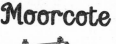

A wide choice of selected and personally inspected self-catering properties in
most areas. APPLY – RECOMMENDED COTTAGES (01751 475547).

WELCOME COTTAGE HOLIDAYS. Hundreds of properties in wonderful
locations at welcoming low prices. Pets, linen and fuel mostly included. For
FREE colour brochure telephone 01756 702209.

DALES HOLIDAY COTTAGES offer a choice of over 400 superb, self catering,
holiday properties in beautiful rural and coastal locations from Bronte, Herriot
and Heartbeat country to Yorkshire's Coastline. Cosy cottages for 2, to a
country house for 10, many open all year. For FREE Brochure contact Dales
Holiday Cottages, Carleton Business Park, Skipton, North Yorkshire BD23 2DG
(01756 799821 & 790919).

Askrigg

TV series based on popular "Vet" stories by James Herriot filmed here. St. Oswald's Church,
"Cathedral of Wensleydale", dates from late 15th and early 16th centuries.

KATE EMPSALL, WHITFIELD, HELM, ASKRIGG, WENSLEYDALE DL8 3JF
(Tel/Fax: 01969 650565). Relax at 950 feet in peaceful surroundings with
spectacular views in B&B (Two Crowns Commended) overlooking Upper
Wensleydale. Waterfalls, high fells and river meadow walks. Cottages at Askrigg
and Hawes (Three Keys Commended), sleep four persons. Non-smoking.

Bentham

Quiet village amidst the fells. Good centre for rambling and fishing. Ingleton 5 miles N.E.

MRS L. J. STORY, HOLMES FARM, LOW BENTHAM, LANCASTER LA2 7DE
(015242 61198). Cottage conversion in easy reach of Dales, Lake District and
coast. Central heating, fridge, TV, washer, games room. 3 Keys Commended. [🐾]

Brompton-by-Sawdon

Quiet village on edge of North Yorkshire Moors. Close to Northallerton.

MRS D. PROCTOR, HEADON FARM, WYDALE, BROMPTON-BY-SAWDON, SCARBOROUGH YO13 9DG (01723 859019). Five spacious character cottages situated in a quiet wooded setting on edge of North York Moors. Open all year from £150 per week. Brochure available.

Clapham

Attractive village with caves and pot-holes in vicinity, including Gaping Ghyll. Nearby lofty peaks include Ingleborough (2,373ft.) to the north. Kendal 24 miles, Settle 6.

NEW INN HOTEL, CLAPHAM, NEAR SETTLE LA2 8HH (015242 51203, Fax: 015242 51496). Friendly 18th century coaching inn. Ideal centre for walking. All rooms en suite, with colour TV and tea/coffee facilities. Restaurant and bar meals. Dogs welcome. [Pets £2 per night]

Coverdale

Small village set in Yorkshire Dales, in heart of Herriot Country.

MRS CAROLINE HARRISON, HILL TOP FARM & LIVERY YARD, WEST SCRAFTON, LEYBURN, COVERDALE DL8 4RU (01969 640663). 4 Keys Highly Commended. You will relax in our converted stone barn — centrally heated, log fires, en suite bathrooms, panoramic views — situated in the Yorkshire Dales National Park. Take part in our farming routines; separate playroom, pets' corner, pony to ride. Fishing, walking; tranquillity guaranteed.4 Keys Highly Commended.

MRS JULIE CLARKE, MIDDLE FARM, WOODALE, COVERDALE, LEYBURN DL8 4TY (01969 640271). Peacefully situated farmhouse. B&B with optional Evening Meal. Home cooking. Pets sleep where you prefer. Ideally positioned for exploring the Dales. [🐕 pw! ⌂]

Easingwold

Small market town with cobbled streets where weathered red brick dwellings are grouped around a large green. 12 miles north-west of York.

MRS R. RITCHIE, THE OLD RECTORY, THORMANBY, EASINGWOLD, YORK YO6 3WN (01845 501417). Ideal for touring Herriot Country, Moors, Dales. TWO SELF CONTAINED COTTAGES sleeping 4/6. Also Bed and Breakfast. 3 spacious bedrooms, 2 en suite. SAE or phone for brochure. [🐕]

GARBUTTS GHYLL, THORNTON HILL, NEAR EASINGWOLD YO6 3PZ (01347 868644). 18th Century working farm located in the Howardian Hills close to Easingwold. Arable and Stock farm. Home cooking with products made on the premises. Open fires. Tranquillity with panoramic views. [🐕 ⌂].

East Ayton

Village four miles south-east of Scarborough.

FORGE VALLEY COTTAGES. Superb stone-built cottages in delightful village on River Derwent, Gateway to the North Yorks Moors and coast, yet only 10 minutes from Scarborough. Highly equipped, cosy and comfortable — the perfect holiday base. 5 Keys Highly Commended. For colour brochure: DAVID BEELEY, WESTGATE, OLD MALTON YO17 0HE (01653 698251).[🐕]

Filey

Well-known resort with sandy beach. Off-shore is Filey Brig. Hull 40 miles, Bridlington 11, Scarborough 7.

MAYFIELD GUEST HOUSE, 2 BROOKLANDS, FILEY YO14 9BA (01723 514557). Close to all amenities; five bedrooms (mostly en suite; one ground floor). Ideal centre for touring. Bed and Breakfast from £17; Dinner £8. Open all year. ETB 3 Crowns. [🐕]

Goathland

Centre for moorland and woodland walks and waterfalls. Village of 19th century houses scattered over several heaths.

JACKIE FEARNLEY, BRERETON LODGE, GOATHLAND YO22 5JR (01947 896481; Fax: 01947 896482). Self catering annexe to country house (sleeps 4/5). Spacious grounds. Moorland walking. Steam railway. Sea 8 miles. Pets welcome. Short breaks off season. Phone for brochure.

MRS MARION COCKREM, DALE END FARM, GREEN END, GOATHLAND, NEAR WHITBY YO22 5LJ (01947 895371). 500-year-old stone-built farmhouse on 140-acre working farm in North York Moors National Park. Rare breeds kept. Generous portions home cooked food. Guest lounge with colour TV and log fire. Homely olde-worlde interior. Many repeat bookings. SAE for brochure. [🐕]

Grassington

Wharfedale village in attractive moorland setting. Ripon 22 miles, Skipton 9.

GRASSINGTON HOUSE HOTEL, THE SQUARE, GRASSINGTON BD23 5AQ (01756 752406; Fax: 01756 752135). A small hotel with a big reputation. All rooms en suite, colour TV, tea making. Parking. Ideal for walking or touring. AA Rosette for Food. 3 Crowns Commended. [🐕]

FORESTERS ARMS, MAIN STREET, GRASSINGTON, SKIPTON BD23 5AA (01756 752349). The Foresters Arms is situated in the heart of the Yorkshire Dales and provides an ideal centre for walking or touring. Within easy reach of York and Harrogate. [🐕]

JERRY & BEN'S HOLIDAY COTTAGES. Seven comfortable properties on private estate near Grassington in Yorkshire Dales National Park. Wooded mountain becks, waterfalls, rocky crags and accessible hill and footpath walking. Brochure from: MRS J.M.JOY, HOLEBOTTOM FARM, HEBDEN, SKIPTON BD23 5DL (01756 752369 Fax: 01756 753370).

Great Broughton

Village 2 miles south-east of Stokesley

RED HALL, GREAT BROUGHTON, MIDDLESBROUGH TS9 7ET (Tel/Fax: 01642 712300). Elegant 17th Century Grade II Listed building. Family run business provides personal service in warm friendly atmosphere. Centrally heated en suite bedrooms. Set in meadows and woodland at foot of North Yorkshire Moors National Park.

Hacknesss

Village five miles west of Scarborough in National Park.

HACKNESS GRANGE HOTEL, HACKNESS, NEAR SCARBOROUGH YO13 OJW (01723 882345). Sensitively restored and idyllically tucked away in National Park. 26 superbly appointed rooms with en suite facilities. Kennels available. AA/RAC ***. [Pets £6 per night.]

Harrogate

Charming and elegant spa town set amid some of Britain's most scenic countryside. Ideal for exploring Herriot Country and the moors and dales. York 22 miles, Bradford 19, Leeds 16.

ABBATT & YOUNG'S HOTEL, 15 YORK ROAD (OFF SWAN ROAD), HARROGATE HG1 2QL (01423 567336). Licensed Hotel with attractive gardens. Colour television, tea/coffee making facilities in all rooms, all with en suite bathrooms. 4 Crowns Commended. AA 2 Stars. [🐕]

ROSEMARY HELME, HELME PASTURE, OLD SPRING WOOD COTTAGES & LODGES, HARTWITH BANK, SUMMERBRIDGE, HARROGATE HG3 4DR (Tel: 01423 780279, Fax: 01423 780994). Country accommodation for dogs and numerous walks in unspoilt Nidderdale. Central for Harrogate, York, Herriot and Bronte country. National Trust area. Illustrated brochure available. ETB 3/4 Keys up to Highly Commended. [pw! Pets £12 per week.]

Luxury cottages and lodges sleeping two to ten people. All equipped to a high standard. Pool, licensed bar, golf and children's playground on estate. Illustrated brochure available. Three/Five Keys. RUDDING HOLIDAY PARK, FOLLIFOOT, HARROGATE HG3 1JH (01423 870439; Fax: 01423 870859). [🐕]

SCOTIA HOUSE HOTEL, 66 KINGS ROAD, HARROGATE HG1 5JR (01423 504361). Owner-managed licensed Hotel five minutes' walk town centre. En suite bedrooms with colour TV, hospitality tray, telephone. Central heating throughout. On site parking. Pets and owners welcome. ETB 3 Crowns Commended, AA, RAC One Star. [pw! 🐕]

Hawes

Small town in Wensleydale. Situated 14 miles south-east of Kirkby Stephen.

STONE HOUSE HOTEL, SEDBUSK, HAWES DL8 3PT (01969 667571; Fax. 01969 667720). This fine Edwardian country house has spectacular views and serves delicious Yorkshire cooking with fine wines. Comfortable en suite bedrooms, some ground floor. Phone for details. [🐕]

MRS S. K. JEFFRYES, SIMONSTONE HALL, HAWES, WENSLEYDALE DL8 3LY (01969 667255). Facing south across picturesque Wensleydale. All rooms en suite with colour TV. Fine cuisine. Extensive wine list. Friendly personal attention. A relaxing break away from it all.

COUNTRY COTTAGE HOLIDAYS, DRYDEN HOUSE, MARKET PLACE, HAWES DL8 3RA (01969 667654). 100 cottages in the lovely Yorkshire Dales. Colour TV, central heating, open fires. Gardens, private parking. Many allow pets. Rents £120-£395 per week. Sleep 1-10.

Hawes near (Mallerstang)

12 miles north west on the Hawes to Kirkby Stephen road.

COCKLAKE HOUSE, MALLERSTANG CA17 4JT (017683 72080). Charming, High Pennine Country House. B&B in unique position above Pendragon Castle in Upper Mallerstang Dale offering good food and exceptional comfort to a small number of guests. Two double rooms with large private bathrooms. 3 acres riverside grounds. Dogs welcome.

Helmsley

A delightful stone-built town on River Rye with a large cobbled square. Thirsk 12 miles.

MRS ELIZABETH EASTON, LOCKTON HOUSE FARM, BILSDALE, HELMSLEY YO6 5NE (01439 798303). 16th century Farmhouse; oak beams, central heating. All rooms washbasins, tea/coffee facilities. Good home cooking. Panoramic views. Bed and Breakfast from £14.50; BB & EM from £24.

MRS SALLY ROBINSON, VALLEY VIEW FARM, OLD BYLAND, HELMSLEY, YORK YO6 5LG (01439 798221). Bed, breakfast and dinner. Working farm, home cooking, table licence, private parking, full central heating, colour TV. Self catering cottages. Kennel and run available. Pets Welcome. [🐕]

BANK COTTAGE. Sleeps 7 plus cot. Beautiful detached stone cottage. Fully equipped kitchen, colour TV, electric heating. Garage and additional parking. Pets by arrangement. Contact: MRS ARMSTRONG'S COTTAGES, GOLDEN SQUARE FARM, OSWALDKIRK, NEAR HELMSLEY, YORK YO6 5YQ (01439 788269).

Scandinavian Pine Lodges, each sleeping up to five persons. Fully centrally heated and double glazed. Set in 60 acres, surrounded by pine forests. Open all year. CRIEF LODGE HOLIDAY HOMES, WASS, YORK YO6 4AY (01347 868207 or Fax: 01347 868202) [pw! 🐕]

CROWN HOTEL, MARKET SQUARE, HELMSLEY YO6 5BJ (01439 770297). Fully residential old coaching inn. Bedrooms are very well appointed, all have tea and coffee-making facilities, colour TV, radio and telephones. Traditional country cooking. AA and RAC 2 Stars. [🐕]

Horton-in-Ribblesdale

Moorland village in the Craven country in the shadow of Pen-y-Ghent (2273 ft.). Many caves and potholes in the vicinity. Settle 6 miles.

COLIN AND JOAN HORSFALL, STUDFOLD HOUSE, HORTON-IN-RIBBLESDALE, NEAR SETTLE BD24 OER (01729 860200). Georgian house standing in one acre of beautiful gardens. All rooms have central heating, washbasins, colour TVs and tea/coffee making facilities. Vegetarians, children and pets also welcome. Bed and Breakfast £16. Evening Meal £8. Self-catering £95-£195.

Huby

Small village 9 miles north of York. Ideal as base for exploring Dales, Moors and coast

THE NEW INN MOTEL, MAIN STREET, HUBY, YORK YO6 1HQ (01347 810219). Ideal base for Yorkshire attractions. Ground floor rooms, en suite, colour TVs etc. Bed and Breakfast from £25 pppn (EM available). Pets welcome. Special 3 day breaks. Telephone for brochure. AA Listed. [🐕]

Kilburn

Village to south of Hambleton Hills. Nearby is White Horse carved into hillside. Helmsley 9 miles, Thirsk 6.

CLAIRE STRAFFORD, CHAPEL COTTAGE, KILBURN, YORK YO6 4AH (01347 868383). Converted farm building in excellent area for touring Moors, Dales and coast. Range of sports facilities and restaurants in area. No children please. ALL PETS VERY WELCOME. [🐕]

Kirkbymoorside

Small town below North Yorkshire Moors, 7 miles west of Pickering. Traces of a medieval castle.

MRS F. WILES, SINNINGTON COMMON FARM, KIRKBYMOORSIDE, YORK YO6 6NX (01751 431719). Newly converted cottages, tastefully furnished and well equipped, on working family farm. Sleep 2/4 from £100 per week including linen and heating. Also spacious ground floor accommodation (teamakers, colour TV, radio alarms). Disabled facilities, separate entrances. B&B from £16. [🐕]

Leeming Bar

Small, pretty village two miles north-east of Bedale.

THE WHITE ROSE HOTEL, LEEMING BAR, NORTHALLERTON DL7 9AY (01677 422707, Fax: 01677 425123). Eighteen bedroom, two-star private Hotel situated in village on A684, half a mile from A1 motorway. Ideal base for touring North Yorks Moors, Dales and coastal resorts. Licensed; Restaurant. 3 Crowns Commended, AA/RAC** [🐕]

Leyburn

Small market town, 8 miles south-west of Richmond, standing above the River Ure in Wensleydale.

BARBARA & BARRIE MARTIN, THE OLD STAR, WEST WITTON, LEYBURN DL8 4LU (01969 622949). Former 17th century Coaching Inn now run as a guest house. Oak beams, log fire, home cooking. En suite from £15. ETB 2 Crowns. [🐕]

WINVILLE HOTEL & RESTAURANT, MAIN STREET, ASKRIGG, LEYBURN DL8 3HG (01969 650515; Fax: 01969 650594). 19th Century Georgian residence in centre of "Herriot" village. Excellent touring centre for Lakes and Dales. Bar, residents' lounge, gardens and car park. B&B from £21.

PEN VIEW FARMHOUSE, THORALBY, LEYBURN DL8 3SU (01969 663319). Fully centrally heated with one single, one twin, one double and one family room, two en suite. Licensed. Ideal for walking or touring Dales. Children and pets welcome. 2 Crowns.

Malham

In picturesque Craven District with spectacular Malham Cove (300ft.) and Gordale Scar with waterfalls. Malham Tarn (N T.) is 4 miles north, Skipton 12 miles.

MRS V. SHARP, MIRESFIELD FARM, MALHAM, SKIPTON BD23 4DA (01729 830414). In beautiful gardens bordering village green and stream. Well known for excellent food. 14 bedrooms, 12 with private facilities. Full central heating. Two well-furnished lounges and conservatory for guests' use.

Malton

17 miles north-east of York. Site of a Roman camp; market square has church dating from Norman times. Castle Howard, designed by Sir John Vanbrugh, lies 4 1/2 miles to the south-west.

BEANSHEAF HOTEL, MALTON ROAD, KIRBY MISPERTON, MALTON YO17 OUE (01653 668614). RAC Merit Award for Comfort. Impressive menus. Gateway to North York Moors. Half an hour from coast resorts, York, Helmsley. Good value for money. AA and RAC 2 Stars [🐕].

Myton-on-Swale

Beautiful, rural surroundings. Very peaceful. Brafferton 2 miles.

MRS R. W. HALL, THE HADDOCKS, MYTON-ON-SWALE, HELPERBY, YORK YO6 2RB (01423 360224). One three-bedroom farm cottage, sleeps 6 plus cot. Fridge/ freezer, microwave, colour TV, open fire, ample parking. Quiet rural surroundings, central for all Yorkshire. [🐾 pw!]

Oldstead

Hamlet 7 miles east of Thirsk in beautiful North Yorkshire Moors.

THE BLACK SWAN INN, OLDSTEAD, COXWOLD, YORK YO6 4BL (01347 868387). 18th-century Country Freehouse offers Chalet-style accommodation, en suite, colour TV, central heating, tea/coffee facilities. Real ale. A la Carte Restaurant. Fine wines. Brochure available. [Pets £1 per night]

Pateley Bridge

Picturesque and friendly small town in the heart of beautiful Nidderdale, bordering the Dales National Park. Excellent walking country and a good centre for touring the Dales, Moors, Herriot Country etc.

RIVULET COURT, PATELEY BRIDGE. ETB rating 5 Keys Highly Commended. Spacious 18th century cottage, comfortable accommodation for six or more. Central heating, fully equipped for self catering with laundry, dishwasher, fridge freezer etc, and situated close to village amenities. Fully enclosed courtyard. Weekly rates £195-£380 incl. For colour brochure contact: ANNE RACK, BLAZEFIELD, BEWERLEY, HARROGATE HG3 5BS (01423 711001). [🐾]

Pickering

Pleasant market town on southern fringe of North Yorkshire Moors National Park with moated Castle (Norm.). Bridlington 31 miles, Whitby 20, Scarborough 16, Helmsley 13, Malton 3.

MRS ELLA BOWES, BANAVIE, ROXBY ROAD, THORNTON-LE-DALE, PICKERING YO18 7SX (01751 474616). Very large stone-built semi-detached house in quiet part of village. Ideal for touring coast, moors, forest and seaside. Three double bedrooms, one en suite, all with washbasin, TV and tea-making facilities; bathroom and toilet; lounge. Car park. B&B from £14 to £17. ETB Two Crowns Commended. [🐾]

VIVERS MILL, MILL LANE, PICKERING YO18 8DJ (01751 473640). Bed and Breakfast in ancient Watermill in peaceful surroundings. Comfortable en suite rooms with beamed ceilings. Tea making facilities. Ideal for Moors, coastline, and York. Bed and Breakfast £23 per day, £145 weekly. [🐾]

SUE CAVILL, BADGER COTTAGE, STAPE, PICKERING Y018 8HR (01751 476108). Comfortable self catering on a small, remote moorland farm. Open plan, well-equipped kitchen, dining and sitting room; spacious bedroom, en suite shower. Linen and power included.

Richmond

One of Yorkshire's most attractive towns, with fine views across the dales to the Vale of York. The Theatre Royal in Friar's Wynd, built in 1788, is one of the oldest surviving theatres in England. Kendal 53 miles, Penrith 52, York 45, Barnard Castle 15, Darlington 12.

THE BRIDGE INN, GRINTON, RICHMOND DL11 6HH (01748 884224). The Hotel is on the River Swale and has its own 1½ miles of private trout fishing. Spectacular views of the hills and moors. Central heating throughout. Large car park. Open all year. Pets welcome. [🐏]

Scarborough

Very popular family resort with fine coast scenery, good sands. Of interest is the ruined 12th century Castle, Wood End Museum and Oliver's Mount (viewpoint). York 41 miles, Whitby 20, Bridlington 17, Filey 7.

PARADE HOTEL, 29 ESPLANADE, SCARBOROUGH YO11 2AQ (01723 361285). Victorian Licensed Hotel with enviable sea views! Comfortable en suite rooms. Bed & Breakfast from £23. Dinner, Bed & Breakfast £32. ETB 2 Crowns Approved. RAC Acclaimed. [🐏]

SCARBOROUGH near. One luxury detached Bungalow, sleeps 2–6, on 170-acre park enjoying wonderful views. APPLY– MRS J. HOLLAND, 32 JOAN LANE, HOOTON LEVITT, ROTHERHAM, SOUTH YORKSHIRE S66 8PH (01709 815102) with SAE. [pw!]

THE PREMIER HOTEL, ESPLANADE, SCARBOROUGH YO11 2UZ (01723 501062). The Premier Hotel is situated on the Esplanade. All rooms have private bath/shower and toilet en suite, colour TV, radio, tea/coffee facilities and full central heating. [Pets £3 per night.]

Skipton

Airedale market town, centre for picturesque Craven district. Fine Castle (14th cent). York 43 miles, Manchester 42, Leeds 26, Harrogate 22, Settle 16.

DALES HOLIDAY COTTAGES offer a choice of over 400 superb, self catering, holiday properties in beautiful rural and coastal locations from Bronte, Herriot and Heartbeat country to Yorkshire's Coastline. Cosy cottages for 2, to a country house for 10, many open all year. For FREE Brochure contact Dales Holiday Cottages, Carleton Business Park, Skipton, North Yorkshire BD23 2DG Telephone (01756) 799821 & 790919.

Over 200 super self-catering Cottages, Houses and Flats throughout Yorkshire Dales, York, Moors, Coast, Peak and Lake District. Telephone for free illustrated brochure. APPLY– HOLIDAY COTTAGES (YORKSHIRE) LTD, WATER STREET, SKIPTON (18) BD23 1PB (01756 700872). [🐏]

Sleights

Village running down to River Esk, 3 miles south-west of Whitby

WHITE ROSE HOLIDAY COTTAGES, SLEIGHTS, NEAR WHITBY. Superior stone village cottages situated near Sleights Bridge. Available all year, including Christmas and New Year. Up to 3 Keys Commended. APPLY: MRS J. ROBERTS (PW), 5 BROOK PARK, SLEIGHTS, NEAR WHITBY YO21 1RT (01947 810763) [pw! £5 per week.]

PARTRIDGE NEST FARM, ESKDALESIDE, SLEIGHTS, WHITBY YO22 5ES (01947 810450). Six caravans on secluded site, five miles from Whitby and sea. Ideal touring centre. All have mains electricity, colour TV, fridge, gas cooker. SAE or phone please. [Pets £5 per week.]

Staithes

Fishing village surrounded by high cliffs on North Sea coast, 9 miles north-west of Whitby.

THE FOX INN, ROXBY, STAITHES, SALTBURN TS13 5EB (01947 840335). Family-run village inn, all rooms colour TV, tea/coffee making. Open all year for B&B from £17.50; Evening Meals on request. Also caravan for hire. [pw! 🐾]

Thirsk

Market town with attractive square. Excellent touring area. Northallerton 3 miles.

FOXHILLS HIDEAWAYS, FELIXKIRK, THIRSK YO7 2DS (01845 537575). Scandinavian, heated throughout, linen provided. A supremely relaxed atmosphere on the edge of the North Yorkshire Moors National Park. Open all year. Secluded site with miles of forest tracks to explore. [🐾]

HIGH PARADISE FARM COTTAGES, BOLTBY, THIRSK Y07 2HT (01845 537353). Well appointed. Sleep 2 to 6 in the "Heart of Herriot Country" near Sutton Bank in Moors National Park. Peaceful seclusion, perfect touring base.

BARLEY GARTH, BALK, THIRSK YO7 2AJ (01845 597524). 18th century mill house. Excellent dog walks. Ideal centre for Moors, Dales, Coast, York. B&B from £16.50, beverage tray, dog bowl. Private bath available. [Pets £1 each per night.]

Wensleydale

Possibly the most picturesque of all the Dales, ideal for touring some of the most beautiful parts of Yorkshire and nearby Herriot Country. Kendal 25 miles, Kirkby Stephen 15.

MRS PAT COOPER, MOORCOTE FARM, ELLINGSTRING, MASHAM HG4 4PL (01677 460315). Three delightful cottages around a sunny courtyard, sleeping 4-6. All equipped to very high standard. Children and pets welcome. Open all year round. [Pets £10 per week.]

MRS SUE COOPER, ST. EDMUNDS, CRAKEHALL, BEDALE DL8 1HP (01677 423584). Set in Swaledale and Wensleydale, these recently renovated cottages are fully equipped and are an ideal base for exploring the Dales and Moors. Sleep 2–7 plus cot. Up to 4 Keys Commended. Brochure available. [🐕]

THE WENSLEYDALE HEIFER, WEST WITTON, WENSLEYDALE DL8 4LS (01969 622322; Fax: 01969 624183). A 17th Century Inn of character and style offering 20 en suite bedrooms and 3 Four Posters. Real Ales with Bistro and Bar Food. Home cooking specialising in Fish and Seafood. 3 Crowns Commended.

West Scrafton

Village 3 miles south of Wensley

ADRIAN CAVE, WESTCLOSE HOUSE, WEST SCRAFTON, NEAR MIDDLEHAM DL8 4RM (0181-567 4862 for bookings). Traditional stone farmhouse. Three bedrooms sleeping six/eight. Storage heating. Microwave, fridge, electric cooker, colour TV. Large barn/playroom and garden. Pets welcome. Ideal for families/walkers. [pw 🐕]

Whitby

Charming resort with harbour and sands. Of note is the 13th-century ruined Abbey. Stockton-on-Tees 34 miles, Scarborough 20, Saltburn-by-the-Sea 19.

MR JOHN HALTON, KIRKLANDS PRIVATE HOTEL, 17 ABBEY TERRACE, WEST CLIFF, WHITBY YO21 3HQ (01947 603868). Bed, Breakfast and Evening Meal. Family-run hotel, good home cooking. Licensed. Some rooms en suite; all have tea/coffee making facilities and colour TV. Pets welcome.

MRS K. E. NOBLE, SUMMERFIELD FARM, HAWSKER, WHITBY YO22 4LA (01947 601216). Between Whitby/Robin Hood's Bay. Six berth caravan. Private farm site. Beach one mile, "Cleveland Way" footpath nearby. Set in secluded safe grassy area. Excellent walking. SAE for details.

SNEATON HALL HOTEL, SNEATON, WHITBY YO22 5HP (01947 605929; Fax: 01947 820177). Small, friendly 2 Star country hotel, three miles south of Whitby. All rooms en suite; tea making facilities, TV. Good food, pleasant gardens, ample car parking. Fully licensed; open to non-residents. Pets most welcome. [🐕]

York

Historic cathedral city and former Roman Station on River Ouse. Magnificent Minster and 3 miles of ancient walls. Many interesting old churches and other notable buildings including Palace Chapel, St. William's College, Merchant Adventurers Hall, St. Anthony's Hall and Treasurer's House. Facilities for a wide range of sports and entertainments. Horse-racing on Knavesmire. Bridlington 41 miles, Filey 41, Leeds 24, Harrogate 22.

ASTORIA HOTEL, 6 GROSVENOR TERRACE, BOOTHAM, YORK (01904 659558). Licensed Hotel, 15 bedrooms, many with private bathroom. Dogs welcome. Private parking. [🐕]

HIGH BELTHORPE, BISHOP WILTON, YORK YO4 1SB (01759 368238; Mobile: 0973 938528). Set on an ancient moated site at the foot of the Yorkshire Wolds, this spacious Victorian farmhouse offers huge breakfasts, open fires, private fishing and fabulous walks. Dogs and owners will love it! One Crown Approved. Open all year. Prices from £15.00 +VAT. [🐕].

MRS S. JACKSON, VICTORIA VILLA GUEST HOUSE, 72 HESLINGTON ROAD, YORK YO1 5AU (01904 631647). Ten minutes' walk from city centre. Comfortable double, twin, single and family bedrooms, all with TV. Children and pets welcome. Open all year. B&B from £13 to £18. [pw! 🐕]

YORK LAKESIDE LODGES, MOOR LANE, YORK YO2 2QU (01904 702346 or 0831 885824; Fax: 01904 701631). Self-catering pine lodges. Mature parkland setting. Large fishing lake. Nearby superstore with coach to centre every 10 mins. ETB 4 Keys up to De Luxe. [Pets £15 per week]

PEGGY SWANN, SOUTH NEWLANDS FARM, SELBY ROAD, RICCALL, YORK YO4 6QR (01757 248203). Friendliness, comfort, and good traditional cooking are always on offer to our guests. The kettle's always on the boil in our kitchen, and a comfortable lounge is yours to relax in at any time. Easy access to York and the Dales and Moors. No smoking please. Day kennelling available. [Pets £1 per night.]

PETER & JUDITH JONES, FOURPOSTER LODGE HOTEL, 68/70 HESLINGTON ROAD, YORK YO1 5AU (01904 651170). Enjoy the relaxing luxury of a four-poster bed and hearty English breakfast at this Victorian villa, convenient for York with all its fascinations. Bed and Breakfast from £25.00 to £27.00. ETB 3 Crowns Commended.

KILIMA HOTEL, 129 HOLGATE ROAD, YORK Y02 4DE (01904 625787). 19th century former rectory within walking distance of city centre and attractions. 15 bedrooms, all with private facilities, colour TV, telephone. Rosette awarded restaurant. Car Park. 4 Crowns Commended. RAC ***, AA **. [🐕]

CLIFTON VIEW GUEST HOUSE, 118/120 CLIFTON, YORK YO3 6BQ (01904 625047). Victorian family-run guest house 12 minutes' walk from City Centre. All rooms have colour TV, tea coffee facilities; most have shower. Private car park. ETB One Crown [🐕]

3 attractive self-catering choices. 12 miles from York. WOODLEA detached house sleeping 5–6, with kitchen, dining area, large lounge and colour TV, bathroom, cloakroom, 3 bedrooms. BUNGALOW adjacent to farmhouse sleeps 2–4. Kitchen, bathroom, lounge/dining room with colour TV and double bed settee. Twin room with cot. STUDIO adjacent to farmhouse, sleeping 2. Kitchen, lounge/dining room with colour TV, twin bedroom, bathroom/toilet. SAE for details: MRS M. S. A. WOODLIFFE, MILL FARM, YAPHAM, POCKLINGTON, YORK YO4 2PH (01759 302172).

WHITEHALL LODGE, YORK (01904 692828). Situated on the outskirts of York yet only 5 minutes from the attractions of this beautiful city. Ideal for touring the Moors and the city of York. Farmhouse B&B from only £16. Pets welcome.

ST. GEORGE'S HOUSE HOTEL, 6 ST. GEORGE'S PLACE, YORK YO2 2DR (01904 625056). Family-run licensed Hotel in quiet cul-de-sac near racecourse. All rooms en suite with colour TV, radio. Tea/coffee facilities. Private parking. Pets welcome. 3 Crowns Commended. RAC, AA. [🐕]

ORILLIA HOUSE, 89 THE VILLAGE, STOCKTON-ON-FOREST, YORK YO3 9UP (01904 400600). Conveniently situated in centre of village 3 miles from York. All rooms with private facilities etc. Bed and Breakfast from £16. Telephone for brochure. [Pets £1 per night.]

ASHCROFT HOTEL, 294 BISHOPTHORPE ROAD, YORK YO2 1LH (01904 659286; Fax: 01904 640107). Set in $2^1/_2$ acres of wooded grounds. All rooms en suite. Pets and owners accommodated in Coach House, giving easy access. 4 Crowns Commended.

Yorkshire Dales

Scenic area stretching from Ilkley in the south to Ingleton in the west, Langthwaite in the north and Kirkby Malzeard tn the east. Peaceful, unspoilt villages, wooded valleys with waterfalls and limestone caves.

DALES HOLIDAY COTTAGES offer a choice of over 400 superb, self catering, holiday properties in beautiful rural and coastal locations from Bronte, Herriot and Heartbeat country to Yorkshire's Coastline. Cosy cottages for 2, to a country house for 10, many open all year. For FREE Brochure contact Dales Holiday Cottages, Carleton Business Park, Skipton, North Yorkshire BD23 2DG (01756 799821 & 790919).

NOTE

All the information in this book is given in good faith in the belief that it is correct. However, the publishers cannot guarantee the facts given in these pages, neither are they responsible for changes in policy, ownership or terms that may take place after the date of going to press. Readers should always satisfy themselves that the facilities they require are available and that the terms, if quoted, still apply.

Calderdale

Administrative district of West Yorkshire. Industrial museum in town.

ASHENHURST COTTAGE. Convenient for town, yet footpaths lead directly to the Moors. Sleeps up to four. Central heating, linen, towels, colour TV all inclusive. Open all year. Well-behaved pets welcome. Brochure from MRS H. M. GRIEVE, ASHENHURST HOUSE, TODMORDEN, LANCS OL14 8DS (01706 812086). [Pets £5 per week.]

Haworth

Town situated above the River Worth Valley. Of interest is the parsonage, one-time home of the Brontë Family, now a museum; the revived Worth Valley Railway runs from Keighley to Oxenhope. Keighley 2 miles.

ROYDWOOD COTTAGES, OXENHOPE, KEIGHLEY. These 200 year old cottages (sleep 2-3) each have a large sitting room, traditional furniture, colour TV and heating. Garden; parking. Long SAE please for brochure toMRS D. S. KINGHORN, 16 SOUTH CLOSE, GUISELEY, LEEDS LS20 8JD (01943 872767). [🐾]

Superb small moorland Cottage, one mile Haworth. Sleeps 4–6. Luxuriously equipped, sunny lounge, patio garden, central heating. Breathtaking moorland views. Children welcome. Available all year round. Price £210 to £300 throughout the year, includes sheets and heating. Tourist Board Category 3. APPLY – MRS P. M. SEABROOK, 30 NEWCOMBE STREET, MARKET HARBOROUGH, LEICESTERSHIRE LE16 9PB (01858 463723).

WALES

NORTH WALES
(Formerly Clwyd and Gwynedd)
Aberconwy and Colwyn, Anglesey, Denbighshire,
Flintshire, Gwynedd and Wrexham

NORTH WALES   *Bala*

The Fairbourne Hotel

Fairbourne, Gwynedd
LL38 2HQ
Tel: 01341 250203

Renowned for its good food and friendly atmosphere, this 300-year-old hotel stands in its own grounds overlooking Cardigan Bay, is fully licensed, has 23 well appointed single, double and family rooms with private bathrooms, tea/coffee making facilities and colour TVs. Large lounge, dining room, bars and games room. Bowls green in grounds. Ideally situated for golf, fishing, horse riding, walking, climbing, sailing, beautiful beach. Pets welcome. Car parking. Open all year. Brochure on request to Mrs Hodson.

☙ ☙ ☙ Highly Commended.

Small Georgian cottage overlooking the magnificent beach at Harlech. Central for unspoiled beaches and countryside, yet within easy reach of Porthmadog and Lleyn Peninsula. Good home cooking. Dinner, Bed and Breakfast at reasonable prices. Pretty bedrooms overlooking sea. Pets welcome.

Fron Deg Guest House, Llanfair, Harlech, Gwynedd LL46 2RE   Tel: 01766 780448

DEVA, 34 TRINITY AVENUE
LLANDUDNO LL30 2TQ

Mrs and Mrs J. Williams

Self contained holiday apartments for 2/3/4 ADULTS only. Bed linen provided. Car Park. Well behaved dogs welcome. Short breaks available early and late season. Highly Recommended. Stamp, please, for brochure, or telephone: **01492 877059**

Hen Dŷ Hotel

10 North Parade, Llandudno, LL30 2LP
Tel: 01492 876184

☙ ☙ ☙ Highly Commended

CHARLES & IRENE WATTS welcome you to the Hen Dŷ Hotel, set on the promenade, opposite the Pier. Wonderful panoramic views over the Bay. All our bedrooms have radio, TV, teamakers, central heating; some en suite. Enjoy the Chef/Proprietor's menu and the cosy Residents' Bar. Tariff from £18.00 to £27.50 per night. Pets welcome by arrangement. We are close to shops, Happy Valley, Dry Ski Slope, Great Orme Summit. Our priority is YOUR comfort and enjoyment.

NOTE

All the information in this book is given in good faith in the belief that it is correct. However, the publishers cannot guarantee the facts given in these pages, neither are they responsible for changes in policy, ownership or terms that may take place after the date of going to press. Readers should always satisfy themselves that the facilities they require are available and that the terms, if quoted, still apply.

SYMBOLS

🛏   Indicates no charge for pets. are welcome free of charge.

£   Indicates that a charge is made for pets: nightly or weekly.

pw!   Shows some special provision for pets; exercise facility, feeding or accommodation arrangement.

⌂   Indicates separate pets accommodation.

WELCOME COTTAGE HOLIDAYS. Hundreds of properties in wonderful locations at welcoming low prices. Pets, linen and fuel mostly included. For FREE colour brochure telephone 01756 702209.

SEASIDE COTTAGES, MANN'S HOLIDAYS (01758 701 702). Large selection of self catering seaside and country cottages, bungalows, farmhouses, caravans etc. offering superb, reasonably priced accommodation for owners and their pets. Please telephone for brochure.

Abersoch

Dinghy sailing and windsurfing centre with safe sandy beaches. Pony trekking, golf, fishing and sea trips.

MR P. W. REES, "QUALITY COTTAGES", CERBID, SOLVA, HAVERFORDWEST, PEMBROKESHIRE SA62 6YE (01348 837871). Cottages set in all coastal areas, unashamed luxury; highest residential standards. Dishwashers, microwaves, washing machines. Log fires. Linen supplied. Pets welcome. [pw!]

Bala

Natural touring centre for Snowdonia. Narrow-gauge railway runs along side of Bala lake, the largest natural lake in Wales. Golf, sailing, fishing, canoeing.

MRS ANN SKINNER, TALYBONT ISA, RHYDUCHAF, BALA LL23 7SD (01678 520234). Bed and Breakfast, optional Evening Meal, on the farm. Also two 6/8 berth Caravans with all modern conveniences. Just two miles from Bala Lake. Ideal for walking, sailing, fishing, golfing. [🐾]

RAFEL, PARC, BALA LL23 7YU (01678 540369). Delightful, cosy, well equipped cottage. Situated in tranquil, picturesque setting. £150 – £260 weekly inclusive of electricity, logs, bed linen. Open all year, short breaks available. [🐾]

Barmouth

Modern seaside resort with two miles of sandy beaches. Surrounding hills full of interesting archaeological remains.

LAWRENNY LODGE HOTEL, BARMOUTH LL42 1SU (01341 280466). Quiet, family-run hotel overlooking harbour and estuary but only 5 minutes from town. Most rooms en suite, all with TV, tea/coffee making facilities and clock radio alarms. Restaurant menu includes vegetarian dishes. Residential licence. Large car park. 3 Crowns Commended. [🐾]

Beaumaris

Elegant little town dominated by castle built by Edward I in 13th century. Museum of Childhood has Victorian toys and music boxes.

MR P. W. REES, "QUALITY COTTAGES", CERBID, SOLVA, HAVERFORDWEST, PEMBROKESHIRE SA62 6YE (01348 837871). Cottages set in all coastal areas, unashamed luxury; highest residential standards. Dishwashers, microwaves, washing machines. Log fires. Linen supplied. Pets welcome. [pw!]

Beddgelert

Delightfully picturesque village in scenic landsape 4 miles south of Snowdonia.

JOAN WILLIAMS, COLWYN, BEDDGELERT, GWYNEDD LL55 4UY (01766 890276). WTB 3 Crowns. Small, friendly 18th century cottage guest house, beams, original stone fireplace; most rooms en suite, white linen, central heating. Overlooking river in picturesque village centre at foot of Snowdon, surrounded by wooded mountains, lakes and streams. Walkers, muddy boots and exhausted dogs welcome. B&B from £17.50- £20.50. Low Season Breaks 4 nights B&B (Mon-Fri) £60pp. Booking usually advisable. Also tiny cottage, sleeps 2, £165 weekly.

Betws-y-Coed

Popular mountain resort in picturesque setting where three rivers meet. Trout fishing, craft shops, golf, railway and motor museums, Snowdonia National Park Visitor Centre. Nearby Swallow Falls are famous beauty spot.

SUMMER HILL NON-SMOKERS' GUEST HOUSE, BETWS-Y-COED LL24 OBL (01690 710306). Quiet location, overlooking river. 150 yards from main road, shops. En suite and standard rooms, tea-making. Residents' lounge. TV. Singles, children welcome. EM available. B&B from £14.00. [Pets £1 per night.]

Blaenau Ffestiniog

Good touring centre amidst dramatic scenery. Well-known slate quarries. Betws-y-Coed 12 miles. Ffestiniog 3.

OFFEREN COTTAGE, BLAENAU FFESTINIOG. Fully equipped 3-bedroomed centrally heated cottage. Sleeps 6 adults plus small child. 2 bathrooms. £80 to £255 per week. Brochure on request from: MRS B.J. PRESTON, 3 BANKS MOUNT, PONTEFRACT WF8 4DN (01977 703092 or 01766 830982). [🐾]

Bodorgan

Location on Anglesey 4 miles south of Gwlachmai.

MRS J. GUNDRY, FARMYARD LODGE, BODORGAN, ANGLESEY LL62 5LW (01407 840977). Comfortable three-bedroomed house, WTB graded 4 Dragons. Enclosed garden. Near beaches, common, forest. Dogs and children welcome. Fully equipped, bedding and electricity inclusive. Colour TV, microwave. [🐾]

Caernarvon

Historic walled town and resort, ideal for touring Snowdonia. Museums, Segontium Roman Fort, magnificent 13th century castle. Old harbour, sailing trips.

Cherished, crafted, comfortable, family mountain cottages, sleep 4/6. Posture beds, patchworked; cots. Fitted kitchens, washing machines; luxury conservatories. Stone-walled peaceful gardens, magnificent views. £130-£325: REVD & MRS E. J. S. PLAXTON, THE VICARAGE, VICARAGE ROAD, LINGFIELD, SURREY RH7 6HA (Tel and Fax: 01342 832021). [🐾]

MRS B. CARTWRIGHT, TAN DINAS, LLANDDEINIOLEN, CAERNARVON LL55 3AR (01248 670098). Comfortable friendly farmhouse. Large grounds. Ideal touring, set between mountains and sea. TV lounge, separate dining room and tables. Open March to October. Bed and Breakfast £15; Evening Meal optional. WTB Listed. [🐕 pw!]

Colwyn Bay

Lively seaside resort with promenade amusements. Attractions include Mountain Zoo, Eirias Park; golf, tennis, riding and other sports. Good touring centre for Snowdonia. The quieter resort of Rhos-on-Sea lies at the western end of the bay.

Popular seafront holiday flats, competitive prices, some discounts. Dogs if house trained and well-behaved. Please send SAE for brochure to THE CONTINENTAL, WEST PROMENADE, COLWYN BAY LL28 4BY (01492 531516). [Pets £10 per week, reduced price for additional dogs.]

EDELWEISS HOTEL, OFF LAWSON ROAD, COLWYN BAY LL29 8HD (01492 532314). Comfortable Country House Hotel set in own wooded grounds close to open parkland; ideal for dog owners. All rooms with en suite facilities. Well-behaved dogs welcome. 3 Crowns Commended. [🐕]

MRS J. MACEY, NANT-Y-GLYN LEISURE, NANT-Y-GLYN ROAD, COLWYN BAY LL29 7RD (01492 531316). Set in a sheltered valley these garden cottages and cedarwood chalets are 15 minutes' walk to the beach and town centre. All pets welcome. SAE for illustrated colour Brochure. [Pets £5 weekly.]

Conwy

One of the best preserved medieval fortified towns in Britain on dramatic estuary setting. Telford Suspension Bridge, many historic buildings, lively quayside (site of smallest house in Britain). Golf, pony trekking, pleasure cruises.

PINEWOOD TOWERS COUNTRY GUEST HOUSE, SYCHNANT PASS ROAD, CONWY LL32 8BZ (01492 592459). Dogs, cats. One of the few Guest Houses catering for animal lovers and their pets, being fully equipped in the right surroundings. 10 acres of gardens and paddocks, with own stream and woods. [pw! 75p per night 🏠]

THE LODGE, TAL-Y-BONT CONWY LL32 8YX (01492 660766; Fax: 01492 660534). Family-run Hotel with lovely en suite bedrooms. Enjoy peace and quiet, superb food and attention from friendly and efficient staff. B&B from £25 to £35; 2 days DB&B from £59.50 to £79.50. Pets welcome. [Pets £2.50 per night]

Conwy Valley

Scenic area with many places of interest.

Self catering cottage in the beautiful Conwy Valley. Sleeps 4; two bedrooms. Well equipped; cosy log fire, storage heaters. Parking. Owner supervised and cleanliness assured. Well behaved pets accepted. Terms £102 to £210; Winter Breaks £16 per night including logs. APPLY MRS M.C. WADDINGHAM, "CEFN", TYN-Y-GROES, CONWY LL32 8TA (01492 650233).

Crafnant

Peaceful scenic area in North Wales with mountains and lakes.

Secluded cottage with log fire and beams. Dogs will love it. Plenty of walks around mountains and lakes. For up to 5 people plus their pet. MRS WILLIAMS, LOW RISBY HOUSE, LOW RISBY, SCUNTHORPE, S. HUMBERSIDE DN15 0BX (01724 733990 or 0831 298448). [🐕]

Criccieth

Popular family resort with safe beaches divided by ruins of 13th century castle. Salmon and sea trout fishing; Festival of Music & Arts in summer.

ABEREISTEDD HOTEL, WEST PARADE, CRICCIETH LL52 OEN (01766 522710; Fax 01766 523526). Sea front position. En suite rooms with colour TV, telephone, tea/coffee. Residents' lounge and licensed bar. Private parking.WTB 3 Crowns Commended, AA/RAC. [🐕]

MRS B. WILLIAMS, GAERWEN FARM, YNYS, CRICCIETH LL52 0NU (01766 810324). Self contained accommodation in furnished farmhouse on dairy/mixed farm situated 4 ½ miles from Criccieth and beaches. Children and pets welcome. SAE for more details. [🐕]

MR P. W. REES, "QUALITY COTTAGES", CERBID, SOLVA, HAVERFORDWEST, PEMBROKESHIRE SA62 6YE (01348 837871). Cottages set in all coastal areas, unashamed luxury; equipped to highest residential standards with dishwashers, washing machines, microwaves. Log fires. Linen provided. Pets welcome. [pw!]

MRS V. WILLIAMS, YNYS GRAIANOG, YNYS, CRICCIETH LL52 ONT (01766 530234). Two stone cottages, 3 & 4 bedrooms set on a small holding in a quiet rural area. Convenient for Lleyn Peninsula and Snowdonia. Plenty of parking space.

MRS A. M. JONES, BETWS-BACH, YNYS, CRICCIETH LL52 OPB (Tel and Fax: 01758 720047/01766 810295). Traditional, stone-built Farm Cottages. Situated in peaceful secluded grounds amidst fine walking countryside. Sleep 2-6. All home comforts. Full heating — open all year. WTB Grade 5. [🐕]

Dulas Bay

On north-east coast of Anglesey, between Amlwch and Moelfre.

MRS G. McCREADIE, DERI ISAF, DULAS BAY LL70 9DX (01248 410536). Beautiful Victorian country house standing in 20 acres of woodland, gardens and fields. High standard of accommodation in two family rooms and one double with en suite. Pets welcome; stabling available. 3 Crowns. [🐕]

Fairbourne

Bright little resort facing Barmouth across the Mawddach estuary. Safe spacious sands. A short distance inland is Cader Idris. Dolgellau 9 miles.

THE FAIRBOURNE HOTEL, FAIRBOURNE LL38 2HQ (01341 250203). Views of Cardigan Bay from own grounds. Licensed. Private bathrooms. Bowls green. Games room. Car park. Open all year. Pets welcome. WTB 3 Crowns Highly Commended. [🐾]

Gaerwen

Village on A5 Holyhead road. Good touring centre for island. Holyhead 18 miles, Bangor 6.

MRS D. WILLIAMS, IFRON, STATION ROAD, GAERWEN, ANGLESEY LL60 6DP (01248 421670/722012). Self catering Cottage, sleeps 5, plus cot. Half a mile from A5, four and a half miles from Menai Bridge. 15 minutes' drive to sandy beach. Pets welcome. Available from May – October. Terms £95-£180. [🐾]

Harlech

Small stone-built town dominated by remains of 13th century castle. Golf, theatre, swimming pool, fine stretch of sands.

MR P. W. REES, "QUALITY COTTAGES", CERBID, SOLVA, HAVERFORDWEST, PEMBROKESHIRE SA62 6YE (01348 837871). Cottages set in all coastal areas, unashamed luxury; highest residential standards. Dishwashers, microwaves, washing machines. Log fires. Linen supplied. Pets welcome. [pw!]

FRON DEG GUEST HOUSE, LLANFAIR, HARLECH LL46 2RE (01766 780448). Small Georgian cottage overlooking beach at Harlech. Pretty bedrooms. Central for unspoiled beaches and countryside within easy reach of Porthmadog. Reasonable terms for Bed and Breakfast, also Dinner. [🐾]

Llanddaniel

Village just off the A5, Menai Bridge 5 miles E.

MRS M. E. WILLIAMS, TYDDYN GOBLET, BRYNSIENCYN, ANGLESEY LL61 6TZ (01248 430296). Secluded farmhouse, uninterrupted views Snowdonia. 3 bedrooms, bathroom, kitchen, living & sitting rooms. Telephone. Modern 34 ft 3 bedroomed caravan very pleasantly and privately situated on smallholding. Shower etc. Also en suite B&B. Ground floor bedrooms. [🐾]

Llanddona

Village on Anglesey 3 miles north west of Beaumaris.

MR P. W. REES, "QUALITY COTTAGES", CERBID, SOLVA, HAVERFORDWEST, PEMBROKESHIRE SA62 6YE (01348 837871). Cottages set in all coastal areas, unashamed luxury, highest residential standards. Dishwashers, microwaves, washing machines. Log fires. Linen supplied. Pets welcome. [pw!]

Llandudno

Premier holiday resort of North Wales coast flanked by Great Orme and Little Orme headlands. Wide promenade, pier, two beaches; water ski-ing, sailing, fishing trips from jetty. Excellent sports facilities: golf, indoor pool, tennis, pony trekking, Leisure Centre. Summer variety shows, Alice In Wonderland Visitor Centre.

MR AND MRS C. WATTS, HEN DY HOTEL, 10 NORTH PARADE, LLANDUDNO LL30 2LP (01492 876184). Experience the warm welcome extended by the proprietors of this charming Hotel, set opposite the Pier, with panoramic views. All rooms with central heating, TV, radio, teamakers; some en suite. Good food. Cosy bar. From £18.00 per night. 3 Crowns Highly Commended. [🐾]

MR AND MRS J. WILLIAMS, "DEVA", 34 TRINITY AVENUE, LLANDUDNO LL30 2TQ (01492 877059). Holiday Flats for 2/4 adults. House-trained pets welcome. Car parking. Colour television. Bed linen provided. Park opposite to walk your dog. Stamp please for brochure. [🐾]

Llanfairfechan

Small resort on Conway Bay midway between Bangor and Conway.

BARBARA & TERRY ALLIX, YENTON, PROMENADE, LLANFAIRFECHAN LL33 OBU (01248 680075). Warm, comfortable, fully equipped, self-contained, seafront family apartments. Sleep 2/6. Bed linen and central heating included. Sandy beach, scenic views, easy seaside or mountain walks, good touring position. [Pets £10.00 per week.]

Llangaffo

Peaceful village 7 miles west of Menai Bridge.

ANN LAMB, PLAS LLANGAFFO, ANGLESEY LL60 6LR (01248 440452). Peaceful location near Newborough Forest and Llandwyn Bay with its miles of golden sands. Sheep, horses and hens kept. Free-range eggs and home-made marmalade for breakfast. Dinner optional. Tea/coffee making facilities. Horse riding available. [🐾]

Llangollen

Famous for International Music Eisteddfod held in July. Plas Newydd, Valle Crucis Abbey nearby. Standard gauge steam railway; canal cruises; ideal for golf and walking.

BRYN DERWEN HOTEL, ABBEY ROAD, LLANGOLLEN LL20 8EF (01978 860583). Warm, friendly welcome for your pet in well-appointed hotel in picturesque Dee Valley. Super walking country, many tourist attractions including Llangollen Steam Railway. Special discounts for *Pets Welcome!* readers.

PEN-Y-DYFFRYN COUNTRY HOUSE HOTEL, NEAR RHYDYCROESAU, OSWESTRY SY10 7DT (Tel. & Fax: 01691 653700). Georgian Rectory set in Shropshire/ Welsh Hills. Seven en suite bedrooms, colour TV. Licensed restaurant. Very quiet and relaxed. 5-acre grounds. Dinner, Bed and Breakfast from £43.00 per person. 3 Crowns. [🐾 pw!]

Llanwrst

Small town on River Conwy 11 miles south of Colwyn Bay

MRS ELEANORE ROBERTS, AWELON, PLAS ISA, LLANRWST LL26 0EE (01492 640047). Small guest house 4 miles north of Betws-y-Coed, 150 yards from A470. 3 well-appointed bedrooms (one en suite) with colour TV and tea-makers. Central for walking and touring Snowdonia. Parking. Sorry, no large dogs. B&B £14.50 to £17; dinner optional.

Morfa Nefyn

Picturesque village 2 miles west of Nefyn.

MR P. W. REES, "QUALITY COTTAGES", CERBID, SOLVA, HAVERFORDWEST, PEMBROKESHIRE SA62 6YE (01348 837871). Cottages set in all coastal areas, unashamed luxury — highest residential standards. Dishwashers, microwaves, washing machines. Log fires. Linen supplied. Pets welcome. [pw!]

Nannerch

Village 4 miles south of Holywell

THE OLD MILL PRIVATE HOTEL, MELIN-Y-WERN, DENBIGH ROAD, NANNERCH, MOLD, FLINTSHIRE CH7 5RH. Small, friendly family-run hotel. All rooms en suite, local hill walks. Watermill conservation area; gardens. Taste of Wales. Special breaks. 3 Crowns Highly Commended, AA**, RAC Highly Acclaimed. Call FREEPHONE 0800 454233 for full details and brochure.

Pentraeth

Picturesque village on Anglesey 5 miles north of Menai Bridge.

ANGLESEY COUNTRY COTTAGES, PENTRAETH, ANGLESEY LL75 8UR (01248 450223). Choice of 12 luxury cottages all with microwave, colour TV and video on a small quiet complex with 20 acres of grass. Heated swimming pool. [pw!]

Porthmadog

Harbour town with mile-long Cob embankment, along which runs Ffestiniog Narrow Gauge Steam Railway to Blaenau Ffestiniog. Pottery, maritime museum, car museum. Good beaches nearby.

MR P. W. REES, "QUALITY COTTAGES", CERBID, SOLVA, HAVERFORDWEST, PEMBROKESHIRE SA62 6YE (01348 837871). Cottages set in all coastal areas, unashamed luxury; highest residential standards. Dishwashers, microwaves, washing machines. Log fires. Linen supplied. Pets welcome. [pw!]

TYDDYN DU FARM HOLIDAYS (PW), GELLILYDAN, NEAR FFESTINIOG, PORTHMADOG LL41 4RB (01766 590281). Beautiful historic 17th century farmhouse situated in the heart of Snowdonia National Park. All rooms have colour TV, tea/coffee and most are en suite. [Pets £2 per night]

BLACK ROCK SANDS, PORTHMADOG. Private site, beach 150 yards.14 Caravans only. Fully equipped 6 berths. Own flush toilets. Showers and TVs. Shop and tavern near. APPLY: M. HUMPHRIES, 251 HEDNESFORD ROAD, NORTON CANES, CANNOCK, STAFFORDSHIRE WS11 3RZ (01543 279583).

Porth Neigel

Bay on south side of Lleyn peninsula, also known as Hell's Mouth.

Attractive cottage set in meadow near beach, quiet rural area. Sleeps 6 , open fire, all comforts. Local carer. Near Abersoch. Details from MRS E.M. COOPER, 18 ST MARY'S LANE, LOUTH, LINCOLNSHIRE LN11 0DT (01507 604408).

Pwllheli

Popular sailing centre with harbour and long sandy beach. Golf, leisure centre, river and sea fishing.

DEUCOCH HOTEL, ABERSOCH, PWLLHELI LL53 7LD (01758 712680; Fax: 01758 712670). Stuart & Barbara White invite you to their comfortable, informal, family-run hotel. Spacious gardens with magnificent views across Cardigan Bay to Snowdonia. Open all year. [🐕].

Red Wharf Bay

Deep curving bay with vast expanse of sand, very popular for sailing and swimming.

MR P. W. REES, "QUALITY COTTAGES", CERBID, SOLVA, HAVERFORDWEST, PEMBROKESHIRE SA62 6YE (01348 837871). Cottages set in all coastal areas, unashamed luxury highest residential standards. Dishwashers, microwaves, washing machines. Log fires. Linen supplied. Pets welcome. [pw!]

BRYN TIRION HOTEL, RED WHARF BAY, ANGLESEY LL75 8RZ (01248 852366; Fax: 01248 852013). Family-run hotel with beautiful views overlooking Red Wharf Bay. All rooms en suite with colour TV, tea/coffee etc. Large garden. Ground floor room. Excellent restaurant. [Pets £2.00 per night.]

Rhos-on-Sea

Popular resort at east end of Penrhyn Bay, adjoining Colwyn Bay to the north-west.

SUNNYDOWNS HOTEL, 66 ABBEY ROAD, RHOS ON SEA, CONWY LL28 4NU (01492 544256; Fax: 01492 543223). A 4 Crown luxury family hotel just 2 minutes' walk to beach & shops. All rooms en suite with colour TV, video & satellite channels, tea/coffee facilities and central heating. Hotel has bar, pool room and car park. [🐕 pw!]

ASHMOUNT HOTEL, COLLEGE AVENUE, RHOS-ON-SEA, COLWYN BAY LL28 4NT (01492 544582; Fax: 01492 545479). Situated close to the picturesque harbour and village of Rhos-on-Sea. Ideal for touring Snowdonia and the North Wales coast. Small, beautiful hotel with elegant restaurant renowned for its cuisine, vegetarian and special diets. 4 Crowns Highly Commended, AA/RAC Two Stars. [Pets £1.50 per night.]

Ruthin

On hill above River Clwyd, with many interesting buildings and modern craft centre producing glass, leather, ceramics and jewellery.

MRS B. QUINN, BERLLAN BACH, FFORDD LAS, LLANDYRNOG LL16 4LR (01824 790732). Meg and Nell, our lovely collies, are delighted to welcome your four-legged friends to their lovely home. En suite rooms with french windows opening into the orchard. Bed and Breakfast from £17.50. 3 Crowns. [🐕]

MRS I. HENDERSON, ESGAIRLYGAIN, LLANGYNHAFAL, RUTHIN LL15 1RT (01824 704047). Stone barn conversion. En suite rooms. Direct access to Clwydian hills. Convenient for Llangollen, Chester, Snowdonia, castles and coast. WTB 3 Crowns. Well behaved dogs welcome free. Owners £16.50! [🐾]

Trearddur Bay

Attractive holiday spot set amongst low cliffs on Holy Island, near Holyhead. Golf, sailing, fishing, swimming.

CLIFF COTTAGES AND PLAS DARIEN APARTMENTS, TREARDDUR BAY LL63 3LD (01407 860789). Fully equipped holiday Cottages, sleeping 4/8 plus cot. Near sea. Children's playground. Indoor and outdoor heated pools. Colour television. Choice of centrally heated apartments or stone-built cottages. Own private leisure complex with bowls, sauna, snooker, table tennis etc. Also tennis, croquet. Adjacent golf course. [🐾]

TREARDDUR HOLIDAY BUNGALOWS, LON ISALLT, TREARDDUR BAY, ANGLESEY LL65 2UP (01407 860494) Good quality self catering holiday bungalows near beach sleeping 3–7. WTB Grade 4. Facilities include indoor heated swimming pool, licensed club and restaurant, site shop, tennis court and children's play areas. [Pets £20 per week]

Trefriw

Hillside village, popular as spa in Victorian times. Local beauty spots at Llyn Crafnant and Llyn Geironnydd. Woollen mill demonstrating traditional techniques.

ANN AND ARTHUR EATON, CRAFNANT GUEST HOUSE, TREFRIW LL27 OJH (01492 640809). Totally non-smoking Victorian country home. 5 en suite double/ twin rooms with drinks tray and TV. Traditional /vegetarian menu. B&B £15-£16. Dogs welcome by arrangement. [Pets £2 per night]

MRS B. COLE, GLANDWR, TREFRIW, NEAR LLANRWST LL27 0JP (01492 640431). Large country house on outskirts of Trefriw village. Good touring area with Llanrwst, Betws-y-Coed and Swallow Falls five miles away. Fishing, walking, golf, pony trekking close by. Comfortable bedrooms, lounge with TV, dining room. Good home cooking. Parking. Bed and Breakfast from £16, Dinner if required.

Tywyn

Pleasant seaside resort, start of Talyllyn Narrow Gauge Railway. Sea and river fishing, golf.

Fully equipped coastal house, close to sandy beach. 3 bedrooms, sleeps five. Gardens; garage. Pets welcome free of charge. APPLY – MR AND MRS WESTON, 18 ELIZABETH ROAD, BASINGSTOKE, HAMPSHIRE RG22 6AX (01256 52364; 01256 412233 evenings).

GILFACH HOLIDAY VILLAGE
THE HOLIDAY VILLAGE ON THE COAST MID-WAY BETWEEN NEW QUAY AND ABERAERON

HORSE AND PONY RIDING

TENNIS COURT ON THE ESTATE

Gilfach is set in lovely unspoiled countryside on the coast midway between the resorts of New Quay and Aberaeron, not far from Aberystwyth, Devil's Bridge and other attractions. There is a choice of modern Bungalows, accommodating up to 6 persons and luxury 2/3 person apartments set in 36 acres of ground. Horse riding to suit all ages is available on the Estate and you can fish from the beach. River fishing is also available nearby. The Estate has its own licensed club, en-tout-cas all weather Tennis court, and boats may be launched from our own beach. Local traders deliver bread, meat, papers, etc. The children have a den and playground and pets are welcome. All the accommodation is fully equipped and includes colour TV, and bed linen is available. For our colour Brochure Pack, write or phone the MANAGER at:

GILFACH HOLIDAY VILLAGE;
LLWYNCELYN, Nr ABEREARON, DYFED SA46 0NN
TEL: LLANARTH (01545) 580288

SYMBOLS

🐕   Indicates no charge for pets. are welcome free of charge.

£   Indicates that a charge is made for pets: nightly or weekly.

pw!   Shows some special provision for pets; exercise facility, feeding or accommodation arrangement.

⌂   Indicates separate pets accommodation.

TYGLYN HOLIDAY ESTATE (Dept. PW)

CILIAU AERON, NEAR LAMPETER, DYFED SA48 8DD
Telephone: (01570) 470684

Tyglyn Holiday Estate nestles in the heart of rural Wales and yet is only four miles from the pretty little seaside town of Aberaeron.

From your holiday bungalow the views up and down the Aeron Valley are awe-inspiring. Beautiful rolling hills rise from the valley through which the river Aeron flows. It passes through the estate for almost a mile and its outfall is at Aberaeron where day or fishing trips can be taken.

The bungalows take pride of place overlooking most of the 120-acre farm and in sight of some of the woodland.

Buzzards nest on the farm, Ravens are regular visitors, Dippers can be seen on the river, Kestrels and the rare Red Kite can be seen in the air. We have Badgers and Foxes breeding on the estate, Otters have been seen in the river, and there are rare butterflies and an abundance of wild flowers.

There is an adjacent pub and restaurant.

Riding can be arranged locally, bowling, tennis, golf and swimming can all be found within a few miles.

While at Tyglyn your accommodation will be provided by one of only 20 award-winning brick-built semi-detached two-bedroom bungalows which include all modern facilities and colour TV. Milk, newspapers and grocery deliveries daily if required. Your pets are welcomed as warmly as you. For further details telephone 01570 470684 for a free colour brochure.

4/6 Berth
£115-£260

NOLTON HAVEN FARM
QUALITY BEACHFRONT COTTAGES/FARM GUESTHOUSE

Quality Beachfront Cottages. The stone, slate and pine constructed Cottages occupy a unique position just 30 yards from Nolton Haven's sandy beach, with extensive lawns leading to the beach which they overlook. The Cottages are equipped with double oven cookers, colour television, steam iron, fridge/freezer, toasters, auto kettles, microwave ovens and fixed heating. The Cottages, fully carpeted and sleeping 4/6, are open all year including Winter Breaks.

Farm Guesthouse. ★ 50 yards sandy beach ★ Colour television lounge ★ Children and pets welcome ★ Babysitting ★ Use of house all day ★ Pub/Restaurant 75 yards ★ Dinner, Bed and Breakfast. En suite rooms available.

J. CANTON, NOLTON HAVEN FARM, Nolton Haven, Haverfordwest, Pembrokeshire, Dyfed SA62 6NH. Tel: (01437) 710263

SAUNDERSFOOT, Mrs Joy Holgate, Carne Mountain Farm, Reynalton, Kilgetty SA68 OPD Tel: 01834 860 546

A warm welcome awaits you at our lovely 200-year-old farmhouse set amidst the peace and tranquillity of the beautiful Pembrokeshire countryside. Pretty, picturesque bedrooms with colour TV, washbasins, tea/coffee tray and central heating. Vegetarians very welcome. Bed and breakfast from £14.00. Wales Tourist Board Commended. Farmhouse Award. Quality 6 berth caravan also available from £90 per week. SAE please.

VINE FARM
The Ridgeway, Saundersfoot SA69 9LA
Tel: 01834 813543

Situated half mile from the village centre and beaches this delightful former farmhouse has been sympathetically modernised whilst retaining its charm. Centrally heated throughout, licensed; ample parking and an exercise paddock for dogs. All five bedrooms are en suite with colour TV, tea/coffee tray and clock/radio. We take great pride in the quality of our food, with choices on all menus, including a 5 course dinner, using local produce and vegetables from our own garden in season.

AA Listed	**B&B from £21 pp. Dinner, B&B from £27 pppd.**	RAC
QQQ	**Also 1-bedroom s/c flat for 2 from £120 per week.**	Acclaimed

---

SYMBOLS

★	Indicates no charge for pets. are welcome free of charge.
£	Indicates that a charge is made for pets: nightly or weekly.
pw!	Shows some special provision for pets; exercise facility, feeding or accommodation arrangement.
⌂	Indicates separate pets accommodation.

Aberaeron

Attractive little town on Cardigan Bay, good touring centre for coast and inland. The Aeron Express Aerial feny offers an exciting trip across the harbour. Marine aquarium; Aberarth Leisure Park nearby.

GILFACH HOLIDAY VILLAGE, LLWYNCELYN, NEAR ABERAERON SA46 ONN (01545 580288). Choice of modern Bungalows (6 persons) or luxury 2/3 person apartments. Fully equipped, linen, colour TV. Horse and pony riding. Tennis. Write or phone for brochure pack to the Manager. [Pets £10 per week.]

Aberporth

Popular seaside village offering safe swimming and good sea fishing. Good base for exploring Cardigan Bay coastline.

MISS M. ALLEN, YR YSGUBOR, PANTYFFWRN, ABERPORTH, CARDIGAN SA43 2DT (01239 810509). Delightful stone cottage on beautiful, unspoilt West Wales coast. Quiet, comfortable; all amenities. Sleeps 2. Large dog-friendly garden. Ample parking. From £60 plus electricity. [🐾]

MRS J. TUCKER, PENFFYNNON, ABERPORTH, CARDIGAN SA43 2DA (01239 810387). Well furnished, comfortable bungalows and large apartments (sleep 2/6), all with sea views; most set in own grounds. Aberporth has two sandy beaches, several pubs and a variety of shops; Cardigan 7 miles. Children and pets welcome. Terms from £100-£300 per week. 3/4 Keys.

MR P. W. REES, "QUALITY COTTAGES", CERBID, SOLVA, HAVERFORDWEST, . PEMBROKESHIRE SA62 6YE (01348 837871). Cottages set in all coastal areas unashamed luxury; highest residential standards. Dishwashers, microwaves, washing machines. Log fires. Linen supplied. Pets welcome. [pw!].

HIGHCLIFFE HOTEL, SCHOOL ROAD, ABERPORTH SA43 2DA (Tel/Fax: 01239 810534). DOLPHINS 'N' DAFFODILS beside our clean, safe sandy beach where dolphins cruise the bay. Olde worlde restaurant, en suite rooms, superb food and special diets. Beach 100 yards, free daily dog chew. [pw! Pets £3 per night]

Bosherston

Village 4 miles south of Pembroke, bordered by 3 man-made lakes, a haven for wildlife and covered in water lilies in early summer.

MR P. W. REES, "QUALITY COTTAGES", CERBID, SOLVA, HAVERFORDWEST, PEMBROKESHIRE SA62 6YE (01348 837871). Cottages set in all coastal areas; unashamed luxury — dishwashers, microwaves, washing machines — highest residential standards. Log fires. Linen provided. Pets welcome. [pw!]

Broad Haven

Attractive little resort on St Bride's Bay in the Pembrokeshire Coast National Park. Superb sandy beach; National Park Information Centre.

PEMBROKESHIRE NATIONAL PARK. Three-bedroom fully furnished holiday house, sleeps 6. Walking distance sandy beaches and coastal footpath. £90 to £220 per week. MRS L.P. ASHTON, 10 ST LEONARDS ROAD, THAMES DITTON, SURREY KT7 0RJ (0181–398 6349). [🐾]

MILLMOOR FARM COTTAGES AND ROCKSDRIFT APARTMENTS. Enjoy a relaxing and peaceful holiday only yards from safe sandy beaches and woodland walks. Personal supervision. Microwaves, fridge freezers, colour TV. Full central heating. Children's play areas, cots, high chairs. Brochure from HELEN MOCK, MILLMOOR, BROAD HAVEN, HAVERFORDWEST SA62 3JB (01437 781507; Fax 01437 781002). [Pets £12 per week.]

SANDRA DAVIES, BARLEY VILLA, WALWYNS CASTLE, NEAR BROAD HAVEN, HAVERFORDWEST, PEMBROKESHIRE SA62 3EB (01437 781254) Comfortable 2 bedroomed accommodation in peaceful, attractive countryside. Central location. All amenities. Linen provided. £90-£150 fully inclusive. B&B also available from £14.50. [Pets £10 per week]

Carmarthen

Town on a bluff above the Tywi, dominated by ruined Norman castle. Site of Roman amphitheatre off Priory Street, and Roman relics in Carmarthen Museum, east of town.

PENDINE SANDS HOLIDAY PARK, NEAR CARMARTHEN (01345 443 443) Heated indoor pool. Live family evening entertainment. Bar, snack food, barbecues and supermarket. Horse riding, bike hire and tennis nearby. Tourers welcome. Call now for a free colour brochure.

Ciliau Aeron

Village in undulating country just inland from the charming Cardigan Bay resorts of New Quay and Aberaeron. New Quay 12 miles, Aberaeron 6.

TYGLYN HOLIDAY ESTATE, CILIAU AERON, NEAR LAMPETER SA48 8DD (01570 470684). In the heart of rural Wales and only four miles from the seaside town of Aberaeron. Twenty award-winning brick-built semi-detached two-bedroom Bungalows with all modern facilities and colour TV. Range of outdoor activities locally. £115-£260 per week.

MR P. W. REES, "QUALITY COTTAGES", CERBID, SOLVA, HAVERFORDWEST, PEMBROKESHIRE SA62 6YE (01348 837871). Cottages set in all coastal areas, unashamed luxury, highest residential standards. Dishwashers, microwaves, washing machines. Log fires. Linen supplied. Pets welcome. [pw!]

Croes Goch

Hamlet 6 miles north east of St Davids.

MRS M. REES, 'CROFTY', CROES GOCH, HAVERFORDWEST, PEMBROKESHIRE SA62 5JT (01348 831441). We offer comfortable beds and a hearty breakfast. Three bedrooms share bathroom, separate toilet, one large ensuite room. All with tea/coffee and TV. From £15 per person. [🐾]

Crymych

Peaceful village in the Pembrokeshire National Park, 8 miles south of Cardigan.

For riders with some experience. Small groups, indoor school, tuition, showjumps and cross-country fences. Spectacular scenery. Own horses welcome. Self catering accommodation. CHRIS OR GILL HIRST, RAVEL FARM, BRYNBERIAN, CRYMYCH, PEMBROKESHIRE SA41 3TQ (01239 891316).

Fishguard

Picturesque Lower Town clusters around the old quayside; Upper Town is spread out on a hill above the harbour. Many craft workshops in the area; ferry to Ireland from nearby Goodwick.

FISHGUARD BAY CARAVAN AND CAMPING PARK, DINAS CROSS, NEWPORT SA42 0YD (Tel: 01348 811 415; Fax: 01348 811 425). Enjoy a stay at our quiet, family-run Park. Ideal walking and touring centre. Modern Dragon Award caravans equipped to high standards. Touring caravans, motor caravans and tents are welcome. {Pets £10 per week in hire cravans]

Haverfordwest

Administrative and shopping centre for the area; ideal base for exploring National Park Historic town of narrow streets; museum in castle grounds; many fine buildings.

MR & MRS PHILIP THOMAS, NOLTON CROSS CARAVAN PARK, NOLTON, HAVERFORDWEST SA62 3NP (01437 710701). Small family-run caravan park on working farm, central for sandy beaches, countryside and coastal walks, horse riding, traditional evenings and water sports. Fully serviced caravans; central children's play area. [🐾]

Little Haven

Village on St Bride's Bay ,10 miles from Haverfordwest.

HAVEN COTTAGES, WHITEGATES, LITTLE HAVEN, HAVERFORDWEST, PEMBROKESHIRE SA62 3LA (01437 781552). Cottages sleep two to twelve. On Coastal Path, 200 yards beach. Linen provided. B&B in fishing village. WTB 4 Dragons. [Pets £12 per week]

Llandovery

Little town on Rivers Tywi and Bran, with ruins of Norman Castle. Picturesque Tywi Valley to the north. Swansea 35 miles, Carmarthen 28, Builth Wells 24, Brecon 21, Lampeter 19.

THE ROYAL OAK INN, RHANDIRMWYN, NEAR LLANDOVERY SA20 ONY (01550 760201; Fax: 01550 760332; e-mail: royaloak@globalnet.co.uk). Family run, small and dog-friendly village inn with fabulous views and surrounded by glorious countryside. En suite accommodation, good food and real ales. Open all year.

Llangrannog

Pretty little seaside village overlooking a sandy beach. Superb cliff walk to NT Ynys Lochtyn, a secluded promontory.

MR P W REES, "QUALITY COTTAGES", CERBID, SOLVA, HAVERFORDWEST, PEMBROKESHIRE SA62 6YE (01348 837871). Cottages set in all coastal areas, unashamed luxury. All equipped to highest residential standards with washing machines, dishwashers, microwaves. Log fires. Linen supplied. [pw!]

Manorbier

Unspoiled village on South Pembrokeshire coast near Tenby. Sandy bay and fine coastal walks. Impressive 12th century moated castle overlooks bay.

AQUARIUM COTTAGE, MANORBIER. Delightful detached country cottage. Two bedrooms, sleeps 6. Also THE LOBSTER POT, MANORBIER. Pleasant modern ground floor flat. Two bedrooms, sleeps 4. Both properties 1/2 mile sea. Pets welcome. Ample parking. Electricity and bed linen included in price. Brochure from: MRS J. HUGHES, ROSE COTTAGE, MANORBIER, PEMBROKESHIRE SA70 7ST (01834 871408). [🐾]

Newgale

On St Bride's Bay 3 miles east of Solva. Long beach where at exceptionally low tide the stumps of a submerged forest may be seen.

MR P W REES, "QUALITY COTTAGES", CERBID, SOLVA, HAVERFORDWEST, PEMBROKESHIRE SA62 6YE (01348 837871). Cottages set in all coastal areas, unashamed luxury; equipped to highest residential standards with dishwashers, washing machines, microwave ovens. Log fires. Linen provided. Pets welcome. [pw!]

Newport

Small town at mouth of the River Nyfer, 9 miles south west of Cardigan. Remains of 13th-century castle.

MR P. W. REES, "QUALITY COTTAGES", CERBID, SOLVA, HAVERFORDWEST, PEMBROKESHIRE SA62 6YE (01348 837871). Cottages set in all coastal areas, unashamed luxury; highest residential standards. Dishwashers, washing machines, microwaves. Log fires. Linen supplied. Pets welcome. [pw!]

Nolton Haven

Hamlet at head of inlet on St Bride's Bay. Fine coastal views.

Quality beachfront Cottages 30 yards from Nolton Haven's sandy beach. Fully equipped, sleeping 4/6. Also nearby Farm Guest House offering Dinner, Bed and Breakfast. APPLY – J. CANTON, NOLTON HAVEN FARM, NOLTON HAVEN, HAVERFORDWEST SA62 6NH (01437 710263).

FOLKESTON HILL HOLIDAY BUNGALOWS. A small group of bungalows in a sheltered valley which winds down to the sea. WTB Graded. Pets welcome – no charge. Brochure from JOHN & CERI PRICE, ST BRIDES BAY COTTAGES, NINE WELLS, SOLVA, HAVERFORDWEST, PEMBROKESHIRE SA62 6UH (01437 720027).

Saundersfoot

Popular resort and sailing centre with picturesque harbour and sandy beach. Tenby 3 miles.

VINE FARM, THE RIDGEWAY, SAUNDERSFOOT SA69 9LA (01834 813543). Former Farmhouse close to village and beaches. Central heating, log fires. All rooms en suite. Pets welcome – garden and paddock. AA Listed QQQ. [pw! Pets £1.00 per night.] Also available, one-bedroomed Self Catering flat for 2.

MRS JOY HOLGATE, CARNE MOUNTAIN FARM, REYNALTON, KILGETTY SA68 OPD (01834 860 546). A warm welcome awaits you at our lovely 200-year-old farmhouse set amidst the peace and tranquillity of the beautiful Pembrokeshire countryside. Bedrooms have colour TV and all facilities. B&B from £14. [One dog free, second pet £1.00 per night.]

Solva

Picturesque coastal village with sheltered harbour and excellent craft shops. Sailing and watersports; sea fishing, long sandy beach.

MRS M. J. PROBERT, YNYS DAWEL, SOLVA, HAVERFORDWEST SA62 6UF (01437 721491). Quality Cottages in Solva near safe, sandy beaches. Highest standards. Enclosed rear gardens. Modern central heating. Resident owners. Particularly warm welcome to Boxer dogs (and others) and their owners. [Pets £7/£10 per week.]

MR P. W. REES, "QUALITY COTTAGES", CERBID, SOLVA, HAVERFORDWEST, PEMBROKESHIRE SA62 6YE (01348 837871). Cottages set in all coastal areas, unashamed luxury, highest residential standards. Dishwashers, microwaves, washing machines. Log fires. Linen supplied. Pets welcome. [pw!]

MRS M. JONES, LOCHMEYLER FARM, PEN-Y-CWM, NEAR SOLVA, HAVERFORDWEST SA62 6LL (01348 837724; Fax: 01348 837622). Modernised farmhouse on 220-acre dairy farm retains all its old character. Smokers' lounge, video library. Choice of menu including traditional farmhouse and vegetarian. Children over 10 welcome. Open all year. B&B from £20. [pw! 🐾]

St David's

Smallest cathedral city in Britain, shrine of Wales' patron saint. Magnificent ruins of Bishop's Palace. Craft shops, farm parks and museums; boat trips to Ramsey Island.

MR P. W. REES, "QUALITY COTTAGES", CERBID, SOLVA, HAVERFORDWEST, PEMBROKESHIRE SA62 6YE (01348 837871). Cottages set in all coastal areas, unashamed luxury; highest residential standards. Dishwashers, microwaves, washing machines. Log fires. Linen supplied, pets welcome. [pw!]

RAMSEY HOUSE, LOWER MOOR, ST DAVID'S SA62 6RP (01437 720321). Mac and Sandra Thompson offer quiet relaxation exclusively for non-smoking adults. Superior en suite rooms with central heating, TV and tea makers. Traditional Welsh cuisine. Licensed bar. Parking. Open all year. Superb beaches and walks nearby – DOGS' PARADISE! 3 Crowns Highly Commended, RAC Highly Acclaimed, AA Selected QQQQ. [🐾]

Delightful farmhouse 6 miles from St David's. 3 bedrooms sleeping 6. Fully equipped except linen. New automatic washing machine. Electricity by coin meter. APPLY: MRS C. E. SKEEL JONES, AROSFYR FARM, DOLGELLAU LL40 2YP (01341 422 355). [First pet free, £15 per week for second pet.]

FELINDRE COTTAGES, LLANRHIAN, ST. DAVIDS, HAVERFORDWEST, PEMBROKESHIRE SA62 5BH (01348 831220). Well-equipped self catering cottages set in peaceful 8 acre location. Sea views. Away from main roads, safe for children and pets. WTB graded. Near sandy beaches, spectacular cliff walks and pub. [Pets £10 per week, pw!]

Tenby

Popular resort with two wide beaches. Fishing trips, craft shops, museum. Medieval castle ruins, 13th-century church. Golf, fishing and watersports; boat trips to nearby Caldy Island with monastery and medieval church.

MR P. W. REES, "QUALITY COTTAGES", CERBID, SOLVA, HAVERFORDWEST, PEMBROKESHIRE SA62 6YE (01348 837871). Cottages set in all coastal areas, unashamed luxury; highest residential standards. Dishwashers, microwaves, washing machines. Log fires. Linen provided, pets welcome. [pw!]

MRS J. N. FRAZER, HIGHLANDS FARM, MANORBIER-NEWTON, TENBY SA70 8PX (01834 871446). Spacious six-berth caravan situated in quiet three-acre meadow. Caravan has electric lighting and TV, gas cooker and heater. Two separate bedrooms, shower, kitchen/diner and lounge. Car essential. Peaceful setting, ideal for children or well-behaved pet. Please write or phone for details.

Whitland

Village 6 miles east of Narberth. Scanty ruins of 12th century Cistercian house remain.

WATKINS, PARC-Y-FFYNNON, CWMFELIN MYNACH, WHITLAND SA34 ODJ (01994 448341). Well appointed six-berth caravan in owner's large garden. Mains services, CTV. Situated in a quiet rural area, within easy travelling distance to beaches. Ideally placed for exploring Carmarthenshire, Pembrokeshire and Cardiganshire. Prices £100-£150 per week inclusive. Brochure on request. [🐴]

POWYS

POWYS   *Corris, Crickhowell*

Braich Goch Hotel & Restaurant
Corris, Near Machynlleth, Powys SY20 9RD

Set in beautiful surroundings in the foothills of Snowdonia on the A487. Ideally situated for touring, steam train enthusiasts, birdwatching, rambling, fishing. Golf, horse riding and clay pigeon shooting all well catered for. World famous Centre for Alternative Technology and King Arthur's Labyrinth (new attraction) close by. Bedrooms en suite or with private facilities; licensed restaurant with extensive menu; cheerful beamed bar is a meeting place for friendly locals. Pets most welcome.

B&B £21pp (double or twin); Autumn and Winter Breaks B,B&EM £25pp.

Tel/Fax: 01654 761229   ☙☙ Commended

Mrs. P. Llewelyn, WHITE HALL, Glangrwyney, Crickhowell, Powys NP8 1 EW

Comfortably furnished and well placed for exploring Black Mountains, Brecon Beacons, Big Pit Mine, Abergavenny and Hay-on-Wye. Double and twin-bedded rooms with TV and tea-making. Terms: from £15. Small single £13.00.

Phone (01873) 811155 or 840267   WTB ☙☙

Brecon

Main touring centre for National Park. Busy market; Jazz Festival in summer. Brecknock Museum, ruined castle, cathedral of interest. Golf, walking, fishing, canal cruising, pony trekking.

MRS ANN PHILLIPS, TYLEBRYTHOS FARM, CANTREF, BRECON LD3 8LR (01874 665329). Warm and cosy, attractively decorated and superbly equipped self catering bungalow, farmhouse or apartments situated amongst spectacular scenery in the Brecon Beacons National Park. Well maintained grounds. Safe children's play area. Ample parking. Personally supervised with cleanliness assured. Short breaks available. Pets by prior arrangement. WTB Grade 4/5. Brochure on request. [Pets £10 per week.]

BEACONS GUEST HOUSE, 16 BRIDGE STREET, BRECON LD3 8AH (01874 623339). Georgian guest house, comfortably furnished, well equipped rooms (most en suite). Cosy bar, spacious dining room, residents' lounge. Excellent Aga-cooked evening meals prepared with care from local produce.Situated two minutes' walk from town centre. Magnificent scenery, wonderful walking country. 3 Crowns Commended, AA QQQ, RAC Acclaimed. [🐾]

Builth Wells

Old country town in lovely setting on River Wye amid beautiful hills. Lively sheep and cattle markets; host to Royal Welsh Agricultural Show.

R. I. AND M. C. WILTSHIRE, BRON WYE GUEST HOUSE, 5 CHURCH STREET, BUILTH WELLS LD2 3BS (01982 553587). Bed and Breakfast; Evening Meals by prior arrangement. Snacks, home cooking. Licensed. TV Lounge. Tea/coffee making all rooms, en suite available. Car park. Children and pets welcome. Bed and Breakfast from £13, en suite £16 per person. Evening Meal £7 per person by arrangement. WTB Three Crowns Commended. [🐾]

MRS LINDA WILLIAMS, OLD VICARAGE, ERWOOD, BUILTH WELLS LD2 3SZ (01982 560680). Beautiful situation just off A470 near Erwood. Spacious rooms with full central heating, beverage trays and washbasins; views over Wye Valley to Black Mountains. Private lounge with games, maps, literature. Bathroom and separate WC. Secluded grounds. B&B £13-13.50; EM by arrangement, own produce. WTB One Crown Commended. [🐾]

Corris

Peaceful village 4 miles north of Machynlleth.

BRAICH GOCH HOTEL & RESTAURANT, CORRIS, NEAR MACHYNLLETH SY20 9RD (Tel/Fax: 01654 761229). Set in beautiful surroundings, in area rich in mountain walks. Ideal for train enthusiasts and birdwatchers; activity holidays can be arranged. Fully licensed restaurant and friendly bar. Pets most welcome.

Crickhowell

Pleasant village in the Usk Valley at foot of Black Mountains. 16th century bridge, fine Georgian houses, fragments of a castle, gateway of a long-vanished manor house, and 14th-cent church with elaborate tombs and memorials.

PRISCILLA LLEWELYN, WHITE HALL, GLANGRWYNEY, CRICKHOWELL NP8 1EW (01873 811155 / 840267). Comfortably furnished and well placed for exploring Black Mountains, Brecon Beacons etc. Double and twin rooms with TV and tea-making. Terms on request. Pets welcome. WTB 2 Crowns. [🐕]

Dinas Mawddwy

Hamlet 8 miles east of Dolgellau.

BUCKLEY PINES HOTEL, DINAS MAWDDWY, NEAR MACHYNLLETH SY20 9LP (01650 531261). Comfortable family-run hotel set in Snowdonia National Park. All rooms with TV and tea/coffee– some en suite. Dogs free of charge, welcome in rooms and bar. Special terms for 3-day breaks. WTB Three Crowns. [🐕]

Garthmyl

Situated on A483 between Welshpool and Newtown in unspoilt countryside.

Self-catering luxury in beautiful log cabins set in 30 acres of unspoilt woodland. Central heating, colour TV, microwave etc. Pets welcome. From £220 to £575 per week. APPLY – PENLLWYN LODGES, GARTHMYL SY15 6SB (01686 640269).

Hay-on-Wye

Small market town at north end of Black Mountains, 15 miles north-east of Brecon.

PETER & OLWEN ROBERTS, YORK HOUSE, CUSOP, HAY-ON-WYE HR3 5QX (01497 820705). RAC Highly Acclaimed, AA QQQ. Enjoy a relaxing holiday in this elegant Victorian guest house quietly situated on the edge of Hay, "Town of Books". Excellent walking country for pets. [Pets £4.00 per visit.]

Llandrindod Wells

Popular inland resort, Victorian spa town, excellent touring centre. Golf, fishing, bowling, boating and tennis. Visitors can still take the waters at Rock Park Gardens.

THE PARK MOTEL, CROSSGATES, LLANDRINDOD WELLS LD1 6RF (01597 851201). In three acres, amidst beautiful countryside near Elan Valley. Luxury, self-contained, centrally heated Chalets. Licensed restaurant open all day. Swimming pool. Children's play area. Pets welcome. [Pets £1 per night, £5 per week.]

Llanfair Caereinion

Small town on River Banwy, 8 miles west of Welshpool.

MRS ANN REED, MADOG'S WELLS, LLANFAIR CAEREINION, WELSHPOOL SY21 0DE (01938 810446). WTB 4 Dragons. Furnished bungalow designed for wheelchair access. Open all year. Also two six/eight berth caravans, available April to November. Farmhouse Bed and Breakfast from £15 per person; Evening Meal £8. [🐾]

Llangurig

Village on River Wye, 4 miles south-west of Llanidloes. Craft centre and monastic 14th century church. Ideal walking countryside.

THE OLD VICARAGE COUNTRY GUEST HOUSE, LLANGURIG, MONTGOMERYSHIRE SY18 6RN (01686 440280). Charming Victorian house, ideal base for exploring the mountains and valleys of this unspoiled area. All bedrooms en suite. Two guest lounges. Warm welcome guaranteed. WTB 3 Crowns Highly Commended. [🐾]

Machynlleth

Set in enchanting position on the Dovey Valley, this spot has been inhabited since the Iron Age and was made capital of Wales by Owen Glendower, who was proclaimed King at a parliament in 1404. Welshpool 38 miles, Newtown 28, Aberystwyth 18, Dolgellau 18, Aberdovey 11.

WYNNSTAY ARMS HOTEL, MAENGWYN STREET, MACHYNLLETH SY20 8AE (01654 702941; Fax: 01654 703884). Traditional coaching inn on edge Snowdonia. Comfortable en suite rooms, cosy bars with traditional ales; excellent bar and restaurant food. Experience the warmest of welcomes.

Presteigne

An attractive old town with half-timbered houses. Ideal for hillside rambles and pony trekking.

MRS R. L. JONES, UPPER HOUSE, KINNERTON, NEAR PRESTEIGNE LD8 2PE (01547 560207). Charming Tudor cottage in lovely Border countryside. 2 miles from Offa's Dyke. Children and pets welcome. Storage heaters, washing machine, microwave, colour TV, log fire. Linen hire optional. Sleeps 5 plus 2 cots. Ample parking. Sun trap garden. On working farm in peaceful hamlet. WTB Grade 3. [🐾]

Talgarth

Small town 7 miles south west of Hay-on-Wye.

Starting from Talgarth, spend one or two weeks exploring the Brecon Beacons National Park in a four berth horse drawn caravan – £450 per week. For brochure contact MR A.GWILLIM, WELSH HORSE DRAWN HOLIDAYS, GREYSTONES, TALGARTH, POWYS LD3 0BP (01874 711346).

Welshpool

Lively market town with medieval streets. Narrow gauge Welshpool and Llanfair Light Railway runs along restored 8 mile track. Shrewsbury 17 miles.

ATTENTION, ALL DOGS IN NEED OF A BREAK! Enjoy a well deserved holiday on our tranquil smallholding. Relax with your owners at our secluded self-catering timber lodge with open fields, wildlife pools, fishing and wonderful views. Phone for FREE leaflet. SONYA WALLACE & BARRY SMITH, LLUEST FACH, FOEL, WELSHPOOL SY21 0PB (01938 820351).

LORDS BUILDINGS FARM, LEIGHTON, NEAR WELSHPOOL. Set in 73 acres with panoramic views. Sleeps 7 plus cot. Everything provided except linen. Ideal touring base. Children and pets welcome. WTB 3 Dragons. MRS M.E. EDWARDS, WINDMILL FARM, HALFWAY HOUSE, NEAR SHREWSBURY, SHROPSHIRE SY5 9EJ (01743 884356). [🐕]

SOUTH WALES
(Formerly Glamorgan and Gwent)
Blaenau Gwent, Bridgend, Caerphilly, Cardiff, Merthyr Tydfil, Monmouthshire, Neath and Port Talbot, Newport, Rhondda Cynon Taff, Swansea, Torfaen, and Vale of Glamorgan

SOUTH WALES   *Llanmadoc*

 Located near the splendid Gower coastline, surrounded by beautiful countryside. "Tallizmand" has tastefully furnished en suite bedrooms with tea/coffee making facilities. Home cooking (vegetarians catered for); packed lunches.
❀❀❀ Highly Commended
Pets welcome.
Mrs A. Main, Tallizmand, Llanmadoc, Gower SA3 1DE (01792 386373)

Abergavenny

Historic market town at south-eastern gateway to Brecon Beacons National Park. Pony trekking, leisure centre; excellent touring base for Vale of Usk.

CHRISTINE SMITH, THE HALF MOON, LLANTHONY, NEAR ABERGAVENNY NP7 7NN (01873 890611). Friendly 17th-century inn. Serves good food and real ale. Enjoy wonderful scenery of Black Mountains. Good base. Walking, pony trekking. Dogs welcome. [🐕]

Gower

Britain's first designated Area of Outstanding Natural Beauty with numerous sandy beaches and lovely countryside to explore.

MRS D. A. STILL, CULVER HOUSE, PORT EYNON, GOWER SA3 1NN (01792 390755). Small, friendly hotel with fabulous food and quality service. Peacefully situated, with superb coast and countryside. En suite, sea views. DB&B from £32.00. WTB 3 Crowns Highly Commended, AA*. [Pets £2 per night.]

Llanmadoc

Village on Gower Peninsula, a secluded area with unspoilt beaches and many bird reserves.

MRS A. MAIN, TALLIZMAND, LLANMADOC, GOWER SA3 1DE (01792 386373). Located near the splendid Gower coastline, surrounded by beautiful countryside Tallizmand has tastefully furnished en suite bedrooms with tea/coffee facilities. Home cooking, packed lunches. Pets welcome. 3 Crowns Highly Commended. [🐕]

Mumbles

Seaside resort of Swansea to west and north west of Mumbles Head

MUMBLES & SWANSEA holiday homes, some with sea views. Flat locations. Well equipped, modern conveniences — carpets throughout. Convenient for beaches, countryside and town's amenities. Personally supervised. WTB Graded Three Dragons. Cottage, maisonette, flat and town house available. MRS JEAN GRIERSON, 112 MUMBLES ROAD, BLACKPILL, SWANSEA SA3 5AS (01792 402278). [🐕]

Pontypool

Town 8 miles north of Newport. Valley Inheritance exhibition centre in former Georgian stable of Pontypool Park House tells story of the valleys.

MRS S. ARMITAGE, TY'RYWEN FARM, TREVETHIN, PONTYPOOL NP4 8TT (Tel & Fax: 01495 785200). A very remote 16th Century Longhouse high in the Brecon Beacons National Park. Spacious en suite rooms, colour TV and beverage tray. Some four-posters. One room with jacuzzi. No smoking. No children. Light supper available. B&B from £20.00. [🐕]

Wye Valley

Scenic area, ideal for relaxation.

MR & MRS J. LLEWELLYN, CWRT-Y-GAER, WOLVESNEWTON, CHEPSTOW NP6 6PR (01291 650700). 1, 4 or more dogs welcome free. Self catering, attractively converted stone buildings of Welsh Longhouse. 20 acres, super views of Usk Vale. Brochure. Three units (one suitable for disabled). Four Dragons Award. [🐕 pw!]

SCOTLAND

SCOTLAND *Aberdour, Aultbea, Aviemore*

Five Crowns Highly Commended
2 The Muirs, Kinross,
Scotland KY13 7AS
Tel: 01577 863467; Fax: 01577 863180

Independently owned holiday hotel, only 5 minutes from the M90. Well-appointed bedrooms and family suites. Restaurant, bar meals. Spacious indoor pool and leisure complex, own 18-hole golf course, two all-weather tennis courts, and world famous trout fishing. Ideal touring base with Edinburgh, Glasgow, Perth, Stirling, St. Andrews, Pitlochry and Highland Perthshire within the hour.

THE ESKDALE HOTEL, LANGHOLM, DUMFRIESSHIRE DG13 0JH
Tel and Fax: (013873 80357)

Commended

Former coaching inn on Scottish Border. All rooms have central heating, colour TV, radio alarm and tea/coffee facilities. En suite available. Quality food in à la carte restaurant. Two bars and lively atmosphere. Golf, shooting, fishing and superb walks.
STB ☼☼☼ *Commended*   **AA ★★**

The Sheiling, Loch Maree

Secluded bungalow in wooded grounds by beautiful Loch Maree in Wester Ross, amidst spectacular scenery. Ideal for fishing, shooting, hill-walking or just relaxing. Accommodation sleeping 5/6 people, with coal fire in lounge, all other rooms heated by electric convectors. The bungalow is totally equipped to high standard; bed linen and towels are supplied. All pets are welcome.
Price: low season from £140 to high season £295.
All electricity consumed paid by £1 coin meter.

For reservations contact: **Mr or Mrs A.Allan, Torguish, Daviot, Inverness IVI 2XQ**
Tel: (01463) 772208 Fax: (01463) 772308

£25 deposit confirms booking; remainder, 2 weeks in advance of arrival.

All the advertisers in PETS WELCOME! have an entry in the appropriate classified section and each classified entry may carry one or more of the following symbols:

🐾   This symbol indicates that pets are welcome free of charge.

£   The £ indicates that a charge is made for pets. We quote the amount where possible, either per night or per week.

pw!   This symbol shows that the establishment has some special provision for pets; perhaps an exercise facility or some special feeding or accommodation arrangements.

⌂   Indicates separate pets accommodation.

PLEASE NOTE that all the advertisers in PETS WELCOME! extend a welcome to pets and their owners but they may attach conditions. The interests of other guests have to be considered and it is usually assumed that pets will be well trained, obedient and under the control of their owner.

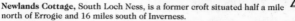

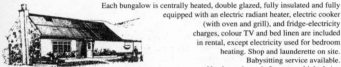

Bunroy Holiday Park,

Roy Bridge PH31 4AG (Tel & Fax: 01397 712332).

In a quiet woodland setting on the River Spean, modern insulated chalets, double glazed and fully equipped for the freedom of self catering for up to four people in comfort. Space for children to play and pets to exercise without traffic worries. Camping and caravans welcome. Ideal base for touring glens and lochs, walking, ski-ing. Chalets from £160 per week. Short Breaks available September to Easter. Visa and Access Cards welcome.

Roy Bridge, Inverness-shire PH31 4AG Tel: 01397 712253

Ideal centre for touring the Scottish Highlands. Nine fully appointed bedrooms with en-suite shower and toilet room, TV and tea maker. Lounge Bar with log fire. Excellent food – full breakfast, à la carte evening meals, bar meals service. Ideal location for touring all areas. Please write or telephone to book and for full brochure and prices.

Terms: B&B from £27 - £32 per night.
Discounts available for 3 nights or more.
All major credit cards accepted.

FHG DIPLOMA
APPROVED to COMMENDED

Be independent with a cottage and a boat on

SKIPNESS ESTATE

This unspoilt, peaceful, West Highland estate with its own historic castle, mediaeval chapel and way-marked walks has traditional seaside estate-workers' cottages to let all year round. Each cottage is well-equipped, including television, rowing dinghy (except in winter months) and open fires, with laundry facilities available alongside the Seafood Cabin at Skipness Castle. Properties sleep four to ten people. Children and pets welcome. All cottages have magnificent views and beautiful surrounding countryside and coastline. Rocky coasts and sandy bays make for safe swimming, with fishing, walks, pony-trekking and golf all nearby. Stalking can be arranged in season. Nearby ferries to Arran, Gigha, Islay and Jura. Apply for rates and further details:

**Sophie James, Skipness Castle, By Tarbert, Argyll PA29 6XU
Tel: 01880 760207; Fax: 01880 760208**

FREE and REDUCED RATE Holiday Visits!
Don't miss our Readers' Offer Vouchers on pages 5 to 18

Aberdeen (Aberdeenshire)

Cathedral and University city on east coast, 57 miles north-east of Dundee. Known as the "Granite City".

SKALA GUESTHOUSE, 2 SPRINGBANK PLACE, ABERDEEN AB11 6LW (01224 572260). Personally run accommodation in quiet city centre location. Convenient for all amenities. All rooms tea/coffee, washbasins, colour TV, CH. STB Listed Commended. Bed & Breakfast from £16 per person. Dogs especially welcome.

Aberdour (Fife)

Small resort on north shore of Firth of Forth 3 miles west of Burntisland. Remains of 17th century castle.

THE WOODSIDE HOTEL, HIGH STREET, ABERDOUR KY3 0SW (01383 860328). You will be made welcome in newly refurbished 3 star comfort. Enjoy the good restaurant, or the tasty food in the bar. You will find the hotel ideally situated for walking your dog. Easy reach to Edinburgh. B&B from £26.50 each.[🐾]

Aberfeldy (Perth & Kinross)

Small town standing on both sides of Urlar Burn near its confluence with the River Tay. Pitlochry 8 miles.

LOCH TAY LODGES, REMONY, ACHARN, ABERFELDY PH15 2HR (01887 830209). STB 4 Crowns Highly Commended. Self catering in village close to Loch. Enjoy hill walking, golf, sailing or touring. Salmon and trout fishing available. Log fires. Pets welcome. Walks along loch shore from house. For brochure, contact MRS G. DUNCAN MILLAR at above address. [🐾]

Appin (Argyll)

Mountainous area bounded by Loch Linnhe, Glen Creran and Glen Coe.

APPIN HOUSE APARTMENTS AND LODGES, APPIN HOUSE, APPIN PA38 4BN (01631 730207; Fax: 01631 730567). We offer 2 cosy lodges and 6 individual apartments adjacent to historic country house. In excellent touring area and surrounded by a large garden. STB 3 Crowns Commended to 4 Crowns Highly Commended. Brochure. [Pets £10 per week.]

Ardbeg (Isle of Bute)

Popular resort reached by ferry from Wemyss Bay. Overlooked by ruined castle; nearby Ardencraig Gardens ane noted for magnificent floral displays; another attraction is Mount Stuart.

ARDMORY HOUSE HOTEL, ARDMORY ROAD, ARDBEG, ISLE OF BUTE PA20 0PG (Tel/Fax: 01700 502346). Nero (Black Labrador) invites friends to share his country retreat of 3/4 acre mature grounds (great sniffs), overlooking Rothesay Bay. 5 well-appointed en suite bedrooms. Restaurant, Bar. Open all year. Bed and Breakfast from £27.50. Bedrooms and Restaurant are NON-SMOKING. STB 3 Crowns Highly Commended, RAC 2 Stars, AA Guild of Master Craftsmen Award.

Auchtermuchty (Fife)

Small town 4 miles south of Newburgh. Site of Roman camp on east side of town.

FOREST HILLS HOTEL, AUCHTERMUCHTY KY14 7OP (Tel and Fax: 01337 828318). Situated in village square, this hotel is an ideal place to stay for pets and owners. Bedrooms with all facilities. Candlelit restaurant. STB 3 Crowns Commended. 20% reduction on accommodation on production of this advert.

Aultbea (Ross-shire)

Village on east shore of Loch Ewe, 5 miles north of Poolewe.

COVE VIEW, 36 MELLON CHARLES, AULTBEA IV22 2JL (01445 731351). Wester Ross is ideal for hill walking or a quiet restful holiday. Two detached cottages in own garden, each with two double bedrooms, sitting room, bathroom and mini kitchen. From £140 per week. B&B from £15.00. A warm welcome awaits you and your pet. [Pets £4 per night]

Aviemore (Inverness-shire)

Scotland's leading ski resort in Spey valley with superb sport and entertainment facilities. All-weather holiday centre with accommodation to suit all pockets. Excellent fishing. Centre for exploring Cairngorms. Edinburgh 129 miles, Grantown-on-Spey 14, Kingussie 12, Carr-Bridge 7.

PINE BANK CHALETS, DALFABER ROAD, AVIEMORE PH22 1PX (01479 810000; Fax: 01479 811469). Cosy Log Cabins and Quality Chalets, situated in a secluded area near the River Spey. Superb Family/Activity Holidays by mountains. Ideal ski-ing, walking, fishing and golf. Sky TV, mountain bikes. Short breaks available. Pets welcome. Open all year. ASSC Member. Brochure. [Pets £20 per week.]

Ballachulish (Argyll)

Impressively placed village at entrance to Glencoe and on Loch Leven. Magnificent mountain scenery including Sgorr Dhearg (3362 ft). Good centre for boating, climbing and sailing. Glasgow 89 miles, Oban 38, Fort William 14, Kinlochleven 9.

BALLACHULISH HOTEL, BALLACHULISH, NEAR FORT WILLIAM PA39 4JY (01855 811606; Fax: 01855 821463). The turreted Ballachulish Hotel will fulfil your dream of the perfect Highland Hotel. Lochside setting, breathtaking mountain views, luxury accommodation, superb restaurant and friendly service. Pets welcome. [pw! £3.00 per night.]

ISLES OF GLENCOE HOTEL AND LEISURE CENTRE, BALLACHULISH, NEAR FORT WILLIAM PA39 4HL (01855 811602; Fax: 01855 821463). Almost afloat, this stylish, modern Hotel nestles on the lochside. Spacious bedrooms offer a commanding panorama of sky, mountain and loch. Delicious cuisine in Conservatory Restaurant. Heated pool & Leisure Centre. [pw! £3.00 per night]

Cottages and Chalets in natural woodland sleeping 4 to 6 people. The Glencoe area is lovely for walking and perfect for nature lovers too. Pets welcome. Regret no smoking. No VAT. Brochure available. APPLY – HOUSE IN THE WOOD HOLIDAYS, GLENACHULISH, BALLACHULISH PA39 4JZ (01855 811379). [🐾]

Ballater (Aberdeenshire)

Village and resort on River Dee 14 miles east of Braemar and 17 miles west of Aberdeen.

THE COYLES HOTEL, 43 GOLF ROAD, BALLATER AB35 5RS (013397 55064). Nestling in a quiet area of Ballater, our small Victorian country hotel will provide every modern facility including luxury accommodation and an excellent menu. En suite guest rooms offer colour TV, radio, tea/coffee facilities and hairdryer.

Ballindalloch (Moray)

Baronial Castle with modern additions and alterations is the most noteworthy building in this area; set on right bank of River Avon near its confluence with River Spey, 7 miles south-west of Charleston of Aberlour.

MRS J. WHITE, BEECHGROVE COTTAGES, TOMNAVOULIN, BALLINDALLOCH AB3 9JA (01807 590220). Traditional Highland Cottages in scenic area. Each sleeps 6 maximum– two double bedrooms, fully equipped dining/kitchen, living room, colour TV. All electric. Linen supplied. Central for coast and ski slopes. Open all year. Car essential. Children and pets welcome. [🐕]

Beattock (Dumfriesshire)

Picturesque Dumfriesshire village, ideally placed for touring Borders region and Upper Clyde Valley.

BEATTOCK HOUSE HOTEL AND CARAVAN PARK, BEATTOCK DG10 9QB (01683 300403). Ideally situated Hotel and Caravan Park for travellers wishing to rest awhile from the busy A74 or to tour the lovely Borders country, Burns Country and the Lake District. Fishing, stalking and rough shooting available. Restaurant; all-day bar licence. AA, RAC.

Biggar (Lanarkshire)

Small town set round broad main street. Gasworks museum, puppet theatre seating 100, street museum displaying old shopfronts and interiors. Peebles 13 miles.

CARMICHAEL COUNTRY COTTAGES, CARMICHAEL ESTATE, BY BIGGAR ML12 6PG (01899 308336; Fax: 01899 308481). Our stone cottages nestle in the woods and fields of our historic family-run estate. Ideal homes for families, pets and dogs. 15 Cottages, 32 bedrooms. Open all year. £160 to £430 per week. [🐕]

MRS MARGARET KIRBY, WALSTON MANSIONS FARMHOUSE, WALSTON, CARNWATH, LANARK ML11 8NF (Tel and Fax: 01899 810338). Friendly and relaxed atmosphere. Good home cooking with home-produced meat, eggs and organic vegetables. Guest lounge with log fire, TV and video. Bedrooms with colour TV. Cot and high chair available. Biggar 5 miles, Edinburgh 24 miles. B&B £13.50, en suite £15.50; Evening Meal £7.50. FHB member. 3 Crowns Commended. [🐕]

Blairgowrie (Perth & Kinross)

Town in picturesque situation near Ericht Gorge. Fine touring centre. Several castles in vicinity. Pitlochry 23 miles, Dundee 20, Forfar 20, Perth 15.

ALTAMOUNT CHALETS, COUPAR ANGUS ROAD, BLAIRGOWRIE PH10 6JN (01250 873324). Modern, fully equipped 1, 2 and 3 bedroom Scandinavian-style Chalets. Colour television. Centrally situated for touring Highlands. Children's amenities on site. Pets welcome. [Pets £1.50 per night.]

Bonchester Bridge (Roxburghshire)

Village 6 miles east of Hawick.

WAUCHOPE COTTAGES, BONCHESTER BRIDGE, HAWICK TD9 9TG (01450 860630). Three detatched cottages (sleeping 2-4) each with kennel in enclosed garden. Quiet location with stunning scenery near Wauchope Forest. Ideal for walking. STB 4 Crowns. [🐾]

Bridge of Cally (Perth & Kinross)

Village on River Ardle 5 miles north-west of Blairgowrie.

MRS JOSEPHINE MACLAREN, BLACKCRAIG CASTLE, BRIDGE OF CALLY PH10 7PX (01250 886251 or 0131-551 1863). Beautiful castle of architectural interest situated in spacious grounds. Ideal centre for touring, walking, golf. Free fishing. Dogs most welcome. B&B £20.50, reductions for children. Open July to early September. [🐾]

Buckie (Moray)

Fishing town and resort on Spey Bay, 13 miles east of Elgin.

ST. ANDREW'S HOTEL, BUCKIE, MORAY AB56 1BT (01542 831227; Fax: 01542 834513). Traditional modernised family-run hotel, children and pets welcome. 15 bedrooms, some en suite. Friendly bars, good home cooking, special diets catered for. Beaches, working harbour, fishing, Highland countryside nearby. STB 2 Crowns Approved. [🐾]

Callander (Perth & Kinross)

Good base for walks and drives around the Trossachs and Loch Katrine. Stirling 14 miles.

E. L. MACLEOD, CRAIGROYSTON, 4 BRIDGE STREET, CALLANDER FK17 8AA (01877 331395). Family-run Guest House. Warm welcome, home cooking. Comfortable rooms, all en suite with tea/coffee facilities, colour TV, central heating. Pets welcome. Prices from £17.50. 2 Crowns Commended. [🐾]

LYNNE AND ALISTAIR FERGUSON, ROSLIN COTTAGE GUEST HOUSE, LAGRANNOCH, CALLANDER FK17 8LE (01877 330638). Bed and good Scottish Breakfast from £15.00 per person. Evening Meal optional. Comfortable accommodation in 18th century Cottage, historic features. Good "walkies" area – dogs are especially welcome. [🐾 pw!]

Carr-Bridge (Inverness-shire)

Village on River Dulnain in Badenoch and Strathspey district, 7 miles north of Aviemore. Landmark Visitor Centre has exhibition explaining history of local environment.

LYNN & DAVE BENGE, THE PINES COUNTRY HOUSE, DUTHIL, CARR-BRIDGE PH23 3ND (01479 841220). Relax and enjoy our Highland hospitality, woodland setting; all rooms en suite. Traditional or vegetarian home cooking. Children and pets welcome. B&B from £16 daily; DB&B from £150 weekly.

LIZ AND IAN BISHOP, SLOCHD COTTAGES, BY CARR-BRIDGE PH23 3AY (Tel & Fax 01479 841 666). Country Cottage, sleeps 6. Wonderful forest and mountain trails. Ideally placed for touring. Close to golfing, fishing, ski-ing etc. From £90 per week. SAE for details. [🐕]

Castle Douglas (Kirkcudbrightshire)

Old market town at the northern end of Carlingwalk Loch, good touring centre for Galloway. Nearby Threave House surrounded by woodland walks and wildfowl refuge.

MR P. W. BALL, BARNCROSH FARM, CASTLE DOUGLAS DG7 1TX (01556 680216). Comfortable Cottages and flats for 2/4/6/8. Fully equipped, including linen. Colour TV. Children and dogs welcome. Beautiful rural surroundings. Brochure on request. [Pets £10 weekly]

MRS CELIA PICKUP, "CRAIGADAM", CASTLE DOUGLAS DG7 3HU (Tel and Fax: 01556 650233). Working farm. Family-run 18th century farmhouse. All bedrooms en suite. Lovely oak-panelled dining room offering Cordon Bleu cooking using local produce such as venison, pheasant and salmon. Trout fishing, walking, and golfing available. Well-behaved dogs £1 per night.

MR AND MRS BARDSLEY, THE ROSSAN, AUCHENCAIRN, CASTLE DOUGLAS DG7 1QR (01556 640269). Small, homely, early Victorian guest house. B&B. Optional evening meal. Organic produce when possible. Ideal centre for bird watching, golf, hill walking, pony trekking locally. STB Listed Approved. Well behaved dogs welcome in bedrooms only. [🐕]

Contin (Ross-shire)

Village in Ross and Cromarty district two miles south-west of Strathpeffer.

COUL HOUSE HOTEL, CONTIN, BY STRATHPEFFER IV14 9EY (01997 421487; Fax: 01997 421945). Skye and Hamish, our lovable labradors look forward to welcoming you. "Taste of Scotland" food, log fires, well-equipped bedrooms. Miles of wonderful walks. 4 Crowns Highly Commended. [🐕 pw!]

Crail (Fife)

Picturesque little fishing town in the East Neuk of Fife.

MRS JEAN COX, CRAIL HOUSE, CRAIL KY10 3SJ (01333 450270; Fax: 01333 450183). Three flats sleeping 4-6. Gardens and parking. Wonderful views. Open all year. From £180 to £350 per week. Short Winter Breaks available. Pets welcome.

Dalbeattie (Kirkcudbrightshire)

Small granite town on Kirgunzeon Lane (or Burn), 13 miles south-west of Dumfries.

BAREND HOLIDAY VILLAGE AND RIVER VIEW PARK, DALBEATTIE (01387 780663– Fax: 01387 780283). Two peaceful sites with Scandinavian-style/timber-built lodges. Accommodation superbly equipped. Facilities at Barend available to both include heated pool, restaurant, riding, fishing. Brochure on request. [Pets £20 per week]

Dalmally (Argyll)

Small town in Glen Orchy. To the south-west is Loch Awe with romantic Kilchurn Castle (14th century) Edinburgh 98 miles, Glasgow 69, Ardrishaig 42, Oban 25, Inveraray 16.

ROCKHILL FARM COUNTRY HOUSE, ARDBRECKNISH, BY DALMALLY PA33 1BA (01866 833218). 17th Century guest house on waterside with spectacular views over Loch Awe. 5 delightful rooms with all modern facilities. First class home cooking with much home grown produce. [Pets £2 per night]

Daviot (Inverness-shire)

Village 5 miles south-east of Inverness, the Highland "capital".

TORGUISH HOUSE & HOLIDAY HOMES, DAVIOT, INVERNESS IV1 2XQ (01463 772208; Fax: 01463 772308). Homely Guest House with generous rooms, some en suite, all with TV, tea/coffee. Large garden. Also, The Steading (self catering cottages sleeping 2–4). Fully equipped kitchen and bathroom. [🐾]

Dunoon (Argyll)

Lively resort reached by car ferry from Gourock. Cowal Highland Gathering held at end of August.

ASHGROVE GUEST HOUSE, WYNDHAM ROAD, INNELLAN, DUNOON PA23 7SH (01369 830306; Fax: 01369 830776). Family-run guest house with extensive grounds and outstanding views. Adjacent forestry walks, minutes from shore. Ponies, goat, poultry, rabbits, etc. Dogs and other small pets very welcome. All rooms en suite. B&B from £17.00. Reductions for children and Senior Citizens. [🐾]

ENMORE HOTEL, MARINE PARADE, DUNOON PA23 8HH (01369 702230; Fax: 01369 702148). Small luxury Hotel with well-tended garden, situated overlooking the beautiful Firth of Clyde. Own shingle beach. Promenade and superb walking in the hills and forests within five minutes' drive. Owners have retriever and standard poodle. STB 4 Crowns Highly Commended. [pw! Pets £3.95 per night.]

Duns (Berwickshire)

Picturesque Borders town with nearby ancient fort, castle, and Covenanters' stone to commemorate the army's encampment here in 1639. Excellent touring centre. Berwick-upon-Tweed 13 miles.

BARNIKEN HOUSE HOTEL, MURRAY STREET, DUNS TD11 3DE (01361 882466). Dogs most welcome, colour TV and tea coffee facilities in all rooms. Luxurious bar, sun lounge, large garden and car park. Central heating. Near spectacular scenery and ideal for walks for dogs. 2 Crowns Commended. [🐕]

Dunvegan (Isle of Skye)

Village at head of loch on north-west coast of Skye. Dunvegan Castle is anciaent stronghold of the MacLeods.

Well equipped detached house offering superb views overlooking Loch Bracadale. Two bedrooms, lounge, fully equipped kitchen. Heating throughout, TV. Enclosed garden. Pets Welcome. Prices from £100 weekly. Contact MR & MRS MACDIARMID, 21 DUNROBIN AVENUE, ELDERSLIE, RENFREWSHIRE PA5 9NW (01505 324460).

Fort William (Inverness-shire)

Small town at foot of Ben Nevis, ideal base for climbers and hillwalkers. West Highland Museum, Scottish crafts.

THE CLAN MACDUFF HOTEL, ACHINTORE, FORT WILLIAM PH33 6RW (01397 702341; Fax: 01397 706174). This family-run hotel overlooks Loch Linnhe, two miles south of Fort William, excellent for touring the rugged mountains of the West Highlands. All rooms have TV, hairdryer and hospitality tray, most with private facilities. 3 nights DB & B from £27.50 pppn. 3 Crowns Commended. Phone or write for colour brochure & tariff. [🐕]

MRS M. MATHESON, THISTLE COTTAGE, TORLUNDY, FORT WILLIAM (01397 702428). Central for touring Highlands– 31/2 miles Fort William, 2 miles Nevis Range. One double and one family bedroom. Large parking area. B&B from £12.00 per night, reductions for children. [🐕]

LINNHE CARAVAN & CHALET PARK, DEPT PW, CORPACH, FORT WILLIAM PH33 7NL (01397 772376). One of the best and most beautiful lochside parks in Scotland. Thistle Award caravans for hire. Graded "Excellent". Private beach, free fishing. Prices from £160; Breaks from £60. [pw! Pets £10 per week]

MR J. FRASER, CROSS COTTAGE, NORTH BALLACHULISH, ONICH, FORT WILLIAM PH33 6RZ (01855 821335). Eight large modern 6-berth caravans, all with full facilities. Small site 200 yards from beach; shops 2 miles. Children and pets welcome. Weekly rates from £135 to £270. SAE for details.

Grantown-on-Spey (Inverness-shire)

Popular ski resort and market town. Excellent trout and salmon fishing in Spey and Dulnain rivers.

MR AND MRS J. R. TAYLOR, MILTON OF CROMDALE, GRANTOWN-ON-SPEY PH26 3PH (01479 872415). Fully modernised Cottage with large garden and views of River Spey and Cromdale Hills. Golf, tennis and trekking within easy reach. Fully equipped except linen. Two double bedrooms. Shower, refrigerator, electric cooker, colour television. Car desirable. Children and pets welcome. Available Easter to October. £80-£90 per week. [🐾]

Haddington (East Lothian)

Historic town on River Tyne 16 miles east of Edinburgh. Birthplace of John Knox, 1505. Renovated Church of St Mary, 14c-15c; St Martin's Church, AM.

THE MONKS' MUIR, HADDINGTON EH41 3SB (Tel and Fax: 01620 860340). Secluded and tranquil amidst beautiful countryside, only 20 minutes from Edinburgh. Tourers, tents and luxury hire caravans. Award winning, lovely facilities, totally 'green', very friendly. Open all year. 5 Ticks EXCELLENT. [🐾]

Innerleithen (Peeblesshire)

An old woollen-manufacturing town set in beautiful Borders countryside. Peebles 6 miles.

MRS JENNIFER CAIRD, TRAQUAIR BANK, INNERLEITHEN EH44 6PR (01896 830425). Stone house with rambling garden, overlooks Tweed. Walking, fishing, riding. Help on farm. Edinburgh ¾ hour. Animals welcome. Bed and Breakfast, Evening Meals by arrangement. STB Listed Commended. [🐾]

Invergarry (Inverness-shire)

Village at foot of Glen Garry. Ruined Invergarry Castle lies to the south east.

A&D GRANT, FAICHEMARD FARM CHALETS, FAICHEMARD FARM, INVERGARRY PH35 4HG (01809 501314). Four Chalets individually situated to give maximum privacy on a working hill farm. Sleep maximum of six. All electric with shower, colour TV. Pets by arrangement. Terms from £110 to £225 per week. [🐾]

Inverlochy (Inverness-shire)

Situated at mouth of River Lochy, 2km north east of Fort William.

MRS A. CAMPBELL, 19 LUNDY ROAD, INVERLOCHY, FORT WILLIAM PH33 6NY (01397 704918). Beautiful views of Ben Nevis. Children and pets very welcome. Tea/coffee in rooms. B&B single from £12; DB&B from £14.

Jedburgh (Roxburghshire)

Small town on Jed Water, 10 miles north east of Hawick. Ruins of abbey founded in 1138.

ALAN & CHRISTINE SWANSTON, FERNIEHIRST MILL LODGE & RIDING CENTRE, JEDBURGH TD8 6PQ (01835 863279). A chalet style guest house set in grounds of 25 acres. All rooms en suite with tea/coffee making facilities. Licensed for residents. Well behaved pets (including horses) welcome by arrangement. STB, AA, RAC, ABRS, TRSS Approved. [🐾 Horses £6 per night]

Kildrummy (Aberdeenshire)

3 miles south of Lumsden.

KILDRUMMY INN, KILDRUMMY, ALFORD AB33 8QS (01975 571227). A small family-run country Inn; good fishing and shooting country, with plenty of hillwalking and pony trekking. Small and cosy with only 4 letting rooms, all with wash basins, tea-making facilities and TV. [🐾]

Kinross (Perth & Kinross)

Town and resort on west side of Loch Leven, nine miles north of Dunfermline. Angling on Loch Leven. Formal gardens at Kinross House.

THE GREEN HOTEL, 2 THE MUIRS, KINROSS KY13 7AS (01577 863467; Fax: 01577 863180). Independently owned hotel with well-appointed bedrooms and family suites. Restaurant, bar meals. Leisure facilities include indoor pool, golf courses, tennis and fishing. M90 five minutes. [🐾]

Langholm (Dumfriesshire)

Small mill town at the junction of three rivers. Common Riding held in July.

THE ESKDALE HOTEL, LANGHOLM DG13 0JH (Tel & Fax: 013873 80357). Former Coaching Inn. All rooms with central heating, colour TV, radio. En suite available. Licensed. Two bars. Restaurant. Games room. Golf, shooting, fishing. AA 2 STARS. 3 Crowns Commended. [🐾]

Lochearnhead (Perth & Kinross)

Popular little touring centre on wooded Loch Earn, dominated by Ben Vorlich (3,244 ft). Edinburgh 65 miles, Glasgow 50, Aberfeldy 30, Crieff 19, Crianlarich 16, Callander 14.

MR ANGUS CAMERON, LOCHEARNHEAD HOTEL, LOCHEARNHEAD FK19 8PU (01567 830229). Small family-run hotel (3 Crowns Commended), restaurant and self-catering chalets (4 Crowns Highly Commended) at the west end of Loch Earn with lovely views across the loch. Excellent golf and touring centre with water ski-ing, sailing and windsurfing on our doorstep. Ample hill walking. AA One Star. [Pets £1 per night]

CLACHAN COTTAGE HOTEL, LOCHSIDE, LOCHEARNHEAD FK19 8PU (01567 830247; Fax: 01567 830300). Ideal holiday venue for pets and their owners. Spectacular Highland scenery, walking, fishing, watersports. Open fires, wonderful food. Three Day, Golf and Off-Season Breaks. [🐕]

Loch Goil (Argyll)

Peaceful loch running from Lochgoilhead to Loch Long.

Five self catering Chalets on the shores of Loch Goil in the heart of Argyll Forest Park. Fully equipped except linen. Colour TV, fitted kitchen, carpeted. Pets welcome. Open all year. DARROCH MHOR, CARRICK CASTLE, LOCH GOIL PA24 8AF (01301 703249/703432).

Lochgoilhead (Argyll)

Village at head of Loch Goil in Argyll

MRS ROSEMARY DOLAN, THE SHOREHOUSE INN, LOCHGOILHEAD PA24 8AJ (01301 703 340). The Shorehouse Inn has seven letting rooms, central heating and double glazing. There is a bar, lounge and licensed restaurant. Local amenities include water sports, fishing, tennis, bowls, golf, swimming pool; good area for walking. Rates from £13.50 B&B. Well trained dogs welcome.

Loch Lomond (Dunbartonshire)

Largest loch in Scotland –23 miles long, up to 5 miles wide, and 630 ft at deepest point – with 30 islands. Pleasure boats and paddle steamer offer rides. Surrounded by beautiful woodland areas.

MRS SALLY MACDONELL, MARDELLA FARMHOUSE, OLD SCHOOL ROAD, GARTOCHARN, LOCH LOMOND G83 8SD (01389 830428). Set on a quiet country lane, surrounded by fields. Friendly and comfortable, where the kettle's always boiling. AA QQQQ, RAC Listed, AA "Landlady of the Year" 1995 Finalist; Winner AA Scotland B&B of the Year 1995. [🐕]

Loch Maree (Ross-shire)

Narrow, very deep loch running from Kinlochewe to near Poolewe in dramatic and unspoiled countryside.

THE SHEILING. Secluded Bungalow in wooded grounds, amidst spectacular scenery. Sleeps 5/6, with coal fire in lounge; equipped to high standard. All pets are welcome. Terms from £140 to £295; electricity by coin meter. APPLY: MR & MRS A. ALLAN, TORGUISH, DAVIOT, INVERNESS IV1 2XQ (01463 772208; Fax: 01463 772308). [🐕]

Loch Ness (Inverness-shire)

Home of "Nessie", extending for 23 miles from Fort Augustus to south of Inverness.

Former croft situated 16 miles south of Inverness. Comfortable lounge, colour TV and open fireplace. Separate dining room. Fully equipped kitchen.Three bedrooms. Central heating. Pets welcome. For a colour brochure contact: ANDY AND ROSEMARY HOLT, ISLAND COTTAGE, INVERFARIGAIG, INVERNESS IV1 2XR (Tel/Fax: 01456 486631). [One pet free 🏠]

Lochranza (Isle of Arran)

Village at north end of Arran.

CATACOL BAY HOTEL, CATACOL, LOCHRANZA (01770 830231; Fax: 01770 830350). Comfortable, friendly, small country house hotel where good cooking is our speciality. Extensive bar menu, meals are served from noon until 10pm. Centrally heated. Open all year. Details of Special Breaks and brochure on request. Les Routiers. Children and pets welcome.

Lockerbie (Dumfriesshire)

Annandale town noted as the scene of a battle in 1593 which ended one of the last great Border feuds. This and the surrounding area comprised the lands of Robert Bruce. Ecclefechan six miles south was the birthplace of Thomas Carlyle. Gretna 15 miles.

LOCKERBIE MANOR COUNTRY HOTEL, LOCKERBIE DG11 2RG (01576 202610). Splendid Georgian mansion house set in 78 acres of beautiful grounds. Ideal base for exploring countryside. Single, twin, double and family rooms, all en suite, and equipped with colour TV, tea-making etc. [pw! 🐕]

Longformacus (Berwickshire)

Village on Dye Water 6 miles west of Duns.

RATHBURNE COTTAGES, LONGFORMACUS, DUNS TD11 3PG (0191 268 0788). Well-equipped self catering cottages in beautiful secluded setting. Large enclosed gardens. Lovely area for wildlife and walking. Pets welcome. [Pets £5 per week.]

Melrose (Roxburghshire)

Picturesque village ideal for touring scenic Borders country. Famous for its medieval abbey. Edinburgh 37 miles, Galashiels 5.

Your pets are welcomed as part of the family at an especially attractive selection of holiday cottages all over Scotland. Please write or phone for our 30-page colour brochure. ECOSSE UNIQUE LTD, THORNCROFT, LILLIESLEAF, MELROSE, ROXBURGHSHIRE TD6 9JD (01835 870779; Fax: 01835 870417). [🐕 or £6 p.n.]

Moffat (Dumfriesshire)

At head of lovely Annandale, grand mountain scenery. Good centre for rambling, climbing, angling and golf. The 'Devil's Beef Tub' is 5 miles, Edinburgh 52 miles, Peebles 33, Dumfries 21, Beattock 2.

MORLICH HOUSE, BALLPLAY ROAD, MOFFAT DG10 9JU (Tel: 01683 220589; Fax: 01683 221032). Set in beautiful 'Burns Country' Morlich House is a superb Victorian country house. Rooms are en suite with TV, radio alarm, tea/coffee and telephone, four-poster available. Private car park. B&B from £16pp, 3 course evening meal from £8.50. Weekly terms. Open Feb/Nov. [Pets £1 per night.]

BARNHILL SPRINGS COUNTRY GUEST HOUSE, MOFFAT DG10 9QS (01683 220580). Early Victorian country house overlooking some of the finest views of Upper Annandale. Comfortable accommodation, residents' lounge with open fire. Situated on the Southern Upland Way half a mile from A74. Bed & Breakfast from £18.50; Evening Meal (optional) from £12.50. [🐕]

Muir of Ord (Ross-shire)

Village 3 miles north of Beauly.

5 bright, cosy chalets designed for 2. One double bedroom, shower room, lounge/kitchen, all linen supplied free of charge.Closed December, January. 3 day breaks available. One pet per chalet. For brochure write to: MRS ANDERSON, KILCOY CHALETS, TORE, MUIR OF ORD, ROSS-SHIRE IV6 7RX or Tel (01349 861456). [🐕]

Nethybridge (Inverness-shire)

Popular Strathspey resort on River Nethy with extensive Abernethy Forest to the south. Impressive mountain scenery. Grantown-on-Spey 5 miles.

MRS M. FRASER, 36 LYNSTOCK CRESCENT, NETHYBRIDGE, INVERNESS-SHIRE PH25 3DX (01479 821312). Modern cottages set in an idyllic spot in Speyside. Fully equipped for 4–8 persons. Car essential. Children and pets welcome. Aviemore 12 miles. STB 4 Crowns De Luxe.

NETHYBRIDGE, STRATHSPEY. Choice of modern cottages or converted smithy. Linen and visitor laundry included. Central heating included in winter. Good walking and touring area. STB 4 Crowns Highly Commended. Write or phone for brochure. MR AND MRS P. W. PATRICK, CHAPELTON PLACE, FORRES, MORAY IV35 0NL (01309 672505). [One dog free, thereafter £15 per week.]

Oban (Argyll)

Popular Highland resort and port, yachting centre, ferry services to Inner and Outer Hebrides. Sandy bathing beach at Ganavan Bay. McCaig's Tower above town is Colosseum replica built in 1890s.

J. AND F. TURNBULL, LAG-NA-KEIL CHALETS, LERAGS, BY OBAN PA34 4SE (01631 562746). One, two or three bedroomed Bungalows or Chalets; fully equipped including linen, colour TV. Free fishing; boat hire. Deer stalking by arrangement. Pets welcome. Up to 4 Crowns Commended.

D. R. KILPATRICK, KILNINVER, BY OBAN PA34 4UT (01852 316272). Three self-catering houses on coastal estate near Oban. Sleep 4–8. All fully equipped; electricity, newspapers, trout fishing included in rental. From £240 including VAT. 4 Crowns. [🐾]

MR HENRY P. WOODMAN, COLOGIN HOMES LTD, LERAGS, BY OBAN PA34 4SE (01631 564501; Fax: 01631 566925). Modern centrally heated timber bungalows, sleep 2-6, all conveniences. Situated on farm, wildlife abundant. Games room, licensed bar with all-day bar meals. Cycle hire, fishing. Live entertainment. [pw! 🐾]

Fully equipped Scandinavian chalets in breathtaking scenery near Oban. Chalets sleep 4–7, are widely spaced and close to Loch Tralaig. Car parking. From £185 per week per chalet. Available March to October. APPLY – GILL AND ANDREW STEVENS, ELERAIG HIGHLAND CHALETS, KILNINVER, BY OBAN PA34 4UX (01852 200225) [🐾]

Onich (Inverness-shire)

On shores of Loch Linnhe. Good boating, fishing. Fort William 10 miles.

INCHREE CHALETS, ONICH, FORT WILLIAM PH33 6SD (01855 821287). Comfortable chalets sleeping up to 6; all facilities. Restaurant and lounge bar. Forest walks from site. Midway between Ben Nevis and Glencoe. Discount for couples. [🐾]

MRS K. A. McCALLUM, TIGH-A-RIGH GUEST HOUSE, ONICH PH33 6SE (01855 821255). Well-equipped, comfortable accommodation in licensed Guest House. Ideal touring centre. Pets and children welcome. Open all year. Bed, Breakfast and Dinner reasonable terms. En suite rooms available. [🐾]

THE LODGE ON THE LOCH, CREAG DHU, ONICH, BY FORT WILLIAM PH33 6RY (01855 821582; Fax: 01855 821238). Enjoying one of the finest panoramas in Scotland, a spell-binding blend of gentle elegance and a delightful, informal atmosphere. Taste of Scotland cuisine.

Pitlochry (Perth & Kinross)

Popular resort on River Tummel in beautiful Perthshire Highlands. Excellent golf, loch and river fishing. Famous for summer Festival Theatre; distillery, Highland Games.

KILLIECRANKIE HOTEL, KILLIECRANKIE, BY PITLOCHRY PH16 5LG (01796 473220; Fax: 01796 472451). Charming small Hotel set in 4 acres. Wonderful views. Superb food, high standard of comfort. Open Christmas and New Year. 4 Crowns Highly Commended. AA 2 Star Rosette. [🐾 pw!]

JACKY & MALCOLM CATTERALL, "TULLOCH", ENOCHDHU, BY KIRKMICHAEL, STRATHARDLE PH10 7PW (01250 881404). STB Approved. Former farmhouse offers comfortable accommodation and good food. One family room with washbasin, one twin with washbasin; one en suite double room. All have tea/coffee facilities and face open country to mountains beyond. Peace and quiet guaranteed. Haven for wildlife and dogs. B&B £14 to £16; optional Dinner £8. [🐾 pw!]

MRS BARBARA M. BRIGHT, CRAIG DUBH COTTAGE, MANSE ROAD, MOULIN, PITLOCHRY PH16 5EP (01796 472058). Pets and guests are welcomed to our family home in a rural setting, one mile from Pitlochry. B&B accommodation, one twin en suite, one double, two singles. All tea/coffee, electric blankets. £13.50/£14.50. [🐾]

Port William (Wigtownshire)

Small resort with quay, on east shore of Luce Bay seven miles south-west of Wigtown.

3 Crown Commended self-catering cottage opposite sea. Sleeps 6. 400 yards from shops. Post Office and pubs with restaurants. Touring, fishing, golf, walking. From £100 to £150 per week. Brochure from: MRS WRIGHT, SHORE COTTAGE, 49 SOUTH STREET, PORT WILLIAM, NEWTON STEWART DG8 9SH (Tel & Fax: 01988 700831). [🐾]

GREENMANTLE HOTEL, MOCHRUM, PORT WILLIAM DG8 9LY (01988 700357). Set in an acre of grounds, we are a family run hotel 11/2 miles from the shores of Luce Bay. Home cooking using local produce., Well placed for walking, birdwatching, fishing, pony trekking and golf. Small pets welcome. [🐾]

Port of Menteith (Stirlingshire)

Village at north east corner of Lake of Menteith, 5 miles from Callander.

MRS MARY WATSON, HOLLY COTTAGE, PORT OF MENTEITH, BY STIRLING FK8 3RA (01877 385604). Bungalow with spacious garden, open views overlooking Lake. 2 rooms en suite, 1 double, 1 twin. Doggie walks, golf, fishing, riding in area. Friendly atmosphere. STB Listed Commended.

Rockcliffe (Kirkcudbrightshire)

Quiet resort on wooded Rough Firth; sandy and rocky bays. Bird sanctuary on Rough Island (N.T Scot). Dumfries 20 miles.

TORBAY FARMHOUSE GUEST HOUSE, ROCKCLIFFE, BY DALBEATTIE DG5 4QE (01556 630403). Our Galloway farmhouse stands in beautiful gardens overlooking the sea. Imaginative cooking and baking using our garden produce and tastefully appointed en suite rooms. Well-behaved dogs welcome. B&B & EM from £28; weekly terms. [Pets £1 per night.]

Roy Bridge (Inverness-shire)

Located in Glen Spean at foot of Glen Roy in Lochaber, 3 miles east of Spean Bridge.

BUNROY HOLIDAY PARK, ROY BRIDGE PH31 4AG (01397 712332). In a quiet woodland setting, modern insulated chalets, double glazed and fully equipped. Camping and caravans welcome. Ideal base for touring. Short Breaks available September to Easter. [Dogs (max 2) £10 per week in lodges]

Fully equipped bungalows (sleep 2-6) £160-£350, and chalets (sleep 8) £200-£475. Set amid heath and birch in Glen Spean; shops and hotels nearby. Discounts for couples and Senior Citizens. Fort William 12 miles. Colour brochure available. 2/4 Crowns Commended. IAN MATHESON, THE LITTLE HOUSES, EAST PARK, ROY BRIDGE PH31 4AG (01397 712370; Fax: 01397 712831). [1st pet free, additional pet £15]

STRONLOSSIT HOTEL, ROY BRIDGE PH31 4AG (01397 712253). Ideal centre for touring Highlands. Nine fully appointed bedrooms with en suite facilities. Lounge bar with log fire, meals service. Excellent food. Discounts available for 3 nights or more. [🐾]

Skirling (Lanarkshire)

Borders village 2 miles east of Biggar.

MRS MARION MCINTYRE, FOREST EDGE, MUIRBURN FARM, SKIRLING, NEAR BIGGAR ML12 6HL (01899 860284). Set half a mile from road in beautiful surroundings. Dog walking in adjacent forest. Good home cooking. Lounge with log fire. Ample parking. Convenient for Glasgow and Edinburgh. B&B: double family room £14, single £12; children 5–11 half price, under 5 years free. 3-course EM £6.[🐾]

Skipness (Argyll)

Picturesque coastal haven on Mull of Kintyre, overlooking Kilbrannan Sound and Isle of Arran.

Peaceful, unspoiled West Highland estate. Traditional Cottages, well equipped including TV, dinghy (not winter) and open fires. Sleep 4–10. Children and pets welcome. Walks, pony trekking, golf nearby. APPLY SOPHIE JAMES, SKIPNESS CASTLE, BY TARBERT PA29 6XU (01880 760207; Fax: 01880 760208). [🐾]

Spean Bridge (Inverness-shire)

At western end of Glen Spean amidst grand mountain scenery. Bridge built by Telford; Commando Memorial nearby. Fort William 10 miles S.W.

MRS M. H. CAIRNS, INVERGLOY HOUSE, SPEAN BRIDGE PH34 4DY (01397 712681). Two spacious 5-berth luxury caravans, highest standard (fridge, shower, TV). 50 acre wooded estate, beautifully secluded overlooking Loch Lochy; beach, fishing, rowing boats, bird watching, lovely walks. Free gas and electricity. Discounts for two occupancy and two-week bookings. Controlled dog welcome. £170-£245 per week. Fort William & Lochaber Tourist Board, British Graded Holiday Parks inspected. SAE for details [🐾]

Staffin (Isle of Skye)

Crofting and fishing village on rocky coast around Staffin Bay, 12 miles north of Portree.

C. M. BOOTH, GLENVIEW INN & RESTAURANT, CULNACNOC, STAFFIN IV51 9JH (01470 562248; Fax: 01470 562211). Traditional island house, ideally situated for exploring north east Skye. Comfortable en suite bedrooms. Restaurant renowned for traditional seafood, ethnic and vegetarian specialities. Dogs most welcome. 3 Crowns Commended. [🐾]

Stanley (Perth & Kinross)

Pretty village on River Tay 8 miles south-east of Dunkeld and 6 miles north of Perth.

MRS A. GUTHRIE, NEWMILL FARM, STANLEY PH1 4QD (01738 828281). On A9 six miles north of Perth. Lounge, sitting room. Twin, double, family rooms, most en suite. Bed and Breakfast from £17. Evening meal on request. Reductions for children. Ideal for touring, fishing, golf. 3 Crowns Commended.

St Andrews (Fife)

Home of golf – British Golf Museum has memorabilia dating back to the origins of the game. Remains of castle and cathedral. Sealife Centre and beach Leisure Centre. Excellent sands. Ideal base for exploring the picturesque East Neuk of Fife.

MRS A. WEDDERBURN, MOUNTQUHANIE HOLIDAY HOMES, MOUNTQUHANIE, CUPAR KY15 4QJ (01382 330 252; Fax: 01382 330 480). Good quality self-catering houses, flats or cottages in tranquil, rural countryside. Central heating modern kitchens, fitted carpets, colour TV, telephone. STB 4 Crowns Commended to 5 Crowns De Luxe. [Pets £10 per week]

Stirling (Stirlingshire)

Historic town dominated by castle standing on 250 ft high rock; nearby are Wallace Monument and Bannockburn Memorial. Excellent road and rail links to Glasgow and Edinburgh.

MRS A. AGNEW, BRAES OF BOQUHAPPLE FARM, THORNHILL, NEAR STIRLING FK8 3QH (01786 850484). This farm is situated on B822 between Thornhill and Callander. It has splendid panoramic views. There are two en suite family rooms. Evening Meals provided by arrangement. Grazing and stabling available for horses, and all well-behaved pets are welcome.

Strathyre (Perthshire)

Village set in middle of Strathyre Forest, just off A84 north of Callander. Information centre and picnic area to south of village.

ARDOCH LODGE, STRATHYRE (01877 384666). Log cabins and cottage in wonderful mountain scenery. Comfortably furnished and fully equipped. Country house accommodation also available. Phone for brochure. Open all year. Pets most welcome. 3 Crowns Highly Commended. [🐕]

Strontian (Argyll)

Beautifully situated at head of Loch Sunart which stretches 20 miles to the sea. In the glen to the north are deserted lead mines. Fort William (ferry) 23 miles.

SEAVIEW GRAZINGS HOLIDAYS, STRONTIAN PH36 4HZ (01967 402191). Quality self catering in Scandinavian log houses overlooking Loch Sunart. Sleep up to 8. TV washer/dryer etc. Pubs/hotels 5 minutes. Pets welcome. Ideal touring centre. send for colour brochure. [🐕]

Tain (Ross-shire)

Small town in Ross and Cromarty district on south shore of Dornoch Firth. 10 miles north-east of Invergordon.

MRS SHIRLEY ROSS, DUNBIUS, MORANGIE ROAD, TAIN IV19 1PY (01862 893010). Comfortable bedrooms, all en suite, colour TV, tea coffee. Off road parking. Good golfing area, horse riding, forest walks. Prices from £16 per person. [🐕]

Tarbert (Argyll)

Fishing port on isthmus connecting Kintyre to the mainland.

WEST LOCH HOTEL, BY TARBERT, LOCH FYNE PA29 6YF (01880 820283). Attractive traditional coaching inn on the shore of West Loch. Bright, comfortable accommodation, cosy atmosphere, superb food and wines. Open February to December. 3 Crowns Commended.

Turriff (Aberdeenshire)

Town at centre of agricultural area, 9 miles south of Banff.

MRS P.E. BATES, HOLIDAY COTTAGES, FORGLEN ESTATE, TURRIFF AB53 4JP (01888 562918/562518 or 563565). Estate on the beautiful Deveron River. Sea only 9 miles away, Turriff 2 miles. 9 cottages sleeping 6–9. £90 to £285 weekly. Special Winter lets. Children and reasonable dogs welcome.

West Linton (Peeblesshire)

Village on east side of Pentland Hills, 7 miles south-west of Penicuik. Edinburgh 18 miles.

MRS C. M. KILPATRICK, SLIPPERFIELD HOUSE, WEST LINTON EH46 7AA (Tel/Fax: 01968 660401). Two excellently equipped converted cottages set in 100 acres of lochs and woodlands. America cottage sleeps 6, Loch Cottage sleeps 4. Car essential. [🐕]

IRELAND

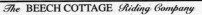
IRISH COUNTRY HOLIDAYS (01502 560688 24 hours). The widest choice.
Individual cottages, castles, hotels and farmhouses. Fishing, golf and River
Shannon cruising. Pets welcome in selected cottages.

Blaney (Co. Fermanagh)

7 miles from Enniskillen.

INNISH-BEG COTTAGES, Four self catering houses available, sleeping 2-9
persons. Fully equipped, central heating, games room, rowing boat with engine
for fishing. Farm surroundings. Holistic treatments available. GABRIELE
TOTTENHAM, INNISH BEG, BLANEY, ENNISKILLEN, CO. FERMANAGH BT93
7AP (013656 41525).

Derrylin (Co. Fermanagh)

Ideal base for a fishing holiday, 10 miles from Belturbet.

KATE'S COTTAGE. Purpose built 4 bedroomed cottage on its own $^3/_4$ acre site.
Open fire with turf supplied. Centrally located in region of leisure and golfing
facilities. Pets welcome. MALCOLM & ROSEMARY CLARKSON,
CORRAMONAGHAN, DERRYLIN, CO. FERMANAGH BT92 9BB (013657 48188).

Dromahair (Co. Leitrim)

Pleasant village 12 miles from Sligo.

THE BEECH COTTAGE RIDING COMPANY, BEECH COTTAGE, DROMAHAIR ,
CO. LEITRIM (00353 71 64110). Riding school and holiday farm on beautiful
estate. Special weekend offer: 3 nights acaommodation in luxurious apartments
and 5 hours riding. Showjumping and trekking available. Full colour brochure
on request.

Dublin

*Capital city of the Republic of Ireland, with many fine buildings, places of historic and cultural
interest, and a wealth of pubs and restaurants to suit all tastes.*

LANSDOWNE LODGE, 6 LANSDOWNE TERRACE, SHELBOURNE ROAD,
BALLSBRIDGE, DUBLIN 4 (00353 1660 5755; Fax: 00353 1660 5662). Superior
3 star executive accommodation in prestigious embassy belt area of Dublin,
15 minute walk from city centre. Bed & Breakfast from £27.50. Ideal for tourists
and business travellers.

SPECIAL SUPPLEMENTS:

Kennels & Catteries and *Holidays with Horses*

If you are having difficulty in locating a kennel or cattery in an area other than your own, then we hope that the special *Kennels and Catteries Supplement* will prove useful. And for the horse lover, the *Holidays with Horses Supplement* provides a selection of accommodation where horse and owner/rider can be put up at the same address — if not actually under the same roof!

We would be grateful if readers making enquiries and/or bookings from these Supplements would mention *Pets Welcome!*.

KENNELS AND CATTERIES

Buckinghamshire

**BEAUMONT KENNELS AND CAT'S INN,
UPHILL FARM, THE HALE, WENDOVER, NEAR AYLESBURY HP22 6QR
(Tel: 01296 623344; Fax 01296 624333)**

Dogs and cats; solid brick and tile kennels; individual cat houses with large runs. All animals must have full inoculations including Intrac for dogs. Extensive exercise facilities on large country estate. Established quarter of a century. Full time residential staff to look after small number of "guests".

Cambridgeshire

**FIELDSVIEW KENNELS AND CATTERY,
FENSTANTON ROAD, HILTON, HUNTINGDON PE18 9JA
(Tel: 01480 830215)**

Dogs, cats and small animals; all have individual kennels and runs; full current inoculation required; pampered pets section and grooming parlour for all breeds – Member of Pet Groomers Association; collection and delivery service available; pets with special diets catered for. All staff qualified to NVQ level 2.

Cornwall

ELIM BOARDING CATTERY
BROADS LANE, MYLOR DOWNS, NEAR FALMOUTH TR11 5UL
(Tel: 01872 865232; Fax: 01872 870071)

Cats only; individual wooden houses with outdoor runs. Normal injections needed.

Essex

ORANGE TREE KENNELS,
OFF CHURCH ROAD, NOAK HILL, ROMFORD RM4 1LB
(Tel: 01708 343054; Fax: 01708 381361)

Dogs (66); cats (30). Dogs in individual pens, exercise areas and grassed paddock area. Heating if necessary. Special diets and vet on call. Cats in individual pens; spacious runs. All pets to be fully inoculated. Clipping and grooming service.

ROSE COTTAGE CATTERY,
COLLIER ROW ROAD, ROMFORD RM5 2BH
(Tel: 0181 590 2278)

Cats only, brick built rooms. Must be fully vaccinated. Single or family rooms available. Pleasant country site close to London. Special diets available. F.A.B. Member.

CROWN FARM KENNELS,
CHURCH ROAD, NOAK HILL, ROMFORD RM4 1JX
(Tel: 01708 342697)

Dogs (100); cats (60); rabbits boarded. Individual pens and exercise areas. Inside and outside kennels. Cats – individual pens and runs. All pets to be fully vaccinated, cards to be shown on arrival. Collection and delivery service, grooming service. Special diets catered for.

Hertfordshire

BRIDGEFOOT FARM KENNEL & CATTERY
BARLEY ROAD, FLINT CROSS, NEAR ROYSTON S98 7PU
(Tel: 01763 208422)

Dogs (70), cats (50); dogs in individual or family kennel, large grass exercise area, heated cat penthouses, outside run. Current inoculation must be shown on arrival, Open all year. Inspection most welcome. Fully licensed.

NATIONAL ANIMAL WELFARE TRUST (AWT TRADING LTD)
TYLER'S WAY, WATFORD BY-PASS, WATFORD WD2 8HQ
(Tel: 0181 950 1320)

Dogs (36) Cats (36) and small domestic pets; concrete kennels with runs for dogs and cats, heated in winter; all dogs must be fully inoculated; cats must be inoculated against feline enteritis and cat flu; inspection welcomed; bathing and grooming available.

Kent

PARK HOUSE ANIMAL SANCTUARY,
PARK HOUSE, STELLING MINNIS, NEAR CANTERBURY CT4 6AN
(Tel: 01303 862622; Fax: 01303 863007)

Dogs, cats & small animals. Viewing welcome by appointment. Individual houses and runs, heating when needed. Full inoculations for dogs, cats and rabbits essential. Veterinary clinic for those on limited income. Sanctuary.

THE ANIMAL INN,
DOVER ROAD, RINGWOULD, NEAR DEAL CT14 8HH
(Tel: 01304 373597; Fax 01304 380305)

Dogs (110), cats (40); daily vet visit as also quarantine. Dogs in individual kennels, all with own covered runs; cats in individual pens; kennels and pens have optional heating. Require proof of vaccination within previous 12 months. Open all year.

Leicestershire

THE GABLE KENNELS
GARLANDS LANE, BARLESTONE CV13 0JD
(Tel: 01530 230278)

Dogs and cats; dogs have individual brick kennels and runs, heated; cats have individual pens; full vaccinations required; bathing and grooming service available.

Nottinghamshire

HILLBANKS KENNELS AND CATTERY,
COMMONSIDE, SELSTON NG16 6FL
(Tel: 01773 860586; Fax: 01773 860586)

36 Dogs, 20 cats, up to two paddocks (ponies, llamas, goats). Small pets boarded. Large kennels with covered runs. Cats have 8' indoor cubicles. Vet on call. Up-to-date vaccination boosters required. Grooming and show preparation. Daily rates.

KENNELS AND CATTERIES

Surrey

WEY FARM,
GIULDFORD ROAD, OTTERSHAW KT16 0QW
(Tel: 01932 873239, Fax: 01932 874758)

Dogs (100), cats (40). Super accommodation in individual runs, heating. Dogs walked daily in 50 acres of Surrey countryside. Usual boosters required up - to - date & Intrac for dogs. Open all year. Inspection welcome.

West Sussex

GATWICK KENNELS
LOWFIELD HEATH, CRAWLEY RH11 0PY
(Tel: 01293 546546)

Cats and dogs in separate facilities, individual and family units, very large runs, infra-red heating, open all year. Individual diets catered for. Vaccination required. Veterinarian in daily attendance. Car parking for Gatwick departures. Established 1964.

West Yorkshire

CARLTON BOARDING KENNELS,
CHURCH HOUSE, CARLTON, YEADON, Nr LEEDS LS19 7BG
(Tel: 0113 250 5113)

Dogs (40); cats (20); concrete individual accommodation with outside runs; heated kennels and cat palaces; dogs walked on lead twice daily in farm land; full vaccination required; trimming by qualified staff.

Dyfed

THE LINKS BOARDING KENNELS,
PEMBREY SA16 0HT
(Tel: 01554 832409)

Dogs and cats; individual heated kennels with large runs; two enclosed grass runs for dogs to run free; heated cattery with covered run. All animals must be inoculated. Other small domestic animals catered for.

Ayrshire

STRUTHERS KENNELS
LONDON ROAD, KILMARNOCK KA3 6ND
(Tel: 01563 533671; Fax: 01563 538824)

Dogs (50) Cats (10) and small animals catered for; individual or family kennels, central heating, additional outdoor runs. Dogs walked 3 times per day. Vaccinations required including infectious bronchitis. Members of the Pet Care Trust.

Perth and Kinross

STRIPSIDE BOARDING CATTERY
LONGLEYS, MEIGLE, BLAIRGOWRIE PH12 8QX
(Tel: 01828 640388)

Individual chalets and runs, insulated and heated beds. Fully insured. All cats must be vaccinated for enteritis and flu. Special diets catered for. Long term boarding; discounts for long stays. Set in open countryside. Veterinary inspected.

Are you having difficulty locating a boarding kennel/cattery in an area other than your own? Have you words of praise (or criticism) for a kennel/cattery you have used? The Boarding Kennels Advisory Bureau is a free service for the general public and monitors progress within the industry. Please write with your enquiry (enclosing SAE) or comments:
The Boarding Kennels Advisory Bureau, c/o Blue Grass Animal Hotel, Little Leigh, Near Northwich, Cheshire CW8 4RJ (Tel: 01606 891303)

HOLIDAYS WITH HORSES

Please note: the entries listed here also have a Display or Classified Advertisement under the appropriate county heading in the main accommodation section of this guide.

Devon/Aylesbeare

MRS H. BALE
GREAT HOUNDBEARE FARM, AYLESBEARE, EXETER EX6 6LH
(Tel: 01404 822771)

Secure stabling and grazing with hay, straw and shavings on arable farm only minutes from Exeter, M5 and coast; B&B or self catering cottage; games room and coarse fishing.

Devon/ Dartmoor.

MRS J. COLTON
PEEK HILL FARM, DOUSLAND, YELVERTON PL70 6PD
(Tel & Fax: 01822 854808)

The gateway to Dartmoor. Sunny, en suite rooms. The biggest breakfast. Packed lunches. Evening meal. Spectacular views. All pets welcomed.

Devon/ South Molton

**MRS JONES
YEO FARM, MOLLAND, NEAR SOUTH MOLTON EX36 3NW
(Tel: 01769 550312)**

On the foothills of Exmoor. Pets welcome including horses. Beautiful, comfortable 17th century farmhouse. Superb hiking/riding on Exmoor. Peaceful yet accessible.

Dorset / Dorchester

**MRS JACOBINA LANGLEY
THE STABLES, HYDE CROOK, FRAMPTON, DORCHESTER DT2 9NW
(Tel: 01300 320075)**

Comfortable equestrian property in 20 acres grounds close to bridleways; grazing and stabling available; en suite accommodation with TV lounge for owners.

Durham / Consett

**LIZ LAWSON
BEE COTTAGE FARM, CASTLESIDE, CONSETT DH8 9HW
(Tel: 01207 508224)**

Working farm in lovely surroundings. Visitors welcome to participate in all farm activities. Ideal for touring. Bed and Breakfast; Evening Meal available.

Durham/ Waterhouses

**MRS P.A. BOOTH
IVESLEY EQUESTRIAN CENTRE, WATERHOUSES, DURHAM DH7 9HB
(Tel: 0191 373 4324)**

Elegantly furnished, comfortable country house set in scenic 220 acres. Near Durham but quiet and very rural. En suite bedrooms. Excellent food. Licensed. Equestrian facilities available.

Norfolk / Mundesley

**JOHN HARRIS
BRIDGE FARM RIDING STABLES, WINDMILL ROAD, GIMINGHAM
NEAR MUNDESLEY NR11 8HL
(Tel: 01263 720028)**

Holidays, hacking, lessons. livery. Bed & Breakfast. Country area near beach.

Northumberland/ Ninebanks

MRS MAVIS OSTLER
TAYLOR BURN, NINEBANKS, HEXHAM NE47 8DE
(Tel: 01434 345343)

Large traditional stabling; excellent grazing with spring water, straw, feed, safe parking for horse transport; wonderful moorland rides; equine references available!

Shropshire / Bishop's Castle

MRS P. ALLBUARY
THE GREEN FARM, WENTNOR, BISHOP'S CASTLE SY9 5EF
(Tel: 01588 650394)

En suite annexe sleeps 2-4. B&B from £15.50. Two inns within 400 yards. Ideal walking country; riding available (extra).

Somerset / Bridgwater

MRS. N. THOMPSON,
PLAINSFIELD COURT, PLAINSFIELD, OVER STOWEY TA5 1HH
(01278 671292; Fax: 01278 671687)

B&B and Self Catering in Farmhouse and Granary dating from 15 century,set in the Quantocks. Magnificent riding country. Stabling, turn out. Dogs welcome.

Somerset / Churchill

MRS HELEN TRIPP
LYNCOMBE LODGE, CHURCHILL BS19 5PQ
(Tel: 01934 852335; Fax: 01934 853314)

BHS Approved centre. Stabling/grass keep. Magnificent countryside. Little /no roadwork. Facilities include Olympic size meneage, showjumping area and extensive cross country course.

Somerset/Dulverton

MRS A. HUMPHREY
HIGHERCOMBE FARM, DULVERTON TA22 9PT
(Tel: 01398 323616).

A 450 acre farm on Exmoor in peaceful setting. Hay/straw grazing and 2 stables available all year. Good off-road riding. Cross country and show jumps.

HOLIDAYS WITH HORSES ▬▬▬▬▬

Somerset/Dulverton

**TARR STEPS HOTEL
HAWKRIDGE, NEAR DULVERTON TA22 9PY
(Tel 01643 851293).**

This delightful Country House Hotel nestles against the wooded slopes of the River Barle. A paradise for walking, riding, fishing. Dogs, horses and children welcome! Superb cuisine, very comfortable en suite rooms.

Somerset/Exford

BRYAN & JANE JACKSON

**HUNTERS MOON, EXFORD, NEAR MINEHEAD TA24 7PP
(Tel: 01643 831695).**

Cosy bungalow smallholding in the heart of Exmoor. Good food (optional Evening Meal), glorious views, friendly atmosphere. Pets welcome, free stabling available. Open all year.

Somerset / Exmoor

JANE & BARRY STYLES

WINTERSHEAD FARM, SIMONSBATH, EXMOOR TA24 7LF

(Tel: 01643 831222; Fax: 01643 831628)

Ideal holiday in the heart of Exmoor for horse and rider, four inspected cottages plus flat with stone stables and grazing. Short Breaks November - March.

East Sussex/Lewes

**MRS A.L. KENNEDY
DUCK BARN HOLIDAYS, 51 SCHOOL ROAD, FIRLE, NEAR LEWES BN8 6LF
(Tel: 01273 858221)**

Beautiful converted Barn, sleeps 8/10; Coach House for 4/5; Cosy Cottage for 2/3. Central heating, woodburners. Exposed beams - pine furniture. Children and horses welcome. Brochure.

Wiltshire /Coombe Bissett

**MR A. SHERING, SWAYNES FIRS FARM,
GRIMSDYKE, COOMBE BISSETT, SALISBURY SP5 5RF
(Tel: 01725 519240)**

Small working farm with cattle, horses and poultry; access to bridleways and footpaths; Ideal for ramblers and horse riders; en suite accommodation available; 7 miles from Salisbury.

North Yorkshire / Goathland

JACKIE FEARNLEY,
BRERETON LODGE, GOATHLAND YO22 5JR
(Tel: 01947 896481; Fax: 01947 896482).

Self catering annexe to country house, (sleeps 4/5). Spacious grounds. Moorland walking. Sea 8 miles. Stable and field. Short breaks off season. Phone for brochure.

North Yorkshire / Grassington

MRS J.M.JOY,
JERRY & BEN'S, HEBDEN, SKIPTON BD23 5DL
(Tel: 01756 752369; Fax: 01756 753370)

Stabling at owner's house for 2 horses in stone stables built for working farm horses. Box parking, some grazing, no labour. Charges by arrangement. Ample parking.

North Yorkshire / Great Broughton

RED HALL

GREAT BROUGHTON, MIDDLESBROUGH TS9 7ET
(Tel/Fax: 01642 712300)

Elegant 17th Century Grade II Listed building. Personal service in warm friendly atmosphere. Centrally heated en suite bedrooms. Set in meadows and woodland at foot of North Yorks Moors National Park.

North Yorkshire / Leyburn

HILL TOP FARM COTTAGE HOLIDAYS
WEST SCRAFTON, LEYBURN DL8 4RU
(Tel: 01969 40663).

Full or part livery grazing on hill farm. BHS Approved. 24hr supervision. Book on bridleways provided. Self catering or B& B. Peace and tranquillity guaranteed.

North Yorkshire / York

HIGH BELTHORPE LIVERY YARD AND B&B,
BISHOP WILTON, YORK YO4 1SB
(Tel: 01759 368238 Mobile 0973 938528)

You and your horse can enjoy wonderful bed and breakfast at our BHS Approved livery yard on a traditional Yorkshire Wolds farm and farmhouse. Fabulous hacking country.

HOLIDAYS WITH HORSES

Dyfed / Crymch

**CHRIS & GILL HIRST,
RAVEL FARM,BRYNBERIAN, CRYMCH, PEMBROKESHIRE SA41 3TQ.
(Tel: 01239 891316)**

For riders with some experience. We offer fit and willing horses and escorted riding through spectacular mountain and moorland scenery. Small groups, indoor school, tuition, showjumps and cross-country fences. Also NEW for 1997 – TRAIL RIDING.

Powys / Welshpool

**Contact: MRS M.E. EDWARDS,
WINDMILL FARM, HALFWAY HOUSE, SHREWSBURY SY5 9ET
(Tel: 01743 884 356)**

Lords Buildings Farm, Welshpool. Self catering cottage, sleeps 7. Ample parking. Stabling and paddock for 3 horses.Hay and shavings available. Beautiful views.

Argyll / Dalmally

**ROCKHILL WATERSIDE COUNTRY HOUSE,
ARDBRECKNISH, BY DALMALLY PA33 1BA
(Tel: 01866 833218)**

17th Century guest house on waterside with spectacular views over Loch Awe. Hanoverian competition horses bred.First class home cooking. Private fishing.

Roxburghshire / Jedburgh

**ALAN & CHRISTINE SWANSTON,
FERNIEHIRST MILL LODGE & RIDING CENTRE, JEDBURGH TD8 6PQ
(Tel: 01835 863279)**

A chalet style guest house set in grounds of 25 acres. Large lounge with TV and log fire. Weekly and short break riding holidays for experienced adult riders. Horses welcome by arrangement. ABRS, TRSS Approved.

Co. Leitrim / Dromahair

**THE BEECH COTTAGE RIDING COMPANY
BEECH COTTAGE, DROMAHAIR, CO. LEITRIM, REP. OF IRELAND
(Tel: 00353 71 64110)**

Riding School and holiday farm on a beautiful estate. Special weekend offer: 3 nights accommodation and 5hrs riding. (showjumping and trekking available. Phone for colour brochure.

THE FHG DIPLOMA

HELP IMPROVE BRITISH TOURIST STANDARDS

You are choosing holiday accommodation from our very popular FHG Publications. Whether it be a hotel, guest house, farmhouse or self-catering accommodation, we think you will find it hospitable, comfortable and clean, and your host and hostess friendly and helpful.

Why not write and tell us about it?

As a recognition of the generally well-run and excellent holiday accommodation reviewed in our publications, we at FHG Publications Ltd. present a diploma to proprietors who receive the highest recommendation from their guests who are also readers of our Guides. If you care to write to us praising the holiday you have booked through FHG Publications Ltd. – whether this be board, self-catering accommodation, a sporting or a caravan holiday, what you say will be evaluated and the proprietors who reach our final list will be contacted.

The winning proprietor will receive an attractive framed diploma to display on his premises as recognition of a high standard of comfort, amenity and hospitality. FHG Publications Ltd. offer this diploma as a contribution towards the improvement of standards in tourist accommodation in Britain. Help your excellent host or hostess to win it!

FHG DIPLOMA

We nominate ....

....

Because

Name ....

Address ....

....Telephone No ....

Are you ready to take the place of her mum?

Leaving Mum can be scary for a small puppy. But if you feed Beta Puppy at least the food's as good as mum's was. For details on the full Beta range call the Beta Petcare Advice Service: Freephone 0800 7382273 or write to PO Box 53, Newmarket, Suffolk CB8 8QF

BETA *petfoods*

Food for Life

The Golden Bowl Supplement for Pet-Friendly Pubs

BETA
petfoods

When Beta Petfoods launched its search for Britain's warmest pet welcome with their Golden Bowl Award Scheme, the response was staggering. Hundreds of people nominated their favourite pubs for a Golden Bowl Award, where kind hearted publicans ensure a fresh bowl of water is available for their canine customers!

The pick of the pet pubs (and hotels) have gone into this Supplement to enable owners travelling, holidaying or just walking their dogs to find a warm welcome for everyone in the party when they stop for refreshment. We only wish we had room to include more!

BETA – THE BETTER WAY TO NUTRITIONAL CARE

Beta Petfoods make caring for your dog easy – at every stage of his life! From puppy to working dog, family pet to older dog, the Beta choice is extensive and the difference between each product clear. Check the Beta complete food packs and you will see each of the seven highly palatable, easily digestible lifestage products has been carefully balanced to meet a dog's different nutritional requirements.

From *Beta Puppy*, high in energy and protein, you can be assured of a smooth nutritional transition in the first six months to *Beta Junior* and then to *Beta Recipe* or *Beta Pet* for the family dog, *Beta Light* for the older or less active dog with a tendency to put on weight, *Beta Field* for the working dog, and *Beta Champion* for breeding and racing dogs.

Beta also produce *Beta Bravo* and *Beta Brutus* – tasty flake foods, plus crunchy wholewheat mixers and delicious treats.

If you want to know more about Beta Petfoods call the Spillers Petcare Service on **Freephone 0800 738 2273.**

Help Your Dog Beat the Heat on the Road

Follow these three tips from John Foster B.VSc., Cert.V.Ophthal., M.R.C.V.S., consultant vet to Beta Petfoods, and you could make your dog's life in the car considerably more comfortable during the summer months.

When travelling with your dog carry plenty of fresh water and a drinking bowl. An average 20kg dog will drink about $1^1/_2$ pints per day. In the heat this can increase by 200-300%.

Always ensure that your dog has plenty of fresh air. Placing a dog in the back of an estate car without an open rear window is undesirable, probably cruel, and may be fatal.

When you leave your car parked in the shade, remember how quickly the sun moves. As the shade disappears, the inside of the car can quickly reach oven-hot temperatures – up to 140 degrees. Heat stroke can happen within minutes.

The Golden Bowl Supplement for Pet-Friendly Pubs

BERKSHIRE

THE GREYHOUND (known locally as 'The Dog')
The Walk, Eton Wick, Berkshire (01753 863925).
Dogs allowed throughout the pub.
Pet Regulars: Include Lady (GSD), at one o'clock sharp she howls for her hot dog; Trevor (Labrador/Retriever), who does nothing; Skipper (Jack Russell), the local postman's dog and Natasha (GSD) who simply enjoys the ambience.

THE QUEEN
Harts Lane, Burghclere, near Newbury, Berkshire (01635 278350).
Dogs allowed throughout the pub.
Pet Regulars: Sam (Border Terrier), makes solo visits to the pub to play with resident long-haired Dachshund Gypsy.

THE SWAN
9 Mill Lane, Clewer, Windsor, Berkshire (01753 862069).
Dogs allowed throughout the pub.
Pet Regulars: Include Luke (Samoyed), enjoys a glass of Tiger beer.

THE TWO BREWERS
Park Street, Windsor, Berkshire (01753 855426).
Dogs allowed, public and saloon bars.
Pet Regulars: Missy and Worthey (Huskies), prefer to remain outside; Sam (Golden Retriever), will retrieve any food and eat it while owner is not looking; Bumble (Highland Terrier), better known as the Highland Hooverer.

BUCKINGHAMSHIRE

WHITE HORSE
Village Lane, Hedgerley, Buckinghamshire SL2 3UY (01753 643225).
Dogs allowed at tables on pub frontage, beer garden (on leads), public bar.
Pet Regulars: Digby (Labrador), the entertainer; Cooper (Boxer), tries hard to better himself - also drinks!

CAMBRIDGESHIRE

YE OLD WHITE HART
Main Street, Ufford, Peterborough, Cambridgeshire (01780 740250).
Dogs allowed in non-food areas.
Pet Regulars: Henry and Robotham (Springer Spaniels), 'pub dog' duties include inspection of all customers and their dogs and, on occasion, seeing them home after last orders.

CHESHIRE

JACKSONS BOAT
Rifle Road, Sale, Cheshire (0161 973 3208).
Dogs allowed throughout with the exception of the dining area.
Pet Regulars: Bix (Labrador), will share pork scratchings with pub cat, chases beer garden squirrels on solo missions; hamburger scrounging a speciality.

CORNWALL

THE WHITE HART
Chilsworthy, near Gunnislake, Cornwall (01822 832307).
Dogs allowed in non-food bar, car park tables, beer garden.
Pet Regulars: Joe (Terrier-cross), sleeps on back under bar stools; Max (Staffordshire-cross), lager drinker; Tatler (Cocker Spaniel), pork cracklings fan; Sheba (GSD), welcoming committee.

WELLINGTON HOTEL,
The Harbour, Boscastle, Cornwall (01840 250202).
Dogs allowed in bedrooms and pub.
Own private 10-acre woodland walk. Dogs welcome free of charge.

NOTE

A few abbreviations and 'pet' descriptions have been used in this section which deserve mention and, where necessary, explanation as follows: **GSD:** German Shepherd Dog. ... **-cross:** a cross-breed where one breed appears identifiable. **57:** richly varied origin. You will also encounter **'mongrel', 'Bitsa'** and **'???!'** which are self evident and generally affectionate.

CUMBRIA

BRITANNIA INN
Elterwater, Ambleside, Cumbria (015394 37210).
Dogs allowed throughout (except dining area).
Pet Regulars: Bonnie (sheepdog/Retriever), beer-mat catching, scrounging, has own chair.

THE MORTAL MAN HOTEL
Troutbeck, Windermere, Cumbria LA23 lPL (015394 33193).
Dogs allowed throughout and in guest rooms.
Pet Regulars: Include James (Labrador) who will take dogs for walks if they are on a lead and Snip (Border Collie), makes solo visits.

STAG INN
Dufton, Appleby, Cumbria (017683 51608).
Dogs allowed in non-food bar, beer garden, village green plus B&B.
Pet Regulars: Bacchus (Newfoundland), enjoys a good sprawl; Kirk (Dachshund), carries out tour of inspection unaccompanied - but wearing lead; Kim (Weimaraner), best bitter drinker; Buster (Jack Russell), enjoys a quiet evening.

WATERMILL INN
School Lane, Ings, near Staveley, Kendal, Cumbria (01539 821309).
Dogs allowed in beer garden, Wrynose bottom bar.
Pet Regulars: Smudge (sheepdog); Gowan (Westie) and Scruffy (mongrel). All enjoy a range of crisps and snacks. Scruffy regularly drinks Theakstons XB. Pub dogs Misty (Beardie) and Thatcher (Lakeland Terrier).

DERBYSHIRE

DOG AND PARTRIDGE COUNTRY INN & MOTEL
Swinscoe, Ashbourne, Derbyshire (01335 343183).
Dogs allowed throughout, except restaurant.
Pet Regulars: Include Mitsy (57); Rusty (Cairn); Spider (Collie/GSD) and Rex (GSD).

RIFLE VOLUNTEER
Birchwood Lane, Somercotes, Derbyshire DE55 4ND (01773 602584).
Dogs allowed in non-food bar, car park tables, beer garden.
Pet Regulars: Flossy (Border Collie), bar stool inhabitant; Pepper (Border Collie), has made a study of beer mat aerodynamics; Tara (GSD), pub piggyback specialist.

WHITE HART
Station Road, West Hallam, Derbyshire DE7 6GW.
Dogs allowed in all non-food areas.
Pet Regulars: Ben and Oliver (Golden Retrievers) drinking halves of mixed; Sid (Greyhound), plays with cats.

DEVON

BRENDON HOUSE HOTEL

Brendon, Lynton, North Devon EX35 6PS (01598 741206).

Dogs very welcome and allowed in tea gardens, guest bedrooms.

Pet Regulars: Mutley (mongrel), cat chasing; Pie (Border Terrier), unusual 'yellow stripe', was once chased - by a sheep! Farthing (cat), 20 years old, self appointed cream tea receptionist. Years of practice have perfected dirty looks at visiting dogs.

THE BULLERS ARMS

Chagford, Newton Abbot, Devon (01647 432348).

Dogs allowed throughout pub, except dining room/kitchen.

Pet Regulars: Miffin & Sally (Cavalier King Charles Spaniels), celebrated Miffin's 14th birthday with a party at The Bullers.

CROWN AND SCEPTRE

2 Petitor Road, Torquay, Devon TQ1 4QA (01803 328290).

Dogs allowed in non-food bar, family room, lounge.

Pet Regulars: Samantha (Labrador), opens, consumes and returns empties when offered crisp packets; Toby & Rory (Irish Setters), general daftness; Buddy & Jessie (Collies), beer-mat frisbee experts; Cassie (Collie), scrounging.

THE DEVONSHIRE INN

Sticklepath, near Okehampton, Devon EX20 2NW (01837 840626).

Dogs allowed in non-food bar, car park, beer garden, family room, guest rooms.

Pet Regulars: Bess (Labrador), 'minds' owner; Annie (Shihtzu), snoring a speciality; Daisy (Collie), accompanies folk singers; Duke (GSD) and Ben (Collie-cross), general attention seeking.

THE JOURNEY'S END INN

Ringmore, near Kingsbridge, South Devon TQ7 4HL (01548 810205).

Dogs allowed throughout the pub.

Pet Regulars: Lager, Cider, Scrumpy and Whiskey (all Terriers) - a pint of real ale at lunchtime between them.

THE ROYAL OAK INN

Dunsford, near Exeter, Devon EX6 7DA (01647 252256).

Dogs allowed in non-food bars, beer garden, accommodation for guests with dogs.

Pet Regulars: Tom Thumb (Jack Russell), pub bouncer - doesn't throw people out, just bounces.

THE SEA TROUT INN

Staverton, near Totnes, Devon TQ9 6PA (01803 762274).

Dogs allowed in non-food bar, car park tables, beer garden, owners' rooms (but not on beds).

Pet Regulars: Billy (Labrador-cross), partial to drip trays; Curnow (Poodle), brings a blanket.

THE WHITE HART HOTEL

Moretonhampstead, Newton Abbot, Devon TQ13 8NF (01647 440406).

Dogs allowed throughout, except restaurant.

Pet Regulars: Poppie, Rosie (Standard Poodles) and Bobby (Collie).

DURHAM

TAP AND SPILE

27 Front Street, Framwellgate Moor, Durham DH1 5EE (0191 386 5451).

Dogs allowed throughout the pub.

Pet Regulars: These include Smutty (Labrador) who brings her own beer bowl and is definitely not a lager Lab - traditional brews only.

ESSEX

THE OLD SHIP

Heybridge Basin, Heybridge, Maldon, Essex (01621 854150).

Dogs allowed throughout pub.

Pet Regulars: Toby (57), monopolising bar stools; Tag (Spaniel), nipping behind the bar for biscuits; Toto (57), nipping behind the bar to 'beat up' owners' Great Dane; Happy (terrier), drinking beer and looking miserable.

THE WINGED HORSE

Luncies Road, Vange, Basildon, Essex SS14 1SB (01268 552338).

Dogs allowed throughout pub.

Pet Regulars: Gina (Newfoundland), visits solo daily for a pub lunch biscuits and a beer; Roxy (Bull Terrier), fond of making a complete mess with crisps and loves a glass of beer. There are 14 canine regulars in all, not including the pub dog Tinka.

GREATER LONDON

THE PHOENIX

28 Thames Street, Sunbury on Thames, Middlesex (01932 789163).

Dogs allowed in non-food bar, beer garden, family room.

Pet Regulars: Pepe (57), fire hog; Cromwell (King Charles), often accompanied by small, balled-up sock. Drinks Websters, once seen with a hangover. Fred (Labrador), would be a fire hog if Pepe wasn't always there first; Oliver (Standard Poodle), still a pup, pub visits are character-building!

THE TIDE END COTTAGE

Ferry Road, Teddington, Middlesex (0181 977 7762).

Dogs allowed throughout the pub.

Pet Regulars: Angus (Setter), "mine's a half of Guinness"; Dina (GSD), guide dog, beautiful, loyal and clever; Harry (Beagle), partial to sausages, a greeter and meeter; Lady (cross), likes a game of tug o' war with Angus.

HAMPSHIRE

THE CHEQUERS

Ridgeway Lane, Lower Pennington, Lymington, Hants (01590 673415).
Dogs allowed in non-food bar, outdoor barbecue area (away from food).
Pet Regulars: Otto (Hungarian Vizsla), eats beer-mats and paper napkins. Likes beer but not often indulged.

THE VICTORY

High Street, Hamble-le-Rice, Southampton, Hampshire(01703 453105).
Dogs allowed throughout the pub.
Pet Regulars: Sefton (Labrador), his 'usual' chew bars are kept especially.

FLYING BULL

London Road Rake, near Petersfield, Hampshire GU33 7JB
(01730 892285).
Dogs allowed throughout the pub.
Pet Regulars: Flippy (Labrador/Old English Sheepdog), partial to the biscuits served with coffee. Status as 'pub dog' questionable as will visit The Sun over the road for a packet of cheese snips.

HERTFORDSHIRE

THE BLACK HORSE

Chorly Wood Common, Dog Kennel Lane, Rickmansworth,
Hertfordshire (01923 282252).
Dogs very welcome and allowed throughout the pub.
Pet Regulars: Spritzy (mongrel), pub hooligan, former Battersea Dogs' Home resident.

THE FOX

496 Luton Road, Kinsbourne Green, near Harpenden, Hertfordshire
(01582 713817).
Dogs allowed in non-food bar, car park tables, beer garden.
Pet Regulars: A tightly knit core of regulars which includes assorted Collies, German Shepherd Dogs and Retrievers. Much competition for dropped bar snacks.

THE ROBIN HOOD AND LITTLE JOHN

Rabley Heath, near Codicote, Hertfordshire (01438 812361).
Dogs allowed in non-food bar, car park tables, beer garden, pitch and putt.
Pet Regulars: Willow (Labrador), beer-mat catcher. The locals of the pub have close to 50 dogs between them, most of which visit from time to time. The team includes a two Labrador search squad dispatched by one regular's wife to indicate time's up. When they arrive he has five minutes' drinking up time before all three leave together.

ISLE OF WIGHT

THE CLARENDON HOTEL AND WIGHT MOUSE INN
Chale, Isle of Wight (01983 730431).
Dogs allowed in pub but not hotel dining room.
Pet Regulars: Guy (mongrel), calls in for daily sausages. Known to escape from house to visit solo. Hotel dog is Gizmo (Spoodle - Toy Poodle-cross King Charles Spaniel), child entertainer.

KENT

KENTISH HORSE
Cow Lane, Mark Beech, Edenbridge, Kent (01342 850493).
Dogs allowed.
Pet Regulars: Include Boozer (Greyhound), who enjoys a beer and Kylin (Shihtzu), socialising. Pub grounds also permanent residence to goats, sheep, lambs, a horse and geese.

THE OLD NEPTUNE
Marine Terrace, Whitstable, Kent CT5 lEJ (01227 272262).
Dogs allowed in non-food bar and beach frontage.
Pet Regulars: Josh (mongrel), solo visits, serves himself from pub water-bowl; Bear (GSD), insists on people throwing stones on beach to chase, will drop stones on feet as quick reminder; Trigger (mongrel), accompanied by toys; Poppy & Fred (mongrel and GSD), soft touch and dedicated vocalist - barks at anything that runs away!

PRINCE ALBERT
38 High Street, Broadstairs, Kent CT10 lLH (01843 861937).
Dogs allowed in non-food bar.
Pet Regulars: Buster (King Charles), a health freak who likes to nibble on raw carrots and any fresh veg; Suki (Jack Russell), Saturday-night roast beef sampler; Sally (Airedale), official rug; Bruno (Boxer), particularly fond of pepperami sausage.

THE SWANN INN
Little Chart, Kent TN27 OQB (01233 840702).
Dogs allowed - everywhere except restaurant.
Pet Regulars: Rambo (Leonbergers), knocks on the door and orders pork scratchings; Duster (Retriever?), places his order - for crisps - with one soft bark for the landlady; Ben (GSD), big licks; Josh (Papillon), hind-legged dancer.

UNCLE TOM'S CABIN
Lavender Hill, Tonbridge, Kent (01628 483339).
Dogs allowed in non-food bar, beer garden.
Pet Regulars: Bob Minor (Lurcher); Tug (mongrel); Bitsy (mongrel); Tilly (Spaniel): 10pm is dog biscuit time!

LANCASHIRE

ABBEYLEE

Abbeyhills Road, Oldham, Lancashire (0161 678 8795).
Dogs allowed throughout.
Pet Regulars: Include Susie (Boxer), so fond of pork scratchings they are now used by her owners as a reward in the show ring.

MALT'N HOPS

50 Friday Street, Chorley, Lancashire PR6 OAH (01257 260967).
Dogs allowed throughout pub.
Pet Regulars: Freya (GSD), greets everyone by rolling over to allow tummy tickle; Abbie (GSD), under-seat sleeper; Brandy (Rhodesian Ridgeback), at the sound of a bag of crisps opening will lean on eater until guest's legs go numb or he is offered a share; Toby (Labrador), valued customer in his own right, due to amount of crisps he eats, also retrieves empty bags.

LEICESTERSHIRE

CHEQUERS INN

1 Gilmorton Road, Ashby Magna, near Lutterworth, Leicestershire (01455 209523).
Dogs allowed throughout the pub.
Pet Regulars: Bracken (Labrador), barmaid; Jessie (Labrador), socialite; Blue (English Setter), 'fuss' seeker.

LINCOLNSHIRE

THE BLUE DOG INN

Main Street, Sewstern, Grantham, Lincs NG33 SQR (01476 860097).
Dogs allowed in non-food bar, beer garden. Dog-hitching rail outside.
Pet Regulars: The Guv'nor (Great Dane), best draught-excluder in history; Jenny (Westie) shares biscuits with pub cats; Jemma (98% Collie), atmosphere lapper-upper; JoJo (Cavalier King Charles), enjoys a drop of Murphys.

MERSEYSIDE

AMBASSADOR PRIVATE HOTEL

13 Bath Street, Southport, Merseyside PR9 ODP (01704 543998).
Dogs allowed in non-food bar, lounge, guest bedrooms.

THE SCOTCH PIPER

Southport Road, Lydiate, Merseyside (0151 526 0503).
Dogs allowed throughout the pub.
Pet Regulars: Pippa (Rescued Russell), one dog welcoming committee, hearth rug, scrounger. Landlord's dogs very much second fiddle.

MIDLANDS

AWENTSBURY HOTEL
21 Serpentine Road, Selly Park, Birmingham B29 7HU (0121 472 1258).
Dogs allowed in non-food bar, car park tables, beer garden.
Pet Regulars: Well-behaved dogs welcome.

TALBOT HOTEL
Colley Gate, Halesowen, West Midlands.
Dogs are allowed throughout the pub.
Pet Regulars: Include Inga, Gil, Jack and Red, all Border Collies. Every Christmas canine customers are treated to gift-wrapped dog chews.

NORFOLK

MARINE HOTEL
10 St Edmunds Terrace, Hunstanton, Norfolk PE36 5EH
(01485 533310).
Dogs allowed throughout, except dining room.
Pet Regulars: Many dogs have returned with their owners year after year to stay at The Marine Bar.

THE OLD RAILWAY TAVERN
Eccles Road, Quidenham, Norwich, Norfolk NR16 2JG (01953 888223).
Dogs allowed in non-food bar, beer garden.
Pet Regulars: Maggie (Clumber Spaniel); Indi (GSD), Soshie (GSD) and pub dogs Elsa (GSD) & Vell (Springer). Elsa is so fond of sitting, motionless, on her own window ledge that new customers often think she's stuffed!

THE ROSE AND CROWN
Nethergate Street, Harpley, King's Lynn, Norfolk (01485 520577).
Dogs allowed in non-food bar, car park tables.
Pet Regulars: A merry bunch with shared interests - Duffy (mongrel); Tammy (Airedale); Bertie & Pru (Standard Poodles), all enjoy pub garden romps during summer and fireside seats in winter.

OXFORDSHIRE

THE BELL INN
High Street, Adderbury, Oxon (01295 810338).
Dogs allowed throughout the pub.
Pet Regulars: Include Wilf (mongrel), supplies full cabaret including talking to people and singing.

SHROPSHIRE

LONGMYND HOTEL
Cunnery Road, Church Stretton, Shropshire SY6 6AG (01694 722244).
Dogs allowed in owners' hotel bedrooms but not in public areas.
Pet Regulars: Sox (Collie/Labrador), occasional drinker and regular customer greeter; Kurt (GSD), entertainments manager; Sadie (Retriever), self appointed fire-guard.

REDFERN HOTEL
Cleobury Mortimer, Shropshire SY14 8AA (01299 270395).
Dogs allowed throughout and in guests' bedrooms.

SOMERSET

THE BUTCHERS ARMS
Carhampton, Somerset (01643 821333).
Dogs allowed throughout the pub.
Pet Regulars: Lobo and Chera (Samoyeds), eating ice cubes and drinking; Emma (Spaniel), a whisky drinker; Benji (Spaniel-cross), self-appointed rug. Jimmy, a pony, also occasionally drops in for a drink.

HALFWAY HOUSE
Pitney, Langport, Somerset TA10 9AB (01458 252513).
Dogs allowed throughout (except kitchen!).
Pet Regulars: Pip (Lurcher), enjoys bitter, cider and G&T; Bulawayo (Ridgeback-cross), the advance party, sometimes three hours in advance of owner; Potter (57), sits at the bar.

THE SHIP INN
High Street, Porlock, Somerset (01643 862507).
Dogs allowed throughout and in guests' rooms.
Pet Regulars: Include Buster, Hardy and Crackers (Jack Russells), terrorists from London; Bijoux (Peke), while on holiday at The Ship enjoys Chicken Supreme cooked to order *every* evening.

SURREY

THE CRICKETERS
12 Oxenden Road, Tongham, Farnham, Surrey (01252 331340).
Dogs allowed in non-food bar, beer garden.
Pet Regulars: Include Lucy (a 'Bitsa'), surreptitious beer drinker and Chocolate Labradors Marston - after the beer and Tullamore Dew - after the whisky.

SUSSEX

CHARCOAL BURNER
Weald Drive, Furnace Green, Crawley, West Sussex RH10 6NY (01293 526174).
Dogs allowed in non-food bar areas and front and back patios.
Pet Regulars: Lucy (Irish Setter), dedicated to cheese snips.

THE FORESTERS ARMS
High Street, Fairwarp, near Uckfield, East Sussex TN22 3BP (01825 712808).
Dogs allowed in the beer garden and at car park tables, also inside.
Pet Regulars: Include Scampi (Jack Russell) who enjoys a social interlude with fellow canine guests.

THE INN IN THE PARK (CHEF & BREWER)

Tilgate Park, Tilgate, Crawley, West Sussex RH10 5PQ (01293 545324).

Dogs allowed in non-food bar, beer garden, upstairs lounge and balcony.

Pet Regulars: Tuffy (Staffordshire Bull Terrier) leans, on hind legs, on bar awaiting beer and nibbles; Ted (Weimaraner), a 'watcher'; Jacko (Dalmatian), a crisp howler who, once given a pack, opens them himself; Meg (Border Collie), hoovers fallen bar snacks.

THE PLOUGH

Crowhurst, near Battle, East Sussex TN33 9AY (01424 830310).

Dogs allowed in non-food bar, car park tables, beer garden.

Pet Regulars: Kai (Belgian Shepherd), drinks halves of Websters; Poppy and Cassie (Springer Spaniels), divided between the lure of crisps and fireside.

THE PRESTONVILLE ARMS

64 Hamilton Road, Brighton, East Sussex (01273 701007).

Dogs allowed in beer garden, throughout the pub (no food served).

Pet Regulars: These include Katie and Susie, a Yorkie and a ???!, who have been known to jump onto the pool table and help out by picking up the balls.

QUEENS HEAD

Village Green, Sedlescombe, East Sussex (01424 870228).

Dogs allowed throughout the pub.

Pet Regulars: Misty (Whippet) partial to Guinness and Bacardi and Coke. Hogs the dog biscuits kept especially for guests' dogs - proceeds to Guide Dogs for the Blind.

THE SLOOP INN

Freshfield Lock, Haywards Heath, West Sussex RH17 7NP
(01444 831219).

Dogs allowed in non-food bar, at car park tables, beer garden, family room, public bar.

Pet Regulars: Pub dogs are Staffordshire Bull Terriers Rosie and Chutney. Customers include Solo (Labrador), crisp burglar, beer drinker; Tania (Rottweiller), sleeping giant. All bedraggled gun-dogs are especially welcome to dry out by the fire.

THE SMUGGLERS' ROOST

125 Sea Lane, Rustington, West Sussex BN16 2SG (01903 785714).

Dogs allowed in non-food bar, at car park tables, in beer garden, family room.

Pet Regulars: Moffat (Border Terrier), beer makes him sneeze; Leo (Border Terrier), forms instant affections with anyone who notices him; Max (Cocker Spaniel), eats crisps only if they are 'plain'; Tim (King Charles Spaniel), quite prepared to guard his corner when food appears. The landlord owns a Great Dane.

THE SPORTSMAN'S ARMS

Rackham Road, Amberley, near Arundel, West Sussex BN18 9NR (01798 831787).

Dogs allowed throughout the pub.

Pet Regulars: Ramsden (Labrador), likes pickled onions. Landlord's dogs will not venture into the cellar which is haunted by the ghost of a young girl.

WELLDIGGERS ARMS

Lowheath, Petworth, West Sussex GU28 OHG (01798 342287).

Dogs allowed throughout the pub.

Pet Regulars: Angus (Labrador), crisp snaffler; Benji (Cavalier King Charles), hearth rug.

THE WYNDHAM ARMS

Rogate, West Sussex GU31 5HG (01730 821315).

Dogs allowed in non-food bar and at outside tables.

Pet Regulars: Henry (wire-haired Dachshund), hooked on Bristol Cream Sherry; Blot (Labrador), welcoming-committee and food fancier; Scruffy (Beardie), completely mad; Oscar (Labrador), floor hog.

WILTSHIRE

ARTICHOKE

The Nursery, Devizes, Wiltshire SN10 2AA (01380 723400).

Dogs allowed throughout pub.

Pet Regulars: Heidi (mongrel), pub tart; Monty (Dalmatian), trifle fixated; Rosie (Boxer), customer 'kissing'; Triffle (Airedale) and Shandy (mongrel) pub welcoming-committee.

THE PETERBOROUGH ARMS

Dauntsey Lock, near Chippenham, Wiltshire SN15 4HD (01249 890409).

Dogs allowed in non-food bar, at car park tables, in beer garden, family room (when non-food).

Pet Regulars: Include Winston (Jack Russell), will wait for command before eating a biscuit placed on his nose; Waddi (GSD), can grab a bowling ball before it hits the skittle pins; Harry 4 Legs (GSD), always wins the Christmas prize draw.

THE THREE HORSESHOES

High Street, Chapmanslade, near Westbury, Wiltshire (01373 832280).

Dogs allowed in non-food bar and beer garden.

Pet Regulars: Include Clieo (Golden Retriever), possibly the youngest 'regular' in the land - his first trip to the pub was at eight weeks. Westbury and District Canine Society repair to the Three Horseshoes after training nights (Monday/Wednesday). The pub boasts six cats and two dogs in residence.

WAGGON AND HORSES
High Street, Wootton Bassett, Swindon, Wiltshire (01793 852326).
Dogs allowed in non-food bar.
Pet Regulars: Include Gemma, a very irregular Whippet/Border collie cross. She likes to balance beer-mats on her nose, then flip them over and catch them, opens and shuts doors on command, walks on her hind legs and returns empty crisp bags. She is limited to one glass of Guinness a night.

YORKSHIRE

BARNES WALLIS INN
North Howden, Howden, East Yorkshire (01430 430639).
Guide dogs only
Pet Regulars: A healthy cross-section of mongrels, Collies and Labradors. One of the most popular pastimes is giving the pub cat a bit of a run for his money.

KINGS HEAD INN
Barmby on the Marsh, East Yorkshire DN14 7HL (01757 638357).
Dogs allowed in non-food bar.
Pet Regulars: Many and varied!

THE FORESTERS ARMS
Kilburn, North Yorkshire YO6 4AH (01347 868386).
Dogs allowed throughout, except restaurant.
Pet Regulars: Ebony (Labrador) and Jess (Labrador), eating ice cubes off the bar and protecting customers from getting any heat from the fire.

FOX INN
Roxby Staithes, Whitby, North Yorkshire (01947 840335).
Dogs allowed throughout including guests' bedrooms, but not in bar.
Pet Regulars: B&B guests include Lucy and Mouse (Jack Russell & Dachshund); Mattie & Sally (Spaniels) and Meg and George (Bassetts); Lady (57) and another Lady, also a Heinz 57.

THE GREENE DRAGON INN
Hardraw, Hawes, North Yorkshire DL8 3LZ (01969 667392).
Dogs allowed in bar, at car park tables, in beer garden, family room but not dining room or restaurant.

THE HALL
High Street, Thornton Le Dale, Pickering, North Yorkshire YO18 7RR
Dogs allowed usually throughout the pub.
Pet Regulars: Include Lucy (Jack Russell), she has her own beer glass at the bar, drinks only Newcastle Brown and Floss (mongrel), partial to Carlsberg.

NEW INN HOTEL

Clapham, near Settle, North Yorkshire LA2 8HH (015242 51203).
Dogs allowed in non-food bar, beer garden, family room.
Pet Regulars: Ben (Collie-cross), a model customer.

PREMIER HOTEL

66 Esplanade, South Cliff, Scarborough, North Yorkshire YO11 2UZ
(01723 501062).
Dogs allowed throughout in non-food areas of hotel.
Pet Regulars: enjoy sharing their owners' rooms at no extra cost. There is a walking
service available for pets with disabled owners.

SIMONSTONE HALL

Hawes, North Yorkshire DL8 3LY (01969 667255).
Dogs allowed throughout hotel except dining area.
Pet Regulars: account for 2,000 nights per annum. More than 50% of guests are
accompanied by their dogs, from Pekes to an Anatolian Shepherd (the size of a small
Shetland pony!) Two dogs have stayed, with their owners, on 23 separate occasions.

THE SPINNEY

Forest Rise, Balby, Doncaster, South Yorkshire DN4 9HQ
(01302 852033).
Dogs allowed throughout the pub.
Pet Regulars: Shamus (Irish Setter), pub thief. Fair game includes pool balls, beer mats,
crisps, beer, coats, hats. Recently jumped 15 feet off pub roof with no ill effect. Yan
(Labrador), a dedicated guide dog; Sam (Boxer), black pudding devotee.

THE ROCKINGHAM ARMS

8 Main Street, Wentworth, Rotherham, South Yorkshire S62 7LO
(01226 742075).
Dogs allowed throughout pub.
Pet Regulars: Tilly (Beardie), does nothing but has adopted the quote of actor Kenneth
Williams- "Sometimes I feel so unutterably superior to those around me that I marvel
at my ability to live among them"; Sasha & Penny (Terriers), enjoy a social coffee; Kate
& Rags (Airedale and cross-breed), prefer lager to coffee; Holly (terrier and pub
dog), dubbed 'the flying squirrel', likes everyone, whether they like it or not!

THE SHIP

6 Main Street, Greasbrough, Rotherham, South Yorkshire S61 4PX
(01709 551020).
Dogs allowed throughout the pub.
Pet Regulars: Include Hans (Guide Dog), reverts to puppy behaviour when 'off duty'
and Ben (Border Terrier), 'frisks' customers for tit-bits.

ROTHERHAM COMPANIONS CLUB
The Fairways, Wickersley, Rotherham, South Yorkshire (01709 548192).
Dogs on leads allowed throughout the pub (some restrictions if wedding party booked).
Pet Regulars: All chocolate fanatics who receive their favourite treat on arrival include Viking (Springer), Duke (Chow), Max (Border Collie) and Willie (Yorkshire Terrier). Viking keeps a box of toys and a ball behind the bar.

THE GOLDEN FLEECE
Lindley Road, Blackley, near Huddersfield, West Yorkshire
(01422 372704).
Dogs allowed in non-food bar, at outside tables.
Pet Regulars: Ellie & Meara (Rhodesian Ridgebacks), starving dog impressions, animated hearthrugs.

WALES

ANGLESEY

THE BUCKLEY HOTEL
Castle Street, Beaumaris, Isle of Anglesey LL58 8AW (01248 810415).
Dogs allowed throughout the pub, except in the dining room.
Pet Regulars: Cassie (Springer Spaniel) and Rex (mongrel), dedicated 'companion' dogs.

DYFED

THE ANGEL HOTEL
Rhosmaen Street, Llandeilo, Dyfed (01558 822765).
Dogs allowed throughoue the pub.
Pet Regulars: Skip (Spaniel/Collie), a Baileys devotee; Crumble (GSD), a devotee of anything edible.

SCOTLAND

ARGYLL

THE BALLACHULISH HOTEL
Ballachulish, Argyll PA39 4JY (01855 811606).
Dogs allowed in the lounge, beer garden and guests' bedrooms, but not in bar.
Pet Regulars: Thumper (Border Collie/GSD-cross), devoted to his owner and follows him everywhere.

INVERNESS-SHIRE

ARISAIG HOTEL

Arisaig, Inverness-shire (01687 450210).

Dogs welcome.

Pet Regulars: Regulars in the public bar include Luar (Lurcher), Cindy (Collie), Whisky (Terrier) and Raith (Jack Russell), plus resident dog Noodle, available for walks at any time.

KIRKCUDBRIGHTSHIRE

CULGRUFF HOUSE HOTEL

Crossmichael, Castle Douglas, Kirkcudbrightshire DG7 3BB (01556 670230).

Dogs allowed in family room, guest bedrooms, but must be kept on leads outside.

Pet Regulars: A cross-section of canine visitors.

MORAYSHIRE

THE CLIFTON BAR

Clifton Road, Lossiemouth, Morayshire (01343 812100).

Dogs allowed throughout pub.

Pet Regulars: Include Zoe (Westie), has her own seat and is served coffee with two lumps and Rhona (Labrador) who makes solo visits.

ROYAL OAK

Station Road, Urquhart, Elgin, Moray (01343 842607).

Dogs allowed throughout pub.

Pet Regulars: Murphy (Staffordshire Bull Terrier) - food bin. Biscuits (from the landlady), Maltesers (from the landlord), sausages and burgers (from the barbecue).

PERTHSHIRE

CLACHAN COTTAGE HOTEL

Lochside, Lochearnhead, Perthshire (01567 830247).

Dogs allowed in all non-food areas.

Pet Regulars: Regulars are few but passing trade frequent and welcome. Previous owner's dog was a renowned water-skier.

CHANNEL ISLANDS

JERSEY

LA PULENTE INN

La Pulente, St Brelade, Jersey (01534 41760).

Dogs allowed throughout the pub.

Pet Regulars: Include Bridie (Border Collie), darts, pool, watching TV, beer-mat skiing, stone shoving. Also responsible for fly catching. Drinks Bass and Guinness.

ONE FOR YOUR FRIEND 1997

FHG Publications have a large range of attractive holiday accommodation guides for all kinds of holiday opportunities throughout Britain. They also make useful gifts at any time of year. Our guides are available in most bookshops and larger newsagents but we will be happy to post you a copy direct if you have any difficulty. We will also post abroad but have to charge separately for post or freight. The inclusive cost of posting and packing the guides to you or your friends in the UK is as follows:

Farm Holiday Guide ENGLAND, WALES and IRELAND
Board, Self-catering, Caravans/Camping,
Activity Holidays. **£5.50**

Farm Holiday Guide SCOTLAND
All kinds of holiday accommodation. **£4.00**

SELF-CATERING HOLIDAYS IN BRITAIN
Over 1000 addresses throughout for
Self-catering and caravans in Britain. **£5.00**

BRITAIN'S BEST HOLIDAYS
A quick-reference general guide for
all kinds of holidays. **£4.00**

The FHG Guide to CARAVAN & CAMPING HOLIDAYS
Caravans for hire, sites and holiday
parks and centres. **£4.00**

BED AND BREAKFAST STOPS
Over 1000 friendly and comfortable
overnight stops. Non-smoking,
The Disabled and Special Diets
Supplements. **£5.50**

CHILDREN WELCOME! FAMILY HOLIDAY & ATTRACTIONS GUIDE
Family holidays with details of
amenities for children and babies. **£5.00**

SCOTTISH WELCOME
Introduced by Katie Woods.
A new guide to holiday accommodation
and attractions in Scotland. **£4.80**

Recommended SHORT BREAKS HOLIDAYS IN BRITAIN
'Approved' accommodation for quality
bargain breaks. Introduced by
John Carter. **£4.80**

Recommended COUNTRY HOTELS OF BRITAIN
Including Country Houses,
for the discriminating. **£4.80**

Recommended WAYSIDE AND COUNTRY INNS OF BRITAIN
Pubs, Inns and small hotels. **£4.80**

PGA GOLF GUIDE Where to play. Where to stay
Over 2000 golf courses in Britain with
convenient accommodation.
Endorsed by the PGA. Holiday Golf in
France, Portugal, Spain and USA. **£9.80**

PETS WELCOME!
The unique guide for holidays for
pet owners and their pets. **£5.50**

BED AND BREAKFAST IN BRITAIN
Over 1000 choices for touring and holidays
throughout Britain.
Airports and Ferries Supplement. **£4.00**

THE FRENCH FARM AND VILLAGE HOLIDAY GUIDE
The official guide to self-catering
holidays in the 'Gîtes de France'. **£9.80**

Tick your choice and send your order and payment to FHG PUBLICATIONS,

ABBEY MILL BUSINESS CENTRE, SEEDHILL, PAISLEY PA1 1TJ (TEL: 0141-887 0428.
FAX: 0141-889 7204). **Deduct** 10% for 2/3 titles or copies; 20% for 4 or more.

Send to: NAME ....

ADDRESS ....

....

....POST CODE ....

I enclose Cheque/Postal Order for £...

SIGNATURE...DATE ....

Please complete the following to help us improve the service we provide. How did you find out about our guides:

❏ Press ❏ Magazines ❏ TVRadio ❏ Family/Friend ❏ Other.

MAP
SECTION

The following seven pages of maps indicate the main cities, towns and holiday centres of Britain. Space obviously does not permit every location featured in this book to be included but the approximate position may be ascertained by using the distance indications quoted and the scale bars on the maps.

Map 1

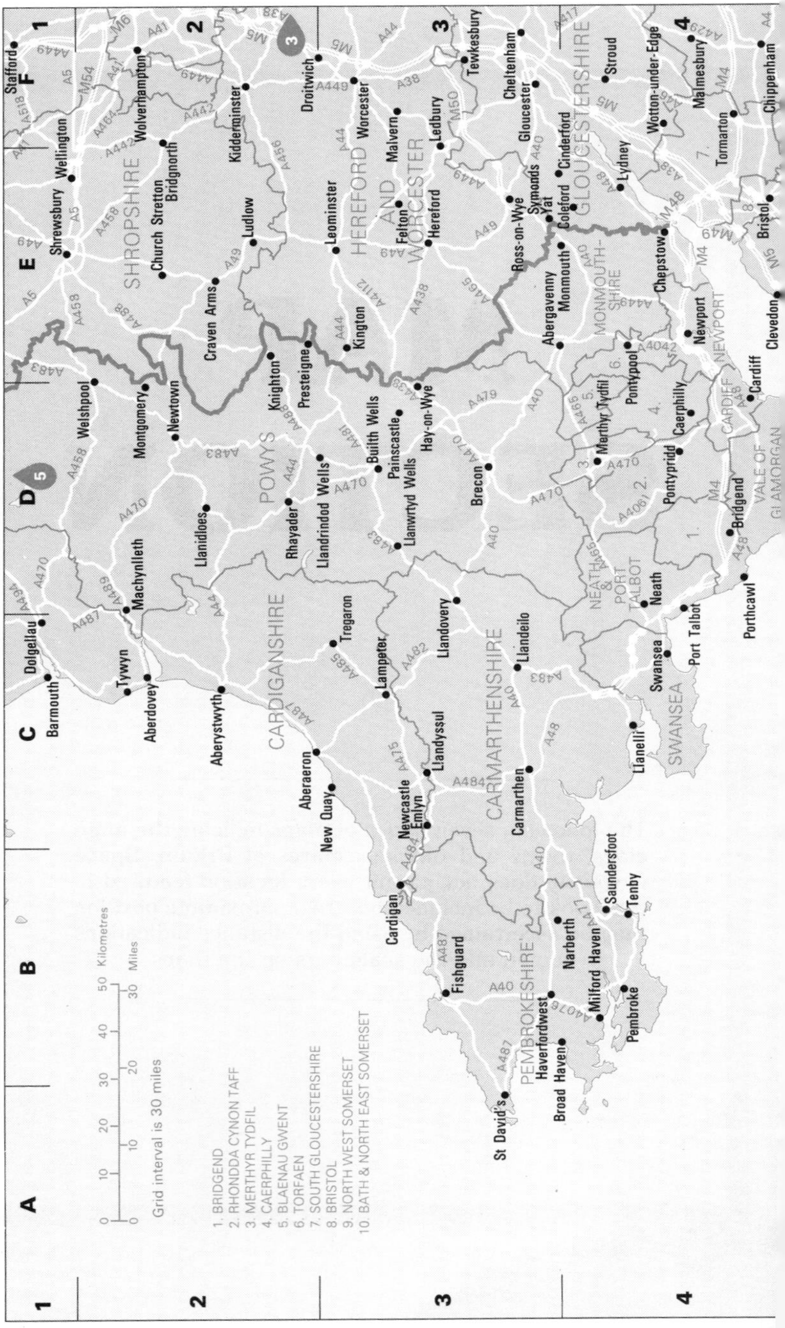

Grid interval is 30 miles
0 10 20 30 40 50 Kilometres
0 10 20 30 Miles
1. BRIDGEND
2. RHONDDA CYNON TAFF
3. MERTHYR TYDFIL
4. CAERPHILLY
5. BLAENAU GWENT
6. TORFAEN
7. SOUTH GLOUCESTERSHIRE
8. BRISTOL
9. NORTH WEST SOMERSET
10. BATH & NORTH EAST SOMERSET
A B C D E F
1 2 3 4
SHROPSHIRE
HEREFORD AND WORCESTER
GLOUCESTERSHIRE
POWYS
CARDIGANSHIRE
CARMARTHENSHIRE
PEMBROKESHIRE
MONMOUTH-SHIRE
NEATH & PORT TALBOT
SWANSEA
CARDIFF
NEWPORT
VALE OF GLAMORGAN
Stafford
Wolverhampton
Shrewsbury
Wellington
Bridgnorth
Church Stretton
Kidderminster
Droitwich
Worcester
Malvern
Ledbury
Tewkesbury
Cheltenham
Gloucester
Stroud
Wotton-under-Edge
Malmesbury
Tormarton
Chippenham
Ludlow
Craven Arms
Leominster
Felton
Hereford
Ross-on-Wye
Symonds Yat
Cinderford
Coleford
Lydney
Monmouth
Abergavenny
Chepstow
Bristol
Newport
Clevedon
Welshpool
Montgomery
Newtown
Knighton
Presteigne
Kington
Hay-on-Wye
Builth Wells
Painscastle
Llandrindod Wells
Llanwrtyd Wells
Brecon
Rhayader
Llanidloes
Machynlleth
Dolgellau
Barmouth
Tywyn
Aberdovey
Aberystwyth
Tregaron
Lampeter
Llandovery
Llandeilo
Aberaeron
New Quay
Llandyssul
Newcastle Emlyn
Carmarthen
Cardigan
Fishguard
Narberth
Saundersfoot
Tenby
Milford Haven
Haverfordwest
Pembroke
Broad Haven
St David's
Llanelli
Swansea
Port Talbot
Neath
Porthcawl
Bridgend
Pontypridd
Caerphilly
Cardiff
Merthyr Tydfil
Pontypool

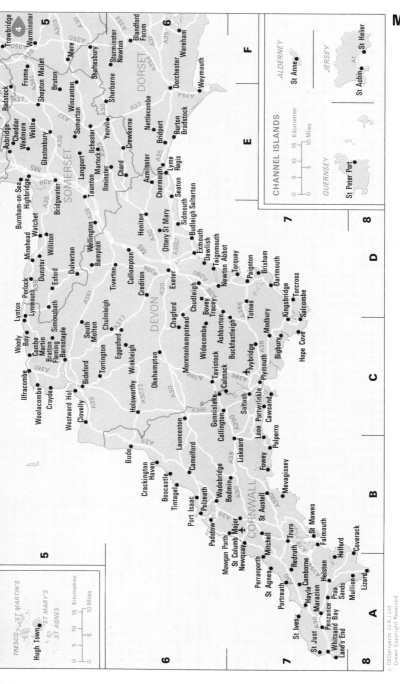

Map 2

Map 3

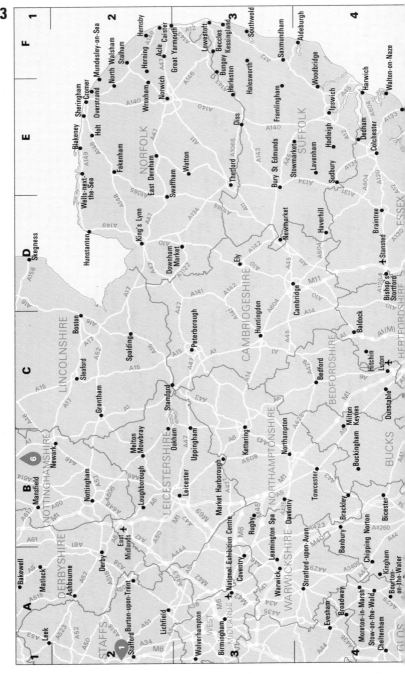

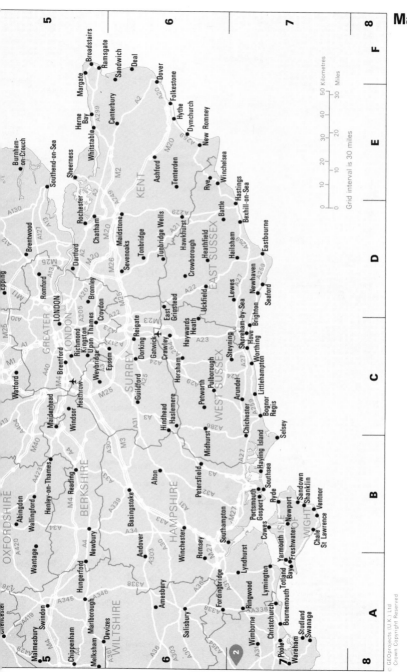

Map 4

© GEOprojects (U.K.) Ltd
Crown Copyright Reserved

Grid interval is 30 miles

0   10   20   30   40   50 Kilometres
0   10   20   30 Miles

Map 5

Girvan

DUMFRIES AND GALLOWAY

Langholm

Bellin
NORT

New Galloway

Dumfries

Annan Gretna Longtown

Greenhead

Newton
Stewart

Castle Douglas

Brampton A69

Wigtown

Gatehouse of Fleet

Silloth

Carlisle

Kirkcudbright

Alston

Port William

Wigton

Maryport

Bassenthwaite

Penrith

Cockermouth

Brampt

Workington

Keswick

Whitehaven

Ennerdale
Bridge

Ullswater

CUMBRIA

Appleby

Shap

Kirkby
Stephen

Ramsey

Gosforth

Little Langdale

Ambleside

Seascale

Hawkshead

Windermere

Peel

Coniston

Kendal

Sedbergh

ISLE OF MAN

Broughton-in-Furness

Newby
Bridge

Kirkby Lonsd

Port
Erin

Douglas

Millom

Ulverston

Grange-over-Sands

Ingle

Castletown

Barrow-in-Furness

Port St Mary

Morecambe

Sett

Lancaster

Fleetwood

Clitheroe

Blackpool

LANCASHIRE

Lytham St Annes

Preston

Blackbu

Southport

Chorley

Bolto

Formby

Wigan

GREATER
MANCHES
Manche

Amlwch

ANGLESEY

Hoylake

Liverpool

MERSEYSIDE

Holyhead

Llanerchymedd

Llandudno

Colwyn
Bay

Rhyl Prestatyn

Birkenhead

Menai
Bridge

Beaumaris

Conwy

Abergele

FLINT-
SHIRE

Knutsford

Llangefni

Bangor

ABERCONWY
& COLWYN

Chester

CHESHIRE

Northwich

Caernarvon

Llanrwst

Denbigh

Llanberis

Ruthin

Betws-y-Coed

DENBIGH-
SHIRE

Nantwich

Newcastle-under-l

Nefyn

GWYNEDD

Portmadoc

Ffestiniog

Corwen

Wrexham

Criccieth

Penrhyndeudraeth

Bala

WREXHAM

Pwllheli

Llangollen

Llanbedrog

Harlech

Aberdaron

Abersoch

Oswestry

Wem

Market
Drayton

Dolgellau

SHROPSHIRE

Wellington

Barmouth

POWYS

Welshpool

Shrewsbury

Tywyn

Machynlleth

A B C D

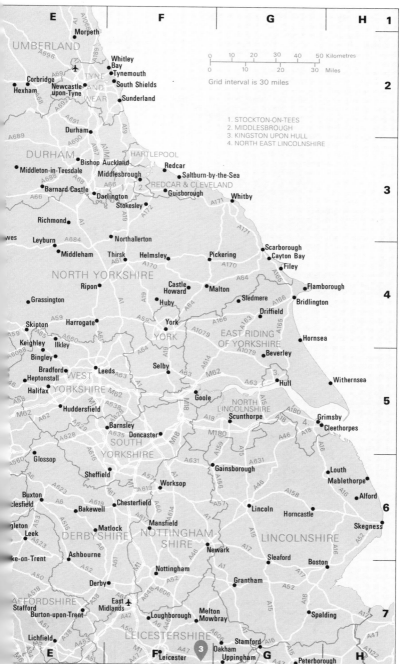

Map 6

1. STOCKTON-ON-TEES
2. MIDDLESBROUGH
3. KINGSTON UPON HULL
4. NORTH EAST LINCOLNSHIRE

0   10   20   30   40   50 Kilometres
0   10   20   30 Miles
Grid interval is 30 miles

Morpeth
UMBERLAND
Whitley Bay
Tynemouth
Corbridge
South Shields
Hexham
Newcastle-upon-Tyne
TYNE AND WEAR
Sunderland

Durham
DURHAM
HARTLEPOOL
Bishop Auckland
Redcar
Middleton-in-Teesdale
Middlesbrough
Saltburn-by-the-Sea
Barnard Castle
REDCAR & CLEVELAND
Darlington
Guisborough
Stokesley
Whitby

Richmond
Leyburn
wes
Northallerton
Middleham
Thirsk
Helmsley
Pickering
Scarborough
Cayton Bay
Filey
NORTH YORKSHIRE
Ripon
Castle Howard
Malton
Sledmere
Flamborough
Grassington
Huby
Bridlington
Driffield
Skipton
Harrogate
York
EAST RIDING OF YORKSHIRE
Keighley
Ilkley
Hornsea
Bingley
Beverley
Bradford
Selby
Heptonstall
Leeds
WEST YORKSHIRE
Halifax
Hull
Withernsea
Huddersfield
Goole
NORTH LINCOLNSHIRE
Barnsley
Scunthorpe
Glossop
Doncaster
Grimsby
SOUTH YORKSHIRE
Cleethorpes
Sheffield
Gainsborough
Louth
Worksop
Mablethorpe
Buxton
Alford
:lesfield
Chesterfield
Bakewell
Lincoln
Horncastle
Skegness
gleton
Matlock
Mansfield
Leek
DERBYSHIRE
NOTTINGHAM-SHIRE
LINCOLNSHIRE
ke-on-Trent
Ashbourne
Newark
Sleaford
Boston
Nottingham
Grantham
Derby
AFFORDSHIRE
East Midlands
Stafford
Burton-upon-Trent
Loughborough
Melton Mowbray
Spalding
Lichfield
LEICESTERSHIRE
Stamford
Oakham
Leicester
Uppingham
Peterborough

Map 7

0 10 20 30 40 50 Kilometres
0 10 20 30 Miles
Grid interval is 30 miles

SHETLAND ISLANDS

1. CITY OF DUNDEE
2. CLACKMANNANSHIRE
3. FALKIRK
4. WEST LOTHIAN
5. CITY OF EDINBURGH
6. MIDLOTHIAN
7. EAST LOTHIAN
8. INVERCLYDE
9. RENFREWSHIRE
10. WEST DUNBARTONSHIRE
11. EAST DUNBARTONSHIRE
12. NORTH LANARKSHIRE
13. CITY OF GLASGOW
14. EAST RENFREWSHIRE

© GEOprojects (U.K.) Ltd
Crown Copyright Reserved